# ART HISTORY & APPRECIATION ACTIVITIES KIT

## Ready-to-Use Lessons, Slides and Projects for Secondary Students

**Helen D. Hume**
*Parkway West High School*
*St. Louis County, Missouri*

The Center for Applied Research in Education
West Nyack, NY

PRINTED IN THE UNITED STATES OF AMERICA

10  9  8  7  6  5  4  3

**Library of Congress Cataloging-in-Publication Data**

Hume, Helen D. [date]
    Art history & appreciation activities kit : ready-to-use lessons, slides and projects for secondary students / Helen D. Hume.
        p.  cm.
    ISBN 0–87628–111–0
    1. Art—Study and teaching (Secondary)—United States.   2. Project method in teaching.   3. Activity programs in education—United States.   I. Title.   II. Title: Art history and appreciation activities kit.
N363.H85   1992
701′.1′071273—dc20                                    92–13923
                                                             CIP

ISBN 0-87628-111-0

**THE CENTER FOR APPLIED RESEARCH
IN EDUCATION**
West Nyack, NY 10994

On the World Wide Web at http://www.phdirect.com

We thank the following for permitting us to use their artwork:

**The National Gallery of Art in Washington, D.C.**
*The Boating Party,* Cassatt; *Untitled (Medici Prince),* Cornell; *Three Motives Against Wall, Number 1,* Moore; *Fanny/Fingerpainting,* Close

**Bernice Steinbaum Gallery in New York**
*Conservatory,* Shapiro; *Pas de Deux,* Shapiro

**The Art Institute of Chicago**
*A Sunday Afternoon on the Island of La Grande Jatte,* Seurat; *Cow's Skull with Calico Roses,* O'Keeffe; *Noah's Ark,* Rembrandt; *The Bath,* Cassatt

**The Nelson-Atkins Museum in Kansas City, Missouri**
*Saying Farewell at Hsün-yang,* Ying; *Faaturuma (Melancholic),* Gauguin; *Landscape After a Song by Yang Hung-hsui The Clearing Sky, the Fading Rainbos and the Red Glow of Sunset,* Tung Ch'i-ch'ang; *Tracer,* Rauschenburg; *Zaga,* Graves; *Tomb Model of a House,* Chinese scroll painting; *Sarah Bernhardt as "La Samaritaine,"* Mucha; *Jane Avril,* Toulouse-Lautrec; *House Post; Untitled,* American Indian

**The Saint Louis Art Museum in St. Louis, Missouri**
*Mummy Cartonnage of Amen-Nestawy-Nahkt, Priest of Amun; African Mask; Still Life,* Claesz; *Charing Cross Bridge,* Monet; *Buddha,* Flack; *Radioactive Cats,* Skoglund; *Flower Hunting Mural,* Munakata; *Horses in Stable, Spring & Autumn,* Haitsu; *Section from a Mosaic Pavement; African Shoulder Mask; Book of Hours, Virgin and Child,* Martinus; *Still Life,* de Susio; *The Louvre, Morning,* Pissarro; *Port-en-Bessin: The Outer Harbor, Low Tide,* Seurat; *Male Portrait Jar; Jug—Human Head; Blanket; The Transformed Dream,* de Chirico; *Isabelle (Dien Bien Phu),* Cornell; *New Continent,* Nevelson; *Private Parking X,* Eddy; *Revenge of the Goldfish,* Skoglund; *Fought Cight Cockfight,* Graves; *Cockfight,* Smith; *Mycenean figurines; The Forty-Seven Ronin at Ryogoku Bridge,* Hiroshige; *Four Seasons,* Keigetsu; *Greek Coins; Wedgewood Vase; Running Artemis; The Street Musicians,* Ochtervelt; *The Huth Factories at Clichy,* Van Gogh; *Vineyard at Auvers,* Van Gogh; *Afternoon Tea Party,* Cassatt; *Air Vent Cover, Fragment from the Stock Exchange Building,* Sullivan; *Totopo Vendors (Group at Market),* Rivera; *Stirrup-Spout Jar in Shape of the God Aiapec; White Lily,* Calder; *The Blue Mandolin,* Braque; *Waterfall,* Escher; *Family Group,* Moore; *Ice Bag, Scale B,* Oldenburg; *Keith,* Close, *Interior of St. Peters' Rome,* Panini

**Art Resource in New York**
*Horses, Bulls and Stags; The Goddess Hathor Places the Magic Collar on Sethi I; Dipylon Vase; Parthenon; Winged Victory of Sumothrace; Colosseum; Les Très Riches Heures de Duc de Berry, May; Chartres Cathedral; The Blue Cloak (Netherlandish Proverbs),* Brueghel; *The Last Supper,* da Vinci; *David,* Michelangelo; *The Sistine Chapel, detail (Creation of Man),* Michelangelo; *The School of Athens,* Raphael; *The Night Watch,* Rembrandt; *View of the Ducal Palace of Venice,* Canaletto; *Yacht Approaching the Coast,* Turner; *Mont Ste. Victoire,* Cézanne; *Portrait of the Artist,* Van Gogh; *The Bedroom of Van Gogh at Arles,* Van Gogh; *Culture of Corn and Preparation of Pancakes,* Rivera; *The Three Musicians,* Picasso; *Kaufmann House, Falling Water,* Wright; *20 Marilyns,* Warhol; *Good Government in the City,* Lorenzetti; *Henry the IV Receiving the Portrait of Maria de Medici,* Rubens; *Guernica,* Picasso

**The Pasta House, St. Louis, Missouri**
*Advertising Poster*

*To*
*my husband, Jack*
*my daughter, Susan*
*my son, David*

## ABOUT THE AUTHOR

**Helen D. Hume** is a teacher and department leader at Parkway West High School, St. Louis County, Missouri. In addition to the art history and photography courses she currently teaches, she has also taught painting, drawing, printmaking, sculpture, ceramics, and commercial art. She currently teaches an art methods course at Florissant Valley Community College.

She has had several articles published in art education publications and is the author of *A Survival Kit for the Secondary School Art Teacher*. A member of the National Art Education Association, she has presented art methods at a number of national conventions. She holds degrees from Webster University.

Mrs. Hume is a member of the Board of Governors of the St. Louis Artists' Guild and specializes in printmaking, photography, and oil painting in her own artwork. While studying painting at Het Vrie Atelier, Antwerp, Belgium, she taught art at the Antwerp International School. She has also taught at the International School in São José dos Campos, Brazil.

# ABOUT THIS RESOURCE

Every teacher's dream is to have a student come in and say, "I really appreciate what you taught me!" Because this rarely happens, especially at the secondary level, most of us are delighted when we see students working creatively, or when a student excitedly brings in a new poster and you find it is an art reproduction, rather than the latest recording star. As a teacher of art history and studio art, I have been thrilled to have students from either class stop me in the hall to talk about the art exhibition they attended, or the museum they visited, and how they liked seeing a certain work they had only seen in slides before.

I prepared the ready-to-use materials and activities in *Art History & Appreciation Activities Kit* to help you get your secondary students excited about great art in its many incarnations from prehistory to the present day, from the "Masters" of Western Art to the distinctive artistry of craftspersons in Asia, Africa, Islam, and the Americas. This kit provides you with 88 student projects and over 100 illustrated worksheets and handouts that help students learn art history by doing simple, hands-on projects, most of which work as well in the regular classroom as in the art studio.

Students enjoy recognizing works by specific artists and trying to understand why the works were created in a certain way. They love being able to put into words why something might look the way it does. There are often more questions than answers. Why did one work of art rather than another catch the public's fancy? Why is one artwork considered better than another? What materials did the artist choose to use for this piece and why? Using original artwork as a springboard to studio projects inspires students to try new ideas and techniques in a variety of media.

Class discussions about their own work and that of others helps students to develop an aesthetic awareness. Teachers of studio art have always realized that students learn in different ways. The same is true in art appreciation and art history instruction. I find that each period is more productive if I use a balance of teaching methods and give more responsibility for learning to the students. It is difficult to hold students' attention for more than twenty minutes of lecturing with slides, though it may be necessary to do this at times. If you first give students information about media and subject matter, such as that provided in the introductory sections of this book, you give them the tools for talking about works in slides and books. Library research projects and other nonstudio projects encourage students to browse through the many beautiful art books (or CD-ROM files). A wide variety of individual and group projects is suggested in "Nonstudio Projects and Activities."

Above all, however, encourage students to create their own artwork. Whether you teach studio art, humanities, art history, social studies, or an interdisciplinary course, the 88 art projects in this book allow students to relate historical examples to their own lives in a way that makes history come alive. For example, students might create a cartouche with their own name in Egyptian hieroglyphics or place themselves in an Egyptian tomb drawing. Making a self-portrait in the manner of an Impressionist can help them always remember and understand how an artist such as Georges Seurat, for example, worked.

*Art History & Appreciation Activities Kit* is arranged chronologically to complement existing art history and social studies textbooks. I encourage you to thumb through and adapt techniques that appeal to you to fit almost any time period. You will find a variety of projects in traditional Western art periods and styles, cross-cultural projects based on non-Western art, and particularly strong sections on modern and contemporary art. (In my experience, these always generate a great deal of student enthusiasm.)

The introductory sections include brief reviews of the elements and principals of art, media, subject matter, and style, as well as tips on grading and testing students. Reproducible worksheets in this section include "The Best and the Worst (Buildings)" and "Personal Art Collection," which ask students to examine their own tastes in art and design. The forty slides included in this kit key into a variety of projects and give an overview of art history. A slide identification script is provided, as well as directions for making your own slides.

The beginning of each section has a reproducible time line and a brief overview of each culture. These aids help students understand the civilization that produced each period of art. Reproducible project handouts include background information and directions for the student, with illustrations that range from small sketches to examples of student work or museum reproductions.

Among the handy appendices in the back of the book are lists of famous artists, famous buildings and their architects, and artists' birthdays.

Use *Art History and Appreciation Activities Kit* with your students and you will be inviting them to a lifetime of enjoyment and appreciation of art!

*Helen D. Hume*

# ACKNOWLEDGMENTS

Much credit for the shaping of this book goes to editors Sandra Hutchison and Win Huppuch of Prentice Hall. As ex-teachers, they knew what was needed, and helped me focus on distilling 30,000 years of the history of art to its essence. My appreciation to Diane Turso, Fred Dahl, and the other professionals at Prentice Hall who saw the book to completion.

I am grateful to the staff of the education department of The Saint Louis Art Museum, and in particular Pam Hellwege, who has helped shaped my approach to teaching Art History through her own dynamic sharing at teacher education workshops. Carol Washburne, Sue Hooker, Cheryl Benjamin, Kate Guerra, and Education Director Dr. Elizabeth Vallance have all contributed to my understanding and love of art history. Special thanks are owed to Pat Woods, the reproductions permissions editor, who can get as excited about helping me select artworks for the book as any teenager could be in selecting a car.

Thanks also to the other professionals who have helped in selecting artworks: Stacey Lynette Sherman and Jan McKenna of the Nelson-Atkins Museum of Art, John Ricco and Ita Gross of Art Resource, JoAnn Isaac of the Bernice Steinbaum Gallery, Ira Bartfield of the National Gallery of Art, and Lieschen Potuznik of the Chicago Art Institute.

Thanks are due to my sounding boards—friends and colleagues who listened to ideas and offered encouragement: Beth Goyer, LuWayne Stark, John Dunivent, Tim Smith, Mary Ann Kroeck, Joan Pirtle, Sharon Stockmann, and Dr. Douglas Turpin. Also to teachers Grant Kniffen, Jerrel Swingle, Clare Richardson, Diana Ziegler-Haydon, Roland Klein, Judy James, Sue Brandenburg, and Parkway West librarians Paula Dull and Barbara Kellams who have assembled a wonderful collection of art books over the years that have been primary resources. Thanks to Dr. Taiyaba Ali who generously obtained a current map of Islam. And, of course, to my students, who have given generously of their talents for illustrations. And last to my husband, Jack, who has explored art history with me, everywhere from prehistoric caves to the Great Wall of China.

# CONTENTS

**FOR THE TEACHERS,** *1*

    **Nonstudio Projects and Activities,** *1*
        *Worksheet: Personal Art Collection, 2*
        *Worksheet: Looking at Architecture, 4*
        *Worksheet: The Best and the Worst, 5*

    **Materials for Teaching Art History,** *6*
        *Suggestions for Testing and Grading Students, 6*

    **A Quick Review of Basic Concepts,** *7*
    Design: The Elements and Principles of Art, *7*
    Media, *7*
        *Handout: Elements and Principles of Art, 8*
        *Handout: Subject Matter and Media, 11*
    Subject Matter in Art, *12*
    Style, *13*
    Architecture, *13*

    **Using the Slides,** *14*
    **Possible Groups of Slides,** *15*
    **Slide Identification Script,** *17*

**Section 1. THE BEGINNINGS OF ART,** *25*

    Prehistory Time Line, *26*

    **Unit 1. The Ancient World (35,000 B.C. to 15,000 B.C.),** *27*
    Project 1-1. Venus, *28*
        *Handout: Project 1-1. Venus, 29*
    Project 1-2. Cave Painting Mural, *30*
        *Slide #1: Detail of Horses, 30*
        *Handout: Project 1-2. Cave Painting Mural, 32*

    **Unit 2. Egypt (7,000 B.C. to 500 B.C.),** *33*
    Egypt Time Line, *34*
        *Handout: Egyptian Architecture, 37*
    Project 1-3. Cartouche, *38*
        *Handout: Egyptian Hieroglyphics, 39*
        *Handout: Project 1-3. Cartouche, 40*
    Project 1-4. Jewelry Fit for a King, *41*
        *Handout: Project 1-4. Jewelry Fit for a King, 42*
    Project 1-5. Pharaoh's Tomb, *43*

*Slide #2: The Goddess Hathor Places the Magic Collar on Sethi I, 43*

*Handout: Egyptian Gods, 45*

*Handout: Project 1–5. Pharaoh's Tomb, 46*

Projects 1–6 and 1–7. The Book of the Dead *and* Mummy, 47

*Slide #3: Mummy Cartonnage of Amen-Nestawy-Nakht, 47*

*Handout: Project 1–6. The Book of the Dead, 48*

*Handout: Project 1–7. Mummy, 49*


**Section 2.   ASIA,** *51*

Asia Time Line, *52*

**Unit 1.   China,** *53*

*Handout: Chinese Dynasties, 54*

Project 2–1. Food for the Gods, *57*

*Handout: Project 2–1. Food for the Gods, 58*

Project 2–2. Houses of Clay, *59*

*Handout: Project 2–2. Houses of Clay, 60*

Project 2–3. Bamboo and Flowers, *61*

*Handout: Project 2–3. Asian Bamboo and Flowers, 63*

Project 2–4. Asian Dragon, *64*

*Handout: Project 2–4. Asian Dragon, 65*

Project 2–5. Scroll Landscape, *66*

*Slide #4: Saying Farewell at Hsün-Yang, 66*

*Handout: Project 2–5. Scroll Landscape, 68*

**Unit 2.   Japan,** *69*

*Handout: Japanese Historical Periods, 69*

*Map of Japan, 70*

Project 2–6. Asian Printmaking, *72*

*Handout: Project 2–6. Asian Printmaking, 74*

Project 2–7. Six-Panel Screen, *75*

*Handout: Project 2–7. Six-Panel Screen, 77*


**Section 3.   MYCENAE AND GREECE,** *79*

Mycenae and Greece Time Line, *80*

**Unit 1.   Mycenae (2300 B.C. to 1100 B.C.),** *81*

*Handout: Greek Architecture, 82*

Project 3–1. The Face of Agamemmnon, *83*

*Handout: Project 3–1. The Face of Agammemnon, 84*

**Unit 2.   Greece (700 B.C. to 100 B.C.),** *85*

Projects 3–2 and 3–3. The Greek Vase *and* The Greek Base as Chair Design, *86*

*Slide #5: Dipylon Vase, 86*

*Handout: Greek Pottery, 88*

*Handout: Greek Vase Painting, 89*

*Handout: Project 3–2. The Greek Vase, 90*

*Handout: Project 3–3. The Greek Vase as Chair Design, 91*

Project 3–4. Wall Painting—Lives of the Greek Gods, 92
*Handout: Project 3–4. Lives of the Greek Gods, 93*
*Handout: Greek Gods, 94*
Project 3–5. Coins and Medallions, 95
*Handout: Project 3–5. Coins and Medallions, 97*
Project 3–6. Classical Architecture, 98
*Slide #6: Parthenon, 98*
*Worksheet: Greek Architecture, 100*
*Handout: Project 3–6. Make It Classi(cal)! 101*
Project 3–7. Toga-Clad Wire Sculpture, 102
*Slide #7: Winged Victory of Samothrace, 102*
*Worksheet: Greek Sculpture, 104*
*Handout: Project 3–7. Toga-Clad Wire Sculpture, 105*
Project 3–8. Toga Party, 106
*Handout: Project 3–8. Toga Party, 107*

**Section 4. ROME AND BYZANTIUM, 109**

Rome and Byzantium Time Line, 110

**Unit 1. Roman Empire (500 B.C. to A.D. 350), 111**
*Handout: Roman Architecture, 114*
Project 4–1. Design a Stadium, 115
*Slide #8: Colosseum, 115*
*Handout: Project 4–1. Design a Stadium, 116*
Project 4–2. Obelisk or Pyramid, 117
*Handout: Project 4–2. Obelisk or Pyramid, 119*
Project 4–3. Mosaic, 120
*Handout: Project 4–3. Mosaic, 122*

**Unit 2. Byzantine Art (A.D. 325 to 1453), 123**
*Handout: Byzantine Architecture, 125*
Project 4–4. Architecture Made Fun, 126
*Handout: Project 4–4. Architecture Made Fun, 128*

**Section 5. AFRICA AND ISLAM, 129**

Africa and Islam Time Line, 130

**Unit 1. Africa, 131**
Project 5–1. African Masks, 133
*Slide #9: African Mask, 133*
*Handout: Project 5–1. African Mask, 135*
Project 5–2. Adinkra Cloth, 136
*Handout: Project 5–2. Adinkra Cloth, 138*

**Unit 2. Islam, 139**
Project 5–3. Islamic Geometric Designs, 141
*Handout: Project 5–3. Islamic Geometric Design, 142*

**Section 6. MIDDLE AGES, ROMANESQUE, AND GOTHIC,** *143*

Middle Ages, Romanesque, and Gothic Time Line, *144*

**Unit 1. The Middle Ages (400 to 1000),** *145*
*Handout: Medieval Architecture, 147*
Project 6–1. Illuminated Frame, *148*
*Handout: Project 6–1. Illuminated Frame, 150*
Project 6–2. Calligraphy, *151*
*Handout: Calligraphy Sample, 151*
*Handout: Project 6–2. Calligraphy, 153*
Project 6–3. Books of Hours, *154*
*Slide #10: Très Riches Heures de Duc de Berry, 154*
*Handout: Project 6–3. Books of Hours (or Months), 155*
Project 6–4. Heraldry, *156*
*Handout: Project 6–4. Heraldry, 157*

**Unit 2. Romanesque (1000 to 1150),** *158*
*Handout: Romanesque and Gothic Architecture, 160*
Project 6–5. Bayeaux Tapestry, *161*
*Slide #11. The Fleet Crosses the Channel, 161*
*Handout: Project 6–5. Bayeux Tapestry, 162*

**Unit 3. Gothic (1100–1400),** *163*
Project 6–6. Rose Window Tracery, *165*
*Slide #12: Chartres Cathedral, 165*
*Handout: Project 6–6. Rose Window Tracery, 166*

**Section 7. RENAISSANCE,** *167*

Renaissance Time Line, *168*

**Unit 1. Northern Renaissance (c. 1350 to 1600),** *169*
*Handout: Renaissance and Baroque Architecture, 171*
*Handout: Symbolism in Gothic, Renaissance, and Baroque Art, 172*
Project 7–1. Illustrate a Proverb, *173*
*Slide #13: The Blue Cloak (Netherlandish Proverbs), 173*
*Handout: Netherlandish Proverbs, 174*
*Handout: Project 7–1. Illustrate a Proverb, 175*

**Unit 2. Italian Renaissance (c. 1400 to 1520),** *176*
Project 7–2. The Golden Rectangle, *178*
*Slide #14: The Last Supper, 178*
*Handout: Project 7–2. The Golden Rectangle, 179*
Project 7–3. Tondo, *180*
*Handout: Project 7–3. Tondo, 181*
Project 7–4. Enlarge a Renaissance Masterpiece, *182*
*Handout: Project 7–4. Enlarge a Renaissance Masterpiece, 183*
Project 7–5. Free the "Slaves," *184*
*Slide #15: David, 184*
*Handout: Project 7–5. Free the "Slaves," 185*

Project 7–6. Fresco, *186*
   *Slide #16: The Sistine Chapel, Detail (Creation of Man), 186*
   *Handout: Project 7–6. Fresco, 188*
Project 7–7. City Planning, *189*
   *Handout: Project 7–7. City Planning, 191*
Project 7–8. Checkerboard Square—Perspective the Italian Way, *192*
   *Slide #17: The School of Athens, 192*
   *Handout: Project 7–8. Checkerboard Square—Perspective the Italian Way, 194*
Project 7–9. Fish Face, *195*
   *Handout: Project 7–9. Fish Face, 196*
Project 7–10. Masterpiece Advertisement, *197*
   *Handout: Project 7–10. Masterpiece Advertisement, 198*

## Section 8.　BAROQUE, *199*

Baroque Time Line, *200*

### Baroque (1590 to 1750), *201*
Project 8–1. Royal Portrait, *204*
   *Handout: Project 8–1. Royal Portrait, 206*
Project 8–2. The Breakfast Piece, *207*
   *Slide #18: Still Life, 1643, 207*
   *Handout: Project 8–2. The Breakfast Piece, 209*
Project 8–3. Dutch Tile Town, *210*
   *Handout: Project 8–3. Dutch Tile Town, 211*
Project 8–4. The Commemorative Portrait, *212*
   *Slide #19: The Night Watch, 212*
   *Handout: Project 8–4. The Commemorative Portrait, 214*
Project 8–5. Old Master Drawings, *215*
   *Handout: Project 8–5. Old Master Drawings, 218*
Project 8–6. City-Scape a la Canaletto, *218*
   *Slide #20: View of the Ducal Palace of Venice and Plaza San Marco, 218*
   *Handout: Project 8–6. City-Scape a la Canaletto, 220*

## Section 9.　ROMANTICISM, REALISM, AND IMPRESSIONISM, *221*

Romanticism, Realism, and Impressionism Time Line, *222*
   *Handout: 19th Century Architecture, 223*

### Unit 1.　Neoclassicism, Romanticism, and Realism (1770 to 1880), *224*
Project 9–1. Sky and Sea, *227*
   *Slide #21: Yacht Approaching the Coast, 227*
   *Handout: Project 9–1. Sky and Sea, 228*

### Unit 2.　Impressionism (1870 to 1905) and Postimpressionism (1886 to 1920), *229*
   *Worksheet: Postimpressionism, 232*
Project 9–2. Impressionist Landscape, *233*
   *Slide #22: Mont Ste. Victoire, 233*
   *Slide #23: Charing Cross Bridge, 233*
   *Handout: Project 9–2. Impressionist Landscape, 235*

Project 9–3. Two-Figure Study in Pastel, *236*

    *Slide #24: The Boating Party, 236*

    *Handout: Project 9–3. Two-Figure Study in Pastel, 238*

Project 9–4. Pointillist Postcards, *239*

    *Slide #25: A Sunday Afternoon on the Island of La Grande Jatte, 239*

    *Handout: Project 9–4. Pointillist Postcards, 241*

Project 9–5. Portrait in the Impressionist Manner, *242*

    *Slide #26: Portrait of the Artist:* Vincent Van Gogh, *242*

    *Handout: Project 9–5. Portrait in the Impressionist Manner, 244*

Project 9–6. Gauguin Look-Alikes, *245*

    *Slide #27: Faaturuma (Melancholic), 245*

    *Handout: Project 9–6. Gauguin Look-Alikes, 246*

Project 9–7. Van Gogh's Bedroom, *247*

    *Slide #28: The Bedroom of Van Gogh at Arles, 247*

    *Handout: Project 9–7. Van Gogh's Bedroom, 248*

**Unit 3. Art Nouveau (1880 to 1910),** *249*

Project 9–8. Poster, *251*

    *Handout: Project 9–8. Poster, 253*

Project 9–9. Art Nouveau, *254*

    *Handout: Project 9–9. Art Nouveau, 255*

Project 9–10. Faces and Flowers, *256*

    *Handout: Project 9–10. Faces and Flowers, 257*

Project 9–11. Sullivan's Stencils, *258*

    *Handout: Project 9–11. Sullivan's Stencils, 259*

**Section 10. TRADITIONAL ART OF THE AMERICAS,** *261*

The Americas Time Line, *262*

**Unit 1. Mesoamerica,** *263*

    *Handout: Mexican and South American Archaeological Sites, 264*

    *Handout: Architecture of the Americas, 265*

Project 10–1. Mayan and Aztec Circles, *267*

    *Handout: Project 10–1. Mayan and Aztec Circles, 268*

Project 10–2. Mural (Based on Mexican Muralists), *269*

    *Slide #29. Culture of Corn and Preparation of Pancakes, 269*

    *Handout: Project 10–2. Mural (Based on Mexican Muralists), 271*

**Unit 2. South America,** *272*

Project 10–3. Peruvian Personality Pot, *274*

    *Handout: Project 10–3. Peruvian Personality Pot, 276*

**Unit 3. Northern Native Americans,** *277*

Project 10–4. Tlingit Totems, *279*

    *Handout: Project 10–4. Tlingit Totems, 281*

Project 10–5. Traders' Muslin Paintings, *282*

    *Handout: Project 10–5. Traders' Muslin Paintings, 284*

**Unit 4.  Pioneer Art,** *285*

Project 10–6.  The Log Cabin Patchwork Quilt, *287*

*Handout: Project 10–6. The Log Cabin Patchwork Quilt, 289*

## Section 11.  MODERN ART, *291*

Modern Timeline, *292*

**Unit 1.  Modern Art (1900 to 1950),** *293*

Twentieth Century Architecture, *296*

Project 11–1.  Matisse Interior, *297*

*Handout: Project 11–1. Matisse Interior, 298*

Project 11–2.  Cubism, *299*

*Slide #30: The Three Musicians, 299*

*Handout: Project 11–2. Cubism, 300*

Project 11–3.  Surrealistic Painting, *302*

*Handout: 11–3. Surrealistic Painting, 304*

Project 11–4.  Box Art, *305*

*Slide #31: Untitled (Medici Prince), 305*

*Handout: Project 11–4. Box Art, 307*

Project 11–5.  I Saw the Figure Five in Gold, *308*

*Handout: Project 11–5. I Saw the Figure Five in Gold, 309*

Project 11–6.  Flowers and Bones, *310*

*Slide #32: Cow's Skull with Calico Roses, 310*

*Handout: Project 11–6. Flowers and Bones, 311*

Project 11 7.  Frank Lloyd Wright's Architecture, *312*

*Slide #33: Kaufmann House, Falling Water, 312*

*Handout: Project 11–7. Frank Lloyd Wright's Architecture, 313*

Project 11–8.  Escher's Tessellations, *314*

*Handout: Project 11–8. M. C. Escher's Tessellations, 316*

Project 11–9.  Homage to Henry (Moore), *317*

*Slide #34: Three Motives Against Wall, Number 1, 317*

*Handout: Project 11–9. Homage to Henry Moore, 318*

## Section 12.  CONTEMPORARY ART, *319*

Contemporary Time Line, *320*

**Contemporary Art,** *321*

Project 12–1.  Combine Painting, *324*

*Slide #35: Tracer, 324*

*Handout: Project 12–1. Combine Painting, 326*

Project 12–2.  Andy Warhol and the Copy Machine, *327*

*Slide #36: 20 Marilyns, 327*

*Handout: Project 12–2. Andy Warhol and the Copy Machine, 328*

Project 12–3.  The Incredible Inedible, *329*

*Handout: Project 12–3. The Incredible Inedible, 330*

Project 12–4. Black, White, or Gold, *331*

Handout: *Project 12–4. Black, White, or Gold, 333*

Project 12–5. Wrap a Building, *334*

Handout: *Project 12–5. Wrap a Building, 335*

Project 12–6. Fingerprint Realism, *336*

Handout: *Project 12–6. Fingerprint Realism, 338*

Project 12–7. Photorealism, *339*

Slide #37: *Buddha, 339*

Handout: *Project 12–7. Photorealism, 341*

Project 12–8. Feminine or Masculine Art? *342*

Slide #38: *Conservatory, 342*

Handout: *Project 12–8. Feminine or Masculine? 344*

Project 12–9. Lime Green Cats, *345*

Slide #39: *Radioactive Cats, 345*

Handout: *Project 12–9. Lime Green Cats, 347*

Project 12–10. Cockfight, *348*

Slide #40: *Zaga, 348*

Handout: *Project 12–10. Cockfight, 350*

Project 12–11. The T-Shirt Generation, *351*

Handout: *Project 12–11. The T-Shirt Generation, 353*

## APPENDICES

A.   How to Create Slides from Books or Magazines, *356*

B.   Ceramics Basics, *357*

C.   How to Mix Plaster, *358*

D.   Artists' Birthdays, *359*

E.   How to Plan a Party, *360*

F.   Famous Artists, *361*

G.   Famous Buildings and Their Architects, *366*

# FOR THE TEACHER

## NONSTUDIO PROJECTS AND ACTIVITIES

As an art teacher, you are interested not only in projects in art history, but also in making students more aware of the history of art. The following nonstudio activities are effective for getting students involved in learning.

- Early in the course, have students begin their "mental art collection" by selecting three favorite artworks that they would own if price and size were no object. These can be sculpture, architecture, paintings, or even the royal barge of the King of Thailand. Remind students that this "collection" can be updated occasionally and is one they can "own" their entire lives. Have them write these in their notebooks along with their reasons or on the worksheet "Personal Art Collection." It is interesting for them to add to the collection from time to time and, at the end of the course, to again select only three that they must have.

- If possible, have a variety of art books in the classroom. Take students to the library and allow them to check some books out.

- Invite artists to your classes, or if possible take students to an artist's studio. If you can't take a field trip during the week, arrange visits to museums. Special exhibitions can be arranged weekends or after school. One teacher meets her students at the art museum on Saturdays. They are responsible for getting transportation there and home again.

- As a course progresses, help the students become aware of their surroundings. Let them know that they will influence what their own world will look like in a few years. There are a few slides on architecture in this book, but there are many wonderful books, and a whole world out there to look at. You can often find experts on local architecture as well, and they are usually pleased to share their knowledge with a class. The worksheet "Looking at Architecture" could be reproduced for students.

- Begin a poster collection. The posters can be laminated with rivets in the corners so they can be used over and over again. Assign students to keep the classroom poster display appropriate to the time period being studied.

- Have students choose their favorite songs. They should select one artwork that perfectly illustrates that song (consider whether it could be appropriately used on the cover of a compact disk or modernized slightly).

- Find a portrait of a literary character, such as Rodin's sculpture of Balzac. Suggest that students research why the portrait was presented in a certain manner.

# PERSONAL ART COLLECTION

Assume you can own any art object anywhere in the world. You may choose to wear it, hang it on your wall, live in it, or display it. You have three choices for your personal collection.

1. Title _____ Location _____

Why? _____

_____

2. Title _____ Location _____

Why? _____

_____

3. Title _____ Location _____

Why? _____

_____

Assume you can upgrade your collection. You still have only three choices. You may "de-access" one or all of your first choices in order to improve your collection. (Museums and art collectors do this from time to time.)

1. Title _____ Location _____

Why? _____

_____

2. Title _____ Location _____

Why? _____

_____

3. Title _____ Location _____

Why? _____

_____

What if a museum decides to sell a painting you especially love to a museum on the other side of the world. Do you feel they have the right, even if they really need the

money to stay open or to "upgrade" their collection? _____

What could you do about it? _____

(continue to other side of page)

- Make a bulletin board for students to bring in advertisements, cartoons, magazine covers, album covers, etc., based on historical works of art (offering extra credit helps this along).

- Have the class collect variations of one famous artwork, such as the *Mona Lisa* or *American Gothic*. Students will send you cards over the years when they find them. Collect funny adaptations of famous artworks, or advertising that is based on famous artwork.

- Choose one day in the year when you could honor an artist by having a birthday party (a list of artists' birthdays is in Appendix D). Talk about the food that might be served, party hats to make, invitations, guests, table decorations, even buttons to wear. This might coincide with an exhibition of artwork created by the class.

- Celebrate black history month with music, dance, stories, and art.

- Investigate the arts and crafts of a particular ethnic/cultural group and present them to the class.

- Announce a "Tacky Day Contest." Offer extra credit for each student who brings in something that is of incredibly poor design. Kitsch is something taken beyond its original intent, such as a Michelangelo's *Pieta* with a clock on the base. It might be jewelry, clothing, a lamp, a souvenir. Offer a prize for the "best" of the worst. (Suitably tacky prizes can be found at garage sales and junk shops.) Explain to students that they will be major consumers very shortly and that this is an opportunity to decide what appeals to them and why. If they become conscious of the artwork as well as the junk around them, you have achieved your goal.

- In contrast to this, have students bring in or find in the room two well-designed functional objects.

- Have students select the five (or two) ugliest buildings in town. They may never have thought about their surroundings, and this gets them thinking about what makes one building better designed than another. The worksheet "The Best and the Worst" could be used in this exercise.

- Divide students into groups and have them dress and pose as a particular painting or sculpture. Take pictures, of course.

- Show thirty slides of works in a variety of media such as oil, watercolor, silkscreen, ink drawing, pencil drawing, and pastel. Have students test themselves in identifying the medium. An artist such as Winslow Homer worked in both watercolor and oil with similar results, but students learn to easily recognize the medium he used.

- Toward the end of the course, have students identify artists from the slides, or tell whether an artwork is romantic or realistic.

- An exercise that students enjoy is to mix slides up chronologically and let them write the approximate century in which they believe something was created. This would need to be done near the end of a course, but they quickly develop an "educated eye." I prefer not to grade this because it is just for fun.

- Collect postcards and mount photos of artwork from art magazines to make several "decks" of 25 to 52 pieces of artwork. Group students, and have them divide the pictured artworks into two logical groups, discussing why they divided them and how. Suggest they might wish to redivide the pictures into four groups. Selecting names for these divisions and sharing them with the class is an interesting exercise. It is surprising how similar each group's results will be. There will probably be divisions such as Realistic-Romantic, Modern-Traditional, or Representational-Abstract.

# LOOKING AT ARCHITECTURE

Select two buildings from the same period or from two different periods in the history of architecture. Supply as much information as you have available.

| BUILDING 1 | BUILDING 2 |

Name

_____ _____

Architect

_____ _____

When was it constructed?

_____ _____

Where is it located?

_____ _____

Basic building material

_____ _____

Innovative features in construction?

_____ _____

_____ _____

_____ _____

Decorative elements?

_____ _____

Based on historic structures?

_____ _____

Site selection?

_____ _____

Describe the structures individually, then explain why they were appropriate for the time in which they were constructed. If some unusual features made them special, even for the time in which they were built, mention those. Use the back of this paper for your answers.

Name: _____     Date: _____

# THE BEST AND THE WORST

If you were to choose the best designed and worst designed buildings in your city or town, which would they be?

**Best**

Why do you think this building is the best design?

_____

_____

Do you know when it was built? _____

Architect? _____

What "style" does it follow, if any?

_____

_____

Best Building
(Do a rough sketch below.)

Name of
Building

_____

_____

**Worst**

What do you think is the worse thing about this

building? _____

How would you change it to make it look better?

_____

If you changed it that way, would it still go with the

neighborhood? _____

When do you think it was built? _____

Architect? _____

If it were your choice, would you tear down the "ugliest" building in town? Why or why not?

Worst Building
(Do a rough sketch below.)

Name of
Building

_____

_____

_____

_____

If a "bad" building has historical significance, should it be protected with historic preservation status?

Why or why not?_____

_____

- Divide the class into groups of five or so (having them draw numbers from a hat is a good way to do this). Give them time to discover what they have in common, something that interests all of them. It may be sports, music, science fiction, movies, etc. Then ask the groups to relate their common interest to some form of art that they can share with the entire class. This is a major undertaking and probably should be a culminating semester project. Their interest can be presented through a play, time machine video, slide presentation, handouts for the entire class, vocal recital with slides in the background, or whatever they can dream up. (I found it worth my effort to videotape these presentations; they were outstanding.)

# MATERIALS FOR TEACHING ART HISTORY

Most studio art teachers already have materials and equipment mentioned in this book. A special (locking) cabinet with simple basic materials enables students to work independently when they have the opportunity. The cabinet should contain:

- Portfolios (a tagboard folder for each student to hold projects in progress)
- Basic art supplies (pastels, oil pastels, conté, colored pencils, charcoal, pencils, black fine-line markers, glue sticks, acrylic paints, watercolor paint, scissors, brushes, X-acto® knives)
- Paper (watercolor paper, paper palettes, drawing paper, tagboard, fadeless paper, vellum)
- Art magazines such as *Art News, Art and Antiques,* National Scholastic's *Art and Man, Architectural Digest*

Students should also have three-ring looseleaf notebooks for handouts and notes. (Let students know you will collect these and grade them.)

## SUGGESTIONS FOR TESTING AND GRADING STUDENTS

- To test students, it is effective to have them read the material and turn in test questions for extra credit (if their questions are used). It helps them appreciate how a good question is worded.
- Students often read a textbook more effectively if they are aware that tests could be taken with their notebooks open. They will jot down important reminders.
- Make up a calendar page for the semester that gives the expected readings, so that students can plan ahead.
- If students wish to contract for a high grade, allow them to sign a contract that spells out what would be expected to make an A. The general level of achievement will astonish you, and even the students who don't quite make the highest grades will achieve considerably more than average.

# A QUICK REVIEW OF BASIC CONCEPTS

### DESIGN: THE ELEMENTS AND PRINCIPLES OF ART

The elements and principles of art are artificial terms applied to the organization of artworks that probably were unheard of until relatively recently. Certainly so-called primitive or naive artists would not know these terms. That does not mean that their art is any less exciting or organized. They simply instinctively did what felt "right" for them at that time. In fact, there were rules of art even in Egyptian times, and it is likely that each culture formulated its own rules.

The conscious effort to organize decorative effects and to combine shapes, line, or color until an object pleases the artist is called *design*. The *elements of art—line, color, value, texture,* and *shape (form)*—are terms probably used more when discussing art than while creating it. The *principles of art* are *variety, space, contrast, rhythm, balance, movement, repetition,* and *emphasis.* Artists instinctively use the principles of art when arranging the elements of art. When an artwork is well done, one sees *unity* or *harmony* in the overall design. The handout "Elements of Art/Principles of Art" helps students recognize how they are combined to create a work of art.

### MEDIA

Some media are more easily recognized than others, based on personal experience. To teach your students quickly about media, divide the class into groups, giving each group responsibility for researching one medium. If the students know that they will have to teach each other about the medium and the artists who used it, they will do a thorough job. If members of the group do a project in that medium, they'll have an even greater understanding.

**Painting.** Painting involves the application of pigment (color) to a prepared ground such as canvas. Over the years the pigment, media, and tools have become more sophisticated than when the cave dwellers smeared earth and lampblack (soot) onto cave walls with hands or wads of moss, but the process and results are similar today.

*Watercolor* is a transparent medium that uses dry cakes or pigment already mixed with water in tubes. *Gouache* is watercolor with white added.

*Tempera* is an opaque water-based medium. It has been used for several thousand years. Pigment was often mixed with egg yolk (egg tempera), which is very durable. To create *fresco,* artists mixed pigment in water or thinned plaster before applying it to a freshly plastered area of wall or ceiling.

*Oil paint* was created in the sixteenth century when ground pigment was suspended in oil. This technique allows for glazing (diluting the paint, which allows the underpainting to show through and gives a "glow" to paint) or impasto (building up texture through the use of undiluted pigment).

*Acrylic paint* is a relatively recent invention. It is water based, but can be thinned to use transparently as watercolor or applied straight from the tube to resemble oil paint.

*Ink and wash* is a medium that falls somewhere between painting and drawing. A wash is thinned ink applied to a paper, combined with lines created with a pen dipped

# ELEMENTS OF ART

| Line | Color | Value | Texture | Shape |
|------|-------|-------|---------|-------|

# PRINCIPLES OF ART

| Space | Contrast | Rhythm | Emphasis | Balance | Variety | Repetition |
|-------|----------|--------|----------|---------|---------|------------|

8

in ink. This common medium gives very uncommon effects in the hands of masters such as Chinese scroll-painters.

**Drawing.** Drawing media have changed very little over the centuries. Although it is possible to "draw" with paint, or "paint" with drawing media such as oil pastel, the basic difference is that drawing media are dry.

*Oil pastels* contain pigment held together with oil. They are opaque and blend to resemble oil paints.

*Pastels* are hard sticks of pigment that can be blended, or left unblended, allowing individual strokes to show.

*Conté crayon* is a synthetic blend of chalk and graphite. It is the forerunner of the modern pencil. It comes in red (sanguine), black, brown (sepia), white, or gray.

*Charcoal* is a medium that has been in use since people discovered fire. Because it smears easily, it must be protected by spraying with fixative or covering with plastic.

**Printmaking.** *Woodcuts* were one of the first means of making multiple images from one "plate." The appearance can vary from the elegant woodcuts of Dürer to the rough, emotional woodcuts of the German Expressionists such as Käthe Kollwitz. Eastern artists also made wide use of woodcuts for prints (such as the Japanese woodcuts that so greatly influenced the Impressionists) and textile decoration.

*Linocuts* (designs cut into linoleum) are a variation of the woodcut. Linocuts are especially effective for student work and offer great sophistication, as illustrated by Pablo Picasso.

*Serigraphy* (silkscreen) uses a block-out system to create multiple images in color. Photo silkscreens such as those done by Andy Warhol show the potential of this medium. Students recognize silkscreen when it is pointed out that most T-shirts are printed this way.

*Intaglio printing* is done on a metal plate that has lines etched or engraved into the surface. Ink is wiped onto the plate, then wiped off. When it is put through a press under pressure, the ink that remains in the depressed lines is forced onto dampened paper. This method was widely employed by Rembrandt and Goya and continues to be popular today. Some methods of intaglio printmaking include *aquatint, line etch, deep etch, sugar lift,* and *engraving.*

**Sculpture.** Natural materials have been sculpted in societies throughout the world. Examples of sculpture in *clay, wood,* and *stone* such as marble can be seen throughout the history of art, and fine examples may be seen in museums throughout the world. The making of jewelry from the lost wax process enabled ancient artisans to make intricate objects of *gold and bronze.* Many examples have been preserved for thousands of years.

Sculpture today takes many new forms, although artists continue to work in traditional media. Artists take advantage of natural materials, as always, but many work in welded metal such as *wrought iron or steel.* Many sculptors, such as Richard Serra, no longer fabricate their own sculpture, but design it and have it made under their supervision in a factory. *Found materials* (which originally were intended for another use but are incorporated into a sculpture) have become commonplace material for today's sculptors, who often are more interested in interpreting an idea than creating a traditional work. Marisol, Louise Nevelson, and Richard Hunt are artists whose sculpture is created from found objects.

**New Media.** Media are constantly changing as science and technology give us new materials. Plastics, acrylics, computer graphics, and photographic images couldn't have been conceived 200 years ago. Art forms that do not even use traditional media such as *environmental or conceptual art, using sound, light, time, or space* would have astonished artists a relatively short time ago. The environmental artist Christo creates artworks which are intended to last only a few days. I'm told of a "laughing floor" installed in front of the Philadelphia Museum of Art. When it is walked on, a recording of laughter comes on, encouraging audience participation.

**Crafts.** The origin of hand-crafted objects is traced back to basic needs such as cooking, wearing, or worship. Then, as now, fine craftspeople incorporated the elements and principles of design to create aesthetically pleasing objects. Although traditional crafts are still produced in all cultures, much that is collected by people today has gone well beyond utilitarian purposes, and is appreciated for its sensory appeal.

*Ceramic* objects originally served as funerary urns, grain storage vessels, water jars, vases, and objects for worship. Peruvian water jars surely were appreciated as objects of beauty that had a secondary purpose (to hold water). I saw an ancient ceramic from China that had begun life as a woven basket, daubed with clay to make it waterproof. Imagine what it must have been like to discover that if clay were fired, it would hold water. Once fired, ceramics have an indefinite life. Much of what is learned about many civilizations comes from the enduring quality of their clay objects.

*Glass blowing* was a craft known to the Egyptians and Phoenicians. *Mosaics,* which were commonplace in ancient Greece and Rome and later in the Renaissance, were made of small squares of glass embedded in mastic. *Beadwork* with glass beads has been practiced throughout the world and has been exquisitely done by Native Americans for generations.

*Fiber arts* include woven clothing, carpets, tapestries, serapes, belts, cloaks, and decorative wall hangings such as those made by the Tlingit Indians of the American Northwest. Decorative tapestries date back centuries, and were created for beauty and warmth. Country people have raised animals such as the alpaca or sheep to produce coverings for themselves and their homes wherever it is cool enough to need warmth. Blankets woven by Peruvian Indians strongly resemble those created by Native Americans because of the colors produced by natural dyes and the results of weaving on a loom.

People have decorated their clothing with batik and other resist-dyeing methods (such as African mud-paste resist), embroidery, and reverse applique (such as molas).

*Basketry,* like some other crafts, has limitations and potential that mean the results will be similar whichever society produces them. Many baskets are so similar in design, even though done on opposite sides of the globe, that only an expert could tell which culture did them. Traditional weaving designs are passed down, and the quality of the grasses or leaves influence what can be done. Some modern artists are stretching the limits by using basketry techniques to create sculpture.

*Wood carving,* while a sculptural technique, is used throughout many cultures for practical objects such as chests and fine furniture, bowls, and utensils. The decorative potential of wood carving is seen throughout Europe, Asia, and Africa.

*Metalwork* ranges from fine jewelry created in gold or silver to wrought iron fireplace tools or cast iron pots. The quality of craftsmanship in metals is demonstrated in museums throughout the world, and one marvels at the quality of work done under so-called primitive conditions. Asian and African bronzes are of such fine quality and detail that they would be difficult to duplicate today.

*Paper* is transformed in many ways, with many contemporary artists hand-casting paper to resemble sculpture. Artists such as Matisse made his famous cut-outs from hand-painted paper. Chinese and Mexican artists continue the tradition of paper cutting

# SUBJECT MATTER

| Narrative | Genre | Fantasy | Religious |
|---|---|---|---|
| | | | |
| Mythological | Human Form | Portraiture | Animal |
| | | | |
| Still Life | Landscape | Abstraction | Expressionism |
| | | | |

# MEDIA

| Oil | Watercolor | Pastel | Weaving |
|---|---|---|---|
| | | | |
| Fresco | Sculpture | Pottery | Jewelry |
| | | | |
| Architecture | Printmaking | Etching | Pencil |
| | | DRYPOINT AQUATINT LINE ETCH DEEP ETCH | |

on thin paper. Papyrus, tapa cloth, and other paperlike materials made from fibers of plants are used in areas such as Egypt, Africa, and Mexico for folk-art paintings.

## SUBJECT MATTER IN ART

**Animals.** The cave dwellers of Altamira and Lascaux did bas-reliefs and paintings of the animals they hunted. Throughout the history of art both wild and domestic animals have continued to be represented in paintings, crafts, and sculpture.

**Religious Art.** Although we often do not know why art was created, we have interpreted paintings of gods who were worshipped by the Egyptians. Grecian wall paintings have been lost, but vases painted with pictures of the Greek gods give us an idea of their wall paintings. The dreaming art of Australian Aborigines is part of the religion—doing the painting itself is religious. Throughout the Middle Ages, Renaissance, and Baroque periods, religious art was one of the few acceptable (or funded) subjects for a painter.

**Mythological, Literary, and Historical Subjects.** Artists illustrated Biblical stories or sayings, as in the works of Pieter Brueghel. Historical occurrences such as Manet's *Execution of the Emperor Maximilian of Mexico,* and myths such as *The Judgment of Paris* by Lucas Cranach were also rich sources for painters. The Pre-Raphaelites wished to return to a realistic depiction of nature, and combined symbolic elements with extreme realism. Politics often were a subject for artists, as they glorified or criticized whoever was in power.

**Portraiture.** Portraits of the pharaohs and their servants were included in Egyptian tombs. Gods, saints, and royalty were depicted throughout history. Religious paintings for Gothic churches began to include portraits of patrons. Portraiture became popular in the Renaissance, and continues today as major subject matter. The *nude* is rarely considered a specific person, but is often a preferred subject of artists simply because of the infinite variety possible and the beauty of the human form.

**Narrative Art.** This type of art tells a story. It too began with the cave dwellers as they painted their hunts on the walls. It was particularly effective in Greek vase painting, and again in the sixteenth and seventeenth centuries when it depicted the exploits of heroes and Gods.

   *Genre* art portrayed ordinary people as they went about their daily lives. It reached a pinnacle in the Netherlands and was also very popular in Victorian England.

**Landscape.** Although Chinese artists painted landscapes shortly after the invention of paper, the landscape really was not considered a subject for Western art except incidentally as the background in religious art until the seventeenth century. English and Dutch artists exploited this subject matter to its fullest. *Seascapes* and *city-scapes* were painted by such artists as Canaletto, and are variations of the landscape.

**Interiors.** These became common subject matter in Dutch art of the sixteenth century, although they were also shown in some religious art of the Middle Ages. Victorian interior watercolors were a genteel form of this art.

**Fantasy Art.** Fantasy art is that which exists only in the artist's mind. One of the earliest artists to depict fantasy was Hieronymus Bosch as seen in his *Garden of*

*Earthly Delights.* Other well-known fantasy artists are Marc Chagall, or *Surrealists* Georgio de Chirico and Salvador Dali.

**Still-Life.** Although many religious paintings contained small areas of still-life, the picture of inanimate objects arranged on a table became most popular in the Netherlands during the 1600s. It continued as a favorite subject of some Impressionists such as Edouard Manet and *Cubists* such as Georges Braque and Pablo Picasso.

The hand-out "Subject Matter/Media" can be useful when you are talking to students about either subject.

## STYLE

Style could be defined as the manner in which an artist composes a picture and whether he or she works realistically or emotionally.

*Romantic art* permitted artists to express their feelings and emotions through paintings and sculpture. It is often a revolt against formal rules, with artists portraying what they imagine. Art vacillates at times between romanticism and realism. Baroque art could be considered romantic, and some of the landscapes that became popular shortly after the excesses of Baroque would be realistic interpretations.

*Realistic art* has existed throughout the history of art, with artists depicting the details of their surroundings as authentically as possible. The advent of photography permitted artists to present accurate, detailed representation that the mind alone could not capture.

*Abstract art* does not always have an apparent subject, though it is possible that one exists. *Cubist art,* for example, used real subjects, which were transformed by distorting lines, fracturing forms and showing movement, and representing different planes or perspectives at the same time. Even the most abstract paintings by Picasso allow students to recognize the subject matter.

*Nonobjective art* has no apparent subject. Jackson Pollock's paintings are nonobjective.

*Classicism* is literally applied to art and architecture that has Grecian or Roman origins of design. It could apply to art that is rationally constructed, using balance and order, or geometric construction.

## ARCHITECTURE

Our houses, shops, churches, and office buildings have all been shaped by the times we live in. It is logical that a shopping mall would belong to a mobile society, just as it was logical in the preautomobile days to cluster everything within walking distance and use space conservatively.

Fortunately the students in most cities can see examples of architecture that date back at least one century, and can be made aware of the changes that have evolved even in their own lifetimes. The computer has changed the face of architecture relatively recently, with many buildings looking somewhat like a child's building blocks.

# USING THE SLIDES

The forty slides included with this package present an overview of the history of art. If you wish to examine your own feelings about art, imagine trying to select only forty to represent the whole of art history! Because I feel comparison is an important part of learning to appreciate art, I have especially included several pieces of sculpture, architecture, and portraits for student discussion. The slides are grouped chronologically. Because students show such a keen interest in "modern times," more than half the slides represent the time from the Renaissance onward.

Each slide will relate to at least one of the projects in the book and may be shown along with several others from the same general time period or same subject matter. In the overview of each period of art I have included the name of several generally acknowledged masterpieces. It is possible to purchase sets of slides that will give an overview, much as this series does, to purchase slides of individual artists or groups of artists, or to photograph your own, as described in Appendix A. I recently purchased groups of slides of artwork by women artists and by various ethnic groups.

While we all have personal opinions about art and artists ("I may not know much about art, but I know what I like!"), we should make every effort to remain impartial when teaching about art. Particularly when you are showing slides of modern art, there are ways of introducing abstract work that help the student to understand what the artist might have been expressing.

Secondary students want to know the names of what they are seeing. They often remember the names and are intrigued. I also read the size of a work of art to them or try to describe the size (comparing it with the screen on which we are viewing the slides). Nothing you ever see in a book will prepare you for the grandeur of Rembrandt's *Night Watch,* nor would most people have expected the *Mona Lisa* to be so small.

Encourage students to talk about art, helping them learn the correct vocabulary and pronunciation. As they learn to talk, they can also learn to write. I find it useful to have a "question of the week" on Friday, when I show one or two slides for them to compare and write about. Several of the reproducible handouts are useful reference material for students. Worksheets can be used to encourage imagination.

# POSSIBLE GROUPS OF SLIDES

### Architecture

Parthenon

Colosseum

Chartres Cathedral

Sistine Chapel

Kaufmann House, Falling Water

### Sculpture

Winged Victory of Samothrace

African mask

David

Untitled, Medici Prince

Three Motives Against the Wall

Radioactive Cats

Zaga

### Painting

Horses, Bulls, and Stags

Mummy Cartonnage of Amen-Nestawy Nakht

The Goddess Hathor Places the Magic Collar on Sethi I

Saying Farewell at Hsün-Yang

Dipylon Vase

Les Très Riches Heures de Duc de Berry

### Renaissance

The Blue Cloak (Netherlandish Proverbs)

The Last Supper

The Sistine Chapel

The School of Athens

### Baroque

Still Life 1643

The Night Watch

View of the Ducal Palace of Venice

### Romantic

Yacht Approaching the Coast

### Impressionist

Mont Ste. Victoire

Charing Cross Bridge

The Boating Party

Sunday Afternoon on the Island of La Grande Jatte

Portrait of the Artist

Faaturuma

The Bedroom of the Artist at Arles

### Modern

Cultivation of Corn

Three Musicians

Skull with Calico Rose

Tracer

20 Marilyns

### Contemporary

Buddha

Conservatory

Radioactive Cats

### Portraits

Mummy, Amen-Nestawy Nakht

Goddess Hathor Placing the Magic Collar on Sethi I

David

Portrait of the Artist

Faaturuma

Untitled, Medici Prince

The Boating Party

20 Marilyns

Conservatory

Tracer

| Groups | Landscape/Seascape |
| --- | --- |
| *Très Riches Heures de Duc de Berry* | *Très Riches Heures de Duc Berry* |
| *The Blue Cloak* | *Charing Cross Bridge* |
| *The Last Supper* | *Yacht Approaching the Coast* |
| *The School of Athens* | *Viaduct of the Ducal Palace of Venice* |
| *The Night Watch* | *Sunday Afternoon on the Island of La Grande Jatte* |
| *The Boating Party* | *Mont Ste. Victoire* |
| *Sunday Afternoon on the Island of La Grande Jatte* | *Saying Farewell at Hsün-Yang* |

# SLIDE IDENTIFICATION SCRIPT

**SLIDE 1.** *Horses, Bulls, and Stags,* Lascaux, France, 14,000–13,500 B.C., Late Paleolithic (Old Stone Age). Animals commonly drawn by early man were bison, mammoths, deer and reindeer, auraux (huge oxen), and horses. *Tarpan* horses such as these still exist in France. The artists, whose work was deep within caves, used colors such as black, red, or ocher. Animals frequently overlapped, and were painted at different times, leading archeologists to speculate that ceremonies were conducted from time to time, possibly to insure a successful hunt, or to bring back vanishing animals. The drawings might have been a form of magic or worship.

**SLIDE 2.** *The Goddess Hathor Places the Magic Collar on Sethi I,* c. 1000 B.C., Fresco. 2.26m high. Thebes, Louvre. The paintings in Egyptian tombs follow the formalized rules of painting of that time, with the figures shown in profile, the shoulders facing front, and all parts of the body showing. If even a hand were not in view, it might not exist in the after-life. The colors were intense, with no shading. The goddess Hathor, who was the patron of art, music, and love, is recognized by the crown with horns and a sun. The hieroglyphics include cartouches that presumably represent Hathor and Seth.

**SLIDE 3.** *Mummy Cartonnage of Amen-Nestawy Nakht, Priest of Awun,* c. 930–880 B.C., 167.6 × 45.1 cm, linen, plaster, and pigments. The Saint Louis Art Museum. The hieroglyphic texts that are seen on the registers describe Amen Nakht's importance, This depiction shows him wearing a wig and collar, with a solar-winged scarab beetle beneath. The four "registers" describe his journey into the afterlife. The top register shows a judgment scene, with him being led into the afterlife accompanied by Anubis, the jackal-headed god of the dead to meet the great god Osiris, lord of the Underworld. The bottom register shows his acceptance.

**SLIDE 4.** *Saying Farewell at Hsün-yang,* (detail), Ch'in Ying, Ming Dynasty (1368–1644), The Nelson-Atkins Museum of Art, Kansas City, Missouri. Although Chinese artists learn how to paint traditional styles of bamboo, pine trees, flowers, and animals, yet there is individual expression. The stylized lines of the fields and mountains is quite modern in appearance, though they were painted four hundred years ago. They are not so different from the color "patches" seen in the fields and mountains painted by Cézanne. The subtle colors could have been painted in almost any season.

**SLIDE 5.** *Dipylon Vase,* c. 700 B.C., 42½ inches high, Metropolitan Museum, N.Y. This very large krater was one of many used in Athen's Dipylon cemetery as grave markers. The bottoms were broken so that visitors to the grave might pour wine or oil as an offering to the deceased. The top band shows the meander, or Greek key design. The largest band represents a funerary scene, with the deceased (in the middle) shown on a bier, surrounded by servants and warriors. The wedge-shaped torsos and stylized figures are typical of the orientalizing phase of Greek vase decoration.

**SLIDE 6.** *Parthenon,* 448–432 B.C., Athens, Greece. The Parthenon is the temple to Athena, and is one of a group of buildings on the Acropolis, a hill that overlooks

Athens. It was designed by Ictinus and Callicrates. The Erectheon is shown in the background. The Parthenon has been a Greek Temple, a Byzantine church, a Catholic cathedral, and a mosque. In 1687 it was almost destroyed when gunpowder that was stored there by the Turks exploded. Many of the beautiful carvings that once graced the outside of the frieze and pediments are now on view in museums. The center of the stepped platform is slightly higher in the center than on the ends, and the columns swell slightly in the middle and lean slightly inward. It is thought that the intentional deviations from normal measurements and building methods contributed to the beauty and grace of this building.

**SLIDE 7.** *The Winged Victory of Samothrace,* 200–190 B.C., 108⅓ inches high, marble, Louvre, Paris. This sculpture of the goddess, Nike, just as she has descended to the prow of a ship is considered the masterpiece of Hellenistic sculpture. With robes whipping about her body, and her form leaning forward, one can almost feel the wind around her. The space that surrounds the form (the negative space) is almost as important as the sculpture itself. The skill with which the robe is carved, and the illusion of "wet" drapery on the form demonstrates vividly the evolution of Greek sculpture from the stiff rigid forms of the archaic period.

**SLIDE 8.** *Colosseum,* 80. A.D., Rome. The beautiful ruin of today's *Colosseum* gives some idea of its former grandeur. It was originally marble-covered, and had an awning to shade spectators. There were 21 principal Roman colosseums built throughout the Roman Empire. The Colossal order (columns that are on more than one story) refers to the Tuscan (similar to the Greek Doric) columns on the bottom, Ionic columns in the middle, and Corinthian columns on the top story. The barrel vault, and the resulting groin vault (when two barrel vaults intersect) are structural elements that contribute to its grace.

**SLIDE 9.** *African Mask,* 20th Century, Ibo Tribe of Nigeria, 8 × 30 inches, The Saint Louis Art Museum. This mask, with its decorative cones is probably the result of a tribal tradition that emphasized a headdress on top of the mask. The wooden mask was only a portion of a costume that was used in rituals, with the body often being covered with grasses. Throughout Africa, masks are recognizable by the region from which they come. Some masks cover the face only, while others are worn on the shoulders and are enormous. The decorative, repetitive design, and unusual arrangement of shapes are the hallmarks of a master carver.

**SLIDE 10.** *Les Très Riches Heures de Duc de Berry,* May, 1413–1416, illuminated manuscript. Pol de Limbourg, Museé du Condé, Chantilly, France. This page, one of twelve that depict the months, vividly demonstrates the life of the Court. The Duke of Berry was the brother of the French King. The outer rim of the blue dome of heaven represents the days of the month. The signs of the zodiac are shown above the chariot of the sun, as well as the phases of the moon. The month of May is represented by showing a royal hunting party in their finery, with a castle in the background. The forest and flowers show an interest in naturalism, combined with the "International Style" that emphasized elongated figures and sumptuous fabrics.

**SLIDE 11.** *Bayeux Tapestry* (detail), c. 1080, 230 feet × 20 inches, Bayeux, France. This embroidered linen tapestry is one of the first known works by women. Created by Queen Matilda and the ladies of her court, it is a visual history of the conquest of England by the Duke of Normandy. This scene shows the fleet setting sail for England, leaving Saint-Velery in the night of September 18, 1066. The tapestry is not woven, but is linen, embroidered in wool. Its stylized design and pattern-filled details, the animals embroidered on the bottom, and the boats filled with horses and warriors, tell a tale of war in a very pleasant manner.

**SLIDE 12.** *Chartres Cathedral,* 1215–1220, Chartres, France. Until the flying buttress and gothic arch were devised, it was impossible to build cathedrals with the great soaring heights, the openness, and the sheer majesty of these buildings. Because these cathedrals sometimes took hundreds of years to complete, many styles of sculpture are found, sometimes even on the same portal, such as is seen on south porch of Chartres. Although the two spires were created some time apart, they do not detract from the beauty of this church, and the south (right) tower is considered one of the most beautiful spires of the Gothic period.

**SLIDE 13.** *The Blue Cloak* (The Netherlandish Proverbs), Pieter Brueghel, 1599, oil on wood, 46 × 64⅛ inches, Staatlich Museen, Berlin Gemaldegalerie. This painting illustrates about 100 Flemish proverbs, many of which are similar to those known by us today (such as the figure in the lower left "banging his head against a stone wall"). Brueghel's figure-filled paintings depicting peasant life often had a moral. The title refers to the figure near the center foreground, illustrating the proverb, "She hangs a blue cloak (lies) around her husband." Attacking foolish behavior through proverbs and humor was a way of teaching morals in the sixteenth century. Can you think of any proverbs that are used today to help improve habits?

**SLIDE 14.** *The Last Supper,* 1495–1498, fresco, Leonardo Da Vinci, Santa Maria della Grazie, Milan, Italy. *The Last Supper* uses one-point perspective, with everything in the picture pointing to the head of Christ. This is supposed to be at the exact moment that He has announced, "One of you will betray me." The figures are reacting to this statement in a variety of ways. The disciples are from left to right: Bartholomew, James, son of Alphaeus, Andrew, Judas, Peter, John, Jesus, Thomas, James, son of Zebedee, Philip, Matthew, Thaddeus, and Simon. Its vibrant colors are dulled because of experimental methods Leonardo used in applying paint, but it is still impressive. The door cut into the painting just below Christ demonstrates that the Friars did not revere this as the masterpiece it is considered today.

**SLIDE 15.** *David,* 1501–1504, 14 feet high, marble, Academia, Florence, Italy. While Michelangelo created many sculptures, this one, created for one of the buttresses for the Florence cathedral, is considered one of his greatest. It represents the youth, David, with his slingshot in his hand, ready to slay the giant, Goliath. The tensed muscles, the determination on the face and mouth, the deliberate exaggeration of the size of the hands, the contrapposto (weight on one leg, which causes one hip to be raised), and delicate balance, all combine to make it one of the most memorable of the Renaissance sculptures.

**SLIDE 16.** *The Sistine Chapel, Detail of Creation of Man,* 1508–1512, fresco, Michelangelo, The Vatican, Rome. Michelangelo was a sculptor, and did not consider himself a painter. He was reluctantly forced by Pope Julius II to paint the Sistine Chapel ceiling. It has recently been restored to Michelangelo's original brilliant coloration. The most famous scene in the Sistine chapel is of God touching the hand of Adam to give him a soul. Adam is on the barren ground, and the figure of God, enveloped in his violet cloak, is rushing toward him through the sky. This depiction of Adam is considered one of the most beautiful figures ever painted. This is one of nine such scenes on the ceiling that tell the story of Christianity. Michelangelo's *The Last Judgment,* also in the Sistine Chapel, shows the Apostle Bartholomew holding a flayed skin. The face on the skin is thought to be a self-portrait of Michelangelo.

**SLIDE 17.** *The School of Athens,* 1510–1511, Raphael, Fresco, Stanza della Segnatura, Vatican Museum, Rome. This painting is seen as the embodiment of classical

High Renaissance. It represents the "Athenian school of thought," and shows several Greek philosophers and their students. Plato, a central figure in red, is pointing toward heaven as the source of ideas. Aristotle, next to him in blue, is pointing toward earth as the object of all observations. Socrates is shown at the upper left. Pythagoras is shown with pupils on the lower left, and on the lower right, Euclid is demonstrating a geometric theorem on a slate. This is often compared to the organization of Leonardo's *Last Supper* because of the groups of figures and their relationship to the architectural setting.

**SLIDE 18.** *Still Life 1643,* Pieter Claesz, 1597, 62.2 × 48.3 cm, oil on panel. The Saint Louis Art Museum. This "Vanitas" painting is typical of Dutch still-life paintings of the seventeenth century. These "breakfast pieces" looked as if a meal had been interrupted, and the person had to leave a half-eaten meal on the table. It was another way of saying that the interruption was death. Morbid thoughts for such a lovely painting! Dutch burghers were proud of their homes and their possessions, and these paintings gave artists an opportunity to show such beautiful objects. Most of the objects had a hidden symbolism, well known to the people of that time. The soft light, the virtuoso painting, and subtle color variations, attest to a "golden age" of painting.

**SLIDE 19.** *The Night Watch* (*The Company of Captain Frans Banning Cocq*) 1642, 12 feet 2 inches × 14 feet 7 inches, oil on canvas, Rembrandt van Rijn. Rijksmuseum, Amsterdam. Rembrandt was a skilled artist, and painted hundreds of portraits during his career. The group portrait of a company of soldiers of a Guild was traditionally a static composition. In the *Night Watch,* he departed from the tradition of showing all faces equally, and grouped the figures as they were organizing for a march. The children playing and the dog barking at the drummer further emphasize the informality of this composition. The diagonal lances, the light falling on some of the faces, served to give drama to this huge painting. When layers of dark varnish were removed, a daylight scene was revealed, though it still had the dark shadows and highlights (chiaroscuro) for which Rembrandt is known.

**SLIDE 20.** *Ducal Palace and Plaza San Marco,* Uffizzi Palace, Florence, Antonio Canaletto. Canaletto's detailed, descriptive paintings of Venice were appreciated and avidly collected, especially by the English. His "moments in time" depicted life in the city and on the canals, and give us an intimate view of eighteenth-century Venice. The pageants and festival show the bustle and vivaciousness of this city. This view of the Doge's Palace and the onion domes on St. Mark's cathedral in the background show the Byzantine influence on the architecture of Venice.

**SLIDE 21.** *Yacht Approaching the Coast,* J. M. W. Turner, c. 1835–1840, 40¼ × 56 inches, Tate Gallery, London. Turner's swirling compositions of colored light on clouds and water results in abstract paintings. He often illustrated historical events or literary themes, suggesting ships, buildings, landscapes, but these were incidental to the portrayal of atmospheric effects such as fires, storms, the smoke of battle, and sunsets. When showing his work, he often accompanied the labels with quotations of poetry—his own and that of others. Most of Turner's work was completed in a studio, though he made quick watercolor sketches when he was outside. The white canvas showing through his oil paintings gave the same luminous effect he could obtain with watercolors.

**SLIDE 22.** *Mont Ste. Victoire,* 1885–1887, Paul Cézanne, Stedelijk Museum, Amsterdam. This favorite subject of Cézanne could be seen from the window of his studio in Aix-en-Provence, France. He painted at least 60 versions of the mountain from a variety of angles. His use of color at times made the mountain seem quite close, but he controlled the distance by enriching details and deepening the color of the landscape in the foreground. His landscapes do not show a time of day, or even the season in which they were painted. His latest efforts were quite abstract. Although he never actually painted one, he theorized that all forms of nature were based on the cone, the sphere, and the cylinder. He was proud of being an Impressionist, and said, "I wish to make of Impressionism something solid and durable, like the art of the museums."

**SLIDE 23.** *Charing Cross Bridge,* 1903, 73.7 × 100.3 cm, oil on canvas. Claude Monet, The Saint Louis Art Museum. Monet was fascinated with the changes in light throughout the day. He did a number of "series" paintings through the years, when he explored one subject through many paintings done at different seasons and times of the day. He created a "water garden" at his home in Giverny, France, and painted there until the end of his life. Other series paintings were haystacks, Rouen Cathedral facade, and fields with poppies. *Charing Cross Bridge* is a "typical" Monet in its rich use of color and contrast. The fog almost obscures the city and boats, yet the bridge contrasts with the background through the use of complementary colors . . . a simple subject, like most of Monet's, yet with infinite variety in the hands of a master.

**SLIDE 24.** *The Boating Party,* Mary Cassatt, 1893–1894, 39½ × 26 inches, oil on canvas, National Gallery of Art, Washington, D.C. *The Boating Party* is typical of Cassatt's compositions that featured two or three people, often mothers and children. The area of flat color in the oarsman's clothing, and the brilliant yellow colors of the boat direct attention to the mother sitting in the bow of the boat, holding her child. Mary Cassatt was the only American who exhibited with the Impressionists. The influence of her friend and mentor, Edgar Degas can be seen in her oils and pastels. Japanese prints were popular in Europe during the time she lived and worked there, and the simplified shapes and patterns in her work show how they influenced her.

**SLIDE 25.** *Sunday Afternoon on the Island of La Grande Jatte,* Georges Seurat, 1884–1886, 207.6 × 308 cm, oil on canvas. Helen Birch Bartlett Memorial Collection. Because George Seurat died at age 32, he did relatively few paintings. *La Grande Jatte* is one of only four large paintings, and is considered his masterpiece. Many small studies were made in black and white and color (often on cigar box lids) before he combined them in a large painting. His "pointillist" (small dot) or "divisionist" method was very time consuming. For many years Seurat worked only in black and white. He was "afraid" of color. In this painting, as in many others, he created a contrasting border of pointillist dots. This painting was shown in the last Impressionist exhibition in 1886.

**SLIDE 26.** *Portrait of the Artist,* 1889–1890, 650 × 545 cm, oil on canvas. Vincent Van Gogh, Louvre, Paris. This was the last self-portrait painted by Van Gogh, completed a few months before his suicide. It was painted in the same year as the famous *Starry Night,* and has the same swirling strokes in the background. The compressed mouth and determined eyes are not particularly different from other self-portraits, but the confidence and boldly painted clothing and background show his mastery of brushwork, and perhaps some of the turmoil he was feeling. The tortured eyes seem to dominate the canvas.

**SLIDE 27.** *Faaturuma (Melancholic),* 1891, 37 × 26⅞ inches, oil on canvas, Paul Gauguin, Nelson-Atkins Museum of Art, Kansas City, Missouri. Gauguin inscribed this title on red-orange on the frame of the painting on the wall. This portrait was executed early in Gauguin's sojourn in the South Pacific, and is still somewhat like his European painting methods and not quite as uninhibited in color as later paintings would be. The rich color, thickly applied paint, and vivid contrasts are a forerunner of some of his later work. This painting conveys the mood of a woman lost in quiet thought.

**SLIDE 28.** *The Bedroom of Van Gogh at Arles,* 1889, 575 × 740 cm, oil on canvas. Vincent Van Gogh, Musée d'Orsay. This painting, completed shortly before his death, is Van Gogh at his best. Sometimes he painted these interior paintings at night, with candles stuck in his hat to provide light. He says, "I have tried to express the terrible passions of humanity by means of red and green." He often painted the rush chairs in these vividly contrasting colors. His use of perspective gives depth to the room, but he isn't terribly concerned if the perspective isn't exactly true. He is more concerned with contrasts. In an earlier version of this painting, he used red and green and yellow-green, where in this painting he contrasted red, yellow, and blue. This was painted in the same time period as *Starry Night.*

**SLIDE 29.** *Culture of Corn and Preparation of Pancakes,* 1950, Diego Rivera, National Palace, Mexico City. Rivera had lived and studied art in Paris, and knew Picasso, Matisse, and other painters who were interested in Cubism and Postimpressionism. The Mexican government commissioned him to do monumental frescoes for public buildings. His work is similar to that of Giotto, with simplified, rounded figures, and reflect his attempt to create a national Mexican style. His work was to influence Mexican painters for years to come. In this mural, Rivera shows all the procedures in the tradition of preparing tortillas. It shows the men doing the digging and cultivation of corn, while the women do all the steps from shelling and grinding the corn to rolling it out and cooking it. The vivid colors, placement of the figures, and the compelling story make this a powerful composition.

**SLIDE 30.** *Three Musicians,* 1921, 80 × 74 inches, Pablo Picasso. Museum of Modern Art, New York. Two versions of this painting were produced simultaneously, and they represent Picasso's Cubism at its best. Color has returned to his palette, and an eerie mood and sense of fantasy pervade the composition. The flat-color shapes appear to have been made from cut paper and arranged. The musicians are Italian circus figures, Harlequin in the diamond-patterned costume, and Pierrot, the white-costumed clown. A masked monk completes the trio. Can you locate the dog in this version?

**SLIDE 31.** *Untitled (Medici Prince),* c. 1953, 17 × 10⅝ × 4⅜ inches, Joseph Cornell, National Gallery of Art, Washington, D.C. This mixed-media construction is one of a series from the "Medici Slot Machine" series, each of which features a famous Renaissance person. Cornell photostated a portrait of Piero de Medici painted by Sofonisba Anguisciola, an Italian mannerist. It is placed behind a blue glass grid. Small photostat portions of this portrait are grouped around the central figure. The map at the prince's feet, the blue cork and wooden orange ball are all representative of Cornell's mysterious symbolism. His careful selection of objects and meticulous arrangement of shapes leave more questions than answers. What emotions do you feel when looking at a work of art such as this?

**SLIDE 32.** *Cow's Skull with Calico Roses,* 1931, 91.2 × 61 cm, oil on canvas, Georgia O'Keeffe. The Art Institute of Chicago. All rights reserved. Gift of Georgia O'Keeffe. Georgia O'Keeffe painted many different subjects, but is especially well known for her paintings of flowers and the desert hills. This painting has portions of several of the images she was painting at this time of her life. She painted black crosses that she saw when she was traveling near her home in New Mexico. The vertical folds could be seen as versions of the hills. O'Keeffe says that when she found beautiful white bones on the desert she picked them up and took them home. It seemed natural to her to combine flowers she found in her garden with other themes from nature such as the sky or hills. She says, "My paintings sometimes grow by pieces of what is around . . . . I have used these things to say what is to me the wideness and wonder of the world as I live in it."

**SLIDE 33.** *Kaufmann House (Falling Water),* 1936, Frank Lloyd Wright, Bear Run, Pennsylvania. Wright was commissioned to build a house *near* a waterfall. He chose to build the house *over* the waterfall. Huge boulders in the side of the hill are part of the house. By using reinforced concrete, he was able to build cantilevered balconies over the water. A stairwell in the living room leads directly down to the water. The contrast of cut stone verticals and cast concrete horizontal forms have made this one of the most famous private residences in modern architecture (now open to the public). He designed the furnishings, integrating them with the design of the building.

**SLIDE 34.** *Three Motives Against the Wall, Number 1,* 1958–1959, $19^{7}/_{8} \times 42^{1}/_{4} \times 17^{1}/_{4}$ inches, bronze, Henry Moore, National Gallery, Washington, D.C. Moore says that there are three fundamental poses of the human figure. One is standing, the other is seated, and third is lying down. He has used all three in this sculpture. Beginning in 1956, Moore created a group of works that included their own setting. The sitting and reclining figures are on benches, and the standing figure is on a base. The wall has irregular windows or openings. These figures are typical of Moore's work, much of which is inspired by bones. He noticed how much bones could resemble people, and his work became more and more abstract. He often took real bones, added plaster here and there, and then used these "maquettes" as models for his castings. He felt that the maquettes worked better than drawings because they allowed him to look at them from every point of view. These were then enlarged into the public sculpture seen in museums around the world.

**SLIDE 35.** *Tracer,* 1963, $84 \times 60$ inches, oil on canvas with silkscreen, Robert Rauschenberg, Nelson-Atkins Museum of Art in Kansas City, Missouri. Rauschenberg's "combine paintings" frequently included reproductions of artwork such as the *Venus and Cupid* by Velàsquez seen here. He applied photographic images with silkscreen or lithography onto a general grid system. His collages were often social commentaries, such as this one that uses familiar images such as street signs, birds in a cage, an eagle, and helicopters. This was painted at a time of increasing United States involvement in Viet Nam. He employs familiar material, using it in serial form from one work to the next.

**SLIDE 36.** *20 Marilyns,* 1962, Andy Warhol, private collection, Paris. Pop Art makes use of material that already is recognized: images such as comic strips or billboards. Warhol repeatedly used the same or similar images in his photo silkscreens. In addition to soup cans, dollar bills, and electric chairs, Warhol used popular icons, such as the Mona Lisa, or well-known movie stars Elizabeth Taylor and Marilyn Monroe or public figures such as Mao Tse Tung and Jacqueline Kennedy. At times he went back over the prints and painted on them. While he was perhaps making fun of them in one way by simply repeating their already familiar faces, the varying ways he applied the paint, sometimes almost obscuring the face, sometimes leaves one feeling uncomfortable.

**SLIDE 37.** *Buddha,* 1975, $70 \times 96$ inches, air-brushed acrylic over polymer, Audrey Flack, The Saint Louis Art Museum, purchase and Contemporary Art Society

Fund. Audrey Flack's thesis, when she was studying with Josef Albers at Yale University was about problems of space and depth. This painting, which was part of her *Gray Border* series, deliberately disorients, with objects projecting out of the picture, and with a very shallow depth of field. When she is photographing still-lifes from which to paint, she suspends objects from string and uses many props to make work stay in place. The glittering surfaces, the deliberately out-of-focus areas, and the choice of symbolic objects reflect her interest in the Baroque Dutch Vanitas paintings that use symbols to encourage people to think about the meaning of life on "conscious and unconscious levels."

**SLIDE 38.** *Conservatory,* 1988, Miriam Schapiro, Miami University Art Museum, Oxford, Ohio. In her *Frida* series, Schapiro "pays homage to and collaborates with women artists of the past." She had a series called *Mary Cassatt and Me.* She sometimes appropriates images created by an artist whom she admires such as Mexican artist Frida Kahlo, who was married to muralist Deigo Rivera. Kahlo was gravely ill, and painted many self-portraits while confined to her studio. This image, *Conservatory,* shows an appropriation of one of Kahlo's self-portraits, surrounded by images that are meaningful to Schapiro such as Tiazolteotl, the Aztec goddess of childbirth, or pots, which would have always been part of women's surroundings. Schapiro describes the relationship between herself and Kahlo. "We were both painters, . . . we were both strong survivors . . . and our paintings came from the depth of our belief systems." (Note: This information was obtained from an address to the National Art Education Association Convention in Atlanta, Georgia, 1991.)

**SLIDE 39.** *Radioactive Cats,* 1980, Cibachrome print, 30 × 37¼ inches, Sandy Skoglund, The Saint Louis Art Museum. Ms. Skoglund creates strange, otherworldly environments that she photographs; this print is one of an edition of twenty. The old couple with their salmon-colored skin, in their gray/brown environment seem almost oblivious to the chaos surrounding them. The cats seem to have taken over the room. Skoglund portrays realistic settings with dreamlike (nightmare?) people and animals, in her combinations of sculpture, painting, and photography. Another of her environments is called *Revenge of the Goldfish;* it shows orange fish floating in a blue bedroom.

**SLIDE 40.** *Zaga,* Nancy Graves, 1983, 72 × 49 × 32 inches, bronze with polychrome patina, Nelson-Atkins Museum of Art. Graves makes use of ordinary items, mostly leaves and other organic forms, that are cast in bronze. She lays the castings out on the floor, and welds the parts together, painting them afterwards. "As parts are welded together, changes in structure, balance, and three-dimensional relationships come into play. The casting may take months, the assembly takes a few hours."

# THE BEGINNINGS OF ART

# PREHISTORY
## TIME LINE

| 30,000 B.C. | 15,000 B.C. | 5000 B.C. | 4000 B.C. | 3000 B.C. | 2000 B.C. | 1000 B.C. |
|---|---|---|---|---|---|---|
| Beginnings of Western Art Prehistoric man 35,000–15,000 | Venus de la Corne | | | Sumerians 3500–2000 B.C. | Iron Age 1400 | Hammurabi's Code of Law 1290 |
| Venus of Willendorf 25,000–20,000 | Cave Paintings Lascaux & Altamira 15,000–10,000 | | Sumer Pictographic writing | Potters wheel 3250 | Babylon 1900–1600 End of Ur Empire 1950 | Babylon Ishtar Gate 575 B.C. |
| | | | | Ur Billy Goat and Tree, 3000 | | Mesopotamia conquered 900–539 |
| **AFRICA** Egyptian Kingdoms 3500–1000 B.C. | | | | | | |
| **AMERICAS** | | | | | Peru Cotton grown 200–1500 | Mexico Olmec Culture 850–150 |
| **ASIA** | | China Yang Shan and Long Shan culture 7000–4000 B.C. | | Xia (Hsia) Culture Wheel thrown Pottery 2180–1750 | Hsia Dynasty 2205–1766 | |
| **EUROPE** | Bison, Altamira. | | | | Stonehenge 1650 | Scythian Stag 700 |
| **NEAR EAST** | | | Sumer Pictographic Writing | | Babylon 1900–1600 | Prince, Persepolis 5th–4th centuries B.C. |

# Unit 1. THE ANCIENT WORLD (35,000 B.C. TO 15,000 B.C.)

## OVERVIEW OF THE VISUAL ARTS

The four earliest known civilizations—the Sumerian, Egyptian, Indian, and Chinese—all developed in great river valleys between approximately 35,000 B.C. and 15,000 B.C. The first known cultures in Europe arose and thrived 35,000 to 10,000 years ago. The people of the Old Stone Age were hunter-gatherers who lived in caves. Not much is known about them except what has been discovered painted on cave walls or from objects that have been excavated.

## PAINTING

The first known artists lived in Europe. Early cave paintings have been discovered all the way from southern Spain and Sicily to southern Siberia. They might have been painted to teach lessons of survival, to portray legends, or to illustrate traditions. Cave art may have been part of initiation ceremonies for young tribesmen or some other rite. Some theorists think that because of their inaccessibility, they represented magical or symbolic figures. Although it is not known if the artists were men or women, it is known that the caves were used for thousands of years, with many surfaces overpainted a number of times.

## MASTERPIECES

*Stags,* c. 15,000 B.C., Lascaux Cave, Montignac, France

*Bison,* c. 15,000–10,000 B.C., cave painting, Altamira, Spain

## SCULPTURE

Small carved stone female forms were found in western Europe. Female figures were also occasionally incised and painted on cave walls. Other naturalistic forms of animals skillfully carved of horn, ivory, or stone have been found throughout Europe.

The Cult of Skulls (7000 B.C.) in Jericho embellished real skulls with clay. Similar works were created in other cultures, such as the Sepik culture in New Guinea, which used sea shell eyes and elaborate patterns.

## MASTERPIECES

*Plastered Skull,* c. 7000–6000 B.C., Jericho, Jordan

*Venus of Willendorf,* c. 15,000–10,000 B.C., Museum of Natural History, Vienna

*Bison,* c. 15,000–10,000 B.C., Museum of National Antiquities, St.-Gemain-en-Laye, France

## ARCHITECTURE

The beginnings of architecture were homes made of wicker, timber, and thatch. Later construction was in wood, brick, and stone. Early stone columns were carved to resemble bundles of reeds that might have been the first "columns." The first known masonry town is Jericho, which was built around 8000 B.C. It had a rough wall and at least one tower 30 feet tall.

The stone circles (cromlechs) found in England are not exactly architecture, but they did serve to enclose space. The most famous of these structures is Stonehenge (2000 B.C.), a circle of large raised stones that were hauled 25 miles by the people who created it. It has a rough form of post and lintel architecture. Stonehenge appears to have been created as a sort of calendar, with the sunrise at the summer solstice coming in at a certain opening. Dolmens were large upright stones used to support horizontal stone slabs. Menhirs (single, large, upright stones) found in Brittany, France (as well as Great Britain), at times arranged in rows, were possibly grave markers and might have been involved in worship.

# PROJECT 1-1: VENUS

### FOR THE TEACHER

"Venus" is a name later given to a group of female forms created by the Upper Paleolithic culture. The *Venus of Willendorf,* which is representative of the "Venus" figures, dates between 30,000 and 25,000 B.C. It is only 4½ inches high and fits easily into the hand. Although their purpose is unknown, these figures were often found in women's graves. The exaggerated breasts, abdomen, and hips indicate their use as fertility figures. (It is assumed through cave paintings that rituals relating to human and animal fertility went on during the Paleolithic times.)

### PREPARATION

Show a slide of the *Venus,* and ask students to write about it for five minutes. Suggest they begin by describing the statue, and what purpose they think it might have served. When they are done writing, ask them to share their theories with the class. Ask them what they know about symbols from the past, and then ask them to discuss symbols of today (the flag and apple pie are examples).

After the project, these forms can be remade into balls and kept in a plastic bag for reuse. If you prefer to have something permanent, have the students use ceramic clay or clay that can be fired in a home oven.

### FURTHER SUGGESTIONS

- Ask them to think of an abstract concept (such as love, space, sadness, or loneliness) and "symbolize" it with the clay, without resorting to obvious symbols such as lips or hearts (for love) or space ships (for space).
- Fertility symbols could be objects other than people. Let them think of a fertility symbol (I usually suggest that they avoid the obvious), and model it in oil clay. You may get (as I did) a fried egg or a flower growing from a bulb.

Name: _____    Date: _____

# PROJECT 1–1:  VENUS

**MATERIALS**

- ½ pound of oil clay (Plasticine)

Probably the first "fertility figures" were nothing more than special egg-shaped "magic" pebbles that seemed to resemble a person or animal. They possessed sacred qualities to early Stone Age humans. Eventually people realized that with flint tools, they could change the shape slightly. It was small enough to hold in your hand, so perhaps sharp corners would not have been comfortable. You will model your fertility symbols by shaping a ball of clay without pinching any of it off. In modeling your "Venus," remember that these were relatively abstract figures. Maybe yours will be tall and skinny.

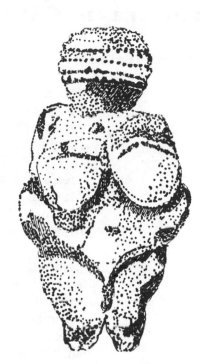

**Venus of Willendorf**

1. Unwrap the clay and hold it in your palms, turning it and trying to shape it into a ball. There is no need to pound it or be in a hurry because it works quite easily after your hands have warmed it for a few minutes.

2. Without removing any of the clay, use your fingers to make a neck and head. Then decide how much detail to make. Many of these figures had detailed hair, and one even had a "woven" skirt, with detail incised (drawn with a pencil) on it. Do you think there was a reason that the real Venus figures did not have faces?

3. You could add texture by impressing objects into the surface. Take the eraser from a mechanical pencil or remove the top of a ball point pen to make circular indentations, or make a pebble surface by lightly "stippling" with a firm brush or pencil tip.

**Venus de Brassenpouy**
**Les Eyzies de Tayac**

**Venus de la Corne**
**Les Eyzies de Tayac, France**

**Venus de Lespugue**
**Les Eyzies de Tayac, France**

# PROJECT 1-2: CAVE PAINTING MURAL

**FOR THE TEACHER**

**Slide # 1: *Horses, Bulls, and Stags.*** Early artists, the ancestors of the Cro-Magnons, painted high on walls and ceilings, using crude scaffolding and lamps of some type (probably hollowed out stones that held wicks of moss and oil). These people had a completely developed language and dealt with complex notions of religion and belief.

The ceiling on the Altamira cave in Spain has been called the Sistine Chapel of prehistoric paintings. There are at least 200 known painted caves in Europe alone. Many of the animals painted in these caves are extinct. Recent excavations show that although the cave dwellers ate mostly reindeer and deer meat, they most commonly drew horses, bison, mammoth, auraux (huge oxen), ibex, and six species of deer.

At times figures (sometimes reclining women) were carved into the wall, then painted. They were outlined in black, then color was applied. Paints used were black and yellow manganese, red and yellow ocher, and occasionally violet. The pigments were mixed with water, egg white, or blood. At times painters used their own hands as stencils, by blowing pigment through a hollow bone at their hands held on the wall. Some of the animals are decorated with mysterious, abstract signs and geometric shapes such as circles, ellipses, dots, and crescents. Animals occasionally overlapped, and many kinds might be shown together.

**MASTERPIECES**

*Wounded Bison,* c. 15,000–10,000 B.C., cave painting, Altamira, Spain

*Hall of Bulls,* c. 15,000–10,000 B.C., Lascaux, France

*Spotted Horses with Negative Hand Imprints,* c. 15,000–10,000 B.C., Pech-Merle, France

**PREPARATION**

To keep the paintings large and bold, make this a huge mural. Students could work on the floor or staple the paper to the wall with undulating forms (stuff newspaper inside in places), as if it were rock, and then paint it. Divide the students into groups. One group might create horses, another bison, another stags, and another hunters. To give an appearance of rocks, crumple the paper the day before painting, brush it with diluted ink or paint, and allow it to dry. The students could take advantage of natural forms found in the creases, just as the cave painters did when they painted.

**FURTHER SUGGESTIONS**

- Make the room dark, and invite others in for a "torchlight tour" of the "cave." To make it a real party, have students figure out what cave dwellers might eat or drink, and have finger food and a movable feast. This could be an evening feature at an open house.

- Make some of the painting implements from natural, "found materials" such as sticks, reeds, yucca or other spiky plants, or animal hair. Use them with ink to draw an animal.

- Petroglyphs are drawings incised on caves and rocks by Native Americans. Make "rocks" by flattening baseball-sized clay with the palm of your hand (so that they are no thicker than 1 inch). Use a pencil or needle-tool to draw scenes of contemporary life. These could be made even more realistic by mixing two colors of clay for a marblized effect.

- To make petroglyph "rock" boxes, form a clay ball. Make the shapes more "rocklike" by flattening some areas on a table before incising petroglyphs on them. Cut the forms in half horizontally with a wire, and hollow them out to ¼-inch thickness. This project and the previous one would need to be fired unless made of self-hardening clay.

## MASTERPIECES

*Stonehenge,* c. 2000 B.C., Winchester, England

*Menhirs and Dolmen,* c. 1500 B.C., Carnac, France

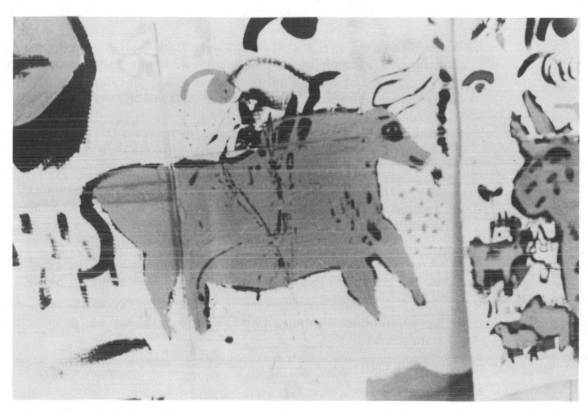

# PROJECT 1–2:  CAVE PAINTING MURAL

**MATERIALS**

- Brown kraft paper, 36 inches wide × 30 feet long
- Diluted ink or brown paint
- Painting instruments: hair taped on a stick, brushes, charcoal briquets, sticks, or bamboo tubes, large brushes 2 to 3 inches
- Flashlights
- Newspapers
- Pigments: brown, reddish brown, yellow, white, and black

Some of the cave dwellers' drawings were stick figures or outlines of their hands. Other paintings were simple and sophisticated, with animals outlined in black and painted in large areas of flat color. Find pictures of wall paintings done by cave dwellers in Lascaux, France, Altamira, Spain, or other areas of the world.

1. Make small, rough pencil sketches of animals (they could be the same animals the early cave dwellers painted, or even your own dog or cat). Choose your best drawing.

2. If you are working with a group, plan ahead. It will make a more effective mural if designs overlap each other so there is no distinct line indicating where one person or group quit and the next began. Look at the previously prepared crumpled paper to see if you "find" an animal already there, or use natural divisions created by the lines.

3. First outline the animal in black, then paint in large flat (unshaded) areas of color. It will look more like a cave wall if large areas of brown paper are left unpainted.

4. Stand back and consider the overall effect. Try to tie areas together with additional animals or people, if needed. You could also use geometric designs, dots, and handprints.

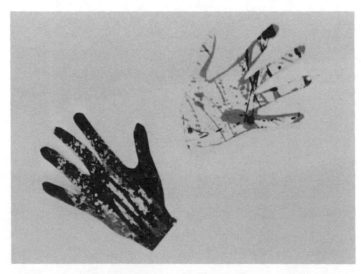

**Photo 1-2. Holman Middle School students outlined their hands and painted the cut-outs for their room-sized mural.**

© 1992 by The Center for Applied Research in Education, Inc.

## Unit 2: EGYPT (7000 B.C. TO 500 B.C.)

**OVERVIEW OF THE VISUAL ARTS**

Egypt is considered the "cradle" of Western civilization, partially because so much of the culture has survived due to its burial customs, climate, and building materials, and because of the way its influence spread to Greece and then throughout Europe. The advent of hieroglyphics gave us one of the first written histories of a culture. The lore of mummies, pyramids, temples, the Rosetta stone, King Tut, and the pharaohs is familiar and fascinating.

Egyptian artists differed from our idea of what an artist is today. Great Egyptian artists followed the rules and did not innovate. The more their art looked like everyone else's, the better the artist was considered. With few exceptions, both sculpture and painting almost always show a young person, though we know many pharaohs lived to old age. The ideal age for the after-life was considered 23, so the deceased person was almost always depicted as young.

Art forms in Egypt were "unified," with temples and tombs designed to be decorated with painting and sculpture. Most paintings and sculpture were created specifically for a site such as a tomb, temple, or building.

**Egypt and Israel**

# EGYPT
## TIME LINE

| 7000 B.C. | 5000 B.C. | 3000 B.C. | 2000 B.C. | 1500 B.C. | 1000 B.C. | 500 B.C. | 1 |
|---|---|---|---|---|---|---|---|

Archaic Period 3500–2800

Old Kingdom 2815–2294

New Kingdom 1650–650

Post Empire 1085–333

Ptolemaic Period 332–30

Upper and Lower Egypt United 3100

Middle Kingdom 2200–1650

Queen Hatshepsut 1480

Alexander the Great conquers Egypt—332

Papyrus 1500

King Zoser Step Pyramids 2780–2720

1365 Nefertiti, Akhenaten c 1360

Tutankhamen 1352

Hippocrates born 469

Hieroglyphic writing 3000

Sphinx 2530

Pyramids 2530–2470

Ramses the Great, 1304

Rosetta Stone 195

Temple of Horus, Edfu

Palette of Narmer, 3000

**Africa**

**Americas**

Silk Production 1500

**Asia**

Shun Dynasty 2300–2205

Chou Dynasty 1122–770

Great Wall of China 214

Chinese Painting 1028

Shang Dynasty 1766–1122

Woodblock printing 618

**Europe**

Scythian Stag 700

**Near East**

Wall of Jericho, Jordan 7000 B.C.

India—Oldest Sanskirt Literature 1500

Israelites leave Egypt 1250

Bull, Sumeria 2800–2600

Moses 1500

**Other**

## PAINTING

Because of Egypt's extraordinarily dry climate, much of the art has survived, giving us an accurate picture of what the paintings of Egypt looked like 5000 years ago. Although much has undoubtedly been lost, the tombs in the Valley of the Kings at Thebes have most of the original paint still intact. The colors are brilliant and clean, though limited in palette.

Elaborate paintings were created for tombs, to make the after-life at least as pleasant for the deceased as real life. The paintings, tomb furniture, and sculpture provided food, entertainment, and worldly goods. Often the life of the personage was recorded, including battles and prisoners taken, or the person making religious offerings. The deceased was shown making a boat journey through the underworld, or sometimes depicted with their protective gods introducing them to netherworld gods. Mummy cases were richly decorated, often with the same stories and details seen in the wall paintings.

## MASTERPIECES OF PAINTING

*The Daughters of Akhenaten*, c. 1365 B.C., Ashmolean Museum, Oxford

*Baboons*, c. 1360 B.C., Tomb of Tutankhamen, Thebes, Egypt

*Tutankhamen Hunting*, c. 1360 B.C., Egyptian Museum, Cairo

## SCULPTURE

The *Sphinx* (a human-headed lion carved of natural rock) is probably the most famous example of ancient sculpture. Guardian statues such as the *Sphinx*, rams, or other animal-headed gods were placed outside the tomb. Several large sculptures, such as the *Colossi of Memnon*, although they were damaged by war or earthquake, remain basically intact today.

Small toylike (effigy) figures were constructed in groups and placed in tombs. Bas-relief (low-relief) carvings were created by applying a thin coat of plaster to the wall, then using a pattern to carve images. Because of hieroglyphics and the Egyptian numbering system, extensive writing on temples told a great deal about the inhabitants and rulers of that time.

Although most sculptures of people were idealized, the concern with the after-life caused sculptors to fashion portrait busts called reserve heads to serve as representations of the body in the event of tomb robbery. Most tombs had either life-sized or smaller effigies.

The sculptures were made mostly from basalt or limestone. Egyptian sculpture was rather stiff in appearance, with figures facing frontward, frequently seated, with hands on the knees. Standing figures had the left foot forward, as if the figure were walking, but with the weight evenly balanced. Most were still attached to the rock from which they were carved, or if basically free-standing, the hands were attached to the sides of the legs. If they were painted, the men were usually reddish brown, while the women were lighter (women stayed indoors all day and were not as dark).

Tutankhamen's (King Tut's) predecessor, Akhenaten, allowed portraits to be made of him that did not follow the accepted "rules" but actually depicted his unique and not very handsome features. In contrast, the sculpture of his wife, Nefertiti is perhaps one of the most beautiful in the world. This brief period of naturalism was short-lived.

## MASTERPIECES OF SCULPTURE

*Chefren,* c. 2530 B.C., Egyptian Museum, Cairo

*The Great Sphinx,* c. 2530 B.C., Giza, Egypt

*Mycernius and His Queen,* c. 2500 B.C., Museum of Fine Arts, Boston

*Nefertiti,* c. 1365 B.C., State Museums, Berlin

*Coffin Cover of Tutankhamen,* c. 1360 B.C., Egyptian Museum, Cairo

*Workmen Carrying a Beam,* c. 1325 B.C., Museo Civico, Bologna

## ARCHITECTURE

The pyramids rising out of the desert on the edge of Cairo at Giza are among the most famous pieces of architecture in the world. They were erected in 2590 to 2470 B.C. to house Pharaohs Cheops, Chefren, and Mycernius. There are numerous smaller pyramids in the vicinity and elsewhere in Egypt, but these are the most famous. The *Pyramid of Chefren* with its vestiges of a polished surface near the top is depicted on the U.S. dollar bill.

Many famous temples still exist. Temples were mostly for the priests' use, though the public was allowed into them on feast days (and there were many feast days!). Great courtyards are enclosed by colonnades. The most common method of building was the post and lintel system, similar to that of Stonehenge. To support a stone roof, the columns were large and close together. Unfortunately, 20 temples were inundated when Lake Nasser was built.

## MASTERPIECES

*Karnak,* Luxor, Egypt

*Pyramids of Mycerinus,* c. 2470 B.C.

*Chefren,* c. 2500 B.C.

*Cheops,* c. 2530 B.C., Giza, Egypt

*Funerary Temple of Hatshepsut,* c. 1480 B.C., Deir-el-Bahari, Egypt

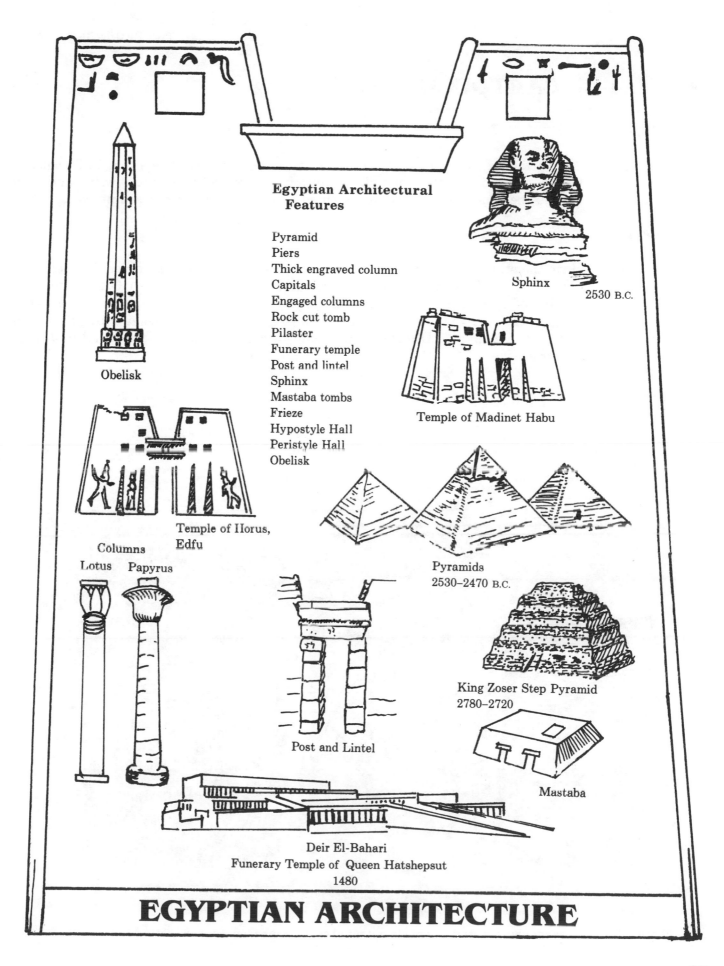

**Egyptian Architectural Features**

Pyramid
Piers
Thick engraved column
Capitals
Engaged columns
Rock cut tomb
Pilaster
Funerary temple
Post and lintel
Sphinx
Mastaba tombs
Frieze
Hypostyle Hall
Peristyle Hall
Obelisk

Obelisk

Sphinx
2530 B.C.

Temple of Madinet Habu

Columns
Lotus    Papyrus

Temple of Horus,
Edfu

Pyramids
2530–2470 B.C.

King Zoser Step Pyramid
2780–2720

Post and Lintel

Mastaba

Deir El-Bahari
Funerary Temple of Queen Hatshepsut
1480

# EGYPTIAN ARCHITECTURE

# PROJECT 1–3: CARTOUCHE

**FOR THE TEACHER**

The cartouche (pronounced "cartoosh") was an oblong form (like a long pill) that contained the name of the pharaoh or king. It was often made into jewelry and worn around the neck, but was also represented on tomb paintings and sculpture.

**PREPARATION**

Have the students research what their name would be in hieroglyphics. (You can also give them the handout, "Egyptian Hieroglyphics," provided here.) Offer students a number of options for making their cartouche. They could make book marks, a sign to hang on the door to their rooms, or a book jacket or decorate a T-shirt (by painting on it with acrylic paint). Directions for making a cartouche in clay are found in *Jewelry Fit for a King*.

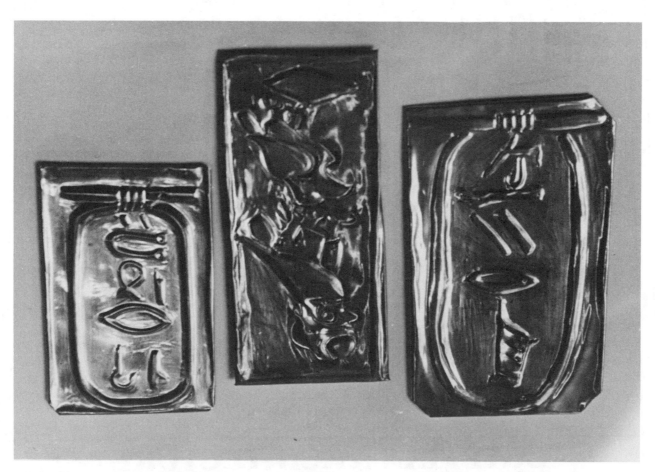

**Photo 1-3. Sue Brandenburg's students made personal cartouches from copper tooling foil.**

# EGYPTIAN HIEROGLYPHICS

© 1992 by The Center for Applied Research in Education, Inc.

| | | | | | | |
|---|---|---|---|---|---|---|
| A | I'YAY | Å | W.U | B | P | F |
| M | N | R | H | H. | Kh | H |
| S | Sch | K. | K | G | T | Tsh |
| D | Dj | L | RÅ | NeB | TA | MeN |
| DjeD | DI | SU | MeR | KhePeR | ANkh | NeFeR |
| NeTeR | HeKA | Weep | Man | Woman | God | Loaf |
| Water | City | Desert | Death | Walk | Child | 1000000 |
| I  II  1  2 | III  IIIII III  3  7 | ∩ ∩∩I  10  21 | 100 | 1000 | 10000 | 100000 |

# PROJECT 1–3: CARTOUCHE

## MATERIALS

**Cartouches from Tomb of Horemheb**

- Newsprint
- Six-ply mat board
- T-shirts
- Brushes
- Pencil
- String
- Acrylic paint
- Newspaper

To make your cartouche, first look at a hieroglyphic chart, or research hieroglyphics in a library. The symbols are arranged vertically. If there is not enough room for your entire name, then use hieroglyphics for your initials. You may also use any common Egyptian symbol, such as the pyramids, Sphinx, Nefertiti, a cat, duck, the lotus, or papyrus. Several commonly used hieroglyphics are shown on the hieroglyphics handout.

1. Before making a pattern, decide on the size and purpose of your cartouche. You could make a sign for your room, a bookmark, or a design to be painted on a T-shirt.

2. Make a pattern by drawing a lozenge, which is a long, vertical, straight-sided rectangle (with rounded top and bottom). Space the symbols equally, and draw them carefully.

**Bookmark.** To make a bookmark, cut a piece of cardboard $2\frac{1}{2} \times 5$ inches. If the edges are rough, smooth them with an emery board or sandpaper. Go over the back of the newsprint pattern with pencil. Turn it over and trace it onto the bookmark. Carefully draw the pattern in pencil, and paint it (and the background if you wish) with acrylic paint, using gold paint for accents. You may do the same design on both sides, or (when the first side is dry) turn it over and paint the back one color. You could put a decorative pattern around the outside. Punch a hole in one end, and make a tassel by folding 5 2-inch long strings. Place this loop through the hole, and put all the cut ends through the loop on the other side. Pull it taut.

**T-Shirt.** To paint a cartouche on a T-shirt, first make the pattern as before. Outline it in black marker. Put a pad of newspaper inside the T-shirt, and place the pattern inside the shirt. you will be able to see the pattern and can draw it onto the shirt lightly with pencil. Place wax paper inside the shirt on top of the pad of newsprint. With acrylic paint, paint your design. The cartouche could be the entire design, or a portion of it. You could make an entire square of hieroglyphics.

## PROJECT 1-4: **JEWELRY FIT FOR A KING**

### FOR THE TEACHER

Egyptian goldsmiths were highly skilled ceramists and glass makers. They blended colors and forms, using semiprecious stones such as amethyst, turquoise, lapis lazuli, cornelian, and jasper. They learned to enamel metal and used brilliant colors. Mummies are found with many faience (turquoise ceramic) and gold amulets within the wrapping cloth. They made beautiful necklaces, headbands, collars, rings, cartouches, and bracelets, in addition to elaborate masks and coffins.

### PREPARATION

Find photographs of Egyptian jewelry. Many of the designs were based on animal forms such as fish, fowl, snakes, beetles (scarabs), or cats.

### FURTHER SUGGESTIONS

- Have the students make large collars such as the Egyptians wore, but use any material they can possibly think of. These collars would be approximately five inches wide, and would be collar shaped (an oval, open at the back), but there the resemblance would end. Begin with a 25-inch cord or wire to go around the neck. Suggested materials to be strung together or pasted on tagboard are safety pins, pictures torn from jewelry catalogues, comics of Mickey Mouse, pictures of eyes, pasta shapes, corks, pull tabs from soda cans, whatever.

- A cartouche could also be made in fired clay, as shown in the next project. If fired ceramics are not feasible, small pieces of prestamped wood or 80-pound watercolor paper shapes are available in hobby shops or through art supply catalogs. Self-hardening clay and plastics also are suitable for this purpose.

# PROJECT 1–4: JEWELRY FIT FOR A KING

**MATERIALS**

- Paper and pencil
- Glue-on pins and epoxy glue
- Silk cord (from hobby shops)
- Needles stuck in a cork (or needle tools)
- Ceramic materials and tools

    Scrapers, clay, dowels or rolling pins,
    underglazes, clear glazes, natural sponges

The jewelry you make could be used as a pin (by gluing on a pin back), pendant, earrings, or key chain. For design ideas, look at tomb paintings and books on Egyptian artifacts. Some examples of the patterns used in Egyptian jewelry and paintings are shown here. Draw several ideas for your Egyptian jewelry.

1. Select a walnut-sized piece of clay. Roll it out to a thickness of approximately ¼ inch. Use a needle to prick any bubbles on the surface. Using a scraper, smooth the surface carefully. This is enough clay to make more than one piece of jewelry. Use the needle to outline the shape of the jewelry. With a knife, cut out the jewelry shape. Smooth the edges with a sponge. Place your initials (in hieroglyphics if you wish) on the back. For decoration, apply thin pieces of clay with slip. Make a hole in the top for hanging.

2. After the unglazed pieces are fired, paint on underglazes, and then cover them with a clear glaze before refiring. The colors most used in Egyptian jewelry were light and dark blue, dark red, turquoise, white, yellow, green, and black. Small amounts of lusters (gold or silver glazes) could be added to a fired, glazed piece before refiring.

**Scarabs.** To make scarabs (beetles), make a small round clay ball. Shape it to a slight oval, and put a thin paper drinking straw through the center. When the piece dries, the straw can be removed, or fired. Flatten the ball on the bottom. Incise the marks found on a beetle. It is effective to glaze these in turquoise to resemble the faience Egyptian scarabs. Put hieroglyphics on the underside. The hole will allow you to string it on a silken cord or leather thong.

**Cartouche.** To make a ceramic cartouche, make a long clay rectangle with rounded ends. Make a hole in the top for hanging (remember that holes shrink when ceramics are fired). This can have names or initials incised and can be painted with underglazes before firing. Apply a clear glaze before firing a second time.

© 1992 by The Center for Applied Research in Education, Inc.

# PROJECT 1–5: **PHARAOH'S TOMB**

## FOR THE TEACHER

**Slide # 2: *The Goddess Hathor Places the Magic Collar on Sethi I.*** The passageways into the pharaohs' tombs in the Valley of the Kings are lined with beautiful paintings. Deep inside the tombs almost every inch is painted, even the ceilings. The paintings are usually organized in "registers," rows that contain a group of figures or hieroglyphics. The Egyptians believed that the Ka, the soul of the deceased, might have gone wandering during the day, but would return to the body at night. They wanted to make the after-life as comfortable as possible, so everything the person enjoyed in daily life was painted there.

The gods were often painted in these registers. The Egyptian Gods handout shows the appearance of the better known gods.

## PREPARATION

Have the registers already cut of posterboard. They can be effectively lined up for display to look almost like the ones at the entrance to a tomb.

Discuss the appearance of Egyptian art. Sometimes the insides of both feet or hands show, with the saying "I have two left feet" being literal. Stylization (nonrealism) was important because the entire body had to be intact for the after-life. Figures were shown rigidly posed, usually in profile with the iris of the eye looking straight out at the viewer. The shoulders face outward, and generally one leg is in front of the other, so the Ka (soul) will have a complete body in the "Field of Reeds" (Egyptian heaven). If a hand or foot were hidden, it might not join the rest of the body. Figures were outlined in black and filled in with flat colors. The colors used were ultramarine (powdered lapis lazuli), red, brown, black, green, yellow, and white. Hierarchical scaling was used, with the more important figures being larger than the others in a scene. Animals and plants were represented far more naturalistically. Perspective did not exist. A pool or lake would have to be shown as seen from above, with the trees all aiming outward, much as a young child might try to draw a swimming pool.

The Hieroglyphic Chart handout shows most letters of the Egyptian alphabet. This could be reproduced and given to each student or photocopied onto an overhead transparency and projected onto the wall. Talk about the symbolism seen in the hieroglyphics, and then discuss modern symbolism. Ask students to name symbols that everyone understands (a caduceus, the shape of a Coca-Cola® bottle, etc.).

## FURTHER SUGGESTIONS

- Make a cardboard pyramid and decorate the inside of it. Or decorate a corner of the room or a closet to look like the inside of a small tomb.
- Students can do a drawing on 9 × 12-inch drawing paper of themselves in modern dress in a modern background drawn in the Egyptian style. These are effective when done with colored pencil.

**Photos 1-4.** Students drawing of themselves wearing modern clothes, but drawn in the manner of a tomb register.

# EGYPTIAN GODS

### AMUN-RA

The hawk-headed sun god wears a sun surrounded by a serpent. Considered by some traditions to be the creator of man.

### ANUBIS

The jackal-headed god of the dead. He was the god of mummification, and assisted souls in the afterworld.

### HATHOR

The "cow-goddess" of love also was the goddess of happiness, dance, and music. She always was seen with horns and a solar disk. Her legs held up the sky.

### ISIS

The wife of Osiris and mother of Horus had great magical powers. She protected children, which made her the most popular goddess.

### KNUM

The ram-headed god fashioned the "world-egg" on his potters wheel. He was the god of fertility and creation.

### OSIRIS

A good god, he was the husband of Isis, and god of the underworld. He was the god of nature, as shown by his green skin.

### PTAH

The god of death was the patron of artisans and artists. He is usually shown as a mummy.

### HORUS

Hawk-headed sky god known as the "uniter of two lands" is wearing the combined crown of upper and lower Egypt.

### THOTH

The ibis-headed god is the patron of science and literature, spokesman of the gods and keeper of their literature.

## PROJECT 1–5: **PHARAOH'S TOMB**

**MATERIALS**

- Posterboard, approximately 11 × 28 inches long
- Oil crayon: black, reddish brown, brown, yellow-gold, green, and blue
- Metal rulers
- Pencil

The assignment is to make a picture of yourself in a tomb "register." Think about the things you do to pass time—watch TV? talk on the phone? eat? fish? Sports, dance, or music might inspire you. Draw yourself in your future life. Include family, friends, teams, etc., if you wish. Consider some modern symbols that mean something to you (things everyone would recognize the meaning of).

1. Use a metal ruler to draw a line 1½ inches from the top and bottom on the piece of posterboard. If everyone in the class uses this same measurement, then when these are all grouped together, they will line up correctly.

2. Draw a border using some of the decorative designs you find in books. Borders frequently used variations of the lotus or papyrus plant (which were symbols of upper and lower Egypt). You may also make up designs to represent contemporary life.

3. Use a pencil to draw an outline of yourself in modern clothing, but with Egyptian style of drawing. Make a profile, with your eye looking out sideways. Use other people, birds, animals, or plants in the drawing. You can draw yourself in several such scenes.

4. To put your own name in the drawing, use a hieroglyphic chart to help spell it. A "cartouche" frequently was shown in tombs. It is a long rectangular shape with rounded corners (a lozenge), with the name or initials shown vertically.

5. Add color, leaving the background white and filling in shapes with intense, plain colors. When you are all done, use black oil pastel or permanent marker to go around all the outlines and add detail such as vertical hieroglyphics. If you put the black on first, it smears.

© 1992 by The Center for Applied Research in Education, Inc.

## PROJECT 1-6: **THE BOOK OF THE DEAD**

## PROJECT 1-7: **MUMMY**

**FOR THE TEACHER**

**Slide # 3: *Mummy Cartonnage of Amen-Nestawy-Nahkt,* Priest of Amun.** Entombment in Egyptian society was ritualized and followed a prescribed procedure. Although earlier dynasties inscribed and painted scenes of the after-life on tomb walls, after the New Kingdom, the *Book of the Dead* was actually enclosed in the sarcophagus. The collection of magic and religious formulas was written on papyrus to provide protection against all the dangers that might be found on a journey through the netherworld. The scrolls often included paintings of the deceased being introduced to the various gods. Fragments of some scrolls have survived more than 5000 years. In later years the magic spells and stories were also painted on the coffin. (The Egyptian *Book of the Dead* has been translated into English and might be available at your library.)

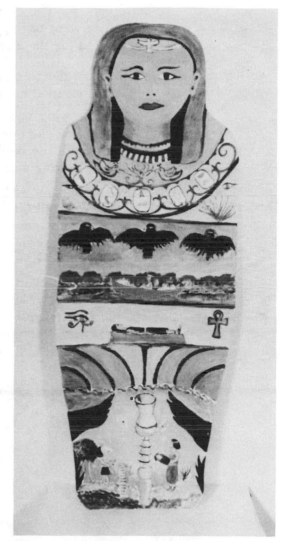

Photo 1-5. Student artwork.

**PREPARATION**

The same general preparation is for either of these projects. Give students hieroglyphic handouts and have them attempt to find photos of tomb scenes. Point out the specific Egyptian rules for painting. Try to find some Egyptian folk tales for students to illustrate. If this isn't feasible, students can illustrate some modern sayings or folk tales or make up a story about themselves. For display, tape a number of the drawings together on the back, and staple them to a dowel at each end to resemble a scroll. Or allow each student to make an individual scroll.

## PROJECT 1–6:  THE BOOK OF THE DEAD

**MATERIALS**

- Tempera
- Rulers
- Gold paint
- ½-inch dowels in 10-inch lengths
- Parchment (yellowish paper) 8½ × ½-inch sheets
- Fine brushes

The *Book of the Dead* was buried with the entombed person. The more wealthy the person, the better the quality of the book. Eventually there was a standard, less expensive version. The book was considered important for an introduction to the after-life. You may want to illustrate a fable, or do a "This Is Your Life" book, similar to the one suggested for the Pharaoh's tomb project.

1. Use a ruler to make a border on top and on the bottom of the paper. Plan to make some vertical hieroglyphics as part of the background.

2. Decide what you will illustrate. The purpose of the *Book of the Dead* was to introduce the dead person to the gods of the netherworld. In addition to a picture of the deceased, the book showed animal-headed gods. Sometimes the deceased was in a boat, making a trip through the netherworld.

3. Draw lightly with pencil, then paint within the lines with flat areas of color. Use very few, but intense colors, such as ultramarine blue, yellow, green, reddish brown, white, and black. When the paint has dried, outline the paint with black marker. Many of the details, such as hieroglyphics, can be added with the marker. If you have gold paint, go over various painted details and highlight some areas.

4. Staple each end to a dowel, and roll the parchment around the dowel on both ends. This could be tied together with a string or piece of tape. Make tassels of string to hang from the dowels by wrapping string around a piece of cardboard 2 × 3 inches 10 times, and tying it together at one end of the cardboard. Use scissors to cut the string at the other end, and tie once again approximately ½ inch from the closed end.

**Photo 1-6. This is a typical scene found in the *Book of the Dead*. It shows the weighing of the deceased's heart against a feather. Collection of the author, purchased from the Papyrus Institute of Cairo.**

## PROJECT 1–7: MUMMY

**MATERIALS**

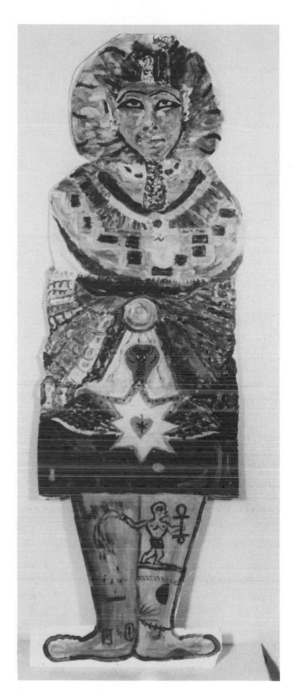

- Foamcore, 48 × 36 inches (makes 2) (or large pieces of cardboard)
- Utility knife
- Acrylic paint
- Brushes

This project can be done in two to three sessions by dividing the work among four to five students. One does the head, one the feet, torso, etc. Discuss whether this is a male or female mummy, and what the color scheme and overall "look" will be. One requirement is that a cartouche representing each person's name be done in hieroglyphics somewhere on the mummy.

1. Use the entire length of the surface of the foamcore or cardboard to make the front of the mummy case nearly life-sized. Draw the outline of the mummy and cut it out, using a utility knife, before doing the painting. Smooth or paint the edges.

2. Allow people to choose the portion of the mummy they will be responsible for painting. Talk about an overall color scheme. To make it easier, you may wish to divide the length of the body into sections (registers) as many mummies were painted. Each register could tell a different story.

3. Decide in advance where the cartouches will be placed. One group might decide to use them as a necklace, or place them in the section painted by each person. They can be large or small. Often they were placed on the shoulder in Egyptian sculpture. It is advised that you draw your designs before applying paint.

**Photo 1-7. Life-sized mummies were completed by groups of five students working together for two class periods.**

4. Try to avoid wasting paint. Put out only the amount you can use in one session, as it dries quickly. Some of the white background could be left, as most real mummy cases were made of a form of plaster and linen, and were white. Sometimes small amulets (good luck charms) were placed within or on the mummy wrappings. They were usually gold or faience (a turquoise ceramic earthenware).

**49**

# Section 2

# ASIA

# ASIA
## TIME LINE

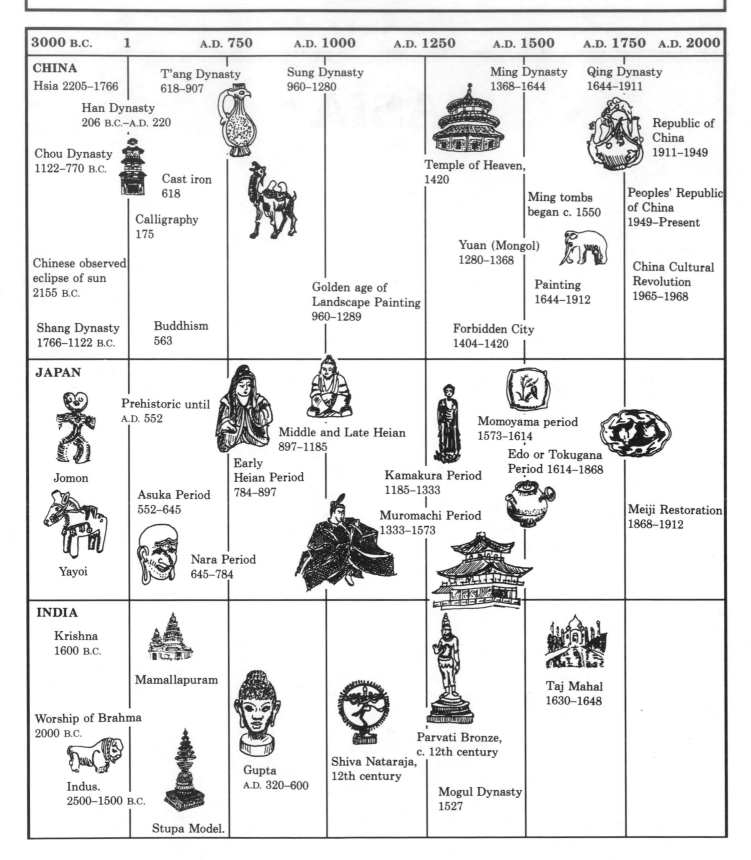

| 3000 B.C. | 1 | A.D. 750 | A.D. 1000 | A.D. 1250 | A.D. 1500 | A.D. 1750 | A.D. 2000 |

**CHINA**

Hsia 2205–1766

Han Dynasty
206 B.C.–A.D. 220

Chou Dynasty
1122–770 B.C.

Chinese observed
eclipse of sun
2155 B.C.

Shang Dynasty
1766–1122 B.C.

T'ang Dynasty
618–907

Cast iron
618

Calligraphy
175

Buddhism
563

Sung Dynasty
960–1280

Golden age of
Landscape Painting
960–1289

Ming Dynasty
1368–1644

Temple of Heaven,
1420

Ming tombs
began c. 1550

Yuan (Mongol)
1280–1368

Forbidden City
1404–1420

Qing Dynasty
1644–1911

Republic of
China
1911–1949

Peoples' Republic
of China
1949–Present

China Cultural
Revolution
1965–1968

Painting
1644–1912

**JAPAN**

Jomon

Yayoi

Prehistoric until
A.D. 552

Asuka Period
552–645

Early
Heian Period
784–897

Nara Period
645–784

Middle and Late Heian
897–1185

Kamakura Period
1185–1333

Muromachi Period
1333–1573

Momoyama period
1573–1614

Edo or Tokugana
Period 1614–1868

Meiji Restoration
1868–1912

**INDIA**

Krishna
1600 B.C.

Worship of Brahma
2000 B.C.

Indus.
2500–1500 B.C.

Mamallapuram

Stupa Model.

Gupta
A.D. 320–600

Shiva Nataraja,
12th century

Parvati Bronze,
c. 12th century

Mogul Dynasty
1527

Taj Mahal
1630–1648

## Unit 1: CHINA

### OVERVIEW OF THE VISUAL ARTS

China's Old Stone Age (Paleolithic) culture flourished from 70,000 to 20,000 B.C. New Stone Age (Neolithic) farming villages appeared about 4500 B.C. The Chinese civilization had been in existence over 2000 years before the Greek civilization was at its height. Civilization emerged in China about 1700 to 1500 B.C. The Shang Dynasty (1766–1122 B.C.) developed a writing system that used over two thousand characters. The Han Dynasty reigned for four centuries from 206 B.C. to A.D. 220 and was comparable to the Roman Empire in Europe in that it unified the vast Chinese Empire. The last dynasty, the Qing (Ching) lasted from 1644 to 1911. During that period trade flourished, and Chinese goods were exported throughout the world. In the middle of the twentieth century, the cultural revolution resulted in artists being sent to the country to work as peasants. Today many of them are once again working at traditional Chinese art forms.

Most art objects are identified with a specific dynasty, such as the Shang or Chou (1122 to 770 B.C.). Artwork from the more recent dynasties—the T'ang, Ming, and Qing dynasties—show the refinements for which Chinese art is known.

### PAINTING

The origin of Chinese painting is from calligraphy, and therefore it is quite linear. It is generally done in ink or watercolor on absorbent materials such as rice paper or silk. Black, with its many variations, is considered a color. Early portraits were of the Buddha and various sages. Early landscape artists attempted to interpret exactly what they saw, so that the viewer might also see it. Chinese painting is generally in one of three forms: horizontal handscrolls, hanging scrolls, and album leaves (stacked, not bound). Favorite subjects were figures, birds, flower and bamboo, and landscape.

The Sung period was considered the high point of landscape painting. Unlike earlier painters, the landscape painters of the Sung era did not try for naturalism, but instead attempted to suggest a mood or feeling. Subject matter varied from traditional subjects such as bamboo, plum flowers, or landscapes, to animals, figures, or historical subjects.

### MASTERPIECES OF PAINTING

*Enjoyment of Chrysanthemum Flowers,* Hua Yen, 1680–1755, St. Louis Art Museum

*The Thirteen Emperors,* Yen Li-Pen, 569–582, Museum of Fine Arts, Boston

*Spring in the Chaing-nan Region,* 1642–1715, Nelson-Atkins Museum of Art, Kansas City

*River and Mountains on a Clear Autumn Day,* Tung Ch'i-ch'ang, 1555–1636, Nelson-Atkins Museum of Art, Kansas City

# CHINESE DYNASTIES

| | |
|---|---|
| Hsia (Xia) | 2205–1766 B.C. |
| Shang | 1766–1122 B.C. |
| Zhou (Chou) | 1122–770 B.C. |
| Spring and Autumn Period | 770–476 B.C. |
| Warring States Period | 476–221 B.C. |
| Qin (Ch'in) | 221–206 B.C. |
| Western Han | 206 B.C.–A.D. 24 |
| Eastern Han | A.D. 25–220 |
| Three Kingdoms Period | A.D. 220–265 |
| Tsin (Jin) | A.D. 265–420 |
|    Western Jin | A.D. 265–316 |
|    Eastern Jin | A.D. 317–420 |
| Southern and Northern Dynasties | A.D. 420–589 |
| Sui | A.D. 589–618 |
| Tang | A.D. 618–907 |
| Five Dynasties and Ten Kingdoms | A.D. 907–960 |
| Sung (Song) | A.D. 960–1280 |
|    Northern Sung | A.D. 960–1127 |
|    Southern Sung | A.D. 1127–1279 |
| Yuan (Mongol) | A.D. 1280–1368 |
| Ming | A.D. 1368–1644 |
| Qing (Ching)—(Manchu) | A.D. 1644–1911 |
| Republic of China | A.D. 1911–1949 |
| People's Republic of China | A.D. 1949–Present |

**Present-Day China**

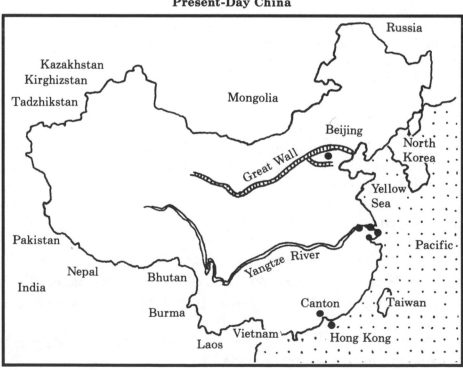

## SCULPTURE

Clay modeling and casting in bronze has continued for over 3000 years. Many of the ceramics, bronzes, and jade carvings were funerary offerings placed in graves, intended to make the after-life more comfortable. Examples of ancient bronze funerary figures show how advanced the civilization was. Ceramic sculpture such as camels or horses from the T'ang Dynasty are lifelike and humorous. The larger-than-life stone animals that guard the pathway to the Ming tombs are prime examples of the stone-carver's art. An imperial bodyguard was created to guard the first Han emperor's mausoleum at Xian. The recently unearthed ceramic army in Xian demonstrates the advanced civilization of that time. The burial chamber contained over 7000 life-sized terra cotta soldiers and horses, equipped with real chariots and bronze weapons.

Large slabs of stone were carved to commemorate special events. These "stele" are similar to those found in Ephesus and other areas of the Middle East. The sculptural tradition in China continues strongly today, as it did in the early days of Buddhism. The earliest Buddhist sculptures resembled the Indian Buddhist sculptures, but eventually came to be simplified. Temples were adorned with stone-carved Buddhas.

## MASTERPIECES OF SCULPTURE

*Tomb Figure of a Horse,* A.D. 618–906, Chicago Art Institute

*Bactrian Camel,* T'ang Dynasty, 618–906, St. Louis Art Museum

*House model,* 106 B.C. to A.D. 221, Nelson-Atkins Gallery of Art, Kansas City

*Xian Tomb Figures,* 220 B.C., Xian, China

## ARCHITECTURE

The best-known Chinese architectural structure, the *Great Wall of China,* was built to separate the south from the north. It is the only manmade structure that can be seen from the moon. Most early Chinese buildings were made of wood and are known chiefly from the copies of them that have survived in Japan. In China there was little difference between secular and religious architecture, with the pagoda being the best known architectural style.

Models of a whole series of buildings ranging from town houses to pagodas and rustic barns, which were found in tombs, tell us something of the Chinese building methods. All Chinese cities had a walled square that was on a north-south axis. The north was viewed as a source of evil, so most of the important buildings were found on the south side of the square. They frequently had a foot-high barrier at the base of the entrance of each door to keep out evil spirits. Private homes of the wealthy consisted of individual one-story pavilions contained within walls. Only the emperors might use brilliant colors; so the roofs and colors of most buildings were gray, while those of royalty used bright reds, greens, yellows, or purple.

## ARCHITECTURAL EXAMPLES

*The Forbidden Palace,* begun 1406, Beijing, China

*The Summer Palace,* rebuilt in 1888, Beijing, China

*The Temple of Heaven,* 1420, Beijing, China

*The Small Wild Goose Pagoda,* 220 B.C. to A.D. 220, Xian, China

**Photo 2-1.** *Tomb Model of a House,* 52 × 33¹/₂ × 27 inches, c. 100 A.D. painted pottery,
Han Dynasty, Nelson Fund, the Nelson-Atkins Museum of Art, Kansas City, Missouri.

# PROJECT 2–1: FOOD FOR THE GODS

## FOR THE TEACHER

The Chinese dynasties from 2205 B.C. to A.D. 220 offer a rich cultural heritage. The sophistication of the bronze objects produced in this time point to a lengthy earlier civilization. People of the Bronze Age were farmers and soldiers. They believed in evil gods, whom they appeased with food sacrifices. Special bronze containers were used for specific foods.

Many of the bronzes had a *t'ao-t'ieh* (ogre) decoration that was based on a tiger, and considered a good luck omen. Dragon designs were common. Rarely, human images appeared on these vessels. As the populace became more civilized, the bronze vessels became more decorative than religious.

## MASTERPIECES

*Wine Container, Fang Lei,* eleventh to tenth centuries B.C., St. Louis Art Museum

*Covered Wine Vessel, Hu,* 480–222 B.C., Chicago Art Institute

## PREPARATION

Modern Chinese ceramics continue to use many of the traditional designs. In the absence of real examples, photocopy pictures of Chinese designs from ceramics and bronzes to pass around. Try to have as many different examples as you have students so these can be used for sketching ideas. For best results, have the students make the pattern and wedge their clay in advance so the basic construction can be done in one day, while the clay is easy to handle and moist. Have slip made in advance also.

## FURTHER SUGGESTIONS

- Use regular or self-hardening clay to make a pendant carved in the Chinese manner with an animal or dragon. Paint it to resemble jade by making several values of green and white acrylic paint. Jade also is black, orange, cloudy white or purple.
- This project could simply be a *drawing* for a vessel, using pencil, marker, or ink. Drawing Chinese designs and shapes of pots is intriguing because it is so different from Western art.
- Copper-colored foil can be cut in a typical bronze-vessel shape and tooled (repoussé technique) with typical designs. Wipe it with thinned blue-green acrylic paint to give a "bronze" patina. Mount it on dark posterboard.

# PROJECT 2–1: FOOD FOR THE GODS

## MATERIALS

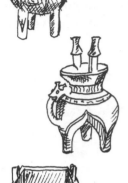

- Clay, 2 pounds
- Paper towels
- Glaze or acrylic paint
- Tagboard
- Masking tape
- Needle tool or knife

- Rolling pins or 1-inch dowels
- Plastic bags
- Brushes
- Scissors
- Sponges
- Sticks, $1 \times \frac{3}{8} \times 12$ inches

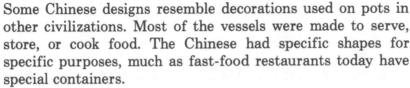

Some Chinese designs resemble decorations used on pots in other civilizations. Most of the vessels were made to serve, store, or cook food. The Chinese had specific shapes for specific purposes, much as fast-food restaurants today have special containers.

1. Decide what food your container will hold. To make a slab container, make a tagboard pattern, taping it together with masking tape to make sure it is the size and shape you want.

2. Wedge the clay by slapping it back and forth between your hands, or kneading it like bread for at least 15 minutes to get rid of air bubbles. Cut through the center of the ball of clay to see if any bubbles are left. Rewedge and form the clay into a ball.

3. Place the clay ball on canvas or paper (to keep it from sticking to the table), and lay a stick on either side to support a rolling pin. Roll the clay to make the slab approximately $\frac{3}{8}$- to $\frac{1}{2}$-inch thick. Lay the tagboard pattern on it and use a sharp point to trace around the outside of the pattern. Use a knife or needle tool to cut the shape from the clay. Keep the clay moist by wrapping it in plastic between working sessions.

4. While the clay is still moist, score (make lines with a sharp point) the edges to be joined, and coat them with slip (clay that has been thinned to the texture of cream). Smooth the joint carefully. Roll "fingers" of clay to place on the insides of the corners of a box. If making a round shape, first make the sides (tube) of the vessel, then place it on a flat piece of clay and cut a bottom to fit.

5. To make Chinese carved designs, use a needle tool to incise the outline, then cut a little deeper with a loop tool or knife, and take away some of the background.

6. After the piece has been bisque fired, you may either paint it with acrylic paint or glaze it to be refired. Chinese bronze vessels were originally a burnished bronze, but after having been buried, most of them have a greenish blue cast (a patina). To achieve this effect with acrylic, paint the ceramic aqua, then rub some green paint on it, then a little brown. Rub the last two colors off while they are still wet to allow the aqua to show through on the raised spots.

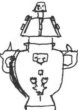

© 1992 by The Center for Applied Research in Education, Inc.

## PROJECT 2-2: **HOUSES OF CLAY**

**FOR THE TEACHER**

This house constructed with slabs can be fairly sizable, with a removable roof to make a box if preferred. It can be constructed to look like a Chinese-type home, with typical roof and decorations such as those seen on temples, or could be a replica of the student's own home.

If a group of students wishes to make a tall pagoda, each one could make a consecutive smaller "box" to set on top of the roof of the one below it. A ¾-inch diameter hole in the flat "roof" and the "floor" of each box would allow the boxes to be held securely in place by a dowel stuck through the middle of several stacked boxes. It would be important to construct this pagoda first in tagboard to make sure of the fit. This would be an appropriate addition to the school's art collection.

**Photo 2-2. Student work by Judy Yuen.**

# PROJECT 2–2: **HOUSES OF CLAY**

**MATERIALS**

- Clay, 2 pounds
- Paper towels
- Glaze or acrylic paint
- Tagboard
- Masking tape
- Needle tool or knife

- Rolling pins or 1-inch dowels
- Plastic bags
- Brushes
- Scissors
- Sponges
- Rulers

Typical early Chinese homes consisted of walled compounds that had a number of one-room pavilions in them. A typical Chinese pagoda roof was sometimes shaped like a pyramid, with a square base and four triangular shapes that met at a point on the top. Many temples are found with conical roofs. Your class could make a city or compound by displaying the individual buildings you have made.

1. Do a quick sketch, either from a photo or your imagination. Make a tagboard pattern and loosely tape it together to make sure it is the size you want. The larger you make it, the more difficult it will be. This project can have either an open base or removable roof. Because it is a box, you will have to be able to get your hand inside to smooth it, and it must have an opening (at least a hole in the bottom) to allow air to escape.

2. Wedge the clay by slapping it back and forth between your hands, or kneading it like bread for at least 15 minutes to get rid of air bubbles. Cut through the center of the ball of clay to see if any bubbles are left. Rewedge and form the clay into a ball. Place the clay ball on canvas or paper (to keep it from sticking to the table), and lay a stick on either side to support a rolling pin. Roll the clay to make the slab approximately 3/8- to 1/2-inch thick.

3. Remove the tape from the pattern and lay it on the rolled out slab of clay. Trace around it with a needle tool or pencil. Hold a knife vertically to cut the sides of the building so they are the exact size of the pattern. Cut the four sides separately and join them by scoring and using slip at the joints. Roll "fingers" of clay to place on the insides of the corners of the box. Cover unused pieces with a damp paper towel and plastic to keep them from drying out.

4. Allow the sections of the roof to become stiff before joining them with slip because they will be at an angle. Use a scraper and sponge to smooth the surfaces. Chinese buildings frequently were richly tiled, so if you intend to incise detail, it is easier to do it before the clay becomes leather hard.

5. While the clay is drying, you may paint details with underglazes. This could also be done after a first firing, but it gives you something to do while the form is drying. After the bisque firing, clear glaze can be painted on the outside. Use a sponge to evenly dampen the surface before glazing to allow the glaze to go on evenly.

© 1992 by The Center for Applied Research in Education, Inc.

## PROJECT 2-3: **BAMBOO AND FLOWERS**

**FOR THE TEACHER**

Chinese and Japanese watercolor painting techniques are similar. The subjects are often based on nature, and the method of using ink wash and limited colors makes it somewhat difficult to tell in which culture the painting was done.

Cultured Chinese painters were also calligraphers, poets, and philosophers. The tradition was passed down through the generations. The Chinese tradition is to learn to copy and follow the rules exactly before beginning to innovate.

**PREPARATION**

Have students sit straight with both feet on the floor (Chinese calligraphers often live to a ripe old age, reportedly because of their perfect posture). The paper should be aligned with the front of the table. In place of traditional ink sticks and grinding stones, give each student a small amount of india ink in the corner of a white styrofoam meat tray (which may also serve as a palette). The brush is held vertically between the thumb and first two fingers.

Have students experiment with using different values in ink. The strokes made must be sure and not overworked. The Chinese had names for their strokes, such as "axe cuts," "bone stroke," "pepper dots," and "horses' teeth."

The bone stroke is the basis for making the bamboo stem. For best results, have students practice strokes many times before combining them into a finished painting. Chinese artists practiced for months on a single stroke.

Asian artists "signed" their paintings by imprinting on them a personal "chop" (printed by dipping a small carved stone stamp engraved with Chinese characters in red cinnabar paste). Some paintings have many red stamps (seals) on them, demonstrating the Chinese custom of showing approval by applying a personal seal on scrolls they treasured (even though they were painted by others). At times, owners of paintings might write a poem directly on the picture expressing personal appreciation. Occasionally a chop representing some special god might also be added, or the artist might have several chops that represented versions of his or her name, so some paintings have numerous small red stamped designs added to the edges.

**FURTHER SUGGESTIONS**

- Many books are available with Chinese characters. Students might enjoy learning to write their own names in Chinese. These characters are attractive additions to a painting of bamboo or landscapes.

- Other traditional Asian subjects that are interpreted frequently are birds, pine trees, mountains, plum blossoms, and other flowers. Show students Asian paintings of these subjects for their interpretation.

**Photo 2-3. Bamboo, ink on rice paper.**

**Photo 2-4. Chrysanthemums, ink on rice paper.**

Name: _____ Date: _____

# PROJECT 2–3: ASIAN BAMBOO AND FLOWERS

**MATERIALS**

- Newsprint
- Cup for water
- Watercolor brushes
- White styrofoam meat tray
- Rice paper or similar absorbent paper

- India ink
- Plasticine clay
- Red ink and pad

Painting bamboo or flowers must be learned in stages before you can put it all together. The Chinese method of copying exactly teaches you the formal rules of painting; then, when you have successfully learned to copy, you may be more creative.

1. *Bamboo:*

   **a.** To make bamboo branches (bones), dip your brush in the water, then ink. Hold the brush at a slight angle, aiming it toward the top left corner of the paper. Push the full part of your brush down, then pull it along on its side toward the upper right; then press again, then flick and lift it. A bamboo stalk is short near the base, then longer, then shorter again at the tip.

   **b.** Dip the tip in dark ink, and make "cartilage" between the bones of the bamboo. Make stems come out from alternate sides of the stalk, in the same manner, but with the tip of the brush or a smaller brush.

   **c.** To make leaves, push the tip down, twist from side to side, pull straight down, pause, and flick the brush off the paper.

2. *Flowers:* In doing a flower painting, remember that you will see flowers from all angles and in all stages of development. There will be full blooms, buds, and the undersides of flowers. The largest flowers are usually near the bottom. Oriental arrangements are noted for their restraint. Three to five blooms are adequate to fill a page.

   To make flowers, use the brush on its side, as in making bamboo. Bring the brush around almost in a circle to "hide the point" of a flower such as a chrysanthemum. To make branches, use the tip of the brush. To make pointed flowers, use a small brush.

3. *Chop:* To make a chop (initial stamp), form a ball of plasticine clay, flattening one side. Use a toothpick to draw initials or another design into the clay. Use this by first inking it on a stamp pad, then stamping it onto a corner of your picture.

# PROJECT 2-4: ASIAN DRAGON

**FOR THE TEACHER**

The dragon was not unique to Asia, but was (and still is) common to folklore in most other cultures. It was the national emblem of China, and the Chinese considered it a symbol of good fortune. A dragon with a pearl symbolized a wish for wealth and good luck. Representations of dragons are found in gardens and homes, and on clothing. The dragon is often seen surrounded by clouds, illustrating the saying, "Clouds follow the dragon, winds follow the tiger."

In Chinese folklore the raised features of a landscape are the veins of a dragon. The dragon inhabits the northwest of the world, its sleep and waking determine night and day, and its breathing regulates the seasons and the wind. Only Chinese emperors could have a dragon with five claws embroidered on their clothing. All other dragons have only four claws.

**PREPARATION**

Ideally you could take students to an exhibition of Chinese art and have them make a number of sketches of dragons from original art. Otherwise find examples of "dragon" art in books on Chinese art. Many versions of dragons are used on clothing or bronze and ceramic vases. Students can make sketches for a painting from photocopied pictures.

**FURTHER SUGGESTIONS**

- Students can research the dragon as it is found in other cultures and show how similar it is in appearance all over the world.
- Have students paint dragon "tattoos" onto each other's arms with acrylic paint. This paint is easily removed by applying wet tissue and letting it soak for a minute.

# PROJECT 2-4: ASIAN DRAGON

**MATERIALS**

- 18 × 24-inch drawing paper cut in half vertically
- Watercolor brushes
- Toothpicks
- Pencils
- Ink
- Paper towels
- Oil clay (plasticine)
- Red stamp pads

The dragon is supposed to have nine parts: the head of a camel, horns of a deer, eyes of a demon, ears of a cow, neck of a snake, belly of a frog, scales of a carp, claws of an eagle, and paws of a tiger. First and foremost the dragon is a snake. The ancient English believed that a dragon was formed when a snake swallowed another snake. As you can see by these sketches (taken from vases, clothing, or architecture), there are many ways to make a dragon, and because on one has ever seen one, you can hardly be wrong.

1. Make several sketches of dragons. Notice how shapes change depending on what they decorate. If they must fit around a vase, they will look very different than if they are on a piece of fabric.

2. Turn the paper vertically and lightly (your pencil marks will show through the ink if they are too dark) draw a dragon the length of the paper. Although it could be drawn horizontally, drawing vertically on the paper will challenge you to be creative with a design you may have copied from a different type of artwork.

3. On a separate paper, practice making marks with the tip of the watercolor brush. Notice that if you add more water, your ink is diluted. Experiment with adding more pigment into wet areas of your drawing (wet-in-wet). Try going back over areas after they have dried to make some of the details.

4. Asian painting is traditionally "loose." Even if you do not have every scale or claw showing, we will know it is a dragon by its shape. There should be variations in value of the ink, ranging from very dark to very light.

5. To make a chop (initial stamp), form a ball of plasticine clay, flattening one side. Use a toothpick to draw initials or a Chinese symbol into the clay. Use this by first inking it on a stamp pad, then stamping it onto your picture.

## PROJECT 2–5: **SCROLL LANDSCAPE**

**FOR THE TEACHER**

**Slide # 4: *Saying Farewell at Hsün-Yang.*** Asian scholars treasured their horizontal roll "books." Many of them can be seen in museums, where a different section is unrolled frequently so you can see a portion at a time. Although the Chinese landscape is stylized, with its pointed mountains, patterned fields, and trees emerging from mists, parts of China actually appear the way they were represented by artists.

Photo 2-5. *Landscape After a Song by Yang Hung-hsui "The Clearing Sky, the Fading Rainbow and the Red Glow of Sunset,"* Ming Dynasty (1368–1644), 24½ × 16 inches, Chinese scroll painting, Tung Ch'i-ch'ang, album leaf, ink and color on paper, Nelson-Atkins Art Museum, Kansas City, Missouri. Acquired through the Hall family Foundations, the William Rockhill Nelson trust (by exchange), and the Hallmark Oriental Operating Fund Surplus.

## MASTERPIECES

*Landscape Handscroll,* A.D. 1661, Ch'eng Cheng-Kuel, Los Angeles County Museum of Art

*Palace Musicians,* A.D. 960–1279, painter unknown, Chicago Art Institute

## PREPARATION

Discuss landscape with students. Ask what they consider a good landscape to be. Probably the surroundings of their own community will come to their minds, or places where they may have vacationed. Remind them that today we take photos or buy postcards of places we want to remember, but centuries ago, landscape artists did paintings to show what far-away (or familiar) places looked like. The Chinese often placed trees, animals, or people in their paintings to give some idea of scale.

## FURTHER SUGGESTIONS

- An entire class could make separate landscapes, which could then be mounted side by side on a long roll of wallpaper to resemble a long oriental scroll. Roll the paper around dowels on each end, and display on a long wall. If you wish, groups of five could work together to make a scroll depicting different locations of the Orient.
- An event (such as a parade, war, race, play, or games) could be depicted on a long roll of paper, with individual students each doing a small portion.
- A visual time line of Chinese or Japanese culture could be made with each student doing a small portion to be pasted onto a long scroll.

Name: _____    Date: _____

# PROJECT 2–5:  SCROLL LANDSCAPE

**MATERIALS**

- Newsprint
- India ink
- Water cups
- Pencils
- Butcher paper, 12 × 24 inches
- Brushes, #7 and #10
- Paper towels

Although you may have people and animals in your landscape, they will probably be rather small. Chinese landscapes usually showed fields, mountains, trees, water, and other familiar landmarks. Some scroll landscapes were made in watercolor, whereas others were in values of black and white.

1. Before beginning the actual landscape, practice painting with ink. Begin with very little ink. It is possible to add ink and build up value, which is much easier than if you make areas too dark in the beginning. Always test the brush on newsprint. If something does get too dark, you can dilute it or blot it with a paper towel.

2. Lightly draw a few lines in pencil to guide your landscape. You can also find try working directly with the brush, as calligraphers do.

3. Think about a focal area that could contain houses, people, or trees that are darker than the overall landscape. A viewer might notice this area first.

4. Make a chop by impressing a design in oil clay. Stamp it on a red ink pad, and affix a "seal" to a landscape.

5. When you are finished, mount the landscape on a piece of wallpaper with wooden dowels on the ends to make it look like an oriental scroll.

© 1992 by The Center for Applied Research in Education, Inc.

**Water Grass**

**Pepper Dots**

**Axe Cuts**

**Hemp Fiber**

**Hook Stroke**

**Bone Stroke**

**Teardrops**

68

# Unit 2: JAPAN

## OVERVIEW OF THE VISUAL ARTS

Relatively recent excavations have shown that Japan also had a Paleolithic culture. A Neolithic culture existed there approximately 8000 to 6000 B.C. Japan's original settlers, the Ainu, and the Japanese assimilated the cultures from migrations of Chinese, Malasians, Korean, and Polynesians. The Japanese culture as a distinct entity came into its own in the fifth century. By the seventh century, universities and monasteries were established.

| JAPANESE HISTORICAL PERIODS | |
| --- | --- |
| Prehistoric period (Jomon and Yayoi) ended | A.D. 552 |
| Asuka period | 552– 645 |
| Nara period | 645– 784 |
| Heian period | 784–1185 |
|    Early Heian | 784– 897 |
|    Middle & Late Heian | 897–1185 |
| Kamakura period | 1185–1333 |
| Muromachi period | 1333–1573 |
| Momoyama period | 1573–1614 |
| Edo, or Tokugawa period | 1614–1868 |
| Meiji Restoration | 1868–1912 |
| Modern times | 1912– |

Shinto is a faith of Japan that is based on ancestor and nature worship. Buddhism was adopted in the seventh century. During the late Nara epoch (A.D. 710 to 784) one in sixty persons in Japan was a monk. The majority of Japanese are Shintoists and also are adherents of Buddhism.

The Japanese artistic heritage is affected by the beauty of the land. Their artwork reflects the great awe they feel for its high mountains, seas and rivers, ancient trees, cliffs and waterfalls, and the silence. In contrast to the Chinese appreciation of perfection, the Japanese appreciate slight imperfections in such artwork as pottery or paintings of nature that remind them of the imperfections in humanity.

## PAINTING

Japanese painters reflected the influence of the great Chinese landscape paintings of the T'ang and Sung dynasties. They also focused on landscape painting, but with subtle differences that reflected the Japanese sensitivity to quiet places and the use of space. Other subjects were symbolic, religious, and historical. Mural painting on screens or for entire rooms became popular in the sixteenth century. Artists also were creating designs for silk weavers and embroiderers.

The Ukiyoye school of the seventeenth to nineteenth centuries was art for the masses. Woodcuts allowed artworks by famous painters such as Hokusai and Iwasa Matabei to be reproduced, sold locally, and exported in quantity. These woodcuts became extremely popular in Europe and greatly influenced the Impressionist painters. Hokusai excelled in portraying atmospheric effects such as rain, sleet, and snow. In addition to nature, other popular subjects were ladies of the court, actors, and great warriors.

## MASTERPIECES OF JAPANESE PAINTINGS AND PRINTS

*Snow at Kambara,* Ando Hiroshige, 1933,

*Irises,* Ogata Korin, Nezu Art Museum, Tokyo, early eighteenth century

## SCULPTURE

In 708 copper became available in large quantity in Japan, making large bronze castings feasible. Indian and Grecian influences led to simplification in style. Most statues of Buddha appear to be asexual, though Buddha was a male. Large bells were also cast in bronze.

**Japan**

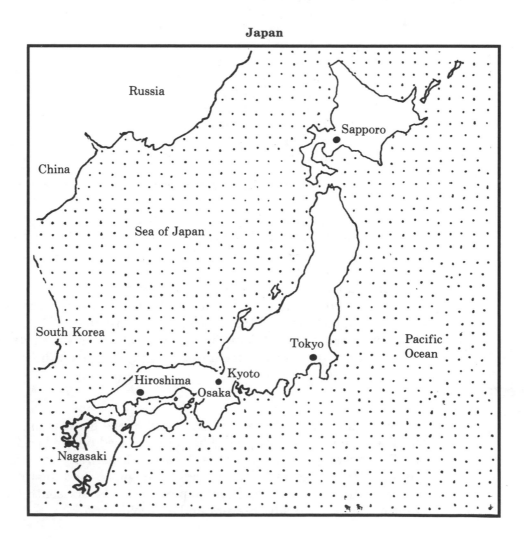

## ARCHITECTURE

The basic structure used in Japanese architecture is a framework of timbers supporting a peaked roof or series of roofs. The roof, as in Chinese architecture, had concave-curved edges that turned up at the corners. Some of the early Buddhist structures exist today because an exact replica has been built every 20 years since the fourth century. Early pagodas, temples, palaces, castles, and monasteries were almost exactly like those of China. Modern Japanese architecture had a tendency toward low structural proportions, with the buildings integrated with a garden. The garden attempted to reproduce nature, in miniature.

## MASTERPIECES OF JAPANESE ARCHITECTURE

*Horyu-ji Temple complex,* begun 607, Asuka, Japan

*Osaka Castle,* late sixteenth century, Osaka, Japan

# PROJECT 2–6: ASIAN PRINTMAKING

## FOR THE TEACHER

Printmaking varies depending on the country in which it was done. The Chinese tended to use repetitious pattern, printing clothing with woodcuts. Japanese printmaking was much more adventurous and admired by Europeans, especially the Impressionists, who were greatly influenced by the bold black lines that enclosed bright color. This influence especially shows up in the work of Vincent van Gogh, Paul Gauguin and Mary Cassatt.

## MASTERPIECES OF ASIAN PRINTMAKING

*Night Rain on Kirasaki Pine,* Utagawa Hiroshige, 1834, Los Angeles County Museum of Art

*Stormy Sea off Kanagawa,* Katsushika Hokusai Takahashi Collection, Japan

*Celebrated Places in Edo,* nineteenth century, Ando Hiroshige

Photo 2-6. *Flower Hunting Mural,* Shiko Munakata, Japanese, block out 1958, impression 1965, 142.5 × 179.8 cm, wood block print and black ink, The Saint Louis Art Museum, gift of Mr. Shiko Munakata in memory of Leo Sirota.

**PREPARATION**

Demonstrate the use of lino-cutting tools. Use a V-gauge to show the line design, then other tools as needed to remove larger areas. It isn't necessary to remove every bit of the surface on top, as that is part of the charm of a linocut or woodcut. *Safety Note: Remind students that the lino-tools will surely slip, and their hands must be behind the tools at all times.*

**FURTHER SUGGESTIONS**

- Instead of a "picture" scene, make characters from the Chinese or Japanese alphabet, printing vertically. Remember they will print backward, so transfer the designs backward.
- Coat the design with acrylic paint and stamp it repeatedly onto a cotton T-shirt. Place a newspaper "pad" in the center of the shirt, to prevent the paint from going through to the other side.

Photo 2-7. *The Forty-seven Ronin at Ryogoliu Bridge,* Ando Hiroshige (date unknown) Wood Block Print, ink and color on paper, The Saint Louis Art Museum.

# PROJECT 2–6: **ASIAN PRINTMAKING**

## MATERIALS

- Linoleum
- Water-based printing ink or tempera
- Piece of plastic or glass for rolling out ink
- Lino-cutting tools
- Drawing paper or rice paper
- Brayers

Your design can be based on things from nature such as flowers, trees, domesticated or wild animals and birds, or on architecture, such as a house or building. The outside shape does not have to be a rectangle, but could be planned ahead to make interlocking prints using a shape such as a square, triangle, or hexagon.

1. Make several thumbnail sketches for your design. Remember that the design will be reversed when you print it. This is not important unless it has words in it. The block can be repeatedly printed on cloth or paper.

2. Decide in advance which parts will remain white and which will be colored. Remove only the portions to remain white. Ideally a block print will have almost half the area colored and half white. Areas that are raised cannot be thin lines (dark), or they may break down when you print them.

3. Transfer the design to the linoleum block by rubbing over the back of the design with pencil and placing that side next to the linoleum. Draw over the front of the design with pencil, thus tracing it onto the linoleum, or you could use carbon paper to transfer the design.

4. Use lino-tools to cut away the part to remain white. You will make normal mistakes. Accept them as "happy accidents" and make them part of your design, changing the design if you have to.

5. To print, squeeze printing ink onto a sheet of glass or plastic. Use a brayer to spread the ink around until it is thin and even. Roll the brayer in the ink, then onto the linoleum. It will probably be necessary to "re-ink" the plate each time you print it.

6. Place a sheet of paper on top of the plate. Use the palm of your hand, wooden spoon, or "baren" (flat Japanese rubbing tool) to rub the back of the paper. This pressure transfers the ink from the lino-cut onto the paper. If you are making a repeat pattern by printing the plate a number of times on one sheet of paper, place the plate in place on the paper, and apply firm pressure to the back of the plate.

7. When you are finished, wash the ink off the plate and store it away. If you wish to change the plate, more of it can be removed before you print again.

© 1992 by The Center for Applied Research in Education, Inc.

## PROJECT 2-7: **SIX-PANEL SCREEN**

### FOR THE TEACHER

The tradition of mural painting on screens that functioned as movable walls began in Japan in the eighth century. Sixteenth-century fortifications and castles had light reflected into their dark rooms by painting on gold surfaces such as ceilings and walls. Many screens were decorated with the eternal Japanese themes of the four seasons, pine trees, mountains, waves, and boats. Other favorite subjects were lions, dragons, tigers, bridges, cranes, gardens, reeds, and flowers. While some screens were quite elaborate, by the late sixteenth century, a six-panel gold screen might have painting on less than a third of the screen, with the subject being the bare essence. Screens were often used as an essential part of the tea ceremony, as a backdrop for a perfect flower arrangement.

### MASTERPIECES OF JAPANESE SCREENS

*The Bridge at Uji,* c. 1700, Tokyo National Museum

*Horses in Stables, Spring and Autumn,* pair of six-fold screens, seventeenth century, The Saint Louis Art Museum

### PREPARATION

Decide on the size of the screens before beginning, based on availability and cost of gold wrapping paper. A small screen would serve as a backdrop for a flower arrangment against a wall, or a large one could be a wall decoration behind a sofa. A very small screen would be effective on a table top. If you wish to keep this project very simple, simply fold a piece of tagboard or watercolor paper into sixths, and paint it with watercolor, not using gold paper.

### FURTHER SUGGESTIONS

- To make a more authentic appearing screen, work in four to six separate rectangles, pasting the paper on front, leaving a small amount to paste around the edges and onto the back. Join with strips of plastic book tape. Cut a piece of patterned paper smaller than the rectangle and paste on the back to hide the tape and pasted edges.

- Use foamcore to make a large Japanese screen. Cover each panel with gold wrapping paper, wrapping it around the edges and mitering the corners. Join the sections together with duct tape "hinges" along the back, after they are covered in gold, then paint an original design with acrylic paint.

- Paint a nature scene on a vertical rectangle of gold paper. Affix it with wallpaper paste or rubber cement to a scroll made of wallpaper. Wrap top and bottom onto a dowel for authenticity.

- Have a "tea ceremony" with one or more of the screens used as backdrops. Discuss the Japanese admiration for the irregular glaze, shapes, and decorations used on tea bowls, and the Japanese reverence for the beauty of art.

- Make a Japanese fan by painting nature subjects with acrylics on gold wrapping paper. Some of the fans used by men were quite large. For authenticity, buy an inexpensive fan, and cut the paper on which you will paint to fit exactly over the old fan. If you carefully remove the paper from the fan, use it as a pattern.

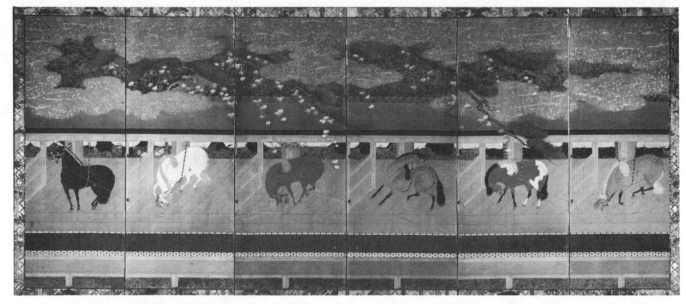

Photos 2-8. *Horses in Stables, Spring & Autumn.* Pair of six-fold screens, 127.0 × 315.7 cm, seventeenth century, ink, color, gold, silver on paper. Purchase: Funds given by Mr. and Mrs. Arthur B. Baer, The Saint Louis Art Museum.

Name: _____ Date: _____

# PROJECT 2–7: SIX-PANEL SCREEN

## MATERIALS

- Tagboard
- Newsprint
- Brushes
- Gold wrapping paper
- Drawing paper
- Acrylic or watercolor paint

The subjects used by Japanese screen painters almost always were based on nature. The reverence the Japanese felt for quiet places and natural objects such as flowers, trees, and animals is shown in the screens they painted.

1. On newsprint, draw a 3 × 6-inch long horizontal rectangle, dividing it into 1-inch vertical segments. This will be the shape of the six-panel screen, to be enlarged. Off to the side, do a number of quick sketches to decide on your subject. It could be animals, mountains, a favorite place in the country you have vacationed, flowers, or the ocean.

2. Decide on a focal point for your design, and on which section it will go. Then decide how you can carry the theme of the focal point to the other sections. You may wish to cover less than one third of the surface of each of the panels. Transfer the design to the newsprint rectangle. If you are doing this on tagboard or drawing paper, use a ruler and the tip of a pair of scissors to "score" the five dividing lines before folding the paper into six sections.

3. Glue gold wrapping paper onto the tagboard, wrapping it over the edges. Fold the "screen" so you will know where the divisions are, then flatten it for painting.

4. Use pencil or chalk to lightly draw your design on the gold paper. To paint with acrylic, squeeze a small amount (less than you would use on a toothbrush) from a tube. You may wish to combine this with permanent marker, which will adhere to a slick background. You may show the five vertical divisions by painting with a dark color.

5. Real Japanese screens have small squares that are caused when thin gold leaf squares are applied. If you would like to try that effect, use brown acrylic paint to *lightly* indicate a few squares. These should barely show.

**Photos 2-9.** *Four Seasons,* 1932, pair of six-fold screens, Matsubayashi Keigetsu, 1876–1973, H. 171.0 × 734.4 cm, The Saint Louis Art Museum, Museum Shop Fund.

# Section 3

# MYCENAE AND GREECE

# MYCENAE AND GREECE
## TIME LINE

| 2800 B.C. | 2000 B.C. | 1000 B.C. | 700 B.C. | 500 B.C. | 300 B.C. | 100 B.C. |
|---|---|---|---|---|---|---|

Mycenae
2300–1100 B.C.

Geometric Period
1100–700

Archaic
700–480

Classical
480–323

Hellenistic
323–30

Orientalizing Phase
735–650

Knossos Palace
1500

Temple of Athena Nike
427–424

Pergamum Altar
c. 175

Aegean
Early Cycladic
1800–2000

Greek Alphabet
800

Minoan
2000–1100

Charioteer of Delphi
500 B.C.

Laocoon
200 B.C.

Roman sack of
Corinth 145

1st Olympics
776

Alexander the
Great, 336–323

Dipylon Vase
800–700

Homer's Illiad
750

Socrates, Plato, Aristotle

Greek speaking
tribes on
mainland
2000

Bull's Head
1500–1550

Theatre of Epidaurus
350

Nike of Samothrace
200–190

Trojan War, 1185

Lion's Gate at
Mycenae 1400

Parthenon
448–432

Socrates drank hemlock
399

Snake Goddess
1550

Calf Bearer
600

Peplos Kore
530

**Africa**

Nok Culture
500 B.C.–A.D. 500

**Americas**

Chavan Culture, Peru
1500

Mayan culture
600

Mound Builders
Ohio Valley
100

Olmecs
850–150

Paracas in Peru
500

**Asia**

First Chinese Dictionary
1100

T'ang Dynasty
618–907

Invention of paper

China
Shang Dynasty
1766–1122

Han Dynasty,
206 B.C.–A.D. 220

Confucius born
551

Chou Dynasty
1027–222

Great Wall unified, 21–210

**Europe**

Etruscan art
750–200 B.C.

Rome settled
1200

Roman art
509–27

**Near East**

India
Diamond Sutra Scroll
868

c. 500 B.C.

Israelites leave Egypt
1250

Susa

**Other**

© 1992 by The Center for Applied Research in Education, Inc.

# Unit 1: MYCENAE (2300 B.C. TO 1100 B.C.)

## OVERVIEW OF THE VISUAL ARTS

Although Doric and other Greek-speaking tribes arrived on the Greek mainland around 2000 B.C., many ancient civilizations contributed to the formation of the Greek culture. The Egyptian influence is seen in architecture and sculpture. A sophisticated civilization existed on the island of Crete from 2000 to 1450 B.C., The Minoans (named for King Minos) had developed indoor bathing and plumbing facilities as seen in the Knossos Palace. This civilization flourished until 1250 B.C., when the center of the Aegean civilization moved to Mycenae on the Greek mainland. The Mycenians, of whom Agammemnon was the King, were highly skilled gold workers, and are known for their "beehive" tombs, lively frescoes and sculpture. Warlike Doric tribes ultimately drove out the Mycenaens.

The handout "Greek Architecture" is useful when discussing the architecture of both Mycenae and Greece as a whole.

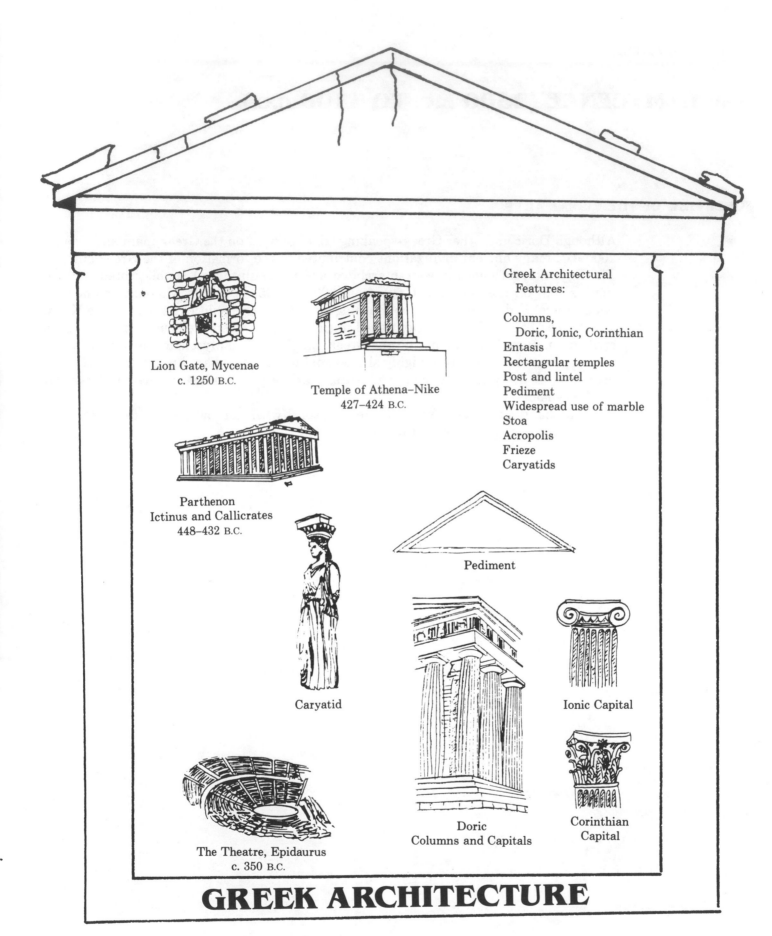

Lion Gate, Mycenae
c. 1250 B.C.

Temple of Athena–Nike
427–424 B.C.

Greek Architectural
Features:

Columns,
Doric, Ionic, Corinthian
Entasis
Rectangular temples
Post and lintel
Pediment
Widespread use of marble
Stoa
Acropolis
Frieze
Caryatids

Parthenon
Ictinus and Callicrates
448–432 B.C.

Pediment

Caryatid

Doric
Columns and Capitals

Ionic Capital

Corinthian
Capital

The Theatre, Epidaurus
c. 350 B.C.

# GREEK ARCHITECTURE

## PROJECT 3–1: **THE FACE OF AGAMMEMNON**

### FOR THE TEACHER

The ruins of Mycenae are on the southeastern shores of the Greek mainland. In 1876 a German archaclogist, Heinrich Schliemann, discovered the palace of Agammemnon. Beehive tombs and circular shaft graves built into the sides of the hills nearby were found to have beautiful repoussé gold masks and other funerary items such as golden cups, daggers, and other items for daily use.

### MASTERPIECES OF MYCENAEAN ART

*Vaphio Cups*, c. 1500 B.C., National Museum, Athens

*Lion Gate*, c. 1250 B.C., Mycenae, Greece

*Burial Mask of Agammemnon*, National Museum, Athens

*Three Dieties*, c. 1500–1400 B.C., National Museum, Athens

### PREPARATION

This is an ongoing project that can be worked on for short periods of time for several days. Show students the slides or photos of some of the repoussé items that were found in the tombs at Mycenae. Students can practice repoussé on heavy duty aluminum foil. It will be about the same weight as colored aluminum foil (which can be purchased through hobby shops).

### FURTHER SUGGESTIONS

- Instead of masks, make designs for modern Vaphio Cups. These could relate to team sports, plays, or other forms of school life. These could be displayed by cutting black mats for them.

- Small faces could be made into pendants. Fill these with plaster-of-Paris so they will keep their shape and be heavy enough to hang well.

Photo 3-1. Student work, repoussé on copper-colored foil.

Name: _____     Date: _____

# PROJECT 3–1: THE FACE OF AGAMMEMNON

**MATERIALS**

- Gold or copper-colored tooling foil
- Pencils or ballpoint pens
- Pads of newspaper

Repoussé literally means "pushed back" in French. It is a technique used in metalwork to create designs by stretching the metal. The Mycenaeans made golden masks for their royalty to be placed in their tombs. In addition they made drinking cups, crowns, and jewelry.

**Drawing after _Burial Mask of Agammemnon_, National Museum, Athens**

1. Before beginning a life-sized mask, experiment on a piece of foil approximately 2 × 3 inches. Place a thick pad of newspaper underneath the foil. A ballpoint pen or dull pencil makes a good tool because you can use the rounded end to smooth areas. Make parallel marks, dots, round circles, patterns of different types. Work from both sides to see what is possible.

2. Draw your mask idea on paper before beginning, because it is possible to overwork the foil.

3. For the mask, use a piece of foil approximately 12 × 12 inches. You will create a three-dimensional mask by stretching the foil. Leave some areas plain.

4. When you are finished, mount the mask on black matboard for an effective display.

© 1992 by The Center for Applied Research in Education, Inc.

# Unit 2: GREECE (700 B.C. TO 100 B.C.)

## OVERVIEW OF THE VISUAL ARTS

The period of Greek history of interest to most people was from 700 B.C. to A.D. 100. It was a time of dramatic changes in government, literature, theater, philosophy, and art. Within a 700-year span, Greek civilization made a transition to new ways of thinking and seeing. The individual began to receive recognition, with philosophers, playwrights, poets, and artists becoming well known. This new humanism was expressed by the philosopher Protagorus in the fifth century B.C. when he said, "Man is the measure of all things."

The Greeks established colonies in countries such as Italy, Turkey, and Egypt. They created new conventions in architecture and sculpture, many of which have set today's aesthetic standards. The symmetry and proportion of Greek architecture and the beauty and purity of its sculpture periodically reappear in "neoclassical" revivals. Today's Greek folk art continues to be produced by craftsmen trained in the old traditions.

**Greece**

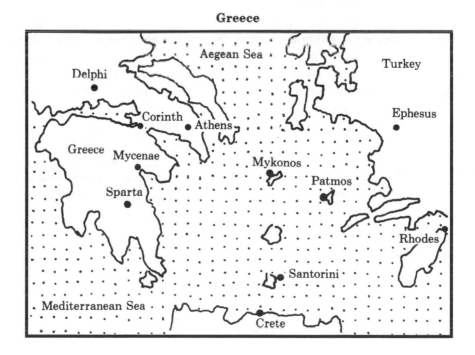

# PROJECT 3-2: THE GREEK VASE

# PROJECT 3-3: THE GREEK VASE AS CHAIR DESIGN

## FOR THE TEACHER

**Slide #5: Dipylon Vase.** In Greek pottery, each shape served a specific purpose. For example, the krater was used to mix wine and water; the hydria was used just for water. The vases ranged in size from 6 inches to 6 feet. Often they were created especially for wedding presents or as grave markers. (Holes were made in the bottoms so visitors to a grave could pour offerings of oil or wine.) Other ceramic pieces included perfume bottles, food containers, stoves, cooking grates, and even high chairs for children. It is hard to imagine, when we see vases and other artifacts from ancient Greece in museums, lined up in cases, that these were treasured household objects.

Much of our knowledge of Greek dress and appearance, religious beliefs, daily life, and battles comes from the study of Greek vase decoration. Many of the vases were signed by the painter or by both the potter and painter. Vases can be approximately dated according to how they are decorated. The iron-rich clay from which the vases were made fires to red, black, or buff. These were usually decorated with thinned clay (slip) in one of these colors.

## PREPARATION

These two projects were placed under the same heading, as they are so closely related and use the same resources. "The Greek Vase as Chair Design," originated by Diana Ziegler-Haydon and used with her permission, gives free reign to creativity, as students translate "design" from one object into a totally different art form. The purpose is to learn about Greek vase painting and to appreciate the intrinsic beauty and simplicity of pottery shapes.

The projects will be made richer if you have books, slides, and pictures of Greek vases for students to use for research. Students might find it interesting to know that terms describing parts of the vase, such as foot, belly, shoulder, waist, neck, and lip, relate it to the human form. Outlines of Greek vases (see the handout) could be printed on an overhead transparency or copied to give to students to get them started. To ensure a variety of decoration, allow students to choose one of the four periods described on the "Greek Vase" handout. The vase shapes changed little over a long period; only the method of decorating them varied. Controlling the number of colors used can make an effective display, no matter which style the students choose. The "Greek Vase" worksheet would be an effective preliminary research project.

If you are interested in obtaining slides, the following list gives a few examples of acknowledged masterpieces of Greek pottery.

## MASTERPIECES OF GREEK POTTERY

*Dipylon Amphora,* 750 B.C., National Museum, Athens

*Owl Perfume Jar,* c. 650 B.C., Louvre, Paris

*Dionysos in a Sailboat,* 540 B.C., Staatliche Antikensammlungen, Munich

*François Vase-Krater,* c. 570 B.C., 26 inches high, Museo Archeologico, Florence

*Heracles Strangling the Nemean Lion,* 520 B.C., Museo Civico, Brescia

*Herakles and Apollo Struggling for the Tripod,* Andokides painter, c. 525 B.C.,

*Mistress and Maid,* Achilles painter, c. 430 B.C., Staatliche Antikensammlungen, Munich

### FURTHER SUGGESTIONS

- On dark red paper, use white crayon to draw a scene of a sporting event or contact sport at school. (The yearbook might have appropriate photos.) The white crayon acts as a resist and represents the incised lines in early vases. This may be filled in with black watercolor marker or black ink.

- Choose a favorite food from a fast food restaurant and design a "classical container" to hold it.

- Consider other Greek motifs to use in designing chairs. Architectural elements or Greek sculpture could also be used for backs or legs.

- Greek vases were often inspiration for jewelry makers. Design dangling earring or key chains in the shape of Greek vases. These could be ceramic, heavy watercolor paper, "Friendly" plastic, or self-hardening clay.

- Create chairs from annealed stovepipe wire (available in a hardware store) that is strong enough to support itself. These sculptures could be approximately 6 to 8 inches high.

Student artwork.

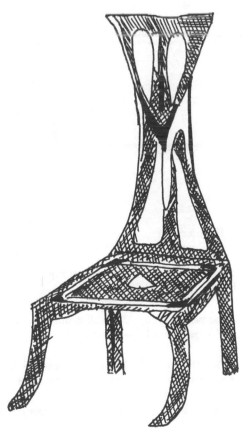

Student artwork.

# GREEK POTTERY

| | | | |
|---|---|---|---|
| **Lekythos** | **Amphora** | **Pyxis** | **Squat lekythos** |
| **Pelike** | **Kylix** | **Lekythos** | **Hydria** |
| **Amphora** | **Oinochoe** | **Bell krater** | **Gamikos** |
| **Bell krater** | **Krater** | **Krater** | **Stemless kylix** |

*Geometric period (850–700 B.C.):* horizontal bands and detailed geometric ornament. Battles, funerals, pageants. Figures were wedge shapes with "stick" arms.

*Orientalizing period (700–600 B.C.):* geometric design only on handles, foot, and lip. Narrative art dominated: battles, funerals, pageants. Figures were loosely arranged.

*Archaic (650–480 B.C.):* mythology and legends. Black figure ware. Figures were painted in black, with internal details incised. White or purple glaze was rubbed into the lines to make them stand out.

*Archaic (500 B.C.):* red figured style. Backgrounds were painted black with a brush, allowing much greater detail.

*Classical (480–323 B.C.):* white ground ware with red, black, and purple glazes. Naturalistic forms were shown.

# GREEK VASE PAINTING

Decorations on the Greek vases were so admired that many potters and painters signed vases. Some artists who created them became quite famous. Over several hundred years a number of different "rules" for vase painting evolved, and the vases of a particular period looked pretty much the same.

*Geometric period (850–700 B.C.):* These were decorated in horizontal bands, with detailed geometric ornament, concentric circles and semicircles, wavy lines, zigzags, net pattern, plain and shaded triangles, lozenges, meander (Greek key pattern), checkers, and swastikas. The scale was extremely miniature. The "prosthesis" (or lying in state by the dead) was often the major subject. Figures were wedge shaped, with "stick" arms. Warships and shipwrecks were often shown.

*Orientalizing phase (700–600 B.C.):* Narrative art dominated, with designs reflecting the oriental and Egyptian influence in animals and people. Popular subjects were battles, funerals and pageants. The figures were composed of simple shapes such as elongated triangles or wedges. Other designs were lotus, rosettes, scrolls, spirals, concentric circles, leaf patterns (laurel and ivy), palmettes, wheels, zigzags, checkers, meander, scale, volutes (scrolls). Figures were loosely arranged, not in bands. Geometric design continued to be used, including some new curved motifs, but only on the vase's handles, foot, and lip.

*Archaic period (650–480 B.C.):* Potters made black and red figure ware with bands of design on the foot, neck, and lip. These vases were smaller than previous ones, because grave markers were now made of stone. Pictorial subjects of mythology showed grouped figures, and legends were incised (scratched) into the red background. Black slip was used as the decoration (black figure ware, 580 B.C.). Later advances allowed the glazes to be painted on with a brush, and some glazing was done in white or reddish purple. Red figure ware (approximately 530 B.C.) reversed the technique, with the black slip being painted onto the background.

*Classical period (480–323 B.C.):* White ground ware vases were primarily used for funerary gifts. They were painted with red, black, or purple after firing, and often showed scenes of daily life such as a woman fixing her hair.

## PROJECT 3–2: **GREEK VASE DESIGN**

**MATERIALS**

- White drawing paper
- Conté crayon (dark red, black, or white) or oil pastels

1. Select one of the periods of vase decoration and if possible, try to find more information or examples of that period. You will be working with limited colors, so decide what your background color will be. If you want to use colored paper and simply draw or paint the designs in just one color (such as black), this could be mounted on a white background for display.

2. Select a shape to decorate, and draw it lightly in pencil on your paper. Use the entire piece of paper. You may find it easier to first make a newsprint pattern. Fold the newsprint in half and cut it out, then trace around it.

3. If you choose to make bands on the vase, notice that the bands will appear to curve as they go around the vase. No need to use a ruler—the Greeks did not.

4. Use your imagination. Rather than portraying a Greek god, try showing a modern musical group or a sports event such as wrestling. Complete the vase, as the Greeks did, by filling in some spaces with lines, and decorations on the foot, neck, and lip of the vase.

Name: _____   Date: _____

## PROJECT 3–3: **THE GREEK VASE AS CHAIR DESIGN**

**MATERIALS**

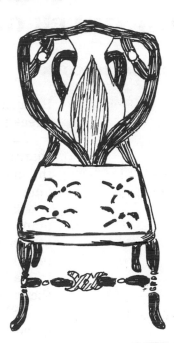

- Paper: minimum 11 × 14 inches; white, black, or dark red construction paper
- Marking instruments: pencils, pastels, crayons, colored markers
- Colored paper (for cutting and pasting)
- Newsprint
- Cardboard
- Scissors

**Drawn from student artwork.**

Many designs from the Greek culture have endured throughout history. The term "classical" comes from the Greek civilization and implies simplicity, restraint, and proportion. Every so often there is a resurgence of interest in Greek art and architecture, and a "Greek revival," or neoclassical period, will occur in furniture and building design.

To learn where designers sometimes go for inspiration, see for yourself how well Greek vase outlines can be adapted for furniture design. Although you might think that these vase backs would make traditional chairs, let yourself go when you are designing. The shapes could be used not only in the center back, but as leg or seat shapes.

1. Choose a vase shape that appeals to you. Don't be afraid to select another if the first one fails to "inspire" you.

2. Make several thumbnail (small) sketches of different chair possibilities. These small designs are "roughs," so don't spend more than 10 minutes drawing them. Select the best. Your chair could be upholstered and made of wood, plastic, foam, or any other material.

3. Whatever the size paper, the design should almost fill it. Draw it lightly in pencil. If you've never drawn a chair, make some sketches from chairs at school or home to get started.

4. Your presentation of the finished chair could be done in many different ways. It can simply be drawn in pencil, colored pencil, crayon, or marker. It is also effective if made of cut-paper or collage. It could be three-dimensional if you draw it on cardboard, and score and fold it.

# PROJECT 3–4:  WALL PAINTING—LIVES OF THE GREEK GODS

**FOR THE TEACHER**

Because of the climate, loss of ancient buildings, and the fragility of panel painting, no Greek painting has endured. We know they existed because of copies found in Etruscan tombs or in Grecian colonies in Italy. This project allows individual research and sharing of knowledge about mythology. Mythology developed as a way of explaining the unexplainable. Why did the sun come up and go down each day? Where did lightning come from?

Students will create individual "wall panels," then join them together with columns, friezes, and caryatids (a supporting column in the form of female figures) created by several of the students to make the interior wall of a Greek villa. These architectural elements should be in white paper, with details painted with gray. (If you wish to marblize, see the directions in "Obelisk," Section 4.) Wide tan kraft paper, or even the insides of tan grocery bags, could be a suitable background.

Show students slides and pictures of Greek vases, sculpture, and architecture that demonstrate how important the deities and heroes were in the lives of the people. The English department may have a world literature or classical literature text that describe them; Edith Hamilton's *Mythology* is an excellent paperback source. Students may be uncertain how to draw the human figure, you could show them how the figure is made up of triangles (or ovals), and have them first draw the figures in motion using ovals, then clothe them in togas.

**FURTHER SUGGESTION**

- Assign students to find interpretations of the lives of the gods in vases, paintings, and sculpture to share with the class (not necessarily just Greek or Roman).

## PROJECT 3-4: **LIVES OF THE GREEK GODS**

### MATERIALS

- Drawing paper 18 × 24 inches or 36-inch wide roll paper
- White 36-inch wide roll paper
- Pastels, conté crayon, or tempera paint
- Fixative

The Greek gods were related to each other, and the ordinary people knew everything about them, even their mortal failings. The Greeks did wall paintings portraying the lives and adventures of the gods. The background colors most commonly seen on the wall paintings were gold, white, dark reddish orange, and light blue. To see how much action there frequently was in these paintings, look at pictures on Greek vases or Greek sculpture.

1. Select one god to research. Or choose a group of gods, such as the three graces or nine muses, or couples such as Zeus and Hera together.

2. Make several thumbnail sketches (rough, taking no more than 10 minutes on this portion of the project). Since no one has ever seen the gods, your interpretation is as good as anyone's, so be creative. Enlarge the sketch you find most interesting.

3. Turn the paper either vertically or horizontally (the entire class should be using the same direction). Use pencil to very lightly draw the general size figures(s) you want. Fill the space well.

4. Outline the main figures in black, and fill in with flat (unshaded) areas of colors such as black, brown, dark red, blue, and gold. If you are using pastel, use the side of the pastel to evenly fill in the background. Observe what your fellow students are doing to make sure everyone is working in approximately the same value (degree of darkness) so that the panels will go together when they are joined on the wall. Two or three colors may be all you need.

5. Before mounting these on the wall, lay them on the floor approximately 10 inches apart, moving them around to show off each individual picture to the best advantage.

6. Take the columns, pediments, and friezes that have been made by other students and place these in appropriate places so that the entire display looks as if it could be a Greek villa.

# GREEK GODS

**Nine Muses**

Clio-Muse of history
Urania-Astronomy
Melpomene-Tragedy
Thalia-Comedy
Terpsichore-Dance
Calliope-Epic poetry
Erato-Love poetry
Euterpe-Lyric poetry
Polyhymnia-Songs to the
    gods

Zeus (Jupiter)
King of the gods,
rules heaven

Hera (Juno)
Queen of the gods

**Zeus's Wives and Loves**

Hera
Themis
Eruynome
Io
Mnemosyne
Leto
Maia
Alcmene
Semele
Demeter
Harmonia

Athena (Minerva)

Poseidon (Neptune)
Rules the sea

Hades (Pluto)
Rules the underworld

Apollo (Apollo)
God of the sun

Hermes (Mercury)
Messenger of the gods

Aphrodite (Venus)
Goddess of love and beauty

Hestia (Vesta)
Goddess of the home

Ares (Mars)
God of war

**Other Gods**

Hephaestus (Vulcan)
    God of fire
Dionysus (Bacchus)
    God of wine
Pan (Faunus)
Chronus (Saturn)
    God of time
Eros (Cupid)
    God of love
Demeter (Ceres)
    Agriculture

Artemis (Diana)
Goddess of the hunt

Persephone
Goddess of underworld

**Three Furies**

Alecto
Tisiphone
Megara

**Three Fates**

Clotho
Lachesis
Atropos

# PROJECT 3-5: COINS AND MEDALLIONS

**FOR THE TEACHER**

Coins were a Greek invention of approximately 650 B.C. when the city-states stamped pieces of metal to guarantee purity, weight, and value. The designs were based on animals, plants, local heroes, or deities. Then, as now, special people were honored by having their faces placed on a coin. Some of the early Greek coins showed people with animals such as horses or dolphins, as well as an occasional Greek word. Many thousands of coins have survived because the Greeks buried their savings (not having banks), and these hoards have been unearthed.

A coin was made by creating a die of thick metal that had the design carved into it. It was held in place on an anvil. A die for the opposite side, also carved, was attached to a metal punch. The coin blanks were heated, placed on the anvil-die, and hammered with the punch-die, making the two-faced coin. Many irregularities were produced, and the coins were thick compared with modern ones. No dates or cities were on the coins, but they can be identified because of the styles and designs. The evolution of Greek art is shown in its coins as well as in other art forms, and these were produced by skilled specialists, just as they are today.

**Photo 3-2.**

**PREPARATION**

Begin this project by discussing familiar coins. What Greek influence carries over today? Students may even want to bring old or foreign coins to discuss. What characteristics do all coins have in common, and what are their differences? Many examples of masterpieces exist. Most had heads or animals on them.

**MASTERPIECES**

*Antimachus of Bactria,* c. 185 B.C., British Museum, London

*Silenus,* c. 460 B.C., British Museum, London

**FURTHER SUGGESTIONS**

- Use large lids such as plastic butter tub lids to cover and make repoussé "commemorative" medallions. Ask students what is being done at their school or community these days that would be worth the awarding of such a medallion. These could even have holes punched in them and be suspended on a tricolored ribbon, like Olympic medals.

- Students could design a clay circle bas-relief to memorialize some famous person for a competition. This could be the "die" for a commemorative edition. If you really wanted to go all out, make a plaster cast of this die, and actually cast several. (See the appendix for instructions on mixing plaster.) Let students know that competitions for designing this type of medal are being held even today.

**Photo 3-3. Greek Coins, 600 B.C. to A.D. 700, The Saint Louis Art Museum, Gift of Mr. Cornelius F. P. Stueck.**

Name: _____ Date: _____

# PROJECT 3–5: COINS AND MEDALLIONS

**MATERIALS**

- Tooling foil, gold or silver
- Bottle caps
- Newsprint
- Scissors
- Scouring pad, steel or plastic
- Tools, dull pencils, empty mechanical pencils
- Newspaper
- Styrofoam (egg cartons)
- Permanent marker

This repoussé coin will be widely circulated, so the image should be something or someone of interest. (You could even use a school photo of yourself as a model.) There will be two sides to the coin, so create two designs that will go together. One side should have the main figure and the other something different such as an animal or a Greek column.

1. Draw around a shallow plastic lid from a medicine bottle. Try a number of quick sketches of various designs. It could be quite detailed. If you are using letters, remember they will be reversed. Select one design.

2. Place the lid on a piece of styrofoam (such as the lid from an egg carton) and press firmly, leaving an indentation. Use scissors to carefully cut inside the lines. Make several of these circles. (You will place one or two pieces of foam inside the lid later.) Cut a square of foil approximately 2 × 2 inches. Use the lid again, and press down on the dull side of the foil to make a circle.

3. Put a pad of newspaper under the foil (shiny side against the newspaper). Practice on the edges, then draw the design inside the circle. You will stretch the foil by repeatedly going over it. It is possible to work on both sides of the foil, pressing some designs in and some out. If you are careful, you can make wonderful detail.

4. When one side is finished, place the lid inside it, and carefully stretch the foil around the lid (which has styrofoam inside it, to make it level). Cut off the excess with scissors. Make the other side in exactly the same manner. When you put it on the lid, press the edges carefully. Remove it and cut the edges so they come exactly to the front of the other side. Put white glue around the edge of the coin and replace the second side, holding and pressing it in place. Wipe off excess glue.

5. Use permanent marker or ink to cover the coin with color. With tissue, wipe off the excess, leaving highlights. It may be necessary to use steel wool to bring up the highlights.

# PROJECT 3–6: CLASSICAL ARCHITECTURE

**FOR THE TEACHER**

**Slide #6: *Parthenon.*** Greek architecture was based on that of Egypt, Crete, and Mycenae, but a difference in materials and tools enabled the Greeks to refine the pure forms and classical designs that have influenced architects ever since. Grecian marble was easier than sandstone to carve, and iron tools were much more efficient than bronze. Today one has the impression that all Greek temples were gleaming white, but brilliant colors once embellished buildings such as the Parthenon. When buildings were created of a material other than marble, a white plaster was used to cover the natural material, and they were sometimes even painted to resemble marble.

Many Greek cities have an acropolis, which was usually a fortified hill, the highest spot in the city. The acropolis was the preferred location for temples, which were entirely created of stone. Civic buildings were usually located below the acropolis. Most of what we know of Greek architecture is based on the remains of temples, theaters, the open market (agora) and meeting places (stoas). Private houses remained relatively modest, often built around a courtyard.

Most temples had columns around the outside and an inner room (cella) where statues of the gods were kept and where offerings might be placed. While Egyptian worship was held inside the temples, Greeks basically worshiped outside the temple. Columns were made by stacking drums of stone on top of each other, holding them in place with metal pieces, before carving them into fluted columns. The familiar "Doric, Ionic, Corinthian" litany refers to the capitals (tops of the columns) and the order in which they were introduced. Corinthian is actually an elaboration of Ionic.

The "Greek Architecture" worksheet will help students researching Greek architecture. A brief overview of important architectural features follows:

*Archaic period (650–480 B.C.):* The Doric column had squat proportions. The columns were set directly on the porch (stylobate), without a base. The Doric column was approximately six times the height of its diameter and was considered "masculine." The temples were approximately 20 feet high.

*Classical period (480–323 B.C.):* In this "Golden Age of Greek Culture," Doric and Ionic temples were constructed. The Ionic column, approximately nine times the height of the diameter of the column, was considered "feminine." Temples were 40 to 60 feet high.

*Hellenistic period (323–30 B.C.):* Ionic and Corinthian orders were most used, and buildings became much larger.

**MASTERPIECES**

*Temple of Apollo,* c. 540 B.C., Corinth, Greece

*Temple of Hera,* 530 B.C., Paestum, Italy.

*Parthenon,* 447–432 B.C., Acropolis, Athens

*Erechtheum,* 421–406 B.C., Acropolis, Athens (Porch of the Maidens)

*Temple of Athena Nike,* 427–424 B.C., Acropolis, Athens

*Altar of Zeus,* Pergamon, c. 175 B.C., Berlin, Germany

**FURTHER SUGGESTIONS**

- Have students design a piece of furniture using architectural elements of design such as columns, friezes, and pediments. Some suggestions are entertainment centers for TV, VCR, etc.), chairs (use the backs as capitals), serving table, coffee table.
- Design wire or clay jewelry to look "architectural."

**Photo 3-4. The use of Grecian architecture as an inspiration for design is seen in this Neoclassical vase. Vase, A.D. 1785–1795, Wedgwood, English, 19.7 × 21.0 × 11.1 cm, The Saint Louis Art Museum, Gift of Mr. and Mrs. Milton L. Zorensky.**

# GREEK ARCHITECTURE

Greek architecture helped define what architects used and continue to use in buildings today. Research and draw the capitals of the three basic styles of Greek columns.

**Archaic Period**
**650–480 B.C.**

**Classical Period**
**480–323 B.C.**

**Hellenistic Period**
**323–30 B.C.**

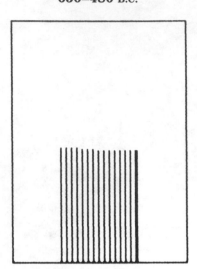   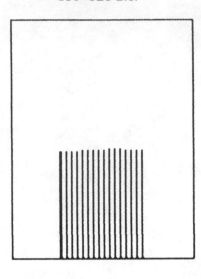   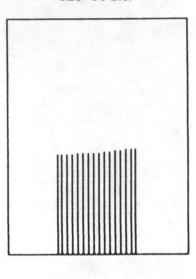

_____    _____    _____

Research and find what the various types of buildings were used for in ancient Greece.

temple _____

stoa _____

agora _____

Define the following terms:

entasis _____

caryatid _____

frieze _____

Design a pediment to fit on your school or home.

Name: _____   Date: _____

## PROJECT 3–6:  **MAKE IT CLASSI(CAL)!**

### MATERIALS

- Rulers
- Tracing paper
- Drawing paper
- Black fine-line markers or chalk

Do research about Greek architecture. Learn to identify the various types of columns and find out something about other architectural elements such as the frieze or pediment. If you can get to a museum, see the Greek architectural ornaments used in furniture design, with columns for legs. Many museums and courthouses in the United States are based on Greek architecture. Although other cultures made greater contributions to the structural elements of building, such as the Roman dome and arch, the Greek decorative elements have dominated classical buildings.

See if there are buildings in your town that reflect the Greek order. Courts and banks often display their dignity and solidity with this type of architecture. The southern mansions with their columns across the front were based on Greek architecture.

1. Select a building such as your house, school, church, a movie theater, or shopping mall in your town. Make a sketch of it as it now stands.

2. Place tracing paper on top of it and see if you can improve it by changing certain elements with the addition of Greek design. Perhaps a frieze across the top, or columns to support a porch with a pediment would improve it.

3. As a different challenge, see what the removal of Greek architectural elements can do to a building that already has them. You (the architect) have been asked to update an old-fashioned building. What can you do to modernize it?

4. When you have made changes on the tracing paper, turn it over and go over the lines with pencil on the underside. When you flip it over again, it is easy to trace only those lines, and transfer it to white paper. Draw with fine-line black marker.

101

# PROJECT 3–7:  TOGA-CLAD WIRE SCULPTURE

**FOR THE TEACHER**

**Slide #7: *Winged Victory of Samothrace.*** Early Greek sculptors were undoubtedly influenced by the Egyptians, but in a relatively short time, they began to make major changes that have influenced sculpture ever since. In contrast to limestone and bronze tools used by the Egyptians, most Greek sculptors carved in marble, using iron tools. Even in early periods, the Greek sculptors removed stone from between legs and the torso and arms, and soon the static quality of archaic sculpture gave way to movement and grace.

Many Greek statues were destroyed because of earthquakes, wars, and foreign invasions. Many famous Greek sculptures are known only because of the Roman copies of the original Greek work. (Romans used a pointing machine to copy statues exactly.) The "Greek Sculpture" worksheet will help students study differences in various periods of Greek sculpture.

**GREEK SCULPTURE CHARACTERISTICS**

*Geometric period (900–600 B.C.):* Sculpture was basically used to decorate temples. Often it was bas-relief, with little freestanding sculpture. The major subjects were animals, warriors, gods and goddesses, and exotic beasts. Materials used were ivory, terra cotta, and bronze.

*Orientalizing phase (700–600 B.C.):* Sculptures of exotic beasts represent the Near Eastern influence. Archaic statues were introduced in this period.

*Archaic period (650–480 B.C.):* The archaic male (kouros) and female (kore) statues were probably used as grave markers and votive offerings for temples. They usually were created of marble and were painted in many colors. The female might have one hand at her side and one across her chest, while the male usually had both hands at his sides. Their eyes appeared to be staring, and their wide mouths were often fixed in a smile. According to the convention of that time, the females were clothed, with three or four braids hanging in front on either side of the shoulders. Their dresses did not appear to really be covering a human form. The unclothed male figures sometimes had the left foot forward, with an even balance of weight, and muscles in tension.

*Classical (480–323 B.C.):* Statues were released from the static poses of archaic times when contrapposto was introduced (contrapposto results when the weight is shifted to one foot, causing one hip to be higher than another). The natural curve this created made the statues become more human in appearance. Facial expressions became more realistic than the empty smile and straightforward stance. The head might now be tilted or turned. Muscles were shown, and the statues often showed movement, or were in athletic poses. The males sometimes appeared to have long tights that ended in folds at the ankles or wrists. Female anatomy was shown with wet-appearing drapery or, later in this period, partially nude.

*Hellenistic period (323–30 B.C.):* Sculpture began to become quite realistic and worldly. Statuary decorated private and civic buildings, as well as temples. Pathos, which found expression in the theater, also began to be shown on the faces of statues, as they expressed emotion. Windblown drapery such as that on the Nike of Samothrace might be seen, and hairstyles were more natural.

Although the figures created in this project will not be realistic, like clay figures, students can still experience making Greek statues. They also may want to add the "props" (attributes) of the various gods, such as winged feet or helmets, made of tag board and covered with paper towels.

## MASTERPIECES OF SCULPTURE

*Deer Nursing a Fawn,* 900–700 B.C., Thebes

*Artemis from Delos,* Nikrandre, c. 660–650 B.C., National Museum, Athens

*Kouros of Sounion,* c. 600 B.C., National Archaeological Museum, Athens

*Calf-Bearer,* c. 570 B.C., 66 inches high, marble, Acropolis Museum, Athens

*La Delicata,* c. 525 B.C., 36 inches high, marble, Acropolis Museum, Athens

*Dying Warrior,* c. 490 B.C., Staatliche Museum, Munich

*Kritios Boy,* c. 480 B.C., Acropolis Museum, Athens

*Charioteer of Delphi,* c. 470 B.C., Museum, Delphi

*Caryatid figures,* 421–405 B.C., Acropolis Museum, Athens

*Three Goddesses,* c. 438–432 B.C., British Museum, London

*Discus Thrower,* Roman copy, c. 450 B.C., Museo Nazionale Romano, Rome

*Nike of Samothrace,* c. 190 B.C., The Louvre, Paris

*Venus de Milo,* c. 200 B.C., Louvre, Paris

*Laocoon and His Two Sons.* c. 200 B.C. to A.D. 100, Vatican Museums, Rome

## FURTHER SUGGESTIONS

- Create archaic (rigid) statues using soda bottles or dishwashing detergent bottles as the body. (Weight plastic bottles with pebbles or sand.) Wrap the arm and shoulder wire around the neck of the bottle, and use the lip as the neck, with a styrofoam egg as the head.
- Bas-relief clay sculptures could be made to fit into a pediment shape, with figures filling the shallow triangular space.
- Very simple sculptures of people and animals such as those made in Mycenae from about 1300 to 1100 B.C. could be made either from fired or self-hardening clay, and painted with the stripes that were a commonly used decoration.

# GREEK SCULPTURE

Observe and compare as art historians and archaeologists do when they analyze a work of art. Choose three pieces of sculpture from different time periods, and give one- or two-word descriptions.

1. _____  2. _____  3. _____

| | Egyptian 900–600 B.C. | Archaic 650–480 B.C. | Classical 480–323 B.C. | Hellenistic 323–30 B.C. |
|---|---|---|---|---|
| Compare heads. | | | | |
| Eyes | | | | |
| Hair | | | | |
| Mouth | | | | |
| Direction | | | | |
| Compare bodies. | | | | |
| Arms | | | | |
| Torso | | | | |
| Movement | | | | |
| Legs | | | | |
| Compare clothing. | | | | |
| Clothed or nude? | | | | |
| Form shown under clothing? | | | | |
| Appearance of drapery | | | | |
| Name two or more famous sculptures in each time period. | | | | |

If you had to choose only one piece of Greek sculpture as your favorite, which would it be?

Name: _____     Date: _____

## PROJECT 3–7: **TOGA-CLAD WIRE SCULPTURE**

### MATERIALS

- Annealed stovepipe wire, 16 to 18 gauge
- Styrofoam eggs
- Wire cutters
- Wallpaper paste
- Paper towels
- White spray paint

- Wood, for bases
- Hammer and tacks
- Old sheeting or muslin
- Straight pins
- Pliers

Your toga-clad "ancient Greek statue" will be approximately 12 inches high.

1. Cut a length of wire approximately 30 inches long. Fold it in half, and make loops on each end for feet, which will be nailed onto a board. If your wire is thin, double or triple the thickness. Make the middle of the wire into a point and stick it halfway into a styrofoam egg (the head).

2. Make loops on each end of a 15-inch piece of wire to make hands, then wrap it just below the neck and make shoulders. Use a little more wire to fill out the upper torso, and reinforce the legs and arms if necessary. Manipulate the wire until it has the action you want in the final product. Tack it to the board.

3. Mix wallpaper paste according to the directions on the package. Dip a paper towel into the paste, wipe off excess paste into the bucket, and center the paper over the head of the figure. Smooth this carefully over the egg, and use the ends to fill out the shoulders, arms and torso. Tear paper toweling to wrap the hand-loops and up the arms.

4. To create the toga, use pieces of 3 × 12-inch torn sheeting or muslin dipped in wallpaper paste. First make draped sleeves, then slit a 12 × 24-inch piece in the middle just to fit over the head. Carefully drape and arrange it to reach to the bottom of the figure (it will give stability to the figure when it dries). If you wish, loosely wrap the bottom of the figure under the toga with paper towels to give more substance.

5. Use yarn dipped in wallpaper paste to make hair, trying to recreate some of the curls and braids seen on statuary. Hold them in place with straight pins pushed into the styrofoam egg. You could put a band around the head.

6. Allow the piece to dry for several days. When it is completely dry, take it outside and spray it with white paint. You may have to spray it a number of times to completely cover the folds. Lightly spray with a second, slightly different color such as beige or gray to make the finish look even more like marble.

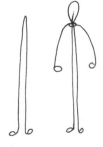  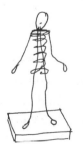    

# PROJECT 3-8: TOGA PARTY

## FOR THE TEACHER

This project could be done at any time during the study of Greek art, but might be an appropriate way to end the unit. Decorating the room with some of the wall paintings and vases adds to the atmosphere. Ask students to wear togas in class and model for the others, who will draw them. Many students may wish to bring finger food such as fruit, cheese, and loaves of bread, which could be grouped on a table in front of the models as part of the picture. If you use only black and white drawing media, this is a good project for demonstrating how volume and form can be shown through differences in value.

Although this project is a celebration of sorts, it still is a working time, and the food should not be eaten until near the end of the period (after drawing). This could be held after school or in the evening if more time is needed.

The dress (toga) was a long wide rectangle of cloth (wool or linen) which could be drawn to the body shape with a belt or pins. There were very detailed rules for draping the cloth, such as pinning it on the left shoulder. A simple shift-like garment called the chiton was worn under the sometimes brightly colored outer cloak. The cloak was laid across the back and shoulders with the corners hanging over the front, then it passed under the right arm so it could be thrown over the left shoulder or held over the left arm. Orators left their right arms free so they could make gestures, and the right arm could be raised to vote only if it was completely free of the draped cloak. Soldiers wore shorter chitons.

Women's clothing was similar, except that their chiton was sometimes slit so part of it could be worn as a hood. Through the years they varied this garment somewhat and wore layers of clothing, pleating and embroidering it, but keeping it relatively simple. In later centuries costumes evolved to many layers of embroidered and woven fabrics. Jewelry such as rings, bracelets (also worn on the upper arm), long earrings, and necklaces were commonly worn, and the pins (fibulas) used to hold the toga in place were decorative. Married women often wore a turban and kept their hair covered. Courtesans and dancers might wear a short tunic rather than the long one worn by respectable women.

## PREPARATION

To give students ideas of how to drape a toga, show them Greek vase paintings and examples of clothed sculptures such as the Nike of Samothrace, caryatids, or the korae (female figures). Have photocopied pictures of various hairstyles, and let them create Grecian hairstyles on the model(s). Sketches on the student page show how to put a toga together.

## FURTHER SUGGESTIONS

- If several students are in togas, have them find a vase painting that appeals to them, and assume the pose on the vase while someone takes instant photographs.
- These figures in togas could be assumed to be gods, and their symbols could be added. For example, Poseidon's trident, Zeus's thunderbolt, Dionysus's (Bacchus's) grape wreath in his hair, or Eros's (Cupid's) bow and arrow could be drawn.

# PROJECT 3–8:  TOGA PARTY

**MATERIALS**

- Plain colored sheets or lengths of fabric for togas
- Drawing paper, 18 × 24 inches
- Charcoal
- Kneaded erasers
- Newsprint
- White chalk
- Fixative

Whenever we think of Greek costumes, we think of the toga, which was not the only garment the Greeks ever wore. It was the outer part of their costume, however, and the draping of it was an art in itself. The Greeks often had elaborate headbands, turbans, and hairdos. They usually wore sandals, and the women wore gold jewelry. To give a feeling of action, allow the human form to show underneath the cloth.

   If you want to draw a "god," you could try one of the known Greek gods, or you could invent one to be in charge of the wind, trees, flowers, or animals. Use your imagination.

1. Make a "viewfinder" by making a rectangle with your hands (thumbs together, index fingers together). Hold this 12 inches away from your eyes, close one eye, and squint through this square at the models. Move it around until you have isolated a section you wish to draw.

2. The assignment is to fill the page. It is not important to draw the entire figure, but to give a mood and a feel through the way you use the charcoal. Redraw some lines to give emphasis. Although you are drawing a light garment, notice how some areas are in shadow, while others reflect light.

3. Use the charcoal to lightly sketch in the outlines. Keep a piece of tissue handy to smear off parts of it if you are not happy, but don't attempt to keep it spotless. Most people who draw with charcoal keep trying for the lines they are after, and it is the repetition of one line over another that gives a drawing life.

4. Use the charcoal in different ways: shade with the side of it, use the end to make small cross-hatching strokes and bold lines, or even totally darken some areas. Use a kneaded eraser to remove the charcoal in some areas to create highlights, or make highlights with white chalk.

5. When you are finished, take the drawing outside and spray it with fixative or hair spray. If you do not fix the charcoal, protect it with newsprint to prevent smearing. It could be mounted behind acetate for protection.

© 1992 by The Center for Applied Research in Education, Inc.

**Photo 3-5.** *Running Artemis*, 323–330 B.C., Greek, Hellenistic, H. 73 cm, The Saint Louis Art Museum.

# ROME AND BYZANTIUM

# ROME AND BYZANTIUM
## TIME LINE

| 750 B.C. | 300 B.C. | 1 | A.D. 100 | A.D. 200 | A.D. 300 | A.D. 450 | A.D. 600 |
|---|---|---|---|---|---|---|---|

Etruscan 700–300

Apollo from Veii 510

Rome founded 753

She-Wolf, 500

Tomb of the Reliefs. Ceveteri, 400

Republic of Rome 200–27

Pantheon 118 B.C.–A.D. 25

Arch of Titus 1

Villa of the Mysteries Pompeii 100 B.C.

Life of Christ 1–30

Colosseum A.D. 72–80

Pont du Gard 1st century A.D.

Equestrian statue of Marcus Aurelius 100

Trajan's Column 106–113

Late Imperial 200–476

Baths of Caracalla 212–216

Arch of Constantine A.D. 312–315

Diocletian's Palace Split, Yugoslavia 300

Emperor Constantine 324

End of Western Roman Empire 476

St. Apollinare in Classe (Ravenna) A.D. 533–549

Hagia Sophia A.D. 532–537

Byzantine Empire 500–1453

Emperor Justinian 527–565

**Africa**

Nok Culture 500 B.C.–500 A.D.

**Americas**

Teotihuacan Mexico 325–700

Maya Civilization 470

Mississippi Valley Culture, 451–500

**Asia**

First Japanese Emperor 230

Han Dynasty 22–220

Calligraphy: China 175

Chinese Bronze 520

Earliest Chinese Scroll Landscape, 535

**Europe**

Scythian Art 6th century B.C.

**Near East**

Constantinople founded 330

**Other**

## Unit 1:  ROMAN EMPIRE (500 B.C. TO A.D. 350)

**OVERVIEW OF THE VISUAL ARTS**

The Roman culture did not spring full-blown upon the countryside of Italy, but evolved slowly, reflecting influences from the Greeks and Egyptians. Etruscan settlements to the north of Rome dominated the area. Most of what we know of the Etruscans comes from their elaborate tombs. Tombs were sculpted into existing rock, and were made to resemble elaborate rooms with the addition of terra cotta decorations and columns.

The Etruscans organized cities by using two main thoroughfares that ran east-west and north-south. The Romans adopted this method for setting up their camps and towns throughout Italy, Western Europe, and North Africa. Rome was established in approximately 500 B.C. Traces of its far-flung empire can be seen today throughout Europe and the Near East in old walls, roads, viaducts, buildings, and amphitheaters.

**The Roman Empire**

## PAINTING

When Mount Vesuvius exploded in A.D. 79, burying the cities of Pompeii and Herculaneum in ash, nearly perfect examples of Roman wall paintings and mosaics were preserved. Their subjects were landscapes, portraiture, battles, and mythological subjects.
The brilliantly colored frescoes have retained their fresh colors. Fake architectural
elements were often painted to resemble real marble, and open "windows," surrounded
by "columns" showed great vistas that used atmospheric perspective (the further away
something was, the more hazy and less distinct). The paintings show the great skill of
Roman painters. They used light from a single source that cast shadows and revealed
form through modeling.

Groups of figures were shown in battle, conversing, or dancing. In figural painting, foreshortening was used (making the portion of the body closest to the viewer
larger than the rest of the body, a form of perspective). Realistic and sensitive portraits have been found on mummy covers of Romans who died while in Egypt.

## MASTERPIECES OF PAINTING

*Portrait of a Boy,* c. A.D. 200–300, Metropolitan Museum of Art, N.Y.

*Scenes of a Dyonysiac Mystery Cult,* 50 B.C., Villa of the Mysteries, Pompeii

*Painted ceiling,* A.D. 300–400, Catacomb of SS Pietro e Marcellino, Rome

*Peaches and Glass Jar,* c. A.D. 50, National Museum, Naples

## SCULPTURE

Although the Romans were greatly influenced by the Greek sculptors in their midst,
and they often copied great Greek sculpture, Roman sculpture came to have its own
identity. Public sculpture memorialized great leaders in busts and larger-than-life-size
statues. Roman portrait busts did not idealize the subject's appearance, but were lifelike, perhaps because of the custom of keeping wax death-masks of ancestors in a
special place in the home. An exception is an 8-foot-tall stone head of Emperor Constantine (it is the only part of his enormous statue that survived). Its staring eyes and
severe facial expression may foreshadow the retreat from realism that characterized
sculpture for the next thousand years. Many scenes of daily life, religious sacrifices,
and battles were carved on Roman sarcophagi (caskets) and triumphal arches. Monuments such as *Trajan's Column* depicted scenes of battles. Bronze equestrian statues
and "orator" statues commemorated the rule of various emperors.

## MASTERPIECES OF SCULPTURE

*She-wolf,* c. 500 B.C., bronze, Capitoline Museums, Rome

*Equestrian Statue of Marcus Aurelius,* A.D. 161–180, Piazza del Campidoglio, Rome

*Head of Constantine,* A.D. 330, Capitoline Museums, Rome

*Arch of Constantine,* A.D. 312–315, Rome (many bas-relief sculptures)

## ARCHITECTURE

Many architectural innovations can be credited to the Romans. Their application of
structural elements such as the arch, dome, and vault enabled them to build enormous

structures such as public baths, sewers, aqueducts, bridges, apartment buildings, forums, and arenas. Although concrete had been invented centuries before, the Romans saw the possibilities of using it to create new forms. It was often decorated with imbedded stones or covered with brick, marble, or smooth plaster. Atriums (enclosed spaces open to the elements) were built in churches and private homes. The ribbed ceiling support, or coffered (boxlike) roof, enabled them to build the large domed temple, the Pantheon.

Roman churches began as modest places of worship, similar to Greek and Egyptian temples, where interiors were basically reserved for the priests. As Christianity grew, however, the basilica form of design used in the public meeting place was adapted to churches to accommodate growing numbers of worshipers inside. Although Egyptians and Greeks had used the rounded barrel vault for strength in underground structures, the Romans adapted it to use in churches.

Roman columns were adapted from the Greek Corinthian form, with a base added. Columns were sometimes attached to the wall, creating an "engaged" column or "pilaster." Arches were commonly used between columns. Many beautiful aqueducts with rounded arches endure today. Niches with rounded tops were created, often for the display of sculpture. The Romans were especially adept at creating mosaic floors by imbedding rocks of various colors in cement to make beautiful designs.

## MASTERPIECES OF ARCHITECTURE

*Colosseum,* A.D. 72–80, Rome

*Trajan's Column,* A.D. 106–113, 40 m. high, marble, Rome

*Arch of Constantine,* A.D. 312–314, Rome

*Pantheon,* A.D. 118–125, Rome

*The Roman Forum,* first to sixth centuries B.C.

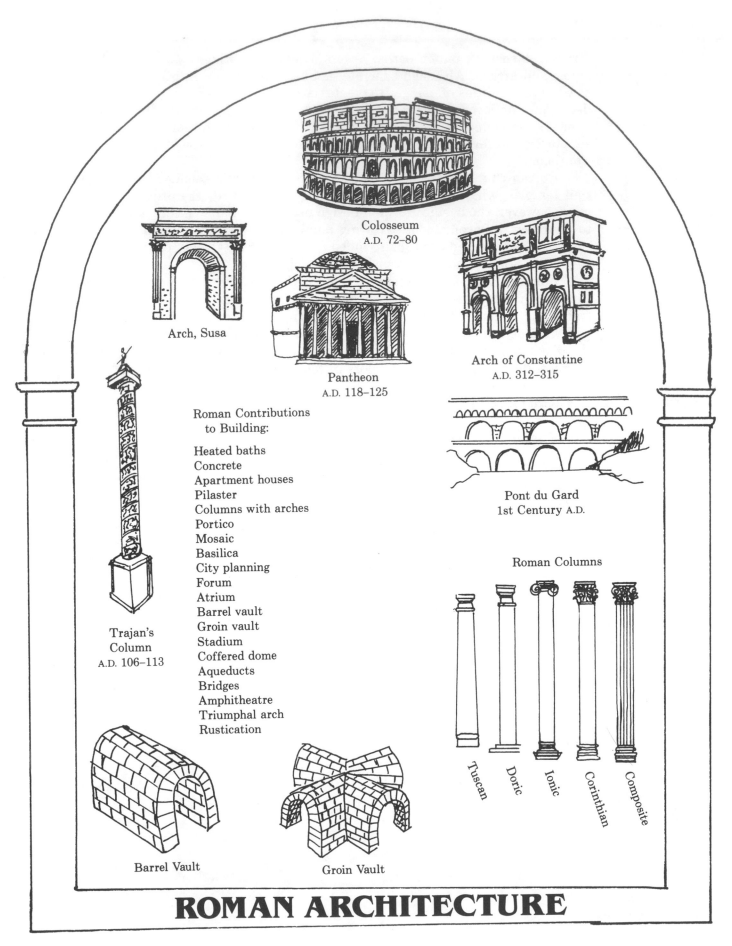

Colosseum
A.D. 72–80

Arch, Susa

Pantheon
A.D. 118–125

Arch of Constantine
A.D. 312–315

Pont du Gard
1st Century A.D.

Roman Contributions
to Building:

Heated baths
Concrete
Apartment houses
Pilaster
Columns with arches
Portico
Mosaic
Basilica
City planning
Forum
Atrium
Barrel vault
Groin vault
Stadium
Coffered dome
Aqueducts
Bridges
Amphitheatre
Triumphal arch
Rustication

Trajan's
Column
A.D. 106–113

Roman Columns

Tuscan  Doric  Ionic  Corinthian  Composite

Barrel Vault

Groin Vault

# ROMAN ARCHITECTURE

# PROJECT 4-1: DESIGN A STADIUM

## FOR THE TEACHER

**Slide # 8: *Colosseum.*** The Colosseum seated approximately 50,000 people, much like today's big city or university stadium. It was finished in A.D. 80. Students can relate the variety of entertainment that took place in the Colosseum to what takes place today. Substitute musical groups, football games, and soccer for lions and gladiators, fights between wild beasts, or even flooding for mock naval battles, and they can understand that their stadium design needs to be multipurpose. As in the United States, arenas exited in most major cities of the Roman Empire.

The Colosseum was based on two Greek amphitheaters (two-thirds of a circle) joined together. It was designed with a different type of column on each of the three levels (the "colossal" orders). The bottom had Tuscan (similar to Doric) columns, the middle Ionic, and the top Corinthian. It had gigantic awnings to shade spectators. There were arches all the way around, and although it is in poor condition today, it must have been magnificent when new. Over the years it was "mined" for marble needed for other construction, so it has lost most of the seats and decorative elements.

## PREPARATION

Demonstrate the use of a paper cutter, straight edge, and compass. Show students how to score the inside of cardboard with the point of scissors to make a neat corner fold. Show them how to make tabs for gluing, and slots for joining pieces together. Talk about architectural elements such as arches, supports for a roof, and aisles. Give each student only one sheet of tagboard, and have them plan ahead on newsprint how to cut it. These stadiums could have a roof added to make a "superdome," or they could be open. Tagboard or six-ply posterboard has sufficient strength and pliability to achieve almost any design.

## FURTHER SUGGESTIONS

- Make a triumphal arch of tagboard. Score the inside arches so they will curve smoothly, making tabs to join them to the front and back of the arch. Cut a long strip, making tabs that will attach to the top, front, and back of the arch. Use pencil and decorate with "bas-relief sculpture."

- Make a miniature Trajan's Column by cutting a piece of paper roughly 5 × 8 inches, and drawing diagonal lines approximately 1 inch apart. Do a narrative of a typical day (or week) starting from getting out of bed in the morning, getting dressed, going to school, seeing friends, having phone conversations, and so on. Organize it so it is a continuous narrative, to be read as you look up the column. Temporarily tape the paper together with removable tape, to understand how the drawing will ascend the column.

# PROJECT 4–1: DESIGN A STADIUM

**MATERIALS**

- Tagboard or six-ply posterboard
- Pencils
- Black fine-line marker
- White glue or rubber cement
- Newsprint
- Compasses
- Rulers
- X-acto® knives
- Scissors

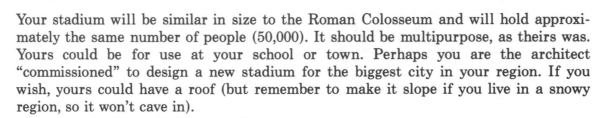

Your stadium will be similar in size to the Roman Colosseum and will hold approximately the same number of people (50,000). It should be multipurpose, as theirs was. Yours could be for use at your school or town. Perhaps you are the architect "commissioned" to design a new stadium for the biggest city in your region. If you wish, yours could have a roof (but remember to make it slope if you live in a snowy region, so it won't cave in).

1.  On newsprint, draw a number of ideas for a stadium, keeping in mind such ordinary items as entrances and exits, ways to get between floors, exterior beauty and ornament, shade or roof, and a view from all seats. The outside can be any shape you wish, such as a rectangle, ellipse, circle, or horseshoe.

2.  Draw the decorations on this stadium while it is flat (before joining the cardboard). Use a ruler to make straight lines for doors, bricks, etc., and draw them lightly in pencil. For stability in an elliptical or circular stadium, make slits and score the bottom to glue it to a shaped base. Make tabs and slots for joining sections together. Protect the table with cardboard when cutting with an X-acto® knife.

    ***Safety Note:*** *When cutting with a knife, keep your noncutting hand behind the blade in case it slips.*

3.  To add strength or decoration, make columns by wrapping long strips around a pencil, then gluing them to the background. Or use pilasters (decorative square columns attached to a wall). To make neat folds, score the inside of the cardboard with the tip of scissors. If you are uncertain how something will work, try making it first in typing paper. If you want a rounded corner, score several vertical lines closely together on the inside, or grasp one end of the cardboard in each hand and run the cardboard back and forth over the edge of a table to make it curl.

4.  Before joining the elements together, go over the decorative pencil lines with a black fine-line marker. If you want colored accents, paint or color the outside with colored pencils.

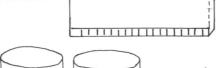

© 1992 by The Center for Applied Research in Education, Inc.

## PROJECT 4-2: **OBELISK OR PYRAMID**

### FOR THE TEACHER

The Egyptians are credited with first creating obelisks, but the city of Rome has made them famous. Several treasured obelisks were brought back from the time of the Roman occupation of Egypt.

### PREPARATION

This project can be simplified by making several sizes and patterns of obelisks that students could trace around for the basic forms. The obelisks could be almost any size they want. Or first allow them to make a tiny obelisk, on a 3 × 5-inch note card, just to show them how easy it is.

Remind students to make tabs to hold the forms together, but not to apply paint on them. Show them how to score the inside of a fold with the point of scissors. If you are using tempera paint (which cracks easily), glue the forms together first, then paint the assembled form. If using acrylic paint, paint the flat form, then fold and glue it.

The "faux-marble" technique of applying paint to plastered walls and wood to resemble marble has long been used in place of more expensive, genuine marble. It helps greatly to have some examples or pictures of real marble for students to look at when they are painting. Faux-marble gift wraps or samples of plastic countertops that resemble marble also make good examples.

### MASTERPIECES OF ART

*Obelisk in front of the Pantheon*, Elephant Base by Bernini, Rome

*Obelisk in front of the Basilica of St. Peter*, Rome

*Obelisk on the Piazza del Popolo*, Rome

*Pyramid Tomb of Caius Cestius*, 12 B.C., Rome

### FURTHER SUGGESTIONS

- Have students work in groups, with each one painting a small sheet of one or two colors of faux-marbling. They can then share colors and cut out pieces to make an elaborate "inlaid" geometric design on a small piece of posterboard. These intricate marble designs are often seen on Italian tables or the exteriors of Italian churches. They could be combined with other pieces of painted paper or tagboard to make a mosaic.

- Find a wall, door, cabinet, box, old lamp, or some other object that students could paint in the faux-marble fashion. After coating with gesso, this could be done with latex paint in closely related colors. Bricks could be "marblized" for use as doorstops or bookends.

### FAUX- (rhymes with "toe") MARBLING

1. After making the pyramid or obelisk, paint it to look like real marble. Do not paint the tabs, as they will be glued together. Mix two or three values of one basic color

(such as rust, gray, or green) or related colors such as beige, white, and gray. Apply the paint smoothly in randomly elongated patches, in the same slating direction. Make some of the patches thick, then thin. Blend the edges.

2. Create the characteristic veining by using a medium brush to apply a darker color along a line formed where two different values meet. While the line is still wet, use the feather to "drag" the paint onto the different colors. On this vein, apply a very thin darker line using a feather or thin brush.

3. When the paint has dried, apply rubber cement to the tab and to the inside of the form, where it will touch the tab. Allow these to dry, then carefully put them together. They will be permanently bonded.

**Photo 4-1. Student artwork.**

# PROJECT 4–2:  **OBELISK OR PYRAMID**

## MATERIALS

- Six-ply posterboard
- Brushes
- Rubber cement
- Scissors
- Acrylic or tempera paints
- Goose or chicken feathers (if available)
- Rulers
- Pencils

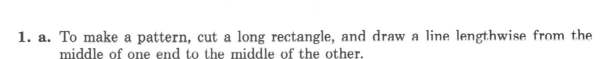

## OBELISK

**1. a.** To make a pattern, cut a long rectangle, and draw a line lengthwise from the middle of one end to the middle of the other.

   **b.** Measure outward from the center and make one end smaller. Use the ruler to mark an angular line from one end to the other on each side.

   **c.** Trim the sides. Make a fold line and score it a short distance from the top.

   **d.** Draw a line from the center of the top to that fold line, and trim away the top to make a triangular shape. Trim away the corners to the fold line.

**2.** Place the pattern on the posterboard. Draw around it. Now flip it over, matching the fold line at the top, and draw around it. Flip it twice more, drawing around it each time. Make 1-inch tabs. Score on the insides of all the lines to make neat folds.

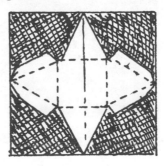

## PYRAMID

Use a ruler to divide a posterboard into nine equally sized squares. The center square will be the bottom of the pyramid. Measure to the center of each square that adjoins the center square and make a mark. Draw a line from the corner of the center square to that mark, making triangular sides. On two of the sides, make a 1-inch tab for gluing. Score each line on the inside of the figure.

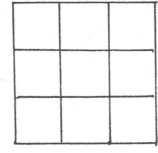

## PROJECT 4-3: **MOSAIC**

**FOR THE TEACHER**

Traces of Roman mosaics exist throughout the Roman Empire. They originated with rounded smooth stones, mostly used on the floor. Early mosaics were of marble and limited to the natural stone variations of browns, whites, grays, rust, and tans. They resembled carpets, with symmetrical borders. Most of them were based on the square grid, so graph paper is appropriate for students to use. Later mosaics depicted animals, birds, flowers, intertwined leaves, portraits of gods, or scenes of battle.

The mosaics seen on walls in churches and homes originally used marble, then evolved to tesserae (small pieces of brilliantly colored glass). Although mosaics might have originally been based on fresco wall paintings, later more elaborate designs were probably inspired by illuminated manuscripts.

### MASTERPIECES OF ROMAN AND CHRISTIAN MOSAIC

*Defeated Persians under Darius from the Battle of Issus,* c. 300 B.C., National Museum, Naples.

*Boy on a Dolphin,* Fishbourne Roman Palace, Chichester, England

*The Good Shepherd,* c. A.D. 425–26, Mausoleum of Galla Placidia, Ravenna, Italy

**Photo 4-2. *Section from a Mosaic Pavement* Syria, Antioch, fifth century, 213.4 cm long, marble, The Saint Louis Art Museum.**

## PREPARATION

This project is not messy and is a good ongoing studio project for short periods. If possible, have pictures of real Roman mosaics for students to see. To make large mosaics, have students make 1-inch grids. Quarter-inch square graph paper could also be used. (If students desire bigger designs, they can use several squares for each line design.)

## FURTHER SUGGESTIONS

- Have students cut colored paper into 1-inch squares (they don't have to be perfect). Include at least one example of marblized or gold (wrapping) paper in harmonizing shades. To make a mosaic design, glue these cut squares onto a large sheet of drawing paper.
- Draw a 1-inch square grid on an 18 × 24-inch piece of paper. Suggest that students paint or use waxy colored pencils to do a city-scape, slightly varying the colors from square to square. The buildings can be a combination of forms from Roman and modern times.
- This project is appropriate for computer graphics. Students enjoy working out the various designs on a graph on a computer screen. The possibilities are endless.

# PROJECT 4-3: MOSAIC

## MATERIALS

- Graph paper, ¼ to ½ inch
- Waxy colored pencils

Although some of these designs seem complicated, follow the steps, and you will be able to complete a design. Try several of the borders before deciding on one. The meander (or Greek Key) is not as difficult as it looks when it is worked out on graph paper. It is easier to begin the design in the center and work outwards.

**1.** *Meander:* Count the squares carefully as you make your design.

**2.** *Double meander*

  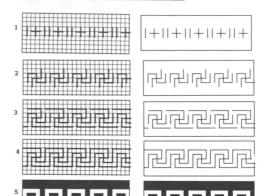

**3.** *Three-square designs*

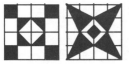    

**4.** *Four-square designs*

**5.** *Five-square designs*

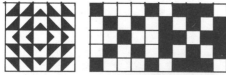   

**6.** *Scrolls, vines, animals, people*

122

## Unit 2:  BYZANTINE ART (A.D. 325 TO 1453)

### OVERVIEW OF THE VISUAL ARTS

The modern city of Istanbul was once Constantinople (named for Emperor Constantine). Before that the city was called Byzantium. In A.D. 323, Emperor Constantine decided to move the capital of the Holy Roman Empire to Byzantium. This resulted in the split of the Christian church into the (western) Catholic church and the (eastern) Orthodox church.

### PAINTING

After the reign of Emperor Justinian (A.D. 527–565), religious images were forbidden. Numerous works of art were destroyed. In spite of this, the "Golden age of Byzantine art" that began during his reign lasted until the end of the ninth century. Byzantine greatness in art came to an end in 1453 when Constantinople (Istanbul) was conquered by the Turks. Much of what we know today of Byzantine art is seen in Ravenna, Italy, Greece, Serbia, and Russia—all of which were under Byzantine rule.

Frescoes were painted on walls, and icons (religious images) were painted on wooden panels. Manuscript illumination was the forerunner to the dramatic mosaic representations later seen in many eastern Orthodox churches. Early Byzantine painting was almost exclusively religious. Figures were portrayed frontally, with large, staring eyes, unsmiling features, and long, narrow faces demonstrating the lack of interest in the human form or realistic portraiture.

### MASTERPIECES OF BYZANTINE MOSAICS

*Justinian and Attendants.* c. A.D. 547, San Vitale, Ravenna, Italy

*Empress Theodora and Attendants.* c. A.D. 547, San Vitale, Ravenna, Italy

*Scenes from Genesis,* c. A.D. 1200, St. Mark's Cathedral, Venice

*Apse mosaic,* A.D. 533–549, Sant'Apollinare in Classe, Ravenna

### SCULPTURE

Sculpture was generally limited to small ivory book covers or small portable, hinged altars ("diptychs," "triptychs," and "polyptychs," depending on the number of panels). Sculpture of the human form was considered idolatrous and was discouraged. Bas-relief decorative carving was used in churches, and beautiful metalwork in gold and silver was created to house the relics of saints. These "reliquaries" were an important part of every church's treasury.

### MASTERPIECES OF SCULPTURE

*Silver-gilt Book Cover,* c. 1020, Treasury of San Marco, Venice, Italy

*Sarcophagus of Archbishop Theodore,* c. seventh century, Ravenna, Italy

## ARCHITECTURE

Byzantine architecture had a far-reaching influence on the construction of churches throughout Europe. A development in the construction of Hagia Sophia, a huge church constructed in A.D. 532–537 in Constantinople, dramatically affected Western architecture. The pendentive (a concave triangular support) allowed a round dome to be placed on square pillars). The central church plan, with its dome over the crossing, evolved. The floor plans were shaped after the Greek Cross (equal sized legs), or the Roman Cross (one leg longer than the other). The rich mosaics used in Hagia Sophia (turned into a Mosque, and currently a museum) were copied throughout churches in Italy. Minarets were added to Hagia Sophia after the Turkish conquest, and it has since served as the model for a number of Islamic mosques.

## MASTERPIECES OF BYZANTINE ARCHITECTURE

*Hagia Sophia,* A.D. 532–537, Istanbul, Turkey

*San Marco,* begun A.D. 1063, Venice, Italy

*Cathedral of St. Basil the Blessed,* A.D. 1544–1560, Moscow

**Early Christian and
Byzantine Architectural Features**

Pendentive
Squinch
Impost block
Onion dome
Gallery
Aisle
Ambulatory
Baptistry
Clerestory
Transept

St. Basil's Cathedral, Moscow
1554–1560

Hagia Sophia, Constantinople, 532–537

St. Mark's, Venice 1042–1085

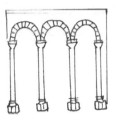

Pendentive

Impost Blocks

Santa Costanza, Rome
A.D. 324

Gracanica, Serbia, 1321

Sts. Michael and
All Saints; Moscow, 1515

Sant' Apollinare in Classe
(near Ravenna)
A.D. 533–549

# BYZANTINE ARCHITECTURE

## PROJECT 4-4: **ARCHITECTURE MADE FUN**

**FOR THE TEACHER**

The changes made in public buildings from Greek temples through Gothic art is an important part of art history, but sometimes difficult for students to relate to. In this project students work in a group to research one specific type of architecture for presentation to the class. Choose a number of examples that vary widely, including Greek, Byzantine, Romanesque, Gothic, and Medieval, so they can see the evolution of building styles.

In addition to involving students in research, the goal is to make a realistic interpretation of a church or other public building by using only stamps made with letters of the alphabet (their initials). One lovely outcome of this might be paintings other than architecture made when students enjoy creating differences in value. For example several of my students did portraiture with their stamps. They also discovered that uncarved erasers made nice squares or rectangles to build up value.

**MASTERPIECES OF ARCHITECTURE**

*Colosseum,* A.D. 72–80, Rome

*Palace of Diocletian,* A.D. 293, Split, Yugoslavia

*Church of San Vitale,* A.D. 525–47, Ravenna, Italy

*San Marco,* begun A.D. 1063, Venice

*Cathedral of St. Basil the Blessed,* A.D. 1544–1560, Moscow

*Mosque of Ahmed I,* c. A.D. 1609–1617, Istanbul

*Taj Mahal,* A.D. 1623–1643, Agra, India

*Cathedral complex,* Pisa, Italy 1063–1164

*Cathedral of Notre Dame,* begun 1163, Paris

*Hagia Sophia,* A.D. 532–537, Istanbul

**PREPARATION**

Photocopy a sheet of pressure-sensitive sans serif lettering, reversed so the letters are backward. (You could also do this by photocopying a page of type from a book onto an overhead transparency, then reversing and photocopying it to make several sheets of reversed letters.)

Although student groups can be organized by many different methods, I found the students enjoyed drawing the name of a famous building from a box and finding the rest of the group members by calling out the building's name. (Put the name of one of the architectural examples given here on three to five slips of paper.) While one member of the group is making a large pencil sketch based on a picture of the building, preparatory to stamping, the other members can be putting together research information to share with the class. (Knowing that a quiz will be given, in which they can use their notes, encourages them to listen closely to their classmates' presentations.) Students might choose to draw or paste up photocopies of some of the architectural features typical of a particular period of architecture to give class members. I would suggest that you collect the erasers and put them back in the box for reuse in the next session.

## FURTHER SUGGESTIONS

- Students can paint acrylics onto these stamps and use them to stamp designs onto cotton T-shirts. They are quite effective, and the initials simply become portions of a design. Naturally they think of other designs to carve onto the stamps. "Fix" the paint with a warm iron, and they can be washed and dried.

- Students enjoy using plain or carved erasers to stamp. Differences in value achieved by how often the stamps are inked make very interesting portraits.

Photo 4-3. Student artwork, ink, stamped with art gum erasers that were carved with initials.

Photo 4-4. Student artwork, ink, stamped with art gum erasers that were carved with initials.

# PROJECT 4–4: ARCHITECTURE MADE FUN

**MATERIALS**

- Art gum erasers
- 5–7 stamp pads
- Ink for pads
- Backwards photocopies of a typeface
- X-acto® knives
- Scissors
- Drawing paper 18 × 24 inches

Each person should carve two letters from a rubber eraser. These may or may not be your own initials. Your alphabet-letter stamps are made for the unique designs that can be made with a variety of curved and straight lines. The letters are the building blocks to create a famous architectural structure.

*Safety Note: X-acto® knives are very sharp. Always keep your fingers away from the blade. Don't hurry, and take away small amounts at a time.*

1. Use scissors to cut closely around the letter patterns you will use. Center the letter on one side of the eraser. Draw around it with a pencil.

2. With the tip of an X-acto® knife, make a thin line around the upper sides of the eraser, approximately ¼-inch from the top. Use the knife tip to also draw gently around the outside of the letter. It is very easy to make a mistake, and the best way to avoid it, until you have a "feel" for carving, is to take a small amount from the top edges of the eraser down ¼-inch to the line you incised around the top sides.

3. To carve the inside of a letter (such as the inside top of an A, R, or P), use the very tip of the knife to gently cut ¼-inch deep. Use the knife tip to take away very small portions at a time. Try to make the edges as neat as possible.

4. Stamp several lines on a practice sheet, using only one eraser letter at a time in a variety of directions. It isn't necessary to stamp ink on it each time, and indeed some of the more interesting areas occur when the stamp begins to run out of ink. Try combinations of your two letters. If you wish, combine letters to make something such a landscape, bicycle, person.

5. To make the large group project, combine your group's stamps in a variety of directions. From time to time stand away from the picture and look to see if you have differences in value. The building should resemble the picture you see in a book. There should be some lines, and some softened areas. The uncut portion of an eraser makes block-like areas and can be used to make stones or sky. Some areas should be left plain—white is also a value.

6. If you wish, make three different views of the same building (or type of architecture) so each person in the group has one to take home. Turn in the best one for a group grade. You will find you get more creative as you have more practice.

# AFRICA AND ISLAM

# AFRICA AND ISLAM
## TIME LINE

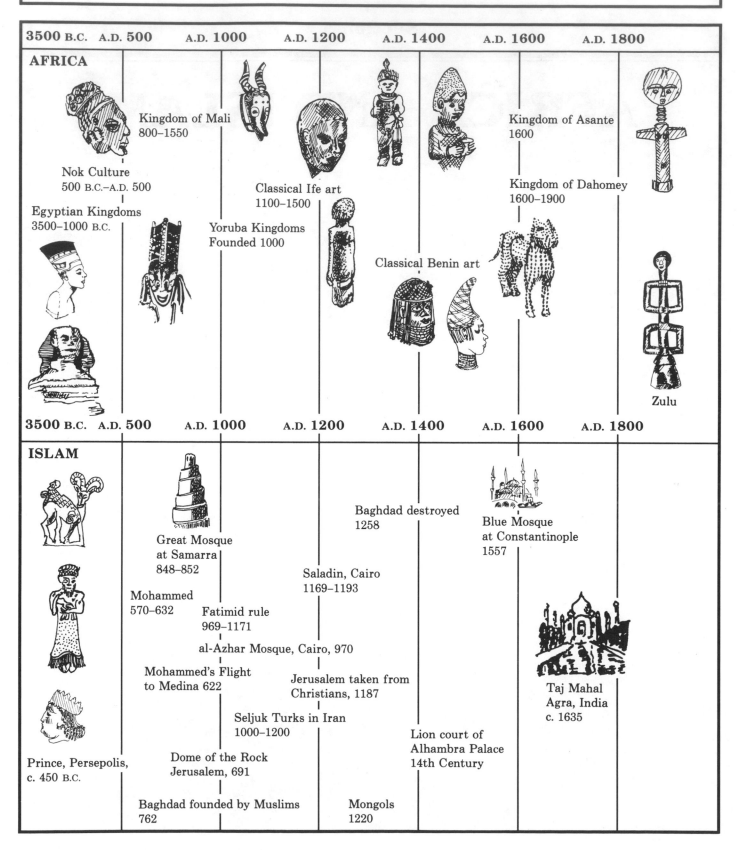

| 3500 B.C. | A.D. 500 | A.D. 1000 | A.D. 1200 | A.D. 1400 | A.D. 1600 | A.D. 1800 |

**AFRICA**

Kingdom of Mali
800–1550

Nok Culture
500 B.C.–A.D. 500

Egyptian Kingdoms
3500–1000 B.C.

Classical Ife art
1100–1500

Yoruba Kingdoms
Founded 1000

Classical Benin art

Kingdom of Asante
1600

Kingdom of Dahomey
1600–1900

Zulu

| 3500 B.C. | A.D. 500 | A.D. 1000 | A.D. 1200 | A.D. 1400 | A.D. 1600 | A.D. 1800 |

**ISLAM**

Great Mosque
at Samarra
848–852

Mohammed
570–632

Fatimid rule
969–1171

al-Azhar Mosque, Cairo, 970

Mohammed's Flight
to Medina 622

Seljuk Turks in Iran
1000–1200

Dome of the Rock
Jerusalem, 691

Prince, Persepolis,
c. 450 B.C.

Baghdad founded by Muslims
762

Baghdad destroyed
1258

Saladin, Cairo
1169–1193

Jerusalem taken from
Christians, 1187

Lion court of
Alhambra Palace
14th Century

Mongols
1220

Blue Mosque
at Constantinople
1557

Taj Mahal
Agra, India
c. 1635

130

## Unit 1: **AFRICA**

### OVERVIEW OF THE VISUAL ARTS

Although Africa is vast there are some similarities in the artwork throughout the continent. Much artwork is based on ancient themes that date back to at least the fifth to first centuries B.C. For example, the head of a figure is generally emphasized, which may signify the respect for their ancestors shown by the Africans. Many carved figures and heads were used on top of containers of the bones of the dead. Some artworks were created as status symbols, such as wooden stools carved for chieftains, or bronze castings to decorate the home.

Outside influences such as Islam (which discourages the representation of living creatures and encourages ornamental designs) and Christianity have affected African art. European trade and the introduction of beads also influenced later work. The result was often the development of new (still African) forms of art. The artwork of many African societal groups was small enough to be carried as the groups moved. Jewelry, woven fabric and clothing, masks and sculpture were all part of their daily lives.

### PAINTING

Although many groups were nomadic, they probably returned seasonally to certain regions where they repeatedly decorated the rocks. Over 30,000 examples of rock engravings and paintings are found in Africa. In addition to painted cave walls, wooden sculpture and masks were richly decorated. In later years the exteriors of homes in some regions were painted in geometric designs.

### SCULPTURE

African sculpture has been a major art form from the stone age to the present. Because of the climate wooden sculpture probably lasts no more than two hundred years under normal circumstances. However, African style is traditional, so relatively recent work probably is similar to that created in ancient times. Sculpture carved to honor ancestors or protect the home might be quite different than that created for ceremonies or dances. In some tribes the sculptor was not seen as an individual artist who expressed himself, but someone who worked for the group, doing what was needed. In addition to masks, sculptural figures, and fetish figures, someone was needed to carve headrests, stools, cups, whisk handles, door posts, and shrines. Some of the sculptors such as the Beni were skilled in casting in bronze by the lost wax technique. Others worked in gold, and the charming gold weights created by the Asante are treasured in many museums. African sculpture was especially appreciated by the cubists, Braque, Gris, Modigliani, and Picasso, and was an inspiration for their work.

### MASTERPIECES

*Head of Ruler,* Ife, British Museum, London

*Figure in Bronze,* Benin, British Museum, London

*Tomb Guardian,* Bakota, British Museum, London

## ARCHITECTURE

Nomadic groups made homes of bamboo and palm thatch. More permanent settlements were made of a form of mud adobe. Some homes in the Nupe region had beautifully carved front doors, while Nigeria has homes decorated with low-relief sculptural designs of mud.

**Modern Africa**

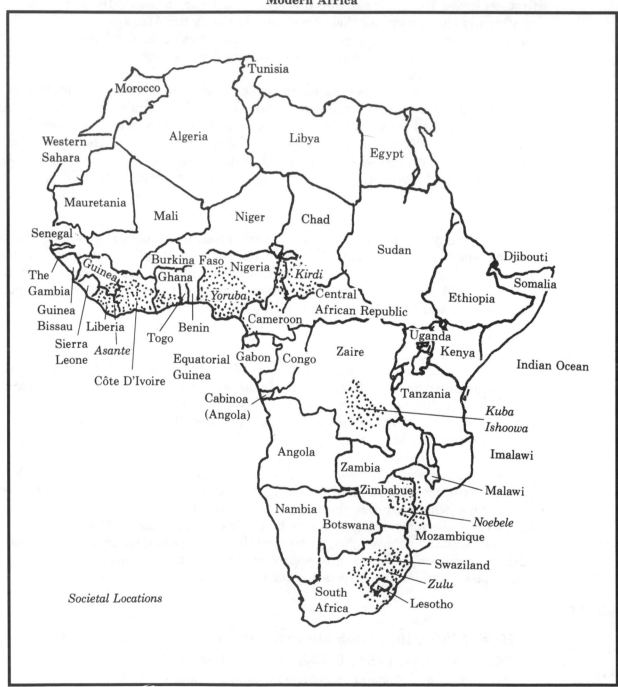

*Societal Locations*

# PROJECT 5–1: **AFRICAN MASKS**

**FOR THE TEACHER**

**Slide # 9: *African Mask.*** Masks served many purposes, and their appearance varied widely according to the societal group that made them, and the purpose they would serve. Because many of the rituals for which they were created are secretive, we may never know their exact purpose. Some were quite smooth inside, and intended to be worn, while others might fit on top of the head, or be held in front of the face by a handle. In many cases they were made to resemble real people who had died. Masks were worn at funerals and festivals, with male dancers sometimes masquerading as females or animals. Many were created to honor ancestors, or for use in boys' and girls' initiation rites.

Photo 5-1. *African Mask,* Nigeria, Ibo Tribe, 26¼ × 8 inches, wood with multicolored patina, The Saint Louis Art Museum, gift of Dr. Donald Suggs.

**MASTERPIECES**

*White-faced Mask,* BaKota, Rietberg Museum, Zurich

**PREPARATION**

If you are doing this with an entire class, spend one day discussing masks while students draw ideas and cut the plaster into strips. The second day make masks on half the students, and the third day on the other half. They can then all decorate them at the same time. Suggest the students bring in materials that can be added to the masks for decoration such as beads, yarn, or feathers.

**FURTHER SUGGESTIONS**

- Rather than making masks, students can make papier-mâché hats with fetish figures on top. These can be painted or clothed with cloth, leather, fur, beads, or other natural materials.

- In addition to the bronze castings of heads, the Benin made bas-relief bronze castings often showing the exploits of warriors. Clay bas-relief scenes of their own "exploits" (team sports, dancing, "snapshots" with a friend) could be fun for students to make.

**Photo 5-2. African shoulder mask, The Saint Louis Art Museum.**

Name: _____    Date: _____

# PROJECT 5-1: AFRICAN MASK

## MATERIALS

- Plaster-impregnated tape
- Water
- Bowl
- Clear plastic wrap
- Scissors
- Tempera or acrylic paint

Your mask may resemble an African mask when you are finished, but it will be based on your own face. The Africans were masters at decoration, however, and you can get ideas by researching masks at the library.

1. Work with partners. The day before making your mask, use scissors to cut "sculpture-tape" into 1½ × 4-inch pieces over a piece of newspaper (to avoid the mess made when plaster sifts out). Wrap these in a piece of paper to be ready for your mask the next day.

2. Have one partner lie down on the table or floor. Cover the face with a 20-inch piece of plastic wrap across the face under the nostrils, down to the table (to keep the hair covered). Place the second piece across the top of the face covering the eyes and hair, so that only the nostrils are uncovered. Remind your partner that the mask can easily be removed at any time.

3. Put a piece of sculpture tape in a bowl of warm water. Hold one end and pull it between your first two fingers to eliminate excess water and straighten it out. Place it on the face. Avoid building too many layers in the center, and try to make it even around the edges. If you will be adding a decoration to the top of the head, you could add tape to the top of the head. You should have at least four even coats of sculpture tape all over the mask. Allow it to harden before removing it. After removal use a Phillips screwdriver to punch holes for eyes and by the ears for ribbons to hang it. If it is too hard to punch, holes can be drilled later with an electric drill.

4. Allow the mask to dry for one day. Use tagboard, papier maché cardboard, and sculpture tape to make it fanciful. Decorative possibilities are yarn, leather strips, beads, paint, or raffia. You could make yours more interesting by the addition of horns, or one of the other decorations such as animals or figures that can be seen in pictures of masks.

5. Before painting, coat the mask with gesso or varnish to prevent absorption of the paint (or plan to give it a second coat of paint). Ordinary latex house paint could also be used.

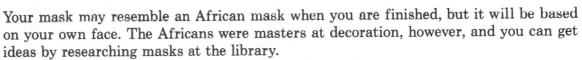

## PROJECT 5–2: **ADINKRA CLOTH**

**FOR THE TEACHER**

Africans have traditionally decorated textiles in dramatic patterns, using a variety of methods. The Asante people of Ghana create adinkra cloth by using "stamps" carved from old calabash pieces to apply black dye to cloth. Traditionally adinkra cloths were worn for funerals, but today are reserved for special occasions. The basic cloth was originally russet brown, terra-cotta, black, or white, but today's machine made cloth comes in many bright colors, although it is still hand-stamped. Each design bears Asante names of historical or magical significance, and consequently were chosen by the wearer to convey a message, much as modern students select T-shirts.

Other traditional African textiles are bakuba, a pile cloth traditionally made in the Congo of woven and embroidered raffia that resembles cut pile velvet. The Bambara people in Mali have devised a dye/discharge method of making designs using an iron-rich mud. People in Nigeria use cassava paste applied as a dye-resist in wonderful patterns. A fine, soft material is also made from the beaten inner bark of certain trees and decorated by stamping. One of the most familiar and colorful textiles is the woven silk kente cloth made by the Asante people in Ghana. This cloth is created from brilliantly colored narrow woven strips which are stitched together.

These cloths were not cut into dresses or shirts as Westerners know them, but left whole, to be wrapped around the body.

Adinkra cloth.

## PREPARATION

Each student could create a pattern by making one stamp and using it in a repeat design on a sheet of paper. These individual designs could be joined together to make a large "cloth" of stamped black designs such as the one shown here. The designs are simple, and many of them have a symbolic meaning.

Add to your collection of stamps each year by having students cut standard designs. Rubber eraser stamps are especially durable, and can be used for many years. It would certainly be possible to make stamps on both sides and the end of an eraser, so one student could cut several designs in one eraser.

## FURTHER SUGGESTIONS

- In place of using stamps and ink, this entire project could be done with fine black marker on colored paper. Permanent marker could be used on cotton cloth.
- Use textile ink or acrylic paint to stamp designs on prewashed T-shirts.
- Make "Kente" cloth by creating multicolored paper strips which are then woven together. Primary colors such as yellow, red, and blue are often dominant.
- Use a stencil to cut these designs, and apply a cassava (or cornstarch) paste through the openings to act as a resist. The cloth should be dyed blue to be authentically African. (The Africans used zinc foil stencils, and applied the paste through the openings with a piece of wood; you could use heavy-duty aluminum foil or plastic.)

# PROJECT 5–2: **ADINKRA CLOTH**

## MATERIALS

- Erasers for stamps (or potatoes, styrofoam, or linoleum)
- X-acto® or paring knives
- Stamp pads (for T-shirts, use acrylic or textile paint)
- Durable paper such as vellum or butcher paper, or cloth
- Black fine-line markers
- Felt, or pad made of folded newspaper

The large adinkra cloths are sectioned into rectangles, separated by borders. Make large stamps for the main motifs in the center squares, and smaller stamps for the borders. The Asante people carved sections of old calabashes (gourds) for designs, attaching handles to fit comfortably in the hand. A rubber or plastic eraser is one of many acceptable modern substitutes.

1. To make an eraser stamp, draw the design on the eraser with pencil, taking care to use as much of the surface as possible. Use the point of an X-acto® knife to cut around the design to a depth of between ¼ and ⅛ inch. Carefully trim from the sides toward the design, removing small amounts at a time. Take your time making the stamp, because you will be using it repeatedly. If you have a *large* eraser, you can make designs on both sides and ends to have four designs. However, don't carve away so much that you cannot hold it comfortably.

2. On a 9 × 12-inch piece of drawing paper, measure to make two borders on all sides, each approximately 1-inch wide. Go over the ruler-drawn lines "free hand" with black marker or ink to get the natural look of handmade cloth. Use one stamp to make a repeat design on the large rectangle by applying color between each application. Stamp smaller designs inside the lines of the borders, leaving the corners plain. You may wish to trade stamps with classmates for some "columns" of your border designs.

3. When a number of rectangles are finished, try to make "quilts" by combining up to twenty of them. These could be attached to a large backing paper by stapling or gluing, or could be taped with very wide masking tape. If you are doing this on cloth, long strips of cloth could be stamped, then sewn together with brightly colored thread.

4. If you would like to stamp these on cloth or T-shirts, wash the fabric first in hot water to remove sizing. For a T-shirt, place a piece of cardboard inside so that the ink doesn't go through. Use textile inks or acrylic paints.

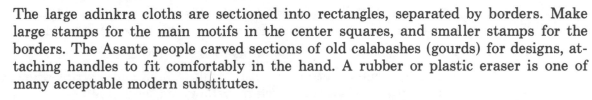

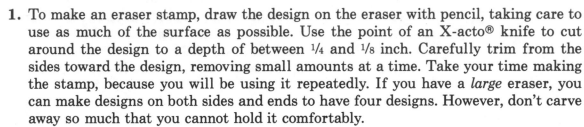

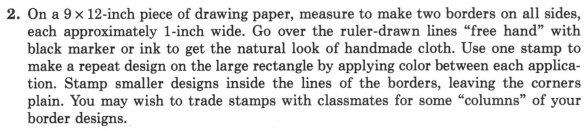

© 1992 by The Center for Applied Research in Education, Inc.

# Unit 2:  **ISLAM**

## OVERVIEW OF THE VISUAL ARTS

The followers of the prophet Mohammed, who was born in 527, are called Muslims (True Believers). The religion they practice is called Islam. The duties of a Muslim include prayer five times daily, fasting during Ramadan, certain dietary restrictions, the giving of alms, and a pilgrimage to Mecca. Muslims did not believe in the priesthood, sacraments, or liturgy. Islam has become a worldwide religion, but continues to be most widely practiced in the Middle East.

Islamic artworks have become a fusion of the cultures of the Turks, Persian, and Arab worlds. The "minor" arts such as ceramics, jewelry, textile and carpet design, demonstrate its richness and diversity. Carpet designs are traditional, with carpet design considered one of the outstanding modern art forms.

Islamic calligraphy was especially important because Mohammed had forbidden the representation of living creatures. Early Islamic manuscripts, metalwork, and ceramics relied almost exclusively on calligraphy and geometric interlace, arabesques, and floral motifs for decoration, with designs originated from a central point. In some cases the text was written as a border on the outside, and the colored decorative work was on the inside.

## PAINTING

Although the Islamic religion forbade representations of humans or animals, at times these forms were abstracted and used in borders or incorporated into calligraphy Painted manuscripts employed beautiful borders and calligraphy. By the thirteen century oriental influences began to affect Islamic illuminated manuscripts, and scenes with people were incorporated into design.

## MASTERPIECES OF PAINTING

*Wall-painting from the Jausak Palace,* 836–839, Samarra

*Painting from a copy of the Warkah wa Gulsha poem,* thirteenth century, Topkapi Sarayi Library, Istanbul

*Frontispiece painting from the Kitab al-diriyak,* 1199, Mosul, Iraq

*Painting from a copy of Hariri's Makamat,* 1237, Baghdad, Iraq

*Painting from a copy of Jami's Haft Aurang,* 1565, Freer Gallery of Art, Washington, D.C.

## SCULPTURE

It was said that Mohammed considered sculpture idolatrous (idol worship); so many statues were destroyed by his followers, and very little sculpture was seen for a time. Mosques and mausoleums in particular did not have figurative representation. The early Muslims were nomadic, so small, easily portable art objects such as carpets, jewelry, and boxes were more commonplace than large objects such as sculpture. The Muslims, however, were very fine artisans in silver and gold, ceramics, and carved ivory. Beautiful Islamic artifacts were brought back to Europe by crusaders and traders and influenced Western decoration in manuscript painting and architecture.

## MASTERPIECES OF SCULPTURE

*Bronze Figure of a Griffin,* eleventh to twelfth centuries, Campo Santo, Pisa, Italy

*Head of a Seljuk Prince,* twelfth century, Metropolitan Museum, New York

*Incense Burner in Form of a Cat,* 1181, Jafar ibn Muhammad ibn Ali, Metropolitan Museum, New York

## ARCHITECTURE

Early Islamic architecture reflected the Byzantine, Greek, Egyptian, and Syrian cultures of the workers brought in to hastily erect huge structures. Four types of buildings were mosques (churches), madrasah (a building for religious and legal instruction), mausoleums (burial places), and palaces. As late as the seventeenth century the great innovations of Islamic builders influenced Christian structures.

Although Hagia Sophia was built as a Christian church, it became a mosque in 1453 when the Turks conquered Constantinople (Istanbul). Earlier mosques were rectangular, with the main axis pointing toward Mecca. They included a minaret (a tower to call the faithful to prayer) and a niche (qibla), toward which Moslems turn to pray. Calligraphy, often consisting of texts from the *Koran,* was used to decorate buildings.

## MASTERPIECES OF ISLAMIC ARCHITECTURE

*Dome of the Rock,* 691, built by Abd-al-Malik, Jerusalem

*Great Mosque of al-Mutawakkil,* 848–852, Samarra

*Mosque of Ahmad ibn Tulun,* 876–879, Cairo

*The Gunbad-i-Kabus,* 1006–1007, Iran

*Madrasah and Mausoleum of Sultan Kalaun,* 1284–1285, Cairo

*Mosque of Sultan Süleyman,* 1550, Istanbul

# PROJECT 5-3: **ISLAMIC GEOMETRIC DESIGNS**

## FOR THE TEACHER

This project was developed by Pamela Smith Hellwege of the Saint Louis Art Museum Department of Education, and is used with her permission and the permission of the museum.

The three major categories of Islamic design are (1) arabesques (stylized florals), (2) calligraphy, and (3) geometric pattern. The geometric patterns are two dimensional and have repeated elements, reflecting the Islamic belief in unity and a universe based on logic and order. There is no perspective or vanishing point, nor is the design created to fit a frame. Designs are sometimes created from patterns of circles, which fit together to make a design similar to mosaic patterns. These designs can be seen in carpets, ceramics, architectural ornament, ivory carvings, and metalwork.

This may be an interesting opportunity to encourage students to discuss similarities between some Islamic rug designs and those of Native Americans.

## MASTERPIECES OF ISLAMIC DESIGN

*Great Mosque,* A.D. 706–715, Damascus, Syria

*Palace at Mshatta,* c. A.D. 743, Jordan

*Mosque at Cordova,* A.D. 786 and 987, Cordova, Spain

*Court of the Lions,* A.D. 1354–1391, The Alhambra, Granada

*Taj Mahal,* c. 1635, Agra, India

## PREPARATION

Provide enlarged copies of geometric patterns such as those shown here for students to place underneath their drawing paper to aid in making floral arabesques or geometric designs. Avoid giving students compasses and straight edges, as you will end up with very predictable results. Encourage them to make several similar designs so they can see how they fit together in a pattern.

## FURTHER SUGGESTIONS

- Each student could design a small Turkish rug, using entirely geometric designs or combining a geometric border with a niche (representing Mecca) such as one sees on Persian prayer rugs. Many mosques have their entire floors covered with such carpets.

- Look at examples of Islamic calligraphy and make an imaginary alphabet using calligraphic pens to "write" an entire design on a page. Students could make an Islamic illuminated manuscript by combining animals and calligraphy, as seen in a fourteenth-century beastiary.

# PROJECT 5-3: ISLAMIC GEOMETRIC DESIGN

**MATERIALS**

- Drawing paper
- Colored pencil or marker
- Patterns made with compasses and rulers

Islamic design was used on a variety of materials ranging from tiles used for the surfaces of buildings, carved ivory, rugs, and fine metal work, to carved architectural ornament. The delicate interlaced designs greatly influenced Western design.

1. Try to find several examples of Islamic design. The designs have unlimited possibilities; so put your imagination to work. Consider how leaves or flowers can look when they are budding or seen from different angles. Inside each leaf, try different decorative effects such as repeated lines, dots, white space, or black space. Combinations of these design elements are used throughout Islamic design.

2. Most Islamic design "grows" outward from the center of a circular design. Although you can make each design different, try to have them resemble each other somewhat so you can tie them together with lines that might resemble the tendrils of a vine.

3. Fanciful animals, human-headed birds, rabbits, deer, and lions might also be found within these circular designs.

4. Make a design using only Islamic calligraphy. You'll be surprised at its beauty.

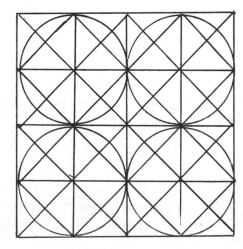

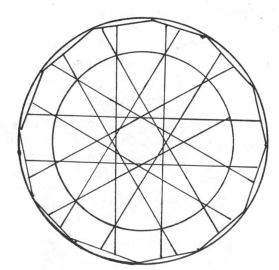

# MIDDLE AGES, ROMANESQUE, AND GOTHIC

# MIDDLE AGES, ROMANESQUE, AND GOTHIC
## TIME LINE

| A.D. 500 | A.D. 750 | A.D. 900 | A.D. 1050 | A.D. 1150 | A.D. 1250 | A.D. 1350 | A.D. 1450 |
|---|---|---|---|---|---|---|---|
| Middle Ages 400–1000 | Carolingian 750–900  Charlemagne 742–814 | Ottonian Rule 900–1150 | Romanesque 1000–1150 | Gothic 1100–1400 | Proto Renaissance 1250–1400 | | Late Gothic 1400 |

Migration art 600

Purse Sutton Hoo 625–633

Animal Head Oseberg Ship-Burial 825

Book of Kells 760–820

Medieval Art 800

Bayeux Tapestry 1073–1083

Mont Ste. Michel 1060–1500

Chartres 1140–1175

Abbot Suger's Chalice 1147

Leaning Tower of Pisa 1153–1283

Madonna & Child, 12th century

Notre Dame c. 1163

Rose Window Chartres

Marco Polo 1271

Madonna & Child 14th century

Giotto 1350

| Africa | | | Yoruba Kingdoms 1000 | Classical Ife Art 1100–1500 | | | Classical Benin Art |
| Americas | | | Leif Ericson in America 1000 | | Incas, Peru 1200–1530 | | |
| Asia  T'ang Dynasty 618–907 | | | Sung Dynasty 960–1280  Japanese Civil War 907 | | | | Ming Dynasty 1368–1644 |
| Europe | | | First Crusade 1096–1099 | | Magna Carta 1215  Marco Polo 1271 | | Gutenberg's Bible 1454  Joan of Arc 1412–1431 |
| Near East  Mohammed 570–632 | | | | Saladin, Cairo 1169–1193 | | | Lion Court, Alhambra Palace 14th century |
| Other | | | | | | | |

144

# Unit 1: THE MIDDLE AGES (400 TO 1000)

## OVERVIEW OF THE VISUAL ARTS

The term "Middle Ages" generally is applied to the period between classical antiquity and modern times. The period from the fifth to the thirteenth centuries was sometimes called the "Dark Ages," referring to the supposed lack of intellectual growth. Medieval life in Europe was shaped by the assimilation of several cultures. The Christian church introduced new religious and ethical concepts and rejected Pagan influences. The Roman Empire contributed strong governmental organization and philosophical, literary, scientific, and artistic influences from classical antiquity. The Germanic tribes contributed ideas of personal freedom and individuality to medieval civilization. Ideas and concepts brought back by the crusaders from the Eastern cultures also added to the intellectual and artistic growth.

## PAINTING

Manuscript illumination was the chief form of painting over a period of several hundred years. Charlemagne, though he was unable to read, was a true patron of the arts in that he supported the copying of classical manuscripts and encouraged the building of churches. Although wall paintings were created during his reign, these have disappeared. With the growth of towns, churches, and a rising middle-class of merchants and artisans, panel paintings for altarpieces became popular. Portraits of royalty and leading citizens were painted. In Italy, the ground of the altarpieces was usually gold (to represent heaven), while the northern artists painted familiar landscapes in the background of their religious paintings.

Wealthy patrons commissioned illuminated books, and the book of hours became the best seller of its day. As artists traveled, an "international style" evolved that had as its ideal elongated figures, sumptuous fabrics, and architectural settings. Women shaved or plucked their hair high on their foreheads to achieve the favored aristocratic look. An interest in naturalism was expressed through realistic painting of foliage and animals.

## MASTERPIECES OF PAINTING

*Madonna,* sixth to seventh centuries, Sta. Francesca Romana, Rome

*St. Matthew the Evangelist,* A.D. 800, British Museum, London

## SCULPTURE

Sculpture played an important part in the decoration of Romanesque and Gothic churches. It was used to decorate columns, the door jambs, and the tympanum (curved arch) above the entrance to the churches. Classical sculpture had been all but lost in history, and Romanesque sculpture revived it as a decorative art. The subjects were largely religious stories and themes such as lives of the saints, the last judgment, or scenes from the life of Christ. Bronze casting was revitalized, and numerous small images of the Madonna and Child or crucifixes were carved of wood, ivory, or stone.

## MASTERPIECES OF SCULPTURE

*The Good Shepherd,* third century, Lateran Museum, Rome

*The Archangel Michael,* sixth century, British Museum, London

*The Harbaville Triptych,* late tenth century, The Louvre, Paris

*Portrait of Eutropios,* c. A.D. 450, Kunsthistorisches Museum, Vienna

*Animal Head* from the Oseberg Ship-Burial, c. A.D. 825, University of Antiquities, Oslo, Norway

## ARCHITECTURE

Some considered architecture to be *the* artistic medium of the Middle Ages. The Middle Ages covered a prolonged time period that saw an evolution of architecture from the early Roman basilica with its flat wooden ceiling, through the Romanesque and Gothic churches. Many churches took centuries to build, so that there rarely was one totally unified style within a single church. The two spires on Chartres Cathedral, for example, were built centuries apart, yet the differences in style do not detract from the whole.

*St. Apollinare in Classe,* 470, Ravenna, Italy

*San Vitale,* 525–547, Ravenna, Italy

*Palace Chapel of Charlemagne,* A.D. 792–805, Aachen, Germany

Alhambra, Segovia, Spain
1333–1391

Abbey Church, Germany
961

Medieval Architecture:
Basilican plan
Westwork (Narthex transept)
Monasteries
Post and lintel arches
Towers over narthex
Groin vaulting
Blind arcade
String course
Pilaster strip
Bay
Chancel
Corbel table
Tall towers
Baptistry
Battlements

Tower, Palazzo Vecchio
c. 1298

Antwerp Cathedral
1352–1416

Palazzo Pubblico, Sienna
1298–1348

Leaning Tower of Pisa
1153–1283

# MEDIEVAL ARCHITECTURE

# PROJECT 6–1: ILLUMINATED FRAME

**FOR THE TEACHER**

Illumination was the art of decorating hand-lettered manuscripts. The Egyptian *Book of the Dead* was the first known illuminated manuscript. The vast majority of western manuscripts were produced in monasteries, which were the centers of learning. The majority of the books were religious, including Bibles, psalm books (psalters), personal prayer and hour books, song books, and antiphonies (responsive reading and song books, often quite large, so that they could be seen by many people). In later years royal patronage encouraged artists to produce books of hours (books containing prayers to be said at certain hours of the day), histories, and romances.

Photo 6-1. *Book of Hours, Virgin and Child* by Martinus, Italian, fifteenth century, ink, gouache and gold on vellum, manuscript, 12.4 × 9.9 cm, The Saint Louis Art Museum, Gift of Mr. and Mrs. John S. Lehmann.

The books were painted on vellum or parchment (fine-grained lambskin, kidskin, or calfskin especially prepared for writing) and often elaborately bound between covers of ivory or gold and enamel embedded with jewels. The text and outlines were done with quill pens in ink. Gold leaf was lavishly used, with the amount of ornament dependent on the price. Later French manuscripts were dominated by architectural concepts, reflecting the interest in Gothic churches. Stained glass windows were often based on compositions from illuminated manuscripts. Charlemagne was crowned the emperor of Rome in 800. He was a patron of the arts, supporting the copying of classical manuscripts by monks and nuns in monasteries, and encouraging the building of churches.

## MASTERPIECES OF ILLUMINATION

*Lindisfarne Gospels,* c. 700, British Library, London

*The Book of Kells,* c. 760–820, Trinity College, Dublin

*The Gospel Book of Charlemagne,* c. 800–810, Kunsthistorisches Museum, Vienna

*Gospel Book of Otto III,* c. 1000, Bavarian State Library, Munich

*Les Très Riches Heures de Duc de Berry,* 1413–1416, Musee Condé, Chantilly, France

## PREPARATION

Purchase precut tagboard mats, or suggest that students purchase precut mats from hobby shops. Many framing places happily donate pieces of left-over matboard. Have students find pictures of illuminated manuscripts, or photocopy and make handouts of initials and design motifs. Encourage students to decide what the border will be used to frame before they begin. A decorated frame for a calligraphy saying might be entirely different from one for a photograph.

## FURTHER SUGGESTIONS

- Students can make a "Fraktur" (a traditional Pennsylvania Dutch illuminated calligraphy version of a family tree, birth certificate, or marriage certificate). These were often decorated with hearts, flowers, birds, and other Pennsylvania Dutch motifs.

- As a good ongoing project, encourage students to make a design motif of their own initials on parchment or vellum, placing it in the center or in a corner and completing it with a border. Waxy colored pencils or watercolors are both effective.

# PROJECT 6–1:  ILLUMINATED FRAME

**MATERIALS**

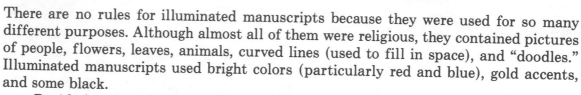

- Mats with precut openings
- Acrylic, tempera paint, or colored pencils
- Gold paint
- Small brushes

There are no rules for illuminated manuscripts because they were used for so many different purposes. Although almost all of them were religious, they contained pictures of people, flowers, leaves, animals, curved lines (used to fill in space), and "doodles." Illuminated manuscripts used bright colors (particularly red and blue), gold accents, and some black.

    Decide before you begin what your decorated frame will be used for. Framing a photograph might be done differently than framing a calligraphy quotation. A "focal point" could be created by making one "picture" or initial in a corner or at the bottom-center of the frame. The rest of the design could be related to the initial.

1. Use pencil to lightly draw lines before painting. If they show, these lines can be erased later.

2. Some suggestions for decorating are:
   a. Variations of the acanthus leaf
   b. Vines with ivy leaves in various colors
   c. Small circles to fill in spaces
   d. Imaginary flowers, joined with vines and curving lines
   e. A "bestiary," incorporating animals such as monkeys, birds, or dragons in the overall design
   f. Elaborate intertwined lines such as those used in Celtic or Islamic manuscripts
   g. An initial in one corner, with designs or calligraphy letters used as the border
   h. Putti (babies with angel wings) intertwined with flowers
   i. A "heraldic" emblem combined with other motifs.

3. Use gold paint to add touches to the edges of flowers or leaves later. Black or white paint can be used to accent some areas.

© 1992 by The Center for Applied Research in Education, Inc.

## PROJECT 6–2: **CALLIGRAPHY**

**FOR THE TEACHER**

Calligraphy (the art of beautiful writing) was the basic method of reproducing the written word until Johannes Gutenberg and other printers invented movable type, printing the first published version of the Bible in 1454. The printing press was invented in 1588. Charlemagne, who could read, but was unable to write, was credited with furthering the cause of literacy through his strong desire to preserve ancient manuscripts.

ABCDEFGHIJKLMN
OPQRSTUVWXYZ
ABCDEFGHIJKLMN
OPQRSTUVWXYZ
abcdefghijkl mnopqrs
tuvwxyz
1234567890

abcdefghijklmnopqrst
uvwxyz

**PREPARATION**

Many of your students will have already had some experience doing calligraphy. Most of them enjoy it and especially will like writing their own names on vellum or parchment in ink. This is an ideal project to teach at the same time you are teaching illumination.

There are a large number of alphabets and rules for learning them, but because time is always limited, I find that secondary students do fairly well if they are given a sample sheet of letters from a book and simple instructions. (See the "Calligraphy Sample" handout.) Use chalk to demonstrate on a board the proper angle to hold the broad-tipped pen, and show them (with the chalk) how holding it at the proper angle will make the lines become thick and thin. Explain that when working, they should sit straight, hold the pen at a 45° angle, start with the pen at the top, and pull it toward the body without turning the pen. Have them practice repeatedly making individual letters before they actually begin a quotation.

While modern Western calligraphy is based on the more easily read Roman alphabet, in which the letters are vertical, students especially enjoy doing more elaborate alphabets such as Italic and Old English. If you are combining this with manuscript illumination, it adds to the "authenticity."

**FURTHER SUGGESTIONS**

- Reproduce Chinese, Islamic, or Egyptian alphabets for students to copy, allowing them to use a brush or calligraphy pen (whichever is most suitable).

- Have them create a "nonalphabet" using forms that might be letters but are not. It would be like reading something you know you should understand, but aren't quite able to.

- Create Books of Hours by folding drawing paper in half (folio), fourths (quarto), and eighths (octavo). See Project 6–3: Book of hours. These could contain calligraphy sayings and illuminations and be sewn together at the folds with an outside cover.

## PROJECT 6–2: **CALLIGRAPHY**

**MATERIALS**

- Paper
- Calligraphy pens
- India ink (if not using marker-type pens)

Calligraphy is something you can enjoy using the rest of your life. It takes repeated practice to become "fluent," and it is a good idea to learn to make one alphabet well before going on to learn others. There is room for creativity in calligraphy after you learn the rules, but it is easier to learn basics by copying what has been done in the past.

Ancient calligraphy used only "upper case" (capital) letters, but this evolved to simplified (small) letters, which are called "lower case." Learn how to make both.

1. Sit straight in your chair, both feet flat on the floor, your back straight, and with your paper placed straight (parallel with the edge) on the table. (These rules practiced by Chinese calligraphers guarantee a long life.)

2. Hold your pen at a 45° angle. Always begin your letters at the top and pull them toward you. Lift the pen to make horizontal marks.

3. Because the shapes of the letters vary, spacing can't be worked out mechanically, but should look pleasing, based on the inside shapes of the letters. Lower case letters are approximately 3/5 the height of a capital letter. Numbers are approximately the size of lower case letters, sometimes going above or below the line. Upper case letters take up different spaces as follows:

    Rectangular letters: H A V N T X Y Z U

    Round letters: O Q D C G

    Wide letters: W M

    Narrow letters: B P R E L F K S

    Very narrow letters: I J

4. Practice making the same letter repeatedly until you make it easily, then go on to the next. This is the first step before writing a quotation or saying.

5. The first time you write a quotation, you might lightly pencil in the letters before you do them in ink, just to make sure they fit on a line. Remember to leave a decent margin on all sides.

6. Alternative lettering suggestions:

    a. Use the same size pen to write one or more lines in oversize capital letters.

    b. Use a larger pen to write the top line.

    c. Place short columns of lettering close together to achieve a "Gothic" appearance.

    d. Begin a piece of writing with several lines of capitals in black or in colored ink.

    e. Make the first letter the size of three lines of writing, as often seen in illuminated manuscripts.

153

## PROJECT 6-3: **BOOKS OF HOURS**

**FOR THE TEACHER**

**Slide #10, *Très Riches Heures de Duc de Berry, May.*** Manuscript illumination enjoyed a resurgence of popularity that lasted from the 1300s to the 1600s. The illustrations reflected the great interest in architecture, and many even resembled stained glass windows, with dark outlines around the figures. Figures were often shown in architectural niches, or great castles might be included in paintings of the countryside.

Books of hours, such as the *Les Très Riches Heures du Jean, Duc de Berry* (the Duc de Berry was the brother of the king of France), were treasured possessions. They contained gospels, prayers, stories of lives of the saints, psalms, and a variety of other reference material such as calendar pages. The months were often illustrated with everyday scenes of peasants working the fields or the nobility hunting. Manuscript illumination was now frequently done by secular painters under the patronage of the nobility.

**PREPARATION**

Discuss with students why people had a book of hours. Ask them why calendars, appointment books, and daily planners play an important part in people's lives today. Suggest they think about the images that are used in today's calendars—photographs of cats, cars, reproductions of artwork, sports figures, the body beautiful, and so on.

Talk with them about what the various months are like in their part of the country: what would they think of in October, for example, or January? Compare these to the calendar pages of a book such as the Duc de Berry's. Appoint groups of students to make a calendar, assigning each student to work on a certain month or months. For very little money, each student could have a personal planning calendar made by the group. (Incidentally, these could be sold to cover expenses.)

Photocopy a blank planning calendar page for each month. To reproduce the calendars, make black and white line drawings to be photocopied. Most schools have a machine to punch holes, for inexpensive plastic binders.

**FURTHER SUGGESTIONS**

1. Try making a calendar in a different shape, such as round or vertical (with all the months on one very long page).

2. Reduce the months in size, glue them to tagboard, and combine them into a small sculpture for the desk. Remind students that calendars have traditionally been given by businesses to attract their customers' attention and show appreciation.

3. Have students research their Zodiac signs, and draw them within an illuminated border. (The slide that goes with this project would be a good example.)

Name: _____   Date: _____

## PROJECT 6–3:  **BOOKS OF HOURS (OR MONTHS)**

**MATERIALS**

- Drawing paper or vellum
- Rulers
- Fine-line black marker
- Newsprint

- Calligraphy pen
- Watercolors or tempera
- Needle and heavy thread

Medieval books of hours were designed to help people plan their days. They contained useful information and ordinary scenes of life. Think about the purpose your book would serve. You can make a daily planner, a weekly planner, or a monthly planning calendar (a group could work together on a calendar, as it is a larger project). Look at planners in stationery departments or bookstores to get ideas on organization.

**CALENDAR**

1. Illustrate a month with an appropriate scene from your own surroundings. For ideas, look through photos of your friends and try to draw them in clothing and locations that are typical of the season you are portraying. For example, in April or July, they might be in bathing suits on a beach, or in December, they might be in ski clothes.

2. Decide in advance with the group whether all the illustrations will be vertical or horizontal. Do thumbnail sketches of several ideas, choosing the best one to develop. If you are working in black and white only, try for a 50/50 black and white balance. After photocopying, color could be selectively added with marker, pencil, or watercolor.

3. Before photocopying the calendar, make sure the illustrations will be right side up when the calendar is opened to be hung (put the illustrations on the backs of the planning pages). This can be bound together with a plastic spine, metal rings, or staples.

**BOOKLET**

1. If you prefer to make a book of calligraphic quotations or cartoons, or an address book, decide in advance how many pages you'll need. If this book will be sewn together, don't make it too thick. Make illustrations appropriate to the purpose of your book, possibly using one only on the cover.

2. Assemble the pages, and use a large needle and heavy thread to sew it together at the fold, as shown here. A cover of marblized paper would be appropriate.

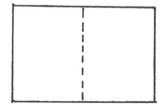 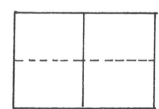 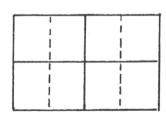 

# PROJECT 6–4:  HERALDRY

## FOR THE TEACHER

Colors and identifying designs were originally worn by knights on a cloak; then "coats of arms" were painted onto a shield used for fighting. This form, in use until 1500, was gradually elaborated upon for decorative purposes. Crests with mantling (which showed a helmet with a short cloak often attached to it) became popular in the thirteenth century. This "cloak" was transformed at times to resemble foliage. Royal arms often showed two "supporters" (figures) on either side of the shield. In modern England, duly recorded grants of arms are given to worthy corporations.

## PREPARATION

Try to get books on heraldry; students will appreciate the beautiful colors and elaborate decorations. Discuss symbolism with them, and ask them to think about their families—where they originated, their position in the family (eldest child, male or female, whether they have brothers and sisters). Suggest they think about their interests—what they like to talk about and do in their spare time. How would they symbolize these interests?

Cut squares or rectangles of posterboard in advance. Explain how they can use the negative shape effectively. The holes left in the colored paper after they have cut out symbols might be one corner of a shield. Show them how to glue neatly with rubber cement. To draw a crest on top of their shield, they can use a rectangle. These could all be displayed together as flags by gluing them to long strips of 14-ply posterboard or stapling them on dowels.

*Safety Note: Rubber cement fumes can be hazardous. Use in a well-ventilated room.*

## FURTHER SUGGESTIONS

- Cut shield shapes in posterboard. Make tagboard cut-outs of shapes such as lions, tre-foils, or lines, and glue them on the posterboard. Cover the form with heavy-duty aluminum foil, smoothing it into place around the cut-outs. Antique it by first wiping on diluted India ink and then wiping off the raised surfaces. Designs can be painted with acrylic paint on the raised areas.

- Make a patch to wear on a jacket by painting a shield onto heavy canvas. This could be ironed onto fabric interlining and stitched (either by hand or on a sewing machine) before cutting out.

- Purchase glazed plain ceramic floor tiles (merchants sometimes will give good prices on odd lots), and have students use acrylic paints to transfer their personal coat of arms to that tile. If you have access to a kiln, paint the tiles with underglaze colors, and apply clear glaze on top before firing.

Name: _____     Date: _____

# PROJECT 6–4: **HERALDRY**

## MATERIALS

- Newsprint
- X-acto® knives
- 12-inch square posterboard
- Rubber cement
- Fadeless or construction paper
- Scissors
- Magazines or cardboard to protect cutting surface

Heraldry was used in the Middle Ages to identify knights and their vassals. Today heraldry is seen on seals used for universities, city and state flags, even class rings. Corporations make use of logos to identify their work and various branches of the armed services have identifying badges with "arms." The drawings on this page show some traditional divisions of space and symbols.

*Safety Note: An X-acto® knife is very sharp. Make sure your fingers are out of the way when you are cutting.*

1. On newsprint make thumbnail sketches of a shape of shield that appeals to you. Before deciding how to divide it, try to come up with some symbols that represent you. Think of your interests and how you can illustrate them. Some suggestions are musical instruments, cars, hats, sports equipment, your house, or favorite musical group. White and yellow are traditionally used to represent the gold or silver background of a shield. Select your favorite color(s) to be combined with these.

2. After selecting a basic shape, use pencil to lightly divide the posterboard in fourths to aid in drawing a symmetrical shield. Draw the shape, trying to make it the full length of the square. The width will vary. You can cut it out later.

3. Although formal rules of heraldry determine how you may place symbols on a shield, you are not bound by these laws and may divide space any way you wish. Use a large symbol, or several smaller symbols. You will probably use a colored background on at least a portion of the paper and may wish to make stripes of harmonizing fadeless paper.

4. Carefully draw the symbols you will use on the front of the fadeless paper and cut out with an X-acto® knife (or scissors). Use a piece of cardboard as a cutting surface to protect the table and the cutting edge of the blade. If you are covering an entire section of the shield with paper, you may wish to trim the edges exactly after it is glued onto the background.

5. To glue the paper to the shield, coat the entire back of your symbols and the area on the shield where the design will go with rubber cement. Allow these to dry so that when you glue them on, they will be permanent. Use a pencil eraser to remove excess rubber cement.

## Unit 2: ROMANESQUE (1000 TO 1150)

### OVERVIEW OF THE VISUAL ARTS

Romanesque art gets its name from the adoption of some of the Roman building forms such as the arch and vault, but the term "Romanesque" now applies only to the eleventh and twelfth centuries, the period between the Roman Empire and the Gothic era. It was a time of growth and expansion for towns and cities in Europe, with the Christian church the center of life for the majority of the people. Wall paintings, hangings, mosaics, carvings and statues, reliquaries (special gem-encrusted containers for relics of the saints brought back from the Holy Land), and painted manuscripts created during that period were objects of great beauty that helped spread the Gospel.

### PAINTING

Manuscript painting continued to dominate and greatly influenced designs on stained glass, which was just beginning to be used in church decoration. Fresco wall painting existed, but few from that era have survived. Mosaics were often used in place of frescoes, reflecting a continued Byzantine influence. An attempt was made to express emotion through exaggerated gestures. Clothing was used to conceal rather than reveal, and faces were passive, with large staring eyes, reflecting an interest in the spiritual rather than human form.

### MASTERPIECES OF PAINTING

*Virgin and Child Enthroned,* c. 1130, fresco, The Metropolitan Museum of Art, New York

*Initial R with St. George and the Dragon,* twelfth century, Citeux, France

*St. John the Evangelist,* c. 1147, Gospel Book of Abbot Wedricus, Societé Archeologique, Avesnes, France

*St. Luke Washing the Feet of Peter,* c. 1000, Gospel Book of Otto III, Bavarian State Library, Munich

### SCULPTURE

Sculpture in bronze reflected some influences from Middle Eastern art brought back by the crusaders. Stone sculpture was an integral part of the church buildings of Romanesque times, being used to decorate the capitals of columns, door entrances, or free-standing figures placed in niches. Figures were elongated and distorted, reflecting the church's continued lack of interest in portraying the human form realistically. Figures were sometimes emaciated to show their poverty and ascetic lives. Favorite subjects were the day of judgment, lives of the saints or Christ, crucifixes, allegories of the months, and zodiac signs.

## MASTERPIECES OF SCULPTURE

*Baptismal Font,* 1107–1118, St. Barthlemy, Liege, Belgium

*Crucifixion,* c. 1087, nave fresco, Sant' Angelo in Foris, near Capua, Italy

## ARCHITECTURE

Romanesque architecture was really the beginning of Gothic architecture, with its use of barrel and groin vaults and columns combined with arches. The Romanesque use of the barrel vault and ribbed cross vaults was the beginning of change in building forms. Geometric forms such as cones, cubes, cylinders, half cylinders, and rectangles were increasingly seen. Because of the necessary thickness of the walls, the height of the church naves was limited. Windows, if any, were small, and consequently church interiors were dark and gloomy. Entrances were at the west end, with the direction of worship facing east (toward Jerusalem). Some of them had a single bell tower or a free-standing bell tower (campanile) such as the Leaning Tower of Pisa. Italian churches often used colored marble on the exterior.

## MASTERPIECES OF ROMANESQUE CHURCHES

*Santiago de Compostela,* 1060–1130, Spain

*St. Sernin,* c. 1080–1120, Toulouse, France

*Cathedral Group,* 1153–1283, Pisa, Italy

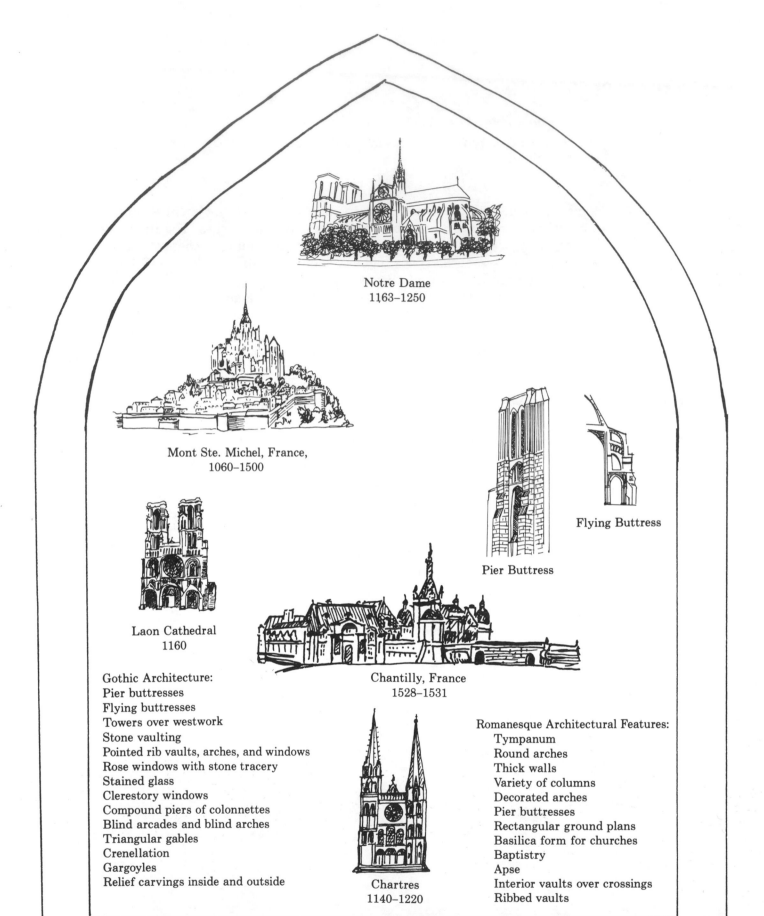

Notre Dame
1163–1250

Mont Ste. Michel, France,
1060–1500

Flying Buttress

Pier Buttress

Laon Cathedral
1160

Chantilly, France
1528–1531

Gothic Architecture:
Pier buttresses
Flying buttresses
Towers over westwork
Stone vaulting
Pointed rib vaults, arches, and windows
Rose windows with stone tracery
Stained glass
Clerestory windows
Compound piers of colonnettes
Blind arcades and blind arches
Triangular gables
Crenellation
Gargoyles
Relief carvings inside and outside

Chartres
1140–1220

Romanesque Architectural Features:
Tympanum
Round arches
Thick walls
Variety of columns
Decorated arches
Pier buttresses
Rectangular ground plans
Basilica form for churches
Baptistry
Apse
Interior vaults over crossings
Ribbed vaults

# ROMANESQUE AND GOTHIC ARCHITECTURE

# PROJECT 6–5: **BAYEUX TAPESTRY**

**FOR THE TEACHER**

**Slide #11:** *The Fleet Crosses the Channel.* The Bayeux Tapestry was probably made in southern England (presumably by an English designer and needlewomen). It is the first known work by women artists and is credited to Queen Matilda, the wife of William the Conqueror, and the women of her court. Bishop Odo, the half brother of William the Conqueror, commissioned it for his cathedral in Bayeux, France. It was embroidered in sections, which were joined together to be viewed when hung clockwise around the nave of the cathedral. For many years it was kept in the treasury of the church, and brought out only on feast days. Today it is in a specially designed room near the cathedral where it can be seen in its full glory.

The tapestry is 230 feet long by 20 inches high and tells its story in a series of vignettes. It is not truly a tapestry (which is woven), but is linen, embroidered in wool, using only two types of stitches. The rich detail, soft colors (terra cotta, blue-green, old gold, olive green, blue, and dark blue or black), and imaginative use of space has made it a world-renowned treasure. It is reminiscent of many illuminated manuscripts, with a border richly embellished with real and imaginary animals. The interlaced branches of trees, the "shorthand" use of symbols for water or land, and the beautiful horses, warriors, and boats all contribute to its beauty.

**PREPARATION**

Explain to the students that you are going to tell a "narrative tale," with each one making a section (8½ × 11 inches), used horizontally. I suggest you split them into groups of five and allow them to work together to tell one part of the "tale." Discuss with them what would be an appropriate event for them to commemorate through such a mural such as the journey of a new student through the school year, Columbus's discovery of America, a sports season, an Olympic festival, or some other current event. Try to have some photocopies of sections of the Bayeux Tapestry, particularly those showing stylized trees, horses, groups of people, etc. Point out the simple patterns that might be used instead of totally filling in everything.

**FURTHER SUGGESTIONS**

1. Make an accordion fold story book by having students draw the "tapestry" on heavy posterboard instead of paper.
2. Have students do caricatures (or cut them out from the newspaper) of today's politicians, making a long comic strip instead of a tapestry.

# PROJECT 6-5: BAYEUX TAPESTRY

**MATERIALS**

- 8½-inch cream or yellow vellum or good bond typing paper
- Waxy colored pencils
- Mineral spirits

The Bayeux tapestry commemorated a great battle in 1066. It was probably designed by one artist and embroidered by a number of different artisans, then the portions joined together. Work in groups of five to give a specific theme to your section.

1. Use newsprint to sketch ideas to share with a group before beginning to work on good paper. Try making "stylized" trees in the manner of the Bayeux Tapestry. Consider putting real or imaginary animals in the border.

2. Some suggestions to unify the mural so that all the individual pieces go together:

   a. Draw on the paper horizontally.

   b. Use limited colors: terra cotta, blue-green, old gold, olive green, blue, and dark blue or black.

   c. Make all upright figures 4 inches in height.

   d. Don't color in faces and hands, but outline them and do features in the darker colors.

   e. Group figures together, and leave some empty space.

   f. Agree in advance what type of decoration will go in the border to unify it.

   g. Leave the background color showing.

   h. Instead of filling in clothing completely, use pattern when appropriate.

   i. Outline clothes and put in details with the same limited colors used throughout the "tapestry."

   j. Use buildings and architectural details. Don't worry about their size in relation to your figures.

3. On scrap paper, experiment with the effects you can get by using colored pencil in different ways.

   a. Try dipping it in mineral spirits to get solid colors.

   b. After you have done a wet area, draw on top of it with a different color.

   c. Although the colors used on the Bayeux tapestry were not shaded, try blending closely related colors (such as shades of green) for richness.

4. When the sections are completed, lay them side by side to come up with the best arrangement. See if you can make them relate to each other by outlining some areas in black fine-line marker. Carefully tape them together on the short sides, and join your portion to that of the rest of the class. Ideally the entire "tapestry" can be hung around the room to give some idea of the size of the real Bayeux Tapestry.

# Unit 3: GOTHIC (1100 TO 1400)

## OVERVIEW OF THE VISUAL ARTS

As Christianity became the dominant religion in Europe, hordes of people traveled a pilgrimage route across Europe to visit the church of Santiago de Compostela in Spain, a Romanesque Church. The six crusades that took place between approximately 1090 and 1228 also had huge numbers of people moving back and forth throughout Europe. The crusaders, with the cross emblazoned across their chests, sought to recapture the Holy Land from the Moslems.

The large churches that developed from the eleventh through thirteenth centuries were an outgrowth of the necessity to accommodate large numbers of people. Countries as such did not exist, but instead regions were ruled by feudal overlords. The bubonic plague (the Black Death) struck in 1348, spreading throughout Europe. Twenty million people died, in some cases entire towns. Small wonder that the Christian church, which promised a life after death, was such a strong influence in people's lives.

## PAINTING

Illuminated manuscripts were commissioned both by the church and wealthy patrons. Although the manuscripts had become more secular, they often continued to serve a religious purpose. Altar paintings on panels, and portraiture became more popular. It was commonplace to see portraits of the donors (often accompanied by their patron saints) incorporated into an altarpiece.

## MASTERPIECES OF PAINTING

*Belleville Breviary,* c. 1323–1326, Bibliotheque Nationale, Paris

*Wilton Diptych,* c. 1377–1413, National Gallery, London

## STAINED GLASS

Stained glass might have been considered the major painting form of this period. It both influenced and was influenced by manuscript illumination. The rich colors have retained their jewel-like quality.

## MASTERPIECES OF STAINED GLASS

*Interior of Sainte Chapelle,* 1243–1248, Paris

*Rose Window,* Notre Dame, 1240–1250, Paris

*Rose and Lancet Windows,* thirteenth century, Chartres Cathedral, Chartres, France

## SCULPTURE

Chartres cathedral had 10,000 carved stone figures. Small religious carvings of the Virgin and Child and small portable altars proliferated. Large carved wooden altarpieces were especially popular in Germany. The exteriors of churches were also rich in carved sculptural elements, including gargoyles (fantasy creatures used as downspouts), tracery used around windows, and statuary.

## MASTERPIECES OF GOTHIC SCULPTURE

*Jamb Figures,* west facade, 1145–1150, Chartres Cathedral, Chartres, France

*Bamberg Rider,* 1240–1255, Bamberg Cathedral, Germany

*Tomb of a Knight,* c. 1260, Dorchester Abbey, Oxfordshire, England

## ARCHITECTURE

Gothic architecture was the first time many innovations used in earlier buildings were brought together. Geometric forms such as rectangles, circles and half-circles, triangles, and squares contributed to the unity and beauty of the churches. Ribbed vaults with pointed arches were typical of Gothic architecture. The pointed intersecting arch, along with the flying buttress, gave strength that enabled the building of enormously high naves (built so high to be closer to heaven). The use of clerestories (outside window walls) and huge windows of jewel-like stained glass gave light to the interiors, representing the "light of heaven" (light symbolized the presence of God).

Great castles and palaces, city halls, and guild halls were constructed during this period. Townhouses were constructed for the upper classes. Towers were used to define corners, and crenellation (battlements, borrowed from Moslem architecture) might be used on the walls of fortresses.

## MASTERPIECES OF GOTHIC ARCHITECTURE

*Abbey Church of St. Denis,* 1140–1144, near Paris, France

*Notre Dame Cathedral,* 1163–1250, Paris, France

*Reims Cathedral,* 1210–1299, Reims, France

*Chartres Cathedral,* 1140–1220, Chartres, France

*Amiens Cathedral,* 1220–1236, Amiens, France

*Canterbury Cathedral,* 1175–1200 and 1397–1400, Canterbury, England

*Salisbury Cathedral,* 1220–1270, Salisbury, England.

## PROJECT 6–6: ROSE WINDOW TRACERY

### FOR THE TEACHER

**Slide # 12: *Chartres Cathedral.*** Stained glass for windows was made by adding various minerals to molten glass to achieve brilliant hues. The resulting small sections were cut, and joined together with strips of lead, emphasizing the design. Some fine details were painted in black. Early designs were strongly influenced by illuminated manuscripts, but eventually the manuscripts began instead to show the influence of the windows, with figures sometimes outlined in black. The windows were usually divided into twelve sections (presumably to represent the apostles).

When advances in Gothic architecture included large clerestories, windows became larger. The rose window became a key feature of the Gothic cathedral. Carved stone was used as a framework for these large round windows. This "tracery," or "rayonnage" (so named for the way it spread out from the center of the window, like rays of the sun), affected the appearance of churches from that time on. It was even used in the ceilings of English churches and in manuscript illumination.

### PREPARATION

Most students will need help in dividing the circle evenly so they can cut openings in the background. Show them how to use a compass and ruler to measure the intersections. Photocopy several photographs from books of illuminated manuscripts onto overhead transparencies for them to see.

### FURTHER SUGGESTIONS

- Make clear overhead transparency reproductions from books for students to color with permanent marker or glass stain or back with colored plastic. Portions could be cut up to form sections of a stained glass window.
- Students can place a sheet of transparent plastic (colored or clear) on top of a suitable image in a book and draw it with a fine black transparency marker. Color can be added later to a clear transparency.

**Photo 6-2. Rose window in Notre Dame, Paris.**

# PROJECT 6–6:  ROSE WINDOW TRACERY

**MATERIALS**

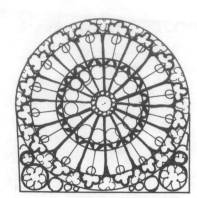

- Clear 8½ × 11-inch overhead transparency
- Six-ply, 10-inch square gray or black posterboard
- Ruler
- Colored plastic          • X-acto® knife
- Compass                  • Rubber cement

Rose windows resemble a rosette shape. The geometric tracery is based on the beautiful shapes (originally cut from stone) that surround and support the stained glass. The circles are divided into twelve sections.

1. Although you may choose to place colored plastic underneath the openings you cut in the posterboard, it is also possible to put designs based on pictures of that time period that you find in books. These can be photocopied onto overhead transparencies or traced onto colored plastic with a black transparency marker. If you use pictures, make your cut-openings large enough to allow them to show through.

2. Use a compass to make as large a circle as possible on the back of black or gray posterboard. Lightly draw a series of concentric circles, one approximately 1 inch inside the outer circle, one approximately halfway from the outside to the middle, and one approximately 1 inch in diameter in the center.

3. With a ruler, measure and evenly space lines from the center to the line next to the outside circle. Some cathedral window designs are shown here. Use an X-acto® knife and ruler to cut through the posterboard. Don't attempt to go all the way through the first time, but repeatedly cut in the same place until it goes through. On circles, make small cuts of less than an inch at a time. It may be possible to go back later with scissors if necessary (to make it neater).

*Safety Note: Always keep your hand behind the X-acto® knife when cutting.*

4. Attach the pieces of plastic behind the openings in the posterboard. Depending on how much space you have, hold these in place with rubber cement or clear tape.

Laon

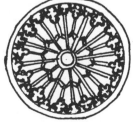

Chartres

Reims, West Portal

Durham, England

Reims

# RENAISSANCE

# RENAISSANCE
## TIME LINE

| A.D. 1250 | 1300 | 1350 | 1400 | 1450 | 1500 | 1550 | 1600 |
|---|---|---|---|---|---|---|---|

Pre-Renaissance
c. 1250–1470

Northern Renaissance 1350–1600

International Style 1400

Early Renaissance
1400–1450

High Renaissance
1495–1520

Mannerism
1525–1600

Last Supper
1495–1498

Cimabue
1240–1302

Henry VIII

Tempietto
1502

Florence
Cathedral
1296–1436

School of Athens
Raphael, 1509

Effects of
Good Government
1338–1340

Jan Van Eyck 1395–1441
Oil painting invented

Michelangelo's David
1504

Peasant Wedding

Pieter Brueghel
1567

Giotto 1267–1337

Mona Lisa
1503–1505

Botticelli's
Venus, 1480

Shakespeare
1558

Ghiberti's
Gates of Paradise
1435

Anglican Church
1534

Tres Riches Heures
Limburgh Brothers, 1400–1430

Palladio, 1567

**Africa**

Ife Art
1100–1500

Benin

Kingdom of
Asante, 1600

Kingdom of
Dahomey, 1600–

**Americas**

Columbus
in
America
1492

**Asia**

Yuan Dynasty
1280–1368

Ming Dynasty
1368–1644

**Europe**

Black plague
1347–1350

Joan of Arc
1412–1431

Gutenberg's Bible
1454

Martin Luther, 1483–1546

Erasmus of Holland, 1511

Spanish Armada
defeated 1588

**Near East**

Seljuk Turks in Iran
1000–1200

Alhambra Palace
14th century

Taj Mahal
Agra, India
c. 1635

**Other**

# Unit 1: NORTHERN RENAISSANCE (c. 1350 TO 1600)

## OVERVIEW OF THE VISUAL ARTS

Transitions in art, such as the movement from Gothic to Renaissance, evolved gradually, influenced by earlier changes. With the migrations across Europe, artists studied in countries other than their own, and an international style came into being. Each culture took something from the other. The rise of Islam was the factor that separated the Middle Ages from the Renaissance.

The Northern Renaissance chiefly took place in Northern France, the Netherlands, and Germany. It consisted primarily of art commissioned by wealthy patrons. Panel paintings such as altarpieces are the most outstanding of these works.

## PAINTING

Many of the early Renaissance painters were unknown by name, although some individuals' styles are recognizable. Such Flemish "anonymous" painters were often named after their masterpieces. The Master of Flemalle, probably Robert Campin (1375–1444), is named for altar paintings done for the city of Flemalle. Two well-known artists were the brothers Hubert (1370–1426) and Jan Van Eyck (1395–1441), whose most famous work is the *Ghent Altarpiece*. Jan Van Eyck is credited with the discovery of oil paint (mixing pigment with oil rather than the usual water or egg yolk). The luminosity achieved through a successive build-up or glazing of layers of paint transformed painting techniques.

## MASTERPIECES OF NORTHERN RENAISSANCE PAINTING

*Merode Altarpiece,* Master of Flemalle (Robert Campin?), 1425–1428, Cloisters Collection, The Metropolitan Museum of Art, New York

*Ghent Altarpiece,* Hubert and Jan Van Eyck, 1432, Church of St. Bavo, Ghent, Belgium

*Giovanni Arnolfini and His Bride,* Jan Van Eyck, 1434, National Gallery, London

*Portinari Altarpiece,* Hugo Van der Goes, 1476, Uffizi Gallery, Florence

*Descent from the Cross,* Rogier Van Der Weyden, 1435, The Prado, Madrid

*Garden of Earthly Delights,* Hieronymus Bosch, 1500, The Prado, Madrid

*Crucifixion,* Matthias Grunewald, 1524, Badische Kunsthalle, Karlsruhe, Germany

## SCULPTURE

Northern Renaissance sculpture was largely confined to wooden and stone pieces such as tombs, pulpits, choir stalls, and wooden altar shrines in churches. Most of these sculptures took their themes from the panel paintings that dominated Northern Renaissance art. Many of the representations of the Virgin Mary and Christ child that came from this time are tender, lifelike representations that reflected aspects of the international style.

## MASTERPIECES OF SCULPTURE

*Well of Moses,* Claus Sluter, 1396–1406, Dijon, France

*Portal of the Chartreuse de Champmol,* Claus Sluter, 1391–1397, Dijon, France

## ARCHITECTURE

There were few innovations in Northern Renaissance architecture. Church architecture was similar to Gothic architecture, featuring stone carving, stained glass windows, vaulted ceilings, and flying buttresses. French architecture blended French elements such as moats and round fortress-like towers with Italian Renaissance ideas.

**Fifteenth-Century Italy**

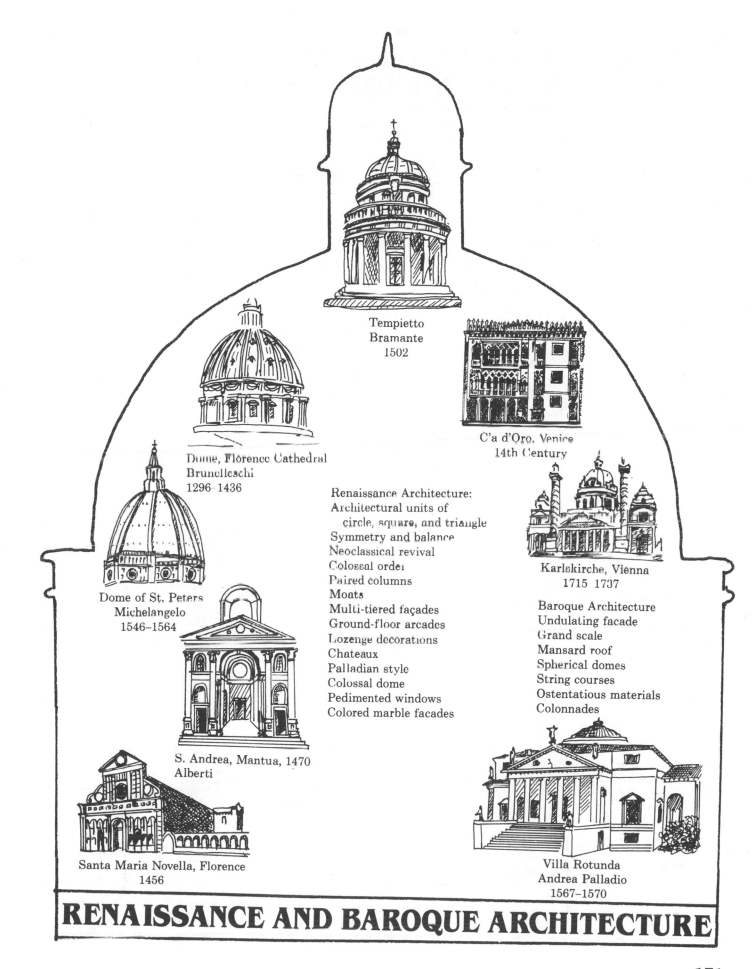

Tempietto
Bramante
1502

C'a d'Oro, Venice
14th Century

Dome, Florence Cathedral
Brunelleschi
1296–1436

Dome of St. Peters
Michelangelo
1546–1564

Karlskirche, Vienna
1715 1737

S. Andrea, Mantua, 1470
Alberti

Santa Maria Novella, Florence
1456

Villa Rotunda
Andrea Palladio
1567–1570

Renaissance Architecture:
Architectural units of
    circle, square, and triangle
Symmetry and balance
Neoclassical revival
Colossal order
Paired columns
Moats
Multi-tiered façades
Ground-floor arcades
Lozenge decorations
Chateaux
Palladian style
Colossal dome
Pedimented windows
Colored marble facades

Baroque Architecture
Undulating facade
Grand scale
Mansard roof
Spherical domes
String courses
Ostentatious materials
Colonnades

# RENAISSANCE AND BAROQUE ARCHITECTURE

# SYMBOLISM IN GOTHIC, RENAISSANCE, AND BAROQUE ART

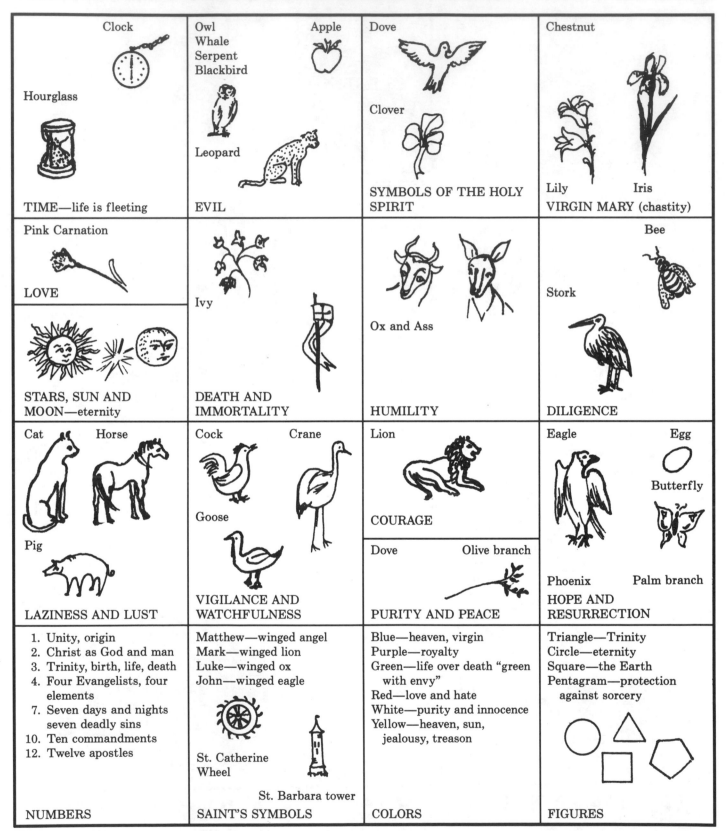

Clock

Hourglass

TIME—life is fleeting

Owl
Whale
Serpent
Blackbird

Apple

Leopard

EVIL

Dove

Clover

SYMBOLS OF THE HOLY SPIRIT

Chestnut

Lily        Iris

VIRGIN MARY (chastity)

Pink Carnation

LOVE

STARS, SUN AND MOON—eternity

Ivy

DEATH AND IMMORTALITY

Ox and Ass

HUMILITY

Bee

Stork

DILIGENCE

Cat        Horse

Pig

LAZINESS AND LUST

Cock        Crane

Goose

VIGILANCE AND WATCHFULNESS

Lion

COURAGE

Dove        Olive branch

PURITY AND PEACE

Eagle        Egg

Butterfly

Phoenix        Palm branch

HOPE AND RESURRECTION

1. Unity, origin
2. Christ as God and man
3. Trinity, birth, life, death
4. Four Evangelists, four elements
7. Seven days and nights seven deadly sins
10. Ten commandments
12. Twelve apostles

NUMBERS

Matthew—winged angel
Mark—winged lion
Luke—winged ox
John—winged eagle

St. Catherine Wheel

St. Barbara tower

SAINT'S SYMBOLS

Blue—heaven, virgin
Purple—royalty
Green—life over death "green with envy"
Red—love and hate
White—purity and innocence
Yellow—heaven, sun, jealousy, treason

COLORS

Triangle—Trinity
Circle—eternity
Square—the Earth
Pentagram—protection against sorcery

FIGURES

# PROJECT 7-1: ILLUSTRATE A PROVERB

## FOR THE TEACHER

**Slide #13: The Blue Cloak (*Netherlandish Proverbs*).** Pieter Brueghel (1525–1569) carried on the narrative tradition that was established by Hieronymus Bosch (c. 1450–c. 1516), the famous Dutch painter. Brueghel painted real people, often in a fantasy world inhabited by strange creatures. His work glorifies ordinary people, perhaps sketched during visits to small villages, where he watched the peasants at their festivals. Subjects that he explored in series were the vices and virtues, illustrations of proverbs, biblical illustrations, seasons of the year, children's games, and lives of the common people.

## MASTERPIECES

*Landscape with the Fall of Icarus*, Pieter Brueghel, 1555, Musées Royaux des Beaux Arts, Brussels, Belgium

*Netherlandish Proverbs* (The Blue Cloak), Pieter Brueghel, 1559, Kaiser Friedrich Museum, Berlin

*Dulle Griet* (Mad Meg), Pieter Brueghel, 1562, Musée Meyer Van den Bergh, Antwerp, Belgium

*Peasant Wedding*, Pieter Brueghel, 1567, Kunsthistorisches Museum, Vienna

## PREPARATION

Brueghel's painting *Netherlandish Proverbs* illustrates approximately 80 Flemish proverbs. Begin this project by asking each student to bring in at least five proverbs (for credit). Discuss these sayings in class. Let each student choose a proverb to illustrate in cartoon style.

## FURTHER SUGGESTIONS

- One of Brueghel's sons was called "Velvet Brueghel" for the beautiful paintings of flowers that he did. Have students try to realistically paint one or more flowers exactly as they see them.

- Brueghel painted daily life and Flemish festivals. Students probably have snapshots of daily life and *their* festivals (basketball games, birthday parties, beach visits, homecoming). Suggest that they design a postage stamp (using a photograph) of their own lives. (Brueghel's work is commemorated on postage stamps.)

## Netherlandish Proverbs

**There are said to be at least 100 Dutch proverbs hidden in this painting.**

1. There the roofs are tiled with pies (a land of plenty)
2. To stick out the broom (celebrate because the owner is gone)
3. Courting under a roof may be shameful, but it is comfortable
4. There hangs the knife (a challenge)
5. The fool gets the trump card (fortune favors fools)
6. They lead each other by the nose
7. Where the scissors hang out (a place where the customer is fleeced—a clip joint)
8. The cross hangs beneath the orb (the world is upside down)
9. It depends on how the cards fall
10. To leave an egg in the nest (keep a nestegg)
11. The herring hangs by its own gills (you take the consequences of your own actions)
12. The sow pulls out the bung (the cat's away, the mice will play)
13. If the eggs have not yet been laid, you can't be sure of getting chickens
14. He will bell the cat
15. She carries fire in one hand and water in the other (contradictory behaviour)
16. A hat on a pillar (a secret under one's hat)
17. She would even tie the devil to a pillow (a shrew)
18. He bangs his head against a stone wall
19. Patient as a lamb
20. One shears sheep, the other pigs (one lives in luxury, one in poverty)
21. One holds the distaff while the other spins (to spread rumors)
22. He carries baskets of light out into the sunshine (coals to Newcastle)
23. She hangs a blue cloak on her husband (deceives her husband)
24. He fills in the well after the calf has drowned (locked the barn door after the horse is stolen)
25. He strews roses before pigs (pearls before swine)
26. One has to squirm if he wants to get through the world
27. He spins the world on his thumb (the world is his oyster)
28. To poke a stick in the wheel
29. He who spills his gruel can't get it all up (don't cry over spilt milk)
30. He is looking for a hatchet (an excuse)
31. He can barely reach from one loaf to the other (can't make ends meet)
32. You don't look for someone in the oven unless you've been there yourself (it takes one to know one)
33. To fall through the basket (to fail)

34. He gives the Lord a flaxen beard (mockery)
35. Two dogs over the same bone rarely agree
36. The pig has been stuck through the belly (he does not know how to kill a pig)
37. He confesses to the devil
38. He lights candles to the devil (to ask a favor of one's enemies)
39. There's a hole in the roof (the whole idea is wrong)
40. Two fools beneath one cap (fools love company)
41. To send one arrow after another (throw good after bad)
42. The pigs run loose in the corn (everything has gone wrong)
43. He hangs his cloak against the wind (an opportunist)
44. To stand looking at the stork (to let an opportunity slip)
45. He plays the violin in the stocks (doesn't see how ridiculous he is)
46. To fall off the ox onto the donkey (to go from the frying pan into the fire)
47. He kills two flies with one blow
48. He opens the door with his backside (doesn't know whether he is coming or going)
49. He fishes behind the net (comes up emptyhanded)
50. The fox dines with the crane
51. The big fish eat the little fish
52. He sits on hot coals (on tenterhooks)
53. He resents the sun shining on the water (is stingy)
54. He throws his money into the water
55. He is dragging the block (is heavy laden)
56. Only fear makes the old lady run
57. The blind lead the blind
58. It is easiest to sail before the wind
59. He has one eye on the sail (is alert)
60. Why do the geese go barefoot (mind your own business)
61. He sees the bears dancing (is hungry)
62. He throws his cowl over the fence (gives up priestly vows)
63. The broadest straps are cut from someone else's hide
64. An eel held by the tail is not yet caught
65. He swims against the tide
66. She takes the hen's egg and lets the goose's go
67. He tries to open his mouth as wide as the oven door (bites off more than he can chew)
68. He sits in his own light (basks in his own glory)
69. He tosses feathers into the wind

Name: _____     Date: _____

# PROJECT 7–1: ILLUSTRATE A PROVERB

**MATERIALS**

- Newsprint
- Six-ply posterboard or drawing paper 5 × 7 inches
- Pencil
- Place fine-line markers
- Watercolor (optional)

In this project you'll draw as if you were a cartoonist. Your drawing will be simple, and will probably involve people or animals. (It is not creative to use someone else's cartoon character.) The object is to illustrate a well-known proverb so that anyone could guess it after seeing the picture.

1. Select a proverb that allows you to create a picture in your mind of how it might be illustrated. If you can envision it mentally, you will be able to draw it well enough for people to understand it. Make several rough sketches on newsprint (use stick figures, if you wish, to get an idea how to arrange them).

2. After you have come up with an idea, make a 5 × 7-inch rectangle on newsprint and draw your idea in detail, including a background. Go over the back of the drawing with pencil so you can transfer it to the posterboard. Place the newsprint on top of the posterboard and draw over your original outline. You should have a faint outline on the posterboard.

3. Use fine-line marker to go over the outlines. Look at newspaper cartoons and notice how areas of dark and light are created. Brueghel frequently worked in black and white. If you can find original reproductions of his work, you can see how he used texture to create variety in his drawings. If you wish, you could go over some of the areas with watercolor. It may cause the ink from the marker to run, but that often adds charm to a finished product.

4. Write the proverb on the back of the posterboard, or do block lettering under the picture. To display these cards, labels with the proverb could be placed under the pictures.

# Unit 2: ITALIAN RENAISSANCE (c. 1400 TO 1520)

## OVERVIEW OF THE VISUAL ARTS

Renaissance, rebirth, the age of humanism, man as the measure of all things, the emergence of the individual—all these are descriptions of the period that brought Italy out of the Middle Ages. Philosophers, writers, and scholars saw this period as a revival of classical antiquity. It was a period that was artistically dominated by giants: Leonardo da Vinci (1452–1519), Michelangelo Buonarotti (1475–1564), Donatello (1386–1466), Raphael Sanzio (1483–1520), Sandro Botticelli (1445–1510), and Filippo Brunelleschi (1377–1446). Their work created dramatic changes in art. The church had essentially dominated the production of art for centuries. Although Renaissance artwork continued to feature religious themes, it also glorified the emergence of the new middle class and recognized the individual. Mythological themes, portraiture, even some genre art were created for new patrons such as merchants, the papacy, and royalty.

## PAINTING

Giotto de Bondone (1266–1337) was considered by some as the first Renaissance artist. He painted scenes from the life of Christ directly into fresh plaster (fresco) at the Arena Chapel in Padua. His work was evidently modeled on real people, as each figure had an individuality rarely seen earlier. He portrayed human suffering and anguish, not only with facial expressions, but also with body language. He was followed by a series of Italian masters, each one of whom contributed something to the evolution of painting.

Under the court patronage of popes and kings, artists fulfilled several functions. Michelangelo, for example, not only painted the *Sistine Chapel*, sculpted masterpieces, and was the architect for the dome of St. Peter's, but also designed the uniforms of the Vatican guards that are still used today.

## MASTERPIECES OF PAINTING

*St. Sebastian*, Andrea Mantegna, 1455–1460, Kunsthistorisches Museum, Vienna

*Mona Lisa*, Leonardo da Vinci, 1503–1505, Louvre, Paris

*Last Supper*, Leonardo da Vinci, 1495–1498, Sta. Maria delle Grazie, Milan

*Sistine Chapel*, Michelangelo, 1508–1512, Vatican, Rome

*Birth of Venus*, Sandro Botticelli, c. 1480, Ufizzi Gallery, Florence

## SCULPTURE

The Italian tradition of sculpture reached back to Roman times, when heroes were glorified by being portrayed in stone. The equestrian statue was also a tradition, portraying the Italian rulers of city-states in all their glory. Sculpture that was created for churches and tombs dated back to the time of the Etruscans.

During the Italian Renaissance, Florence was a center of commerce and culture. Its enlightened atmosphere fostered creativity in every aspect of art. Artistic competitions were held when a special need was seen, such as a design for the doors of the baptistry or the dome of the cathedral.

## MASTERPIECES OF SCULPTURE

*Gattemelata* (Equestrian Statue of Erasmo da Narni), Donatello, c. 1445 1450, Padua

*Equestrian Monument of Bartolomeo Colleoni*, Andrea del Verrocchio, c. 1483–1488, Venice

*David*, Michelangelo, 1501–1504, Galleria dell' Accademia, Florence

*Moses*, Michelangelo, c. 1513–1515, St. Peter in Chains, Rome

*Pieta*, Michelangelo, 1499–1500, St. Peter's, Vatican, Rome

*David*, Donatello, c. 1430–1432, National Museum, Florence

*Gates of Paradise*, Lorenzo Ghiberti, c. 1435, Baptistry, Florence

*Tomb of Lorenzo and Giuliano de Medici*, Michelangelo, 1524–1534, Florence

*Madonna and Child*, Luca della Robbia, c. 1455–1460, Florence

## ARCHITECTURE

Architecture in Italy during the Renaissance was refined and inventive. The architects made extensive use of geometric units such as the rectangle, square, and triangle. They combined round arches with pedimented windows (rounded or triangular arches at the top) and multitiered facades. Ground floor arcades provided protection from the sun. Colored marble was often used to create rich horizontal stripes and designs on the façades of the churches, bell towers, and baptistries.

## MASTERPIECES OF ARCHITECTURE

*Dome of Florence Cathedral*, Filippo Brunelleschi, 1420–1436, Florence

*Ufizzi Palace*, Giorgio Vasari, 1560–1580, Florence

*Campidoglio Plaza* (Capitoline Hill), Michelangelo, 1537, Rome

*St. Peter's*, Michelangelo, 1546–1564, Rome

*Villa Rotonda*, Andrea Palladio, 1567–1570, Vicenza, Italy

# PROJECT 7-2: THE GOLDEN RECTANGLE

**FOR THE TEACHER**

**Slide #14: *The Last Supper.*** The golden section, or golden rectangle, was a canon of proportion developed by the Egyptians and used by the Greeks as early as the fifth century B.C. Leonardo felt that even the human figure could be divided into two golden sections (from the top of the head to the navel, and from the navel to the soles of the feet).

**PREPARATION**

If you do not have right-angle triangles, cut some from tagboard on a paper cutter. Few compasses are large enough to make a large golden rectangle, so have students make a small rectangle and simply draw to scale to get the dimensions for one larger. It is roughly in proportions of 8 to 13 and can be obtained using a right-angle triangle and compass. To save time, you could precut the large drawing paper, but still give students the experience of making a small golden section using a compass and triangle.

**FURTHER SUGGESTIONS**

- Renaissance artists felt everything could be explained by geometry. Leonardo's famous drawing of a human figure in a circle illustrates this. A purely geometric composition, with overlapped shapes, would be a guaranteed success for everyone. Suggest that students work in a monochromatic color scheme, with one small shape colored in a complementary color.

- Have students design a public building using only geometric shapes for doors, windows, and decorations. This building could be a new city hall, a mall, new telephone building, or school. Many of the buildings that are now designed on a computer have these geometric relationships.

Name: _____     Date: _____

# PROJECT 7–2: THE GOLDEN RECTANGLE

## MATERIALS

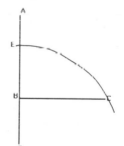

- Compass
- Ruler
- Pastels
- Triangle (or tagboard triangle)
- White drawing paper

Renaissance artists applied geometry and perspective in many of their paintings, placing figures within a pyramidal or triangular arrangement within a "golden section." Ancient Greeks and Renaissance artists considered these shapes to be in perfect proportion. They were often used in designing churches and paintings. Most drawing paper is in roughly this same proportion.

1. Make a golden rectangle as follows
   a. Draw two lines of equal length at right angles to each other (AB, BC).
   b. Extend a line half the length of AB, creating BD.
   c. With D at the center, use a compass to make an arc CE, intersecting line AB at point E.
   d. To make a rectangle, draw a line from E parallel to BC and from C parallel to BE. These meet at point F, forming rectangle BCFE.

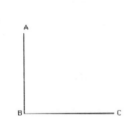 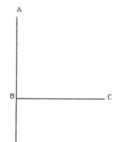 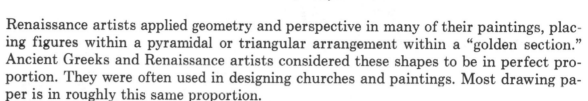 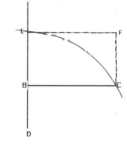

2. Before deciding on a specific subject, make several geometric divisions within the rectangle. You could make more rectangles, triangles, pyramids, or circles. Many Renaissance paintings showed people, religious, or mythological subjects. Some suggestions to help with composition and subjects are:
   a. Find some of the intersections where the geometric figures overlap, and draw a person at an intersection.
   b. Create a complete abstraction with no recognizable subject.
   c. Draw a room you are familiar with, such as your bedroom or the classroom.
   d. Use one-point perspective like Leonardo used in his Last Supper.
   e. Make simple contour drawings of figures, overlapping them and painting them in "flat" areas of color.
   f. Illustrate a myth.
   g. Do a portrait (such as a friend drawn in the pose of the Mona Lisa).

**179**

# PROJECT 7-3: **TONDO**

## FOR THE TEACHER

The tondo, or circle, was sometimes used by Renaissance artists for painting, ceramics, and decorative architectural elements. They also composed paintings within a half-circle (lunette) or a rectangle with a rounded top. Particular care was taken in arranging elements of design within the circle, or it could almost appear to roll. Most tondos were religious, with the majority having a Madonna and Christ child. Early in his career Michelangelo carved religious medallions, and his painted tondo of the holy family resembles sculpture.

## MASTERPIECES OF TONDO PAINTING

*Holy Family,* Michelangelo, 1506, Ufizzi Gallery, Florence

*Madonna of the Chair,* Raphael, 1515–1516, Pitti Palace, Florence

*Madonna and Child,* Luca Signorelli, 1490, Ufizzi Gallery, Florence

*Madonna of the Magnificat,* Botticelli, c. 1483, Ufizzi, Florence

## PREPARATION

The circle will be used as an organizational format to contain figure drawings. A thumbnail sketch is advisable.

For the actual painting, I have found that simply tracing around a stool or barrel lid gives a good-sized circle, or (to speed up the project) you could make circular patterns for students to use.

## FURTHER SUGGESTIONS

- Any subject can be "poured" into a circle and made to fit it. It is fun to take a subject such as a car or animal and distort it so it touches the outside edges of the circle.

- Do a take-off on Leonardo's human figure that fits within the circle. Let it be someone in uniform such as a band member, football player, or cheerleader.

## PROJECT 7–3: **TONDO**

### MATERIALS

- Magazines
- Rubber cement
- Compass
- Drawing paper
- Watercolor or colored pencils

Use your own sketches or photographs, or find several figures from magazines to paste together, overlapping and organizing them to fit within a circular format. Don't be concerned about how people are dressed until later. Renaissance artists often composed their figures in a pyramid or triangle and usually had most of the "weight" in the bottom half of the circle. Often they drew a horizontal line on the lower third of the circle to keep it from appearing to "roll."

1. If you use magazine pictures, cut out three to five figures from magazines, without paying much attention to size, but rather to the positions the figures are in. You will probably use the figures just to give you ideas as you draw them to fit within a circle. Overlap the figures, trying to place the heads more or less in a triangle or pyramidal scheme. Glue them to the background with rubber cement. If you are using your own figure drawings, simply arrange them the same way.

2. Draw a circle around the composition. Look closely at the organization of the figures. Could you make some smaller or larger?

3. Do a quick sketch of the entire composition; see if there are changes you could make so that the sketch will work a little better. Make a circle as large as your paper will allow. Enlarge your drawing to fit within the circle.

4. Consider what the figures are wearing. They could all be part of a team or be wearing modern dress, hats, or headdresses. What about making them part of a landscape, with a horizon line, or moving some of the figures to follow the contour of the line?

5. Paint the figures and background within the circle. Try "modeling" the figures by shading clothing and skin to show roundness. If you have been working with color photographs, you can discern how an illusion of roundness is created.

6. Cut out the circle, and mount it on a square of dark paper for display.

# PROJECT 7-4: ENLARGE A RENAISSANCE MASTERPIECE

**FOR THE TEACHER**

Modern painting really began during the Renaissance. The small panel or portable painting hardly existed before that time. For hundreds of years painting was generally religious, mostly created for churches and private chapels. Renaissance painters were commissioned to do religious paintings and painted subjects to the taste of the emerging middle class. Students will be able to name a number of Renaissance paintings they have seen such as Leonardo's *Mona Lisa* or *Last Supper*.

**PREPARATION**

Many students have had little experience painting; so attempting to exactly reproduce a small "abstract" portion of a painting is fun. Because they will be enlarging only a section of an actual painting, they are not threatened by having to make it look exactly like a "real" picture.

Select at least one "masterpiece" (a small reproduction) to cut into pieces. Number and place directional arrows on the back of each cut-up section so you will be able to join the enlarged sections, piecing together the original later. Attach each piece to a separate 3 × 5-inch card to preserve it. Students don't need to know what they are reproducing. The surprise when it is assembled is half the fun. In advance, cut drawing paper into pieces that are in exact proportion to the size of the small section each student will receive. Your finished masterpiece can be very large, or modest in size, depending on the time you have to do it. Show students how to make a grid for enlarging on both the small section and large drawing paper. Naturally the finished enlargements will not line up exactly, nor will the colors be exactly the same, but that contributes to the charm.

If you have a large class, two or three masterpieces may be reproduced at the same time.

**FURTHER SUGGESTIONS**

- Students can make an abstract interpretation of a Renaissance masterpiece by placing tracing paper over a masterpiece and drawing lines or shapes through major figures. The colors could be similar. The original would be merely a starting point (just as Picasso loosely interpreted the work of Velásquez).

- A small reproduction (such as a postcard or ad) of an original can be glued anywhere on a piece of drawing paper, and "extensions" of the original painting can be made. Lines can be extended out to the edges of the drawing paper, and colors or scenes can be added. If colors are faithfully reproduced, the original can become part of the whole picture and not be noticeable unless you look closely.

- Of course each student can literally enlarge a single masterpiece by projecting a slide onto the paper or with the grid system. If they select one that has people in it, they can substitute their own face, or people in modern dress instead. Two of my students did a parody on Manet's *Luncheon on the Grass,* substituting a nude male surrounded by fully dressed women in jeans, with the picnic consisting of Perrier water, crackers, and cheese.

## PROJECT 7–4:  ENLARGE A RENAISSANCE MASTERPIECE

**MATERIALS**

- White drawing paper or posterboard
- Wide masking or duct tape
- Oil pastels, tempera, or acrylic
- Brushes
- Pencils
- White note cards
- Postcard or magazine reproductions of original artwork

Renaissance paintings portrayed a variety of subjects, though most of them have people in them. Take the time to try to faithfully reproduce the coloring and shading that you see on your portion of the "masterpiece." Keep your original section so the entire original painting can be pieced together and mounted next to your masterpiece.

1. When you receive your section, use a ruler to make a grid on it in pencil. Carefully measure from the bottom left, drawing one-half-inch squares. Now take the large sheet of drawing paper, and lightly draw a grid in exact proportion to your section. For example, if you have one-half-inch squares on the original, then your grid could be enlarged at a scale of one-half inch equals 2 inches.

2. Use a pencil to lightly sketch the original onto the large piece of paper. Look at each square of the small grid and make the marks in the related square on the large sheet of paper. You may wish to number each square of both grids to keep track of the enlarging. Accept the fact that it is not possible to be totally accurate when enlarging by hand.

3. If you are working in tempera or acrylic paint, attempt to reproduce exactly the colors used in the original. If you are working in oil pastel, come as close as you can to the original. In either case, pay careful attention to use the "modeling" (shading) that you see in the original.

4. When they are finished, join the sections together with wide tape. Rejoin the original small sections, and display the large masterpiece and the original masterpiece on the same wall.

# PROJECT 7-5: FREE THE "SLAVES"

## FOR THE TEACHER

**Slide #15: *David.*** Michelangelo felt that he never really designed a piece of sculpture, but that he simply released the figure by taking away the stone that surrounded it. Most of his early sculptures, including the *Pieta,* were highly polished. Late in his life he did a number of bound "slaves" that were never totally freed from the stone in which they were imprisoned.

## MASTERPIECES OF SCULPTURE BY MICHELANGELO

*Moses,* c. 1513–1515, St. Peter in Chains, Rome

*The Rebellious Slave,* 1513–1516, Louvre, Paris

*David,* 1501–1504, Galleria dell' Academia, Florence

*Pieta,* 1498–1499, St. Peter's, Rome

## PREPARATION

Show students slides of Michelangelo's work. Point out to them the angles caused by different levels of the shoulders and knees, the twists in the torso, the turning of a head. Because they will be beginning with a block of material, it is difficult for students to envision that their sculpture is not just on one surface, but probably deep within, bent, twisting, and alive.

I recommend that you try an Oasis® carving yourself before explaining it to students, as this will help you describe it.

Ask students if they have ever tried soap carving. If they have, they may know that you cannot remove large amounts of material at once without ending up with a pile of soap chips. Explain before beginning that the material limits the amount of detail possible, and that the sculpture should be fairly simple. Advise students to work over the entire block at one time, removing small amounts, and not making deep indentations such as a neck or waist (which will cause those areas to become fragile) until the work is almost finished.

## FURTHER SUGGESTIONS

- Luca della Robbia (1400–1482) was a Renaissance sculptor who created ceramic flowers and fruits, organized in swags or wreaths, and glazed blue and white. These ceramics sometimes framed portrait sculpture, and were often used to ornament buildings and palaces. Students could create a della Robbia wreath by bringing in fruit and flowers (real or fake), then either draw it or sculpt it in clay (if you are limited for time, each student could do only one fruit or flower).

- You could make a Modigliani-style portrait in Oasis® with the long face typical of his work. It is said that these were based on one type of African mask that was distorted in this manner.

## PROJECT 7–5: **FREE THE "SLAVES"**

**MATERIALS**

- Newsprint
- Newspaper
- Paring knives
- "Oasis" floral foam $3 \times 4 \times 8$ inches
- Pencil
- Gesso

Because this is an easily worked material, you could destroy it in a half hour. Don't be in a hurry; take your time, and stop occasionally to consider what you will do next. You may spend as much time planning what you will do next as you spend actually carving. Leave the thinnest cuts (such as a neck) until you are all finished, as they will be fragile. You will make mistakes, so be flexible about your carving. Changing your mind is half the fun.

1. Do thumbnail sketches before "freeing" the figure within the "stone." Draw a cube the shape of the plastic foam. Envision your figure within it. It could be seated, standing, bent, or in motion. Try to keep arms close to the body, since they are likely to break off if they are too thin (just as the Venus de Milo lost her arms).

2. Use a knife to make light lines on the outside of the cube, determining where the head, neck, waist, buttocks, knees, and feet will be. Accept the fact that your final sculpture will be almost half changed from your original concept. No matter how abstract your "figure," it will still look human if it has indentations at the neck and waist, and is tapered somewhat inward at the bottom. If you make it too thin at the bottom to support it, attach it to a base for stability.

3. Work on a newspaper to make clean up easy. With a paring or X-acto® knife, take away small amounts (never more than one-fourth inch) of material from all over the sculpture. Remember that the figure is buried deeply within the block. You can control how deeply you cut by making "stop-cuts." (Cut straight in one-fourth inch, then make a slice toward the cut.)

4. When you have finished cutting, use the broad side of a blade to smooth out edges. (Edges, or "planes," may also be left in, as frequently seen in modern sculpture.)

5. If you are going to paint the sculpture, coat it first with gesso (a material similar to plaster). To make a foam base, cut a piece of foam $4 \times 4 \times 2$ inches, and attach it to the base of the statue with long wooden toothpicks or skewers.

# PROJECT 7-6:  FRESCO

**FOR THE TEACHER**

**Slide #16:** *The Sistine Chapel, Detail (Creation of Man).* The technique of fresco was known in Egypt as early as 3000 B.C. Applying colored pigment into freshly prepared plaster walls meant that the paint actually became part of the plaster. Some of the colors applied several thousand years ago remain almost as fresh as when they were first painted.

The traditional method of painting fresco was to first create a cartoon (a drawing on paper with small holes outlining the design). The artist then mixed and applied to the wall only the amount of plaster that could be painted in one day.

Students enjoy doing fresco painting in the traditional manner and will understand and appreciate the challenge it must have been to work high on a scaffold, such as that used by Michelangelo, while lying on your back. Explain that a great deal of the plaster mixing, pigment grinding, and so on would have been done by apprentices, while the master would have done the important portion of the painting.

**MASTERPIECES OF FRESCO**

*Arena Chapel,* Giotto, 1305–1306, Padua

*Tribute Money,* Masaccio, c. 1427, Brancacci Chapel, Florence

*Discovery and Proving of the True Cross,* Piero Della Francesca, c. 1460, S. Francesco, Arezzo

*Sistine Chapel,* Michelangelo, 1508–1511, Vatican, Rome

*Last Supper,* Leonardo da Vinci, c. 1495–1498, Sta. Maria delle Grazie, Milan

**PREPARATION**

Make life easy for yourself by purchasing premixed dry wall compound (you can buy it in large quantity, and it lasts years). In experimenting with various types of pigments, my students found that although they could make powder from pastels (by scraping them with a knife or pair of scissors), the best results were achieved with ordinary tempera, which was essentially what the masters used. If authenticity is important to you, try mixing powdered tempera with egg yolk. Because we worked a little larger than average (18 × 24 inches), few students were able to complete a *buon fresco* ("true fresco," painted into damp plaster) painting in one class period. Painting into dry plaster (*fresco secco*) can continue at any time.

**FURTHER SUGGESTIONS**

- Tape white kraft paper on the underside of tables or desks, and let students experience personally how Michelangelo must have felt always painting above his head. (This could be done with markers to avoid drips of paint into hair, clothes, etc.)

- Let each student paint a life-sized figure on kraft paper, cut it out, then overlap them to create a wall-sized mural to resemble that of the *Last Judgment* on the end wall of the Sistine Chapel. Select a theme before beginning so that the figures appear to have something in common.

# PROJECT 7–6: **FRESCO**

## MATERIALS

- Canvas board, masonite, or plywood
- Premixed dry wall plaster compound
- Plaster spatula or 14-ply cardboard
- Tracing wheel and/or yarn needles
- Muslin square 12 × 12 inches
- Rubber band
- Tan kraft paper
- Brushes
- Hair dryer
- Charcoal
- Foam egg carton
- Newsprint
- Tempera paint

What to paint is often the most difficult part of any painting. You are using an ancient technique, yet you may not wish to do a traditional painting. Select a subject such as people, flowers, clouds, trees, or something from nature that resembles historic frescoes but would not have to be precise. You will be working quickly, and the subject needs to be "forgiving."

### Day 1

1. Make several thumbnail sketches, then select one. Draw it in pencil on a piece of tan kraft paper cut the exact size of the board. This drawing is called a "cartoon." Plan your colors ahead by writing them on the cartoon.

2. Prick holes in the paper along the lines of your drawing (not further apart than ½ inch) with a tracing wheel or needle. Then the design is ready to transfer to the damp fresco the next day. Prepare the "pounce" (powdered charcoal applicator) by placing charcoal in a square of muslin, closing the ends with a rubber band, and pulverizing the charcoal with a hammer.

### Day 2

3. Use a putty knife to scoop premixed plaster onto the board. Spread it into a thin coat (one-sixteenth inch) using either a wide metal putty knife or a wide, heavy piece of matboard. Allow it to dry approximately 15 minutes (or until none comes off onto your palm when you touch it; a hair dryer speeds up drying). Prepare your paint in the egg carton while waiting for the plaster to dry slightly. When you are done for the day, close the carton to keep the paint moist.

4. Place the paper cartoon on the plaster. Pat the charcoal pounce onto the holes punched into the paper. It may be necessary to gently rub the pounce over the holes if they are not large enough. This will transfer a dot pattern onto the plaster.

5. Use a large brush to apply paint as quickly as possible over the entire surface. You can go back later and refine the details, but the base colors will last hundreds of years if they are applied into the wet plaster.

© 1992 by The Center for Applied Research in Education, Inc.

## PROJECT 7–7: **CITY PLANNING**

**FOR THE TEACHER**

It is impossible to think of the Renaissance without considering its architecture. The growth of cities around churches, the rise of the merchant class, and international commerce all affected the look of cities. This can be a great lesson in city planning, as you ask students to think about what is needed in a city to make it function.

Italian cities (like most cities in the world), are built near a source of fresh water such as the Tiber River (Rome) or the Arno (Florence). They usually have churches, palaces, plazas, schools and universities, private homes, bridges, monuments, apartments, towers, arcades, city walls, city gates, a stadium, etc. Most are laid out on a north-south axis, as were ancient Roman cities. Although some cities, such as Paris, or Washington, D.C., have streets radiating at angles from a central point, most cities are built much as the Romans did.

**Photo 7–1.** *Good Government in the City,* 1338–1340, Ambrogio Lorenzetti, fresco, Palazzo Publico, Siena. Art Resource, NY.

**MASTERPIECES RELATED TO
RENAISSANCE ARCHITECTURE**

*The Tempietto,* Donato Bramante, 1502, S. Pietro in Montorio, Rome

*Square Court of the Louvre,* Pierre Lescot and Jean Goujon, 1546, Paris

*Good Government in the City,* Ambrogio Lorenzetti, 1338–1340, Palazzo Pubblico, Sienna

*S. Andrea,* Leone Battista Alberti, 1470, Mantua

## PREPARATION

Each student will contribute to the city. Decide on a scale (an average house might be 2 to 3 inches square). As the class names types of buildings or other structures, write each one on the board. You may also wish to decide on an overall color scheme. Many cities have a general color that is determined by nearby building materials. For example, Florence is mainly buff in color, with red-orange tile roofs. Edinburgh, Scotland, is dark gray, the color of the surrounding stone.

When they are ready to begin, have each student select one type of building so you will have a variety. If you have more students than types of buildings, assign several to make palaces or churches or houses. Two or three students will need to be city planners, making the streets, parks, and plazas, rivers, etc., to accommodate the buildings. They could assign someone to make decorative elements for a plaza such as a fountain or statue (these could be made of plasticine or self-hardening clay). Have each student give the "city planners" a piece of paper the size of the base of their individual building to help them in their planning.

## FURTHER SUGGESTIONS

- Several experimental self-sufficient cities already exist in the United States. City planning for the future is happening now. Students could plan a complete city to be built out in the suburbs, on a space station, or under the sea.

- With land at a premium in most cities, suggest that students come up with innovative ways to accommodate more people in less space. This idea could provoke a thoughtful discussion, as they try to creatively solve "space for people."

## PROJECT 7-7: CITY PLANNING

### MATERIALS

- Newsprint
- Rubber cement
- X-acto® knives
- Tagboard or posterboard
- 14-ply mountboard or Foam-core® as a base

- Compasses
- Pencils
- Scissors
- Rulers
- Colored pencil or tempera

Most buildings are rectangles of various sizes. Some are quite tall, such as town towers (often with a clock on them), others squat, single-family dwellings. In the Renaissance, churches often were the largest buildings in town, with small houses and shops attached to them. Renaissance architects used decorative elements such as colored marble, columns and arches, pilasters, and carvings. In addition to polished marble, stone was a common building material, often purposely left rough (rusticated). City walls and bridges were often quite elaborate.

1. Do a thumbnail sketch of a type of building you would like to make. Draw it to scale on a piece of newsprint, and make a pattern to lay on a piece of tagboard. Be sure to add tabs on the sides of your boxes to make them easy to join.

2. Draw around the pattern, then use an X-acto® knife or scissors for cutting out windows and doors.

   **Safety Note:** *Remember to keep your hand behind the cutting edge of the knife. It is an easy habit to get into and will prevent accidents. Also remember to place a magazine or piece of cardboard underneath where you are cutting to protect the table.*

3. Before gluing, decorate the building with colored pencil, marker, or paint. Roof tiles could be made by painting a piece of tagboard, then cutting it into small pieces to glue individual "tiles" to the roof. You can use pencil to draw "stones" on the sides of the buildings.

4. When the buildings are all made, arrange them on the city's foundation. Discuss where things should go, and make adjustments until most class members are content with the city. Although everything could be glued in place, you might find opportunities to exhibit it if it were easily portable. Have a competition to name the city.

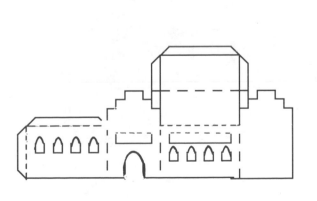

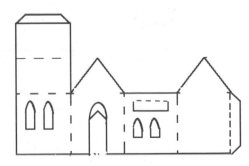

# PROJECT 7–8: CHECKERBOARD SQUARE: PERSPECTIVE THE ITALIAN WAY

**FOR THE TEACHER**

**Slide #17: *The School of Athens.*** Although perspective had been used for several hundred years, linear perspective was haphazard until the Renaissance. An Italian, Filippo Brunelleschi (1377–1446), formalized the "rules" of perspective. He designed many well known churches in Florence and other Italian cities. He and other Renaissance architects applied the science of geometry in designing churches by using multiples of simple squares, rectangles, and circles to achieve perfect symmetry. His greatest achievement was the building of the dome of the great church in Florence.

Another type of perspective used by Renaissance artists was aerial perspective, the hazy appearance of objects far in the distance. Leonardo da Vinci was a master of this *sfumato* (smoky) effect.

**RENAISSANCE PAINTINGS THAT DEMONSTRATE PERSPECTIVE**

*St. Sebastian,* Andrea Mantegna, c. 1455–1460, Kunsthistorisches Museum, Vienna

*Holy Trinity with the Virgin and St. John,* Masaccio, 1425, Sta. Maria Novella, Florence

*Delivery of the Keys,* Pietro Perugino, 1482, Vatican, Rome

*School of Athens,* Raphael, 1510–1511, Stanza della Segnatura, Vatican, Rome

Photo 7–2. *Interior of St. Peter's,* Rome, 1731, 145.2 × 227.5 cm, oil on canvas, Giovanni Paolo Panini.

## PREPARATION

This project could be worked on 15 minutes at a time and is a good ongoing project. Try it first yourself before giving it to students, and of course encourage students to become creative with the placement of objects in the drawing. One of my students used this system to do a room interior for an interior design class.

## FURTHER SUGGESTIONS

- Use geometric forms to design a building. It could be completely modern and absolutely symmetrical, with half-circles, squares, and triangles.
- Make a fantasy drawing using linear perspective. Use columns, obelisks, people, animals, distorted fruit, machines, watches (a la Dali)—any unlikely combination of objects.

**Photo 7-3. This Dutch interior scene demonstrates that the use of perspective was one of the hallmarks of a successful painter.** *The Street Musicians,* 1665, 68.6 × 57.2 cm, oil on canvas, Jacob Ochtervelt, The Saint Louis Art Museum, Gift of Mrs. Eugene A. Perry.

# PROJECT 7–8: CHECKERBOARD SQUARE—PERSPECTIVE THE ITALIAN WAY

**MATERIALS**

- Drawing paper
- Pencil
- Black fine-line marker, black ballpoint, or colored pencils
- Rulers or yardsticks

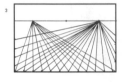

Draw very lightly in pencil so you can erase the guidelines after you have gone over the drawing in marker or ink. When you are doing vertical or horizontal lines, remember to keep the ruler parallel to the edges of the outside rectangle. It looks much more difficult and confusing than it is. Simply complete one step at a time, and you'll be amazed as your picture recedes into space.

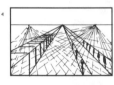

1. *Figure 1.* Measure along the *bottom* of the paper and mark every half inch to create a base line. Mark along the lower *sides* of the paper every half inch to halfway up.

2. *Figure 2.* Approximately one-quarter of the way from the top, lightly draw a horizontal line (the guideline). Place three points on it, one at the center, and one on each side between the center and the outside edge of the paper.

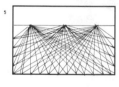

3. *Figure 3.* Use a ruler to draw from the left corner of the baseline to the guideline vanishing point on the opposite side of the page. Do this from each corner.

4. *Figure 4.* To get correct spacing for parallel *vertical* lines so they appear to recede into the distance, draw a line from the baseline and from a point (or points) on the side to the center vanishing point. Draw vertical lines from the lower line (bottom to vanishing point), to the upper line (side to vanishing point). These vertical lines could represent buildings, trees, or people.

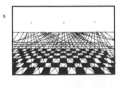

5. *Figure 5.* To make "checkerboard squares," draw horizontal lines through the guidelines from each side of the square, going through the Xs formed by the diagonal lines.

6. *Figure 6.* Lightly draw a horizon line near the center of the paper. Line up the ruler between the center vanishing point and the marked baseline. Draw from each intersection on the baseline to the horizon line, leaving the center unlined. Fill in every other square to look like a checkerboard.

7. *Figure 7.* Erase guidelines from top of the horizon line and erase the vanishing points and line. You may draw buildings on the horizon line and fill in the entire composition with people, buildings, trees, and checkerboard squares.

© 1992 by The Center for Applied Research in Education, Inc.

## PROJECT 7–9:  FISH FACE

### FOR THE TEACHER

Fantasy paintings existed long before the Renaissance, but one Renaissance painter in particular, Giuseppe Arcimboldo (1527–1593), is appreciated today and frequently included with the Surrealists. He was a court painter to several Austrian emperors; so undoubtedly created many competent, "normal" portraits. He is especially remembered, though, for the faces he created using such bizarre elements as fish, flowers, vegetables, or fruit to create facial characteristics. A particularly interesting series portrayed the seasons, using (for example) fall vegetables as the features of a face for autumn.

### MASTERPIECES OF RENAISSANCE FANTASY PAINTING

*Winter,* Giuseppe Arcimboldo, 1563, Kunsthistorisches Museum, Vienna

### PREPARATION

Students will benefit from seeing reproductions of the work done by Arcimboldo and other artists who created fantasy paintings. Have a class discussion about researching similar objects to get variety and authenticity. Suggest looking in an encyclopedia for a wide variety of birds, butterflies, fish, flowers, trees, etc. Magazines such as *National Geographic* and *Smithsonian* would be good reference sources. Discuss how almost any related objects could be used to fill in an outline of a face.

### FURTHER SUGGESTIONS

- Students could cut related objects from a magazine and paste them together to make a face. One problem with magazine collages is that they tend to all look alike. They are best used as a springboard for a drawing copied from the collage. Drawing pencil or colored pencils could allow this to be an ongoing project.

- As some Italian Renaissance artists did, use a face outline as a basis for a "fantasy landscape." The idea is to hide the face, with it being immediately visible only to very discerning viewers.

- A life-sized ceramic or papier-mâché bust based on Arcimboldo's work could be put together by a group, each creating a different fruit or vegetable, and putting them together in the form of a bust. (I recently saw one of these, glazed all white.)

# PROJECT 7–9:  FISH FACE

## MATERIALS

- Newsprint
- Watercolor or drawing paper
- Pencil
- Glue stick or rubber cement
- Watercolor or tempera paint

Decide on a theme to use for the elements of the face. These do not necessarily have to be fruit, fish, flowers, and so on, but could be such things as kitchen utensils, artists' supplies, carpentry tools, or any other items that have something in common. You can always change the scale later if need be.

1. On a piece of newsprint draw a human face. It can be your own face, or one drawn from imagination. The outline will change as you add materials to it, so don't spend much time on it.

2. Assuming you have chosen a theme, do a series of drawings of various related objects (such as fish, fruit, or vegetables). You can cut these up and move them around to fit within the face. It may be necessary to change the size of some. Glue them to the outline.

3. Look carefully at your drawing to see how you could emphasize some features or add something humorous. These collage paintings were not beautiful, so surely they were considered witty.

4. Tape the newsprint drawing collage to a window, and tape drawing paper over it. Transfer your design to drawing paper. Try to make the theme elements used on the face as realistic as possible.

5. With watercolor or colored pencil, paint the face. When you are done, stand back and look at it from a distance. You can emphasize some areas by adding darker values. It is also effective to use watercolor and colored pencil together.

**Summer, Giuseppe Arcimboldo, 1563 Kunsthistorisches Museum, Vienna**

**Winter, Giuseppe Arcimboldo, 1563 Kunsthistorisches Museum, Vienna**

## PROJECT 7-10: MASTERPIECE ADVERTISEMENT

### FOR THE TEACHER

Because paintings of the Renaissance are so well known, they are fair game for advertisers, who adapt them for their eye-catching familiarity. Since Leonardo painted his Mona Lisa, how many artists have made versions of it, and how many birthday cards and ads have used this image through the years?

### PREPARATION

Have students bring in ads that contain references to established works of art. Suggest they consider what they would like to advertise (rule out anything related to cigarettes or alcohol as against school regulations). Have them come up with slogans, etc. To encourage creativity, have them list words that the product reminds them of. Then have them try to find a well-known artwork that relates, even remotely, to the product.

This ad should contain both lettering and an illustration. Now that do-it-yourself copy centers are available in most cities, students might be able to do a paste-up by combining letters from an ad with an image. This could then be hand copied with tracing paper, or a hand-colored photocopied ad could be the final product.

### FURTHER SUGGESTIONS

- Almost daily one finds cartoons that are plays on famous paintings. If students prefer to do a cartoon rather than an ad, it could be an acceptable substitute. As a starting point, suggest they select one painting that appeals to them, then try every way they can think of to make it funny. For example, in a parody on Rembrandt's *Anatomy Lesson of Dr. Tulp*, a satirist has shown Dr. Tulp holding a hammer instead of a scalpel. Substituting one object in the picture could make an amusing change.
- Suggest they do a take-off on a famous work of Renaissance art and design either a dress or shirt. Point out to them how often fabric designers refer to the past for inspiration. Recently a very elegant store had an ad for matching shoes and purse with a famous artwork design (these sold for almost more than the artwork originally sold for).

# PROJECT 7–10:  MASTERPIECE ADVERTISEMENT

## MATERIALS

- Drawing paper
- Colored pencil, acrylic, or watercolor
- Magazines

Drawing after
*Arrangement in Gray and Black No. 1*
James Abbott McNeill Whistler, Louvre.

When your ad is finished, anyone should be able to look at it and have a pretty good idea which famous painting was your inspiration.

1. Select a product to advertise. Some suggestions are cars, food, soft drinks, shoes, clothes, electrical appliances, album from a musical group, jeans, backpacks, cameras, musical instruments, furniture, candy or other snack food, and so on. Once you have something in mind, begin looking at famous works of art.

2. When you have chosen a work of art, decide how you can make an ad of it. You may be able to substitute your product for one feature in the artwork, or you may have the main figure in the artwork holding your product.

3. To come up with a slogan, write a list of words that either your artwork or your product make you think of. Try combining these words in various ways. If you simply cannot think of words that relate to the artwork, then let the artwork demonstrate the product.

4. This is one time when photocopying a work of art would be permissible. You can add pressure-sensitive or photocopied letters. Tape the photocopied work onto a window, and trace it onto a piece of drawing paper. It does not have to be large, as it is made to go into a magazine.

5. Some suggested media for finishing the artwork are:
   a. Acrylic paint
   b. Fadeless paper cut out and glued, outlined with black fine-line marker
   c. Watercolor paint
   d. Colored pencil (for an intense color, dip in turpentine)
   e. Ink and wash

6. It isn't necessary to color in the entire artwork. An area left white (an interesting "negative" shape) might make the ad more eye-catching.

Drawing after *David,*
Andrea del Castagno,
National Gallery of Art.

Drawing after *American Gothic,*
Grant Wood,
Art Institute of Chicago.

Drawing after *Mona Lisa,*
Leonardo da Vinci, Louvre, Paris.

Drawing after *Mt. Fuji and Great Waves,*
Hokusai, Museum of Fine Arts, Boston.

# BAROQUE

# BAROQUE
## TIME LINE

| A.D. 1600 | 1625 | 1650 | 1675 | 1700 | 1725 | 1750 | 1775 |
|---|---|---|---|---|---|---|---|

Baroque
1590–1750

Rembrandt's
Night Watch
1642

Gallileo
1633

Cervantes
Don Quixote
1605–1615

The Jester
Judith Leyster

San Carlo Allo
Quatro Fontana

East Facade of
Louvre, 1667

Versailles Palace
1669–1685

Ecstasy of St. Theresa
Bernini, 1645–1652

Velásquez'
Las Meninas
1656

Frans Hals' The Jolly Toper, 1627

Rococo, 1700–1800

St. Paul's Cathedral
Christopher Wren

Church of Invalides,
Paris, 1680–1691

Gulliver's Travels
1726

Houdon. Voltaire
(Candide, 1759)

| **Africa** | | | | | | | |

Kingdom of Asante, 1600

Kingdom of Dahomey, 1600–1900

| **Americas** | | | | | | | |

Pilgrims in Jamestown
1607

Harvard founded
1636

Quakers settled
1668

American
Revolution
begins 1775

| **Asia** | | | | | | | |

Qing (Ching) Dynasty
1644–1911

Tokugawa Shoguns
Japan, 1603–1868

| **Europe** | | | | | | | |

King James Bible
1611

Royal Academy of Paris
1648

Dutch East India Co. 1602

Watt's Steam
Engine 1769

| **Near East** | | | | | | | |

Taj Mahal
Agra, India c. 1635

| **Other** | | | | | | | |

## Unit 1:   BAROQUE (1590 TO 1750)

**OVERVIEW OF THE VISUAL ARTS**

The Baroque period had several things in common with the Renaissance. The church, government, and aristocracy continued to employ artists, and both cultures created much the same types of artwork. There was a demand for large sculptures, fountains, churches, decorations for palaces, and portraiture. The Baroque even had its own giants such as Caravaggio, Bernini, Rembrandt, Velásquez, and Rubens. Local traditions, the wishes of the patrons, and the official religion and wealth of the country led to major differences in the work done in different regions. For example, in largely Catholic countries, the shapes of the churches themselves, the dramatic uses of light, and religious paintings and sculpture were important means of teaching the Christian religion. In Protestant countries, all religious images were destroyed, and although the buildings were left intact, the interiors were whitewashed and stark.

Design characteristics were reminiscent of classical Rome, but lacked restraint. The painting, sculpture, and architecture was characterized by swirling, lively composition, rather than the formal geometry of the Renaissance. The compositions relied greatly on light and shadow for dramatic impact and were filled with intense colors and texture and rich brush work.

"Rococo" (1700–1800) was a term applied to the decorative arts popular in the time of Louis XV of France. This term has also become a derogatory reference to excessive decoration. Rococo art typically was asymmetrical, with the use of S-curves and C-scrolls, ribbons, and naturalistic designs from plants, rocks, shells and flowers.

**PAINTING**

Each country had its own unique version of Baroque painting, largely influenced by the region's political and economic situation. Subject matter generally continued to be figure paintings based on mythology, the classics, and the Bible. The designs often appeared to be in dynamic motion, with elements placed around the edges, or diagonally, rather than parallel to the picture plane.

Because of the differences in various countries, a brief description of each region's artwork and its best-known practitioners is given here.

**Italy.** The church, as chief patron of the arts, commissioned artists to decorate churches and palaces. Religious paintings were often painted in a "genre" manner, with ordinary people in contemporary clothing. Ceiling paintings contained swirling clouds that appeared to open the way to heaven. The tenebrism (use of dark and light) of Michelangelo Amerighi da Caravaggio (1569–1609) was to influence painters such as Rembrandt, Velásquez, and de La Tour, who adopted and refined his dramatic use of shadow and light.

**Holland.** The rise of middle-class merchants and tradesmen, and their pride in owning paintings led to a real explosion of genre art. The formal group portrait, paintings of interiors, moral lessons, the still life, landscapes, and church interiors were some of the specialized subjects that were so admired by the Dutch. Rembrandt van Rijn (1606–1669) was the only Dutch artist who continued to create religious compositions.

**Flanders.** The patrons of Flemish artist Peter Paul Rubens (1577–1640) were the aristocracy, the church, and the middle-class burghers of Antwerp. His emotional paintings, rich colors, and spiraling compositions made him very well known. His "school," in which many of his students worked on his paintings, strongly influenced Flemish Baroque painters. His best-known student, Anthony Van Dyck (1599–1641), became one of the major court painters in England.

**France.** The French court, with its excesses, encouraged a type of romantic painting that portrayed its interest in leisure activities and plays. Elegantly dressed figures were shown in garden settings. Themes of love, romance, and fantasy dominated French paintings.

**Spain.** Diego Velásquez (1599–1660), a court painter, also painted ordinary workmen with great sympathy. He, and other Spanish painters such as Francisco de Zurbaran (1598–1662) and José de Ribera (1588–1656), showed an interest in the use of light and shade such as that used by Caravaggio, Rembrandt, and Rubens.

## MASTERPIECES OF PAINTING

*Judith with the Head of Holofernes,* c. 1625, Artemisia Gentileschi, Detroit Institute of Art

*The Night Watch,* Rembrandt van Rijn, 1642, Rijksmuseum, Amsterdam

*Calling of Saint Matthew,* Caravaggio, c. 1599–1600, S. Luigi dei Francesi, Rome

*Allegory of the Art of Painting,* Jan Vermeer, c. 1670–1675, Kunsthistorisches Museum, Vienna

*View of Haarlem,* Jacob van Ruisdael, c. 1670, Mauritshuis, The Hague

*The World Upside Down,* Jan Steen, c. 1663, Kunsthistorisches Museum, Vienna

*Still Life,* Willem Claesz Heda, c. 1648, Fine Arts Museum of San Francisco

*Banquet of the Officers of the Saint George Guard Company,* Frans Hals, 1616, Frans Hals Museum, Haarlem

*Boy with Flute,* Judith Leyster, 1630, National Museum, Stockholm

*Garden of Love,* Peter Paul Rubens, c. 1638, Prado Museum, Madrid

*Charles I in Hunting Dress,* Anthony Van Dyck, 1635, Louvre, Paris

*Marie Antoinette and Her Children,* Elizabeth Vigeé-Lebrun, 1788, Museé National du Chateau de Versailles

*Holy Family on the Steps,* Nicolas Poussin, 1648, National Gallery of Art, Washington, D.C.

*A Pilgrimage to Cythera,* Jean-Antoine Watteau, 1717, Louvre, Paris

*Newborn,* Georges de la Tour, 1630, Musée des Beaux-Arts, Rennes, France

*Las Meninas,* Diego Velásquez, 1656, Prado Museum, Madrid

*Triumph of Bacchus,* Diego Velásquez, c. 1628, Prado Museum, Madrid

## SCULPTURE

Baroque sculpture is almost synonymous with Gianlorenzo Bernini (1598–1680). Rome is filled with his work, ranging from various fountains to the many pieces commissioned for the interior and exterior of St. Peter's. Many that bear his name were actually executed by the 39 sculptors who worked under his supervision on the interior of St. Peter's. Most Baroque sculpture is similar to the paintings, with lively movement and light used dramatically to affect the emotions.

## MASTERPIECES OF BAROQUE SCULPTURE

*David,* Gianlorenzo Bernini, 1623, Galleria Borghese, Rome

*Apollo and Daphne,* Gianlorenzo Bernini, 1622–1624, Galleria Borghese, Rome

*Ecstasy of Saint Theresa,* Gianlorenzo Bernini, 1645–1652, Sta. Maria della Vittoria, Rome

## ARCHITECTURE

Baroque church architecture drew on classical forms such as columns, entablatures, and pediments, but combined these with the arch and dome to create an entirely new form. The size and scale were grand and demonstrated the power of the Catholic church. In some of the Italian churches, the undulating facade, the second-story porch, exterior pilasters, and the use of ovals and elliptical forms were a dramatic departure from the balanced geometry of the Renaissance. After the development of the Baroque architectural form, it was used for centuries in public architecture.

## MASTERPIECES OF BAROQUE ARCHITECTURE

*Sant'Agnese in Piazza Navona,* Francesco Borromini, 1653–1666, Rome

*S. Carlo allo Quatro Fontane,* Francesco Borromini, 1665–1667, Rome

*Colonnade of St. Peter's,* Gianlorenzo Bernini, 1656, Rome

*Whitehall Palace,* Inigo Jones, 1619–1622, London

*St. Paul's Cathedral,* Christopher Wren, 1675–1710, London

*Church of the Invalides,* Jules Hardouin-Mansart, 1676–1706, Paris

*Palace of Versailles,* Jules Hardouin-Mansart and Charles LeBrun, 1669–1685, Paris

*East Facade of the Louvre,* Claude Perrault, 1667–1670, Paris

*Karlskirche,* Johann Bernhard Fischer von Erlach, 1716–1737, Vienna

*Benedictine Abbey,* Jakob Prandtauer, 1702, Melk, Austria

# PROJECT 8-1: ROYAL PORTRAIT

**FOR THE TEACHER**

Court painters such as Peter Paul Rubens and Diego Velásquez not only were hired to paint royalty and members of the aristocracy, but also acted as ambassadors between the courts of Europe. Alliances were formed through intermarriage of royalty throughout Europe. It seemed natural that the painter, who had access to various courts, should act at times as a go-between. Portraits and miniatures of royalty were often used for selecting prospective royal brides and bridegrooms.

Photo 8-1. *Henry the IV Receiving the Portrait of Maria de Medici*, P. P. Rubens, 1622–1625, 156¼ × 117 inches, oil on canvas, The Louvre, Paris, Art Resource, NY.

## MASTERPIECES OF ROYAL PORTRAITURE

> *Portrait of Charles I in Hunting Dress,* Anthony Van Dyck, 1635, Louvre, Paris
>
> *Henry the IV Receiving the Portrait of Maria de Medici,* Peter Paul Rubens, 1621–1625, Louvre, Paris
>
> *The Princesse de Polignac,* Elizabeth Vigeé-Lebrun, The National Trust, Waddesdon Manor, England

## PREPARATION

Playing cards for sale in some European countries today have miniature paintings of their royalty. The kings, queens, and jacks of modern playing cards probably stem from actual miniatures. Ask students to bring in old playing cards so they can see the many ways artists decorate face cards.

## FURTHER SUGGESTIONS

- Have students bring in rich fabrics (clothing) such as velvet, satin, shiny nylon, sequined fabric, or sheer fabrics. The people in Baroque paintings were often dressed in clothing of these materials. Each student can make a personal still life by placing one or two items on a piece of fabric. A very small colored drawing or painting will teach them how folds, highlights, and shadows are shown through values of one color and give them an appreciation of the virtuosity of Baroque painters.
- Challenge students to make a design based on the patterns found on the kings, queens, and jacks in playing cards. If several different decks of cards are available, this should offer plenty of variety. They could design a new ace or joker or make a design for the backs of the cards.

# PROJECT 8–1:  ROYAL PORTRAIT

## MATERIALS

- Unlined 3 × 5-inch cards
- Colored pencils
- Tracing paper
- Deck of cards
- Rulers
- Wallet-sized portraits

During the Baroque period, artists were often matchmakers, painting portraits of royal families, and especially the young unmarried princes and princesses. These portraits were taken to prospective brides and bridegrooms, often by the painter.

1. Use a small piece of tracing paper to trace your own yearbook photo (or that of a friend). Trace over the back of the drawing with pencil.

2. On an index card or 3 × 5-inch white posterboard, draw a line ½ inch around the outside edge as a border. Place the drawing of the face near the top center, and trace it onto the card. You can now make a simple portrait by adding fanciful Baroque clothing. If you prefer, you can make a "playing card" by drawing the same face on the bottom of the card.

3. With pencil, lightly complete the drawing. Now you can draw crowns, patterns, and so on to complete your royal portrait.

4. With colored pencil, fill in the faces and designs. It is all right to leave some of the white showing if you have been able to keep from smearing it, but you may need to fill in the background also. You can make a Baroque gold frame around the outside by using two or three shades of yellow and gold.

5. When you finish, if you prefer to have a miniature portrait, cut the drawing in an oval shape (make an oval pattern first, which you can trace around and cut out). Use rubber cement to mount the oval on black paper or board.

© 1992 by The Center for Applied Research in Education, Inc.

## PROJECT 8–2: **THE BREAKFAST PIECE**

**FOR THE TEACHER**

**Slide # 18:** *Still Life 1643.* Because of the Dutch passion for owning paintings, Dutch artists became specialists in doing one subject, such as cows, church interiors, portraits, ice-skating scenes, ships, tavern interiors, and landscapes. One such speciality was the "breakfast piece." It often had only snack foods such as bread, wine, shellfish, and cheeses and also was an opportunity for the artist to show the beauty of a glowing white cloth, lovely crystal, or gleaming silver.

What was visible in the picture was only partially what the painting represented. For all their appreciation of the good life and beautiful things, the Dutch were stern moralists. The half-eaten bread, a half-peeled lemon, almonds, the spilled wine or broken glass, an insect on the table, a butterfly—all had meanings to the people of that

Photo 8-2. *Still Life,* Lodewijck Susi, 1619, 34.9 × 46.5 cm, oil on panel, The Saint Louis Art Museum.

time. The breakfast piece demonstrated that life lasted but a moment, that it could be interrupted at any time. The mortality of humankind was represented by the obscure (to us) symbolism.

Another type of painting that showed mortality was the flower picture. The Dutch went through a period of "tulip-mania," when they were enchanted with this new flower. Their flower paintings combined tulips with other flowers of all types (regardless of season), insects, butterflies, and snails, all of which were symbols of mortality included, perhaps, to "mar" such perfection a little.

## MASTERPIECES OF DUTCH STILL LIFE

*Still Life,* Pieter Claesz, 1643, St. Louis Art Museum

*Still Life,* Willem Claesz Heda, 1634, Boymans-van Beuningen Museum, Rotterdam

*Flowers,* Balthasar van der Ast, 1622, St. Louis Art Museum

## PREPARATION

Suggest that students bring in garden catalogs, or photocopy pictures of flowers from magazines or encyclopedias. They can work from photographs or bring in real items such as lemons, French bread, wine glasses, and a tablecloth. Use a photo flood light or lamp to add light to the still life from one side.

## FURTHER SUGGESTIONS

- Discuss modern symbolism. Students can talk about how designs on T-shirts advertise something about the person wearing them, or how corporate logos symbolize something about a company.
- If fresh flowers are available, students could make outsized paintings of a single flower, such as those made by Georgia O'Keeffe.

## PROJECT 8–2: **THE BREAKFAST PIECE**

**MATERIALS**

- Drawing paper
- Tempera paint or colored pencil
- Still life materials

You will have to use your imagination, as the Dutch artists did, to add symbols to represent death. Most "breakfast paintings" depicted real food, but also showed a broken glass, an insect on the glass, a wormy apple, mice nibbling on almonds, or flies on the bread, to show that the person had "left the table" (died). You may wish to make up your own symbols. Add some little "creatures" to the food for a little humor.

If you choose to do a Dutch flower painting instead, you could combine flowers from all seasons, but be sure to include insects, snails, butterflies. These little details also symbolized mortality. It is interesting that such pretty paintings represented such depressing ideas.

1. Because the Dutch paintings were so realistic in appearance, you should work from real food, glasses, or serving pieces. Perhaps you can find pictures in magazines that would also allow you to work realistically.

2. This still life should be carefully composed, with a central grouping on a table, and open space behind. Have some areas quite light (such as bread or a lemon) and some quite dark, for contrast.

3. To paint glass, you have to paint exactly what you see—not what you "know" is there. Show every reflection (perhaps even your own) and every variation of color in the glass. The same technique is used for painting metal such as copper or silver. Reflections are the only way to show the texture and quality.

4. Many of the Dutch paintings used soft, related colors that had slight variations. If you use undiluted tempera paint, it will be a harsh color. Instead, "gray" the colors slightly by adding a complementary color. (Add a touch of red to green, for example, then add white to it, to make a soft shade of green. Add yellow to that combination for another variation of green.)

5. Pay careful attention to the effects of lighting. The Dutch often used side lighting, carefully rendering light and shadow.

# PROJECT 8-3: DUTCH TILE TOWN

## FOR THE TEACHER

The new art patrons of the north, the burghers of Holland, were very proud of their houses. The houses come right to the sidewalk, or sometimes had a tiny garden in front, with a larger, private courtyard in back of the house. People are usually included in the paintings to give meaning to these house portraits.

## MASTERPIECES

*View of Delft,* Jan Vermeer, c. 1662, Mauritshuis, The Hague

*Street in Delft,* Jan Vermeer, c. 1660, Rijksmuseum, Amsterdam

*A Country Cottage,* Pieter de Hooch, c. 1665, Rijksmuseum, Amsterdam

*View of the Martelaarsgracht in Amsterdam,* Jan Van Der Heyden, 1637, Rijksmuseum, Amsterdam

*Haarlem,* Gerrit Berckheyde, 1638, Rijksmuseum, Amsterdam

## PREPARATION

Discuss architectural building materials and techniques. Brick and stone were common building materials in the Netherlands. Most houses had red tile roofs and shutters on the windows.

## FURTHER SUGGESTIONS

- Roll clay approximately ¼-inch thick, and make miniature pins in the shapes of houses.
- Make papier-mâché houses by covering corrugated cardboard or matboard with paper towels dipped in wallpaper (or Pritt™) paste. Add details with string, paper twine, or screenwire, using cardboard chips for tile roofs.

## PROJECT 8–3: **DUTCH TILE TOWN**

**MATERIALS**

- Clay
- Rolling pin or 1-inch dowel
- Two battens, $1/4 \times 1^1/4 \times 12$ inches
- Knife
- Burlap or newsprint

Dutch townhouses were sometimes narrow three- or four-story homes, sharing a wall with the house next to them. The Baroque details such as stepped roofs, a wheel on top of the chimney with a stork nest, brick facades, and shutters on the exterior give them charm.

1. Make several thumbnail sketches of the shape of your house and details of the exterior. Cut a tagboard pattern.

2. Wedge the clay to remove air bubbles. Either knead it on the table, or slap it firmly between your hands for 10 to 15 minutes. Place the ball of clay on a piece of burlap or canvas, between two parallel sticks. Flatten the ball with a rolling pin, using the sticks as "tracks" to make an even slap $1/4$- to $3/8$-inch thick.

3. Place the piece of tagboard on top of the clay, and cut around it with a knife. Use the tip of the knife for details such as brick. Roll thin pieces of clay to add such details as window and door frames, people leaning out windows, or animals. Attach these to the tile with slip (clay that has been diluted with water and mixed to the thickness of cream).

4. When all the details have been added, place a dampened paper towel on the tile and keep it loosely covered with plastic. Tiles will dry from the outside inward, and unless they are dried slowly, they will curl up on the edges. Sometimes you can leave them uncovered for an hour or so, but keep lightly dampened towels around the edges so the center can dry. Ideally, allow several days for them to dry so they will be flat.

5. With a pencil, make a hole in the top for hanging. The hole will shrink after drying, so make sure it is large enough.

6. When the tiles are leather hard, you can apply underglazes. Cover with a clear glaze and fire.

# PROJECT 8–4: THE COMMEMORATIVE PORTRAIT

## FOR THE TEACHER

**Slide # 19: *The Night Watch* (The Company of Captain Frans Banning Cocq).** In the Baroque period there were many portrait artists. Well-to-do Dutch burghers and members of guilds often commissioned well-known artists to paint a commemorative group portrait. Each member of the group would pay equally for his or her share of the portrait. The "line-'em-up-and-grin" paintings (which students easily relate to yearbook group photos) gave everyone in the portrait equal importance.

Rembrandt broke with this tradition when he painted *The Company of Captain Frans Banning Cocq.* He grouped the company as if they were preparing for a parade or battle. Because of heavy varnish, soot, and oxidation of the paint, the painting appeared for years much darker than Rembrandt intended and was called *The Night Watch.* When cleaned after World War II, it appeared to be a daylight scene, though it did have dark shadows and warm highlights that were typical of Rembrandt's use of chiaroscuro (darks and lights).

## MASTERPIECES OF DUTCH GROUP PORTRAITURE

*The Syndics of the Drapers' Guild,* Rembrandt van Rijn, 1662, Rijksmuseum, Amsterdam

*The Anatomy Lesson of Dr. Tulp,* Rembrandt van Rijn, 1632, Rijksmuseum, Amsterdam

*The Women Regents of the Old Men's Almshouse,* Frans Hals, c. 1664, Frans Hals Museum, Haarlem

*Banquet of the Officers of the Saint George Guard Company,* Frans Hals, 1616, Frans Hals Museum, Haarlem

*Las Meninas,* Diego Velásquez, 1656, Prado Museum, Madrid

## PREPARATION

Discuss types of groups. Students have little trouble relating to group portraits such as those of musicians on album covers, or yearbook photos of the jazz band, so this portrait could be almost any group of that type and can include props that help it "hang together."

This will take a little effort on the part of the teacher (or an aide) to collect everyone's yearbook photo and print them (several at a time) on the copy machine. Try to schedule this as soon as the yearbook photos come out, and offer extra credit for turning it in on the day requested. Photocopying works with both color and black and white photos. You can print the smallest version, or the wallet size, reducing or enlarging as you wish. I have even printed an entire page of school photos of one student, for a variation on the project (a group portrait using the same face in many different poses and costumes).

When the collages are completed, you may wish to copy them on the machine again so the students can color them with pencils. This step is not a necessity. you can reduce the faces so each student receives a page that has all the students' portraits on it. Each student should have at least seven faces to use in a group portrait.

This could also be done with cut-outs of heads from a magazine, pasted onto a sheet for copying.

**FURTHER SUGGESTIONS**

- Have small group portraits of four or five students in costume or with props. These could be photographed with a Polaroid or a regular 35mm camera. As a further extension of this project, students could draw from these photographs.

**Photocopies of yearbook photos were pasted and combined with a colored pencil drawing in this "commemorative portrait."**

# PROJECT 8–4:  THE COMMEMORATIVE PORTRAIT

**MATERIALS**

- Wallet-size photographs of everyone in class
- Copy machine copies of these photos
- White drawing paper
- Colored pencil
- Rubber cement

Your commemorative group portrait needs to have a theme. Rembrandt's *Night Watch* was painted as if the men were preparing for a parade. Although they were in similar clothes, the colors varied, and one was holding a flag. Rembrandt's *Anatomy Lesson of Dr. Tulp* was a group portrait of physicians clustered around a cadaver.

Your group could be part of a circus company, a musical group (for an album cover), a group of old women, as in Frans Hals's *The Women Regents of the Old Men's Almshouse,* or a ballet troupe—anything your imagination can come up with.

1. Cut out the heads you will use. Trim them very closely. Move them around on the page. Decide what kind of setting you will use, what they will be wearing, and any props that would add to the setting.

2. Use rubber cement to glue the portrait heads in place. With pencil, draw clothing, and surroundings for your group portrait. When the collage is completed in black and white, you might wish to make a new copy on a copy machine. (Some machines are capable of making enlargements if you prefer.) This step is not absolutely necessary.

3. Use colored pencil to color some areas. Don't forget to repeat color at times. For intense colors, you can paint on a small amount of mineral spirits and color directly into it. Blend closely related colors together to add to the richness of the portrait. It isn't necessary to fill it in totally with color.

4. When your picture is finished, place it in a mat and give it an interesting "group" title.

© 1992 by The Center for Applied Research in Education, Inc.

# PROJECT 8–5: OLD MASTER DRAWINGS

### FOR THE TEACHER

Caravaggio and Rembrandt both influenced painting for generations because of their dramatic use of light and shadow. Caravaggio's tenebrism placed much of the composition in shadow, while a shaft of light coming in from one side cast intense light on a few figures. Rembrandt's chiaroscuro used light and shadow to call attention to the center of interest and create dramatic effects.

Photo 8-3. Rembrandt Harmensz. van Rijn, Dutch, 1606–1669, Noah's Ark, reed pen and brown ink, with brush and brown wash, heightened with traces of white gouache, on buff laid paper, c. 1660, 19.9 × 24.4 cm, Clarence Buckingham Collection, 1953.36. © 1992 The Art Institute of Chicago, All Rights Reserved.

**MASTERPIECES OF BAROQUE LANDSCAPES**

> *Three Trees,* 1643, Rembrandt van Rijn, The Metropolitan Museum of Art, New York
>
> *The Omval,* 1645, Rembrandt van Rijn, Bibliotheque National, Paris

**PREPARATION**

Before making an actual composition, students need to experiment with making ink washes. "Found" drawing instruments such as cotton swabs or sharp sticks make interesting lines. Steel-tipped pens are always good. Show students how to create texture with a pen by cross-hatching, stippling, or using parallel lines. Dutch landscape artists such as Rembrandt used "scribble" marks to make foliage.

**FURTHER SUGGESTIONS**

- Have students draw several trees off in the distance (or from a photo), making only scribble marks in ink to show leaves. They will learn that to show value differences, they simply need to make the scribbles more dense, or make them over and over in the same place.

- Have students make their own bamboo drawing pens by using an X-acto® knife to make a point on one side (use a purchased one as a guide). They could also make quill pens from turkey feathers (feathers can be purchased from hobby stores). They will be pleasantly surprised at the variations in their lines when they draw with instruments that have to be repeatedly dipped in ink.

*Safety Note: These should be cut when placed on a surface rather than held in the hand for carving.*

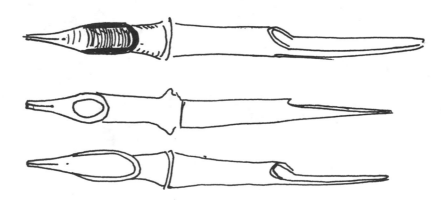

## PROJECT 8–5: OLD MASTER DRAWINGS

**MATERIALS**

- Brown ink
- Ink pens
- Newsprint
- Brushes
- Drawing paper

1. Before beginning an actual composition, experiment with different ways of making marks.

   **a.** Make an ink wash with a brush with undiluted ink.

   **b.** Dilute the ink and make a wash. Blot it with paper towels, or allow it to dry and add more ink to it.

   **c.** Draw into the ink while it is wet; the line you make will spread.

   **d.** Wait until the ink wash dries, and draw into it.

   **e.** Do cross-hatching with a pen.

   **f.** Make marks with various kinds of instruments such as a cotton swab, toothpick, stick, bamboo pen, or quill pen (a bird feather that you have sharpened).

   **g.** Draw on top of an ink wash with graphite pencil.

2. Select a subject such as a still life, portrait, a figure drawing, city-scape, or land-scape. It may be easier to make something realistic rather than abstract.

3. Briefly make a thumbnail sketch, envisioning which parts of it could be made very dark and which parts should be left entirely white. Enlarge this sketch on drawing paper.

4. Use a brush to make an ink wash. Start out with a light wash, and make it darker if needed. It is far easier to add ink than to take it away. Make a sincere effort to make use of "chiaroscuro" (dark and light areas) as the old masters did. Even if from 10 feet away you cannot tell what your subject is, the areas of light and dark can make an effective composition.

5. You may choose to use only ink wash on many areas. With a pen or other marking instrument, draw details into the ink or into areas that did not have ink on them.

    a       b       c       d       e       f       g

## PROJECT 8-6:  **CITY-SCAPE A LA CANALETTO**

**FOR THE TEACHER**

**Slide # 20:** *View of the Ducal Palace of Venice and Plaza San Marco.*
Giovanni Antonio Canal (called Canaletto) (1697–1768) was an artist who specialized
in "town-scapes" of Venice. These paintings were very popular and in great demand
throughout Europe, especially in England. Canaletto also made several painting trips
to England and was elected a member of the Royal Academy in 1763. He lived there for
four years. He was one of the first artists to use the "camera obscura" (a box-like
device with mirrors) that aided him in determining proper perspective. Because he had
a nephew (Bernardo Bellotto) who also went by the name of Canaletto, and a large
workshop that helped produce his paintings, the number of "Canalettos" is incredible
and of varying quality.

The paintings showed the same views for which Venice is famous today, as well as
its little known areas. His luminous, broad sweeps of sky and water included minutely
detailed buildings, festivals, and people.

## MASTERPIECES

*Stonemason's Yard,* Giovanni Antonio Canaletto, National Gallery, London

*Feast of the Ascension in Venice,* Giovanni Antonio Canaletto, Crespi Collection, Milan

## PREPARATION

Discuss with the class what a city-scape should include. They may choose their own town, but they could also select a city such as San Francisco. Demonstrate how to mix watercolor wash in the lid of the box. Then show them how to paint with different pieces of cardboard for varied effects. Although they may prefer to cut their own cardboard, it will help if you have a little box of small pieces (approximately $1 \times 3$ inches). They should vary in thickness from matboard to corrugated cardboard, with some of the edges jagged.

## FURTHER SUGGESTIONS

- These city-scapes can be made three-diminsional by cutting out the buildings, re-grouping them, and gluing a small accordion-fold of paper on the back of each that will make them stand out when glued to a new base.

- Any subject is suitable for cardboard painting, and students might enjoy trying to paint a still life or figure drawing using a cardboard "brush." It will be more challenging than working with a brush, but can give them an idea of planes. They quickly make discoveries that it would not have occurred to you to demonstrate.

# PROJECT 8–6: CITY-SCAPE A LA CANALETTO

**MATERIALS**

- Drawing or watercolor paper
- Watercolors
- Brushes
- Cardboard (various types)
- Water

1. Add water to each color in the box to soften it slightly. With the brush, carry color to the lid, where you can mix it with a small amount of water.

2. Use the brush only for mixing color. Dip the end of the cardboard into the paint. Hold the cardboard upright, and apply paint with the cardboard bottom edge. The cardboard will get soggy eventually. Just throw it away and get another.

3. To make the city-scape, you needn't even draw it in advance. To make water, paint horizontal strokes of various "sea" colors, blue, violet, green, or mixtures of all of them. Leave some white showing. The water is usually slightly darker than the sky. When making sky, simply leave areas white for clouds.

4. Venetian buildings were light in color. First make various shapes of buildings, allow them to dry slightly, then use small cardboard "brushes" to make darker windows and details.

5. To paint people and other details, use a narrow piece of cardboard or the tip of a brush.

# ROMANTICISM, REALISM, AND IMPRESSIONISM

# ROMANTICISM, REALISM, AND IMPRESSIONISM
## TIME LINE

| 1750 | 1775 | 1800 | 1825 | 1850 | 1875 | 1900 | 1925 |
|------|------|------|------|------|------|------|------|

Neoclassicism
1770–1820

Romanticism
1800–1850

Realism
1850–1880

Art Nouveau
1880–1910

Postimpressionism
1886–1920

Impressionism
1870–1905

Manet
1866

Van Gogh, 1899

Degas

Symbolism

Toulouse-Lautrec
1899

Jefferson's
Monticello 1770–1782

Fauvism
1905–1907

The Opera House
1861–1874

The Scream
Munch, 1895

Pompeii and Herculaneum
discovered, 1745

Eiffel Tower

Expressionism
1890

| | | | | | | | |
|---|---|---|---|---|---|---|---|
| **Africa** <br><br> See Chapter 5 | | | | | | | |
| **Americas** <br><br> Revolutionary War <br> 1775 | | Louisiana Purchase <br> 1803 <br><br> Simón Bolivar <br> 1822 | Oregon Trail <br> opens, 1842 | Civil War, USA <br> 1861–1865 | Telephone <br> patented, 1876 <br><br> Light bulb, 1879 | Sullivan's <br> Skyscraper <br> 1890–1891 | |
| **Asia** | | Edo <br> Period | | | Boxer Rebellion <br> 1899–1900 | | |
| **Europe** <br> French Revolution <br> begins 1789 | 1890 <br> Paine, The <br> Rights of Man | Electricity <br> 1800 <br><br> Napoleon's <br> Waterloo, 1815 | Daguerrotype <br> 1839 | Queen Victoria <br> Crowned <br> 1837 | | | |
| **Near East** <br><br> See Chapter 2. | | | | | | | |
| **Other** | | | | | Schliemann <br> excavates <br> at Troy <br> 1872 | | |

© 1992 by The Center for Applied Research in Education, Inc.

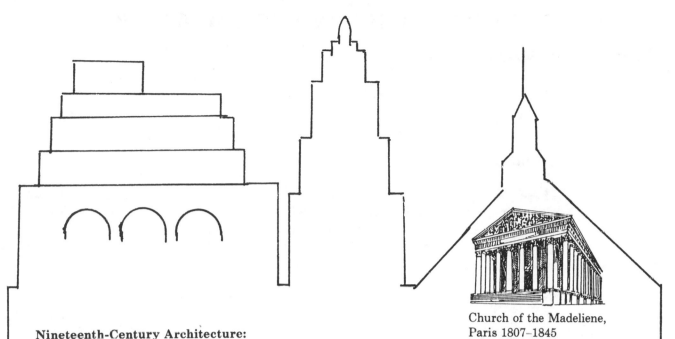

**Nineteenth-Century Architecture:**

Introduction of elevator
Skyscraper
Metal "skeletons" with glass or concrete walls
Art Nouveau
Cast iron buildings
Structural steel
Prefabricated structural elements
Large exhibition halls and office buildings
Neoclassicism
Gothic Revival
Neobaroque
Victorian
Concrete and metal used together

Church of the Madeliene,
Paris 1807–1845
Alexander-Pierre Vignon

The Opera, Paris, 1874
Charles Garnier

Carson Pirie, Scott Bldg. Chicago, 1899
Louis Sullivan

Crystal Palace
1850–1851

Brighton Pavilion
1815

Church of Sagrada Familia,
Barcelona 1883–1926

Eiffel tower
1889

# 19TH CENTURY ARCHITECTURE

# Unit 1: NEOCLASSICISM, ROMANTICISM, AND REALISM (1770 TO 1880)

## OVERVIEW OF THE VISUAL ARTS

These "isms" cover an exciting period when artists were experimenting with new techniques in painting and sculpture. Labels such as Neoclassicism, Romanticism, Realism, Impressionism, and Postimpressionism were applied to the work of artists of the time. The groups often overlapped, and some long-lived artists (such as Monet) produced art during several of these periods.

**Neoclassicism (c. 1770–1820).** The Neoclassical revival of the design principles of ancient Greece and Rome was a reaction against the excesses of Baroque and Rococo. It affected architecture and painting. Painters returned to subjects such as history and mythology.

**Romanticism (1800–1850).** Romanticists were committed to personal interpretation and vision and rejected the principles of Neoclassicism. Whether it was French artists such as Eugene Delacroix (1798–1863) and Theodore Gericault (1791–1834) painting heroic and patriotic subjects of the Revolution, or Spaniard Francisco Goya (1746–1828) painting the horrors of war, the artists were commenting through their art on the life around them. British artists, such as Joseph Mallord William Turner (1775–1851) and John Constable (1776–1837), painted landscapes, though with quite different interpretations.

**Realism (c. 1850–1880).** Realists did not use the bright colors of the Romanticists, but tried to use colors as they occurred in nature. They were opposed to portraying history, mythology, or religious art. They preferred to portray genre (everyday) scenes and landscape. Well-known realists were Jean Francois Millet (1814–1875), Jean Baptiste Camille Corot (1796–1875), Honoré Daumier (1808–1879), and Americans Winslow Homer (1836–1910), and Thomas Eakins (1844–1916).

## PAINTING

Neoclassical paintings reflected a return to the rules of composition and design of the Greeks and Romans. In addition to showing restraint and order, the paintings often included classical columns or were placed in architectural settings. They were often linear in quality and displayed symmetrical balance.

Romanticism in painting allowed freedom of imagination, rejecting an adherence to any one style. It was characterized by almost-Medieval paintings of adventure, war, realism, and emotionalism. France was engaged in revolution, and the paintings of Jacques Louis David (1748–1825) and Jean-Auguste Dominique-Ingres (1780–1867) inspired patriotic fervor. French Romanticists such as Theodore Gericault, Eugene Delacroix, and Honoré Daumier (1808–1879) also reflected the trauma and emotional turmoil that their country was suffering.

In England, John Constable painted realistic landscapes while J. M. W. Turner's vivid clouds and seas often featured sea battles or cities as focal points. In Spain, Francisco Goya influenced generations to come with his wide-ranging choices of subject, from social protest to royal portraiture.

American painters included John Singleton Copley (1738–1815), Benjamin West (1738–1820), and George Bingham (1811–1879). Realists simply painted what they saw. If they were inspired by any historical period, it might have been the Baroque, when the still life, genre, and landscapes were popular. Certainly the matter-of-fact representation of nature was an inspiration to the Impressionists.

## MASTERPIECES OF NEOCLASSICAL, ROMANTIC, AND REALISTIC PAINTINGS

### Neoclassicism

*Coronation of Napoleon and Josephine,* Jacques Louis David, 1805–1807, Louvre, Paris

*Comtesse d'Haussonville,* Jean-Auguste-Dominique Ingres, 1845, Frick Collection, New York

### Romanticism

*Greece on the Ruins of Missolonghi,* Eugene Delacroix, 1826, Musée des Beaux-Arts, Bordeaux

*Tiger Hunt,* Eugene Delacroix, 1854, Louvre, Paris

*The Third of May,* Francisco Goya, 1814–1815, Prado, Madrid

*Mounted Officer of the Imperial Guard,* Theodore Gericault, 1812, Louvre, Paris

*The Slave Ship,* J. M. W. Turner, 1840, Museum of Fine Arts, Boston

*Rain, Steam, and Speed,* J. M. W. Turner, 1844, National Gallery, London

*Stoke-by-Nayland,* John Constable, 1844, Art Institute of Chicago

### Realism

*The Sower,* Jean Francois Millet, c. 1850, Museum of Fine Arts, Boston

*The Third Class Carriage,* Honoré Daumier, c. 1850, The Metropolitan Museum of Art, New York

*The Morning Bell,* Winslow Homer, 1866, Yale University Art Gallery, New Haven, Connecticut

*The Croquet Game,* Winslow Homer, 1866, Art Institute of Chicago

*The Gross Clinic,* Thomas Eakins, 1875, Jefferson Medical College, Philadelphia

*Arrangement in Black and Gray* (Whistler's Mother), James McNeil Whistler, 1871, Louvre, Paris

*Nocturne in Black and Gold,* James Whistler, 1871, Detroit Institute of Arts

## SCULPTURE

Romantic sculptors continued to follow the precepts of classical sculptors, faithfully rendering likenesses and breaking little new ground, although their poses were somewhat theatrical and exaggerated. Sculpture mostly consisted of monuments to heroes or commemorated recent events. Faithful adherence to the Greek manner of sculpture caused the eyes to look somewhat vacant.

## MASTERPIECES OF SCULPTURE

*George Washington,* Jean Antoine Houdon, 1788–1792, State Capitol, Richmond, Virginia

*Pauline Borghese as Venus,* Antonio Canova, 1788–1792, Borghese Gallery, Rome

## ARCHITECTURE

The architecture constructed during the nineteenth century reflected a tremendous variety of influences and designs of the past. New technology and materials such as cast iron, glass, and steel allowed artists to try styles that had previously not been possible. Public buildings reflected Neoclassical, Neobaroque, and Gothic Revival styles. The skyscraper was invented.

## MASTERPIECES OF ARCHITECTURE

*Neoclassicism*

*Monticello,* Thomas Jefferson, 1770–1784, and 1796–1806, Charlottesville, Virginia

*Church of the Madeleine,* Pierre Vignon, 1806–1843, Paris

*Chiswick House,* Lord Burlington and William Kent, 1725, London

*Neogothic*

*The Houses of Parliament,* Sir Charles Barry and A. Welby Pugin, 1836, London

*The Royal Pavilion,* John Nash, 1836, Brighton, England

*Neobaroque*

*The Opera,* Charles Garnier, 1861–1874, Paris

## PROJECT 9–1: SKY AND SEA

### FOR THE TEACHER

**Slide # 21: *Yacht Approaching the Coast.*** Joseph Mallord William Turner (1775–1851) was utterly fascinated by the play of light on clouds, sunsets, and water. He once had himself tied to a mast during a storm so he could feel the spray of waves and wind. He began as a watercolorist and throughout his career continued to make watercolor "sketches" that he translated into finished oil paintings in his studio. The looseness of his oil painting technique resembled his watercolor sketches, and his use of white underpainting gave his paintings a luminosity. His paintings were often based on historical events and contained subjects such as ships, cities, trains, bridges, and people, but these were only incidental to his real subject, which was the brilliance of light and color. His output was prodigious, consisting of over twenty thousand paintings, drawings, and watercolors.

### MASTERPIECES BY J. M. W. TURNER

*Yacht Approaching the Coast*, 1835–1840, Tate Gallery, London

*Venice: The Piazzetta from the Water*, c. 1835, Tate Gallery, London

*The Slave Ship*, c. 1839, Museum of Fine Arts, Boston

### PREPARATION

Allow students to experiment with watercolor or pastels before actually beginning a painting. To paint an "atmospheric" painting such as those painted by J. M. W. Turner, they should think about the colors sometimes seen in the sky—not just the blue of midday, but the colors that are sometimes seen at sunset or sunrise or during a storm. Subject matter was usually incidental to Turner's paintings, taking up a small space, but it was essential for a focal point. Suggest students think of a focal point as a starting place for the turbulence of the water and clouds.

### FURTHER SUGGESTION

- This is an ideal subject for pastels. Have students use a knife to scrape old pastels into little piles of powder on a piece of paper. Use cotton balls to apply the pastels for sky and trees. (An ideal project for a day [not windy] outdoors sketching landscape.)

# PROJECT 9–1: SKY AND SEA

## MATERIALS

- Watercolor paper, white construction paper, or drawing paper
- Watercolors
- Pastels or oil pastels
- Paper towels
- Brushes, #7, #10, #3

1. Experiments are necessary before beginning your actual painting. Keep a sheet of paper nearby to test your color before applying it to the painting.

*Watercolor Experiments*

   a. Wet in wet: brush clean water onto the paper. Add pigment to the wet areas. Add more color and notice how it changes. It can be blotted with a paper towel.

   b. Local color: use very diluted pigment to apply light color in certain areas. These areas can be added to repeatedly to make differences in value.

*Pastel Experiments*

Pastels are vibrant when you use colors side by side or cross-hatch to make shadows. Let the viewer's eye do the mixing.

   a. Draw parallel marks in one color. Use a complementary color to do cross-hatching. See what happens when you cross-hatch in a different direction with a third color.

   b. Make short, small strokes of one color next to strokes of a complementary color to make a third color (example, blue next to yellow makes green).

*Watercolor and Pastel Combination*

   a. Make a background wash of watercolor. Allow it to dry before using pastel on top of the watercolor. Experiment also by drawing with pastel into wet areas.

   b. Use *oil* pastel as a resist. If it is applied firmly, it will prevent watercolor from touching the paper.

2. Use pencil to lightly sketch your subject matter near the horizon line. Subjects could be boats, a cityscape, people, bridges, trees in the distance (something rather small, as your chief subject matter should be sky and sea).

3. Work over the entire paper, rather than completing one area before going to the next. Gradually develop areas of dark, middle, and light values. If you draw water, remember that it is usually slightly darker than the sky, but often reflects its color. From time to time look at your painting from across the room. Close your eyes, then open them and see what the eye is first attracted to—is there a definite focal point? (It could be the lightest, darkest, or most colorful area, but there should be one.)

# Unit 2:  IMPRESSIONISM (1870 TO 1905) AND POSTIMPRESSIONISM (1886 TO 1920)

## OVERVIEW OF THE VISUAL ARTS

A group of (mostly) French artists were called "Impressionists" after a group of them had an exhibition, "Salon des Refusés" (artists whose work was rejected from the annual French salon exhibition). Claude Monet's painting *Impression, Sunrise* inspired the derogatory title. Their work reflected their interest in changes in the light and atmosphere. They frequently painted landscapes, at that time not a very "genteel" subject matter. Without question they were influenced by the advent of photography and the "snapshots" taken outdoors.

The movement originated in France, with the first exhibit in 1863 and the last in 1886. The varying group of exhibitors included Edouard Manet (1832–1883), Claude Monet (1840–1926), Camille Pissarro (1830–1903), Edgar Degas (1834–1917), Berthé Morisot (1841–1895), Pierre-Auguste Renoir (1841–1919), Paul Cézanne (1839–1906), and Mary Cassatt (1844–1926).

## PAINTING

The Impressionists' intent was to show exactly what the eye sees, rejecting the emotional effect so favored by the Romanticists. Impressionists usually painted outdoors, reflecting a fascination with the play of light and color. Pure color was applied to the canvas with little blending and loose brush strokes. The patches thus formed allowed the viewer's eye to mix the color.

The painters were influenced by each other, and at times it is difficult to see differences between their painting styles. Each of the major Impressionists is identified by certain paintings that showed an individual manner or subject, but when two painters did the same scene, standing almost side by side, their pictures strongly resembled each other's.

Although there were only eight artists who exhibited together in the seven "Impressionist exhibitions," a number of artists are called Neoimpressionists or Postimpressionists so the movement takes in a number of artists whose work was widely divergent. The following list gives a very brief synopsis of the portraiture styles of some of the leaders of the movement.

*Edouard Manet:* dramatic contrast; often depicted people in a "snapshot" effect; basically realistic; sometimes used a neutral background and flat colors

*Claude Monet:* pastel colors; smallish strokes of color; painted people early in his career, but mostly did landscapes later

*Edgar Degas:* pastels; subjects often were ballet dancers and horses: dramatic lighting; short, parallel, diagonal strokes; sculpted clay in much the same manner

*Pierre Auguste Renoir:* a portrait artist; frequently painted members of his family, flowers, Mediterranean landscapes, and holiday scenes

*Mary Cassatt:* frequently painted portraits of women and children, using pastels or oils; the only American who exhibited with the Impressionists; work resembled Japanese woodcuts at times

*Paul Cézanne:* "patches" of color, relationships of forms and patterns.

*Georges Seurat:* small dots of color placed closely together, "mixed by the eye"

*Paul Gauguin:* black outlining; somewhat unrealistic; bright colors and patterns; and flat areas of color

*Vincent Van Gogh:* vivid colors applied in a thick impasto; swirling brush strokes; arresting portraits

*Redon Odilon:* isolated the face against a plain background, then filled in around the edges of the picture plane with flowers

*Henri de Toulouse-Lautrec:* often painted in cafes; used pastels in short, slanted, parallel strokes on a tan background, allowing the strokes to show through

**Photo 9-1.** *The Louvre, Morning,* **Camille Pissarro, 1901, 29 × 36½ cm, oil on canvas, museum purchase, The Saint Louis Art Museum.**

## SCULPTURE

Because Impressionism was a school of *painting,* it is hardly thought that sculpture could have been classified as "Impressionistic." The work of Auguste Rodin (1840–1917) is an exception. Rodin sculpted in clay (later cast in bronze), working much as an Impressionist painter. He captured "impressions" of models as they strode around his studio, trying to give "life" to fleeting glimpses. His work was considered scandalous, as he sought to give a living vitality to a one-color material, departing from the classical serene sculptures of only a generation earlier.

Edgar Degas's sculptures demonstrated his manner of capturing movement and life. His works were created in wax or clay and not cast in bronze until after his death.

## SCULPTURAL MASTERPIECES

*Burghers of Calais,* Auguste Rodin, 1884–1886, Hirschhorn Museum, Washington, D.C.

*The Gates of Hell,* Auguste Rodin, 1840–1845, Musée Rodin, Paris

*Balzac,* Auguste Rodin, 1840–1845, Hirschhorn Museum, Washington, D.C.

*Little Dancer of Fourteen Years,* Edgar Degas, 1840–1845, Saint Louis Art Museum

## ARCHITECTURE

Cast iron and structural steel architecture opened the way to commercial structures and exposition halls. The skyscraper was invented, and public buildings became more important than churches and palaces. Cast iron buildings were created, and fanciful Victorian architecture was at its most flamboyant.

## MASTERPIECES OF ARCHITECTURE OF THE NINETEENTH CENTURY

*Eiffel Tower,* Gustave Eiffel, 1889, Paris

*Galerie des Machines,* 1889, Paris International Exposition

## POSTIMPRESSIONISM (c. 1886 TO 1920)

Postimpressionism was a label given in 1914 to all painters after 1880. Many Impressionists were also Postimpressionists. Artists such as Paul Cézanne, Georges Seurat, Paul Gauguin, Vincent van Gogh, Henri de Toulouse-Lautrec, and Henri Rousseau (1844–1910) are sometimes included in the Impressionist roster because of their continued use of bright patches of color, but each one had a unique style that demonstrated a departure from Impressionism.

The worksheet "Postimpressionism" can help students appreciate the distinct techniques of a variety of Postimpressionist painters.

# POSTIMPRESSIONISM

The Postimpressionists developed individual, easily recognizable styles of applying pigment. Of the nine Postimpressionists listed here, select at least six, and make "typical" drawings in each artist's style. Do not put the name at the bottom, but leave it blank, to see if others can guess who it is by your drawing and description.

EDVARD MUNCH, HENRI MATISSE, VINCENT VAN GOGH, HENRI TOULOUSE-LAUTREC, GEORGES SEURAT, PAUL CÉZANNE, HENRI ROUSSEAU, AUBREY BEARDSLEY, AND PAUL GAUGUIN

|  |  |  |
|--|--|--|
|  |  |  |
|  |  |  |
|  |  |  |
|  |  |  |
|  |  |  |
|  |  |  |
|  |  |  |
|  |  |  |
|  |  |  |

## PROJECT 9–2: IMPRESSIONIST LANDSCAPE

### FOR THE TEACHER

**Slide # 22: *Mont Ste. Victoire***

**Slide # 23: *Charing Cross Bridge*.** When we talk of Impressionist paintings, we sometimes think of delicate colors, light filtered through trees or reflected on water, beautiful groups of people, and city streets of Paris. Yet close your eyes and picture the tremendous variations in the work of Monet, Renoir, Manet, Sisley, Boudin, Pissarro, and Cézanne. These artists lived and worked in France, painted together, yet basically each is remembered for a distinctive style of working. The Impressionists were influenced by photography which was relatively new, and "captured the moment," as well as by Japanese woodcuts that had become so popular and were notable for their linear quality, flat areas of color, and rich patterns.

### MASTERPIECES OF IMPRESSIONIST LANDSCAPES

*The Beach at Trouville,* Eugene Boudin, 1863, Ittleson Collection, New York

*The Orchard,* Camille Pissarro, 1877, Louvre, Paris

*The River,* Claude Monet, 1868, The Art Institute of Chicago

*Impression Sunrise—Le Havre,* Claude Monet, 1872, Musée Marmottan, Paris

*Rouen Cathedral in Fall Sunlight,* Claude Monet, 1892–1893, Museum of Fine Arts, Boston

*Water Lilies,* Claude Monet, 1920, Carnegie Institute, Pittsburg

*Dejeuner sur l'Herbe* (Luncheon on the grass), Edouard Manet, 1863, Louvre, Paris

*Young Man in the Forest of Fontainebleu,* Pierre-Auguste Renoir, 1886, Museum of São Paulo, Brazil

### POSTIMPRESSIONIST LANDSCAPES

*Mont St. Victoire,* Paul Cézanne, 1885–1887, Stedelijk Museum, Amsterdam

*The Dream,* Henri Rousseau, 1910, Museum of Modern Art, New York

*The Starry Night,* Vincent Van Gogh, 1889, Museum of Modern Art, New York

*Bathers at Asnieres,* Georges Seurat, 1883–1884, National Gallery, London

*Vision After the Sermon,* Paul Gauguin, 1888, National Gallery of Scotland, Edinburgh

*The Day of the God,* Paul Gauguin, 1894, The Art Institute of Chicago

### PREPARATION

Allow individual students (or groups of students) a day to research and present the work of different Impressionists. They can show the work with slides, posters, postcards, or books. A one-page (or one paragraph) handout on each artist (researched by students) can be reproduced and given out. *Or you can lecture!* Posters are especially effective, and you may find that many students have such a reproduction at home.

Most of the Impressionists did oil paintings, but oil pastel is a satisfactory substitute. The pastels of Edgar Degas are wonderful teaching tools. Have students examine them closely to see the many different ways he used this dry medium. You could also use acrylic, oil, or tempera paint for this project.

## FURTHER SUGGESTIONS

- Have students purchase favorite Impressionist slides to make pins. With acrylic paint, carefully "extend" the slide onto the edges of the slide mount, creating a border. Add a pin backing to the top back of the slide. (Or marblize the slide mounts, selecting appropriate colors for each slide.)

- Paint a T-shirt with acrylic paint to "advertise" an Impressionist painter's exhibition. (All the best museums do this, and they are great sellers.) Find a copy of the artist's signature, and "sign" the painting.

**Photo 9-2.** *The Huth Factories at Chichy,* Vincent Van Gogh, 53.9 × 72.8 cm, oil on canvas, The Saint Louis Art Museum.

Name: _____   Date: _____

# PROJECT 9–2:  IMPRESSIONIST LANDSCAPE

**MATERIALS**

- Drawing paper
- Tempera or oil pastels

**Drawing after Paul Cézanne, Mont Sainte-Victoire, Metropolitan Museum of Art.**

The Impressionist manner of working was to place complementary colors (such as blue next to red to make violet, or two different values of blue) side by side, allowing the spectator's eye to mix the colors. Your subject can be a place you have been, or right outside your home or schoolroom. Claude Monet spent 26 years painting his water garden at Giverny. He did series paintings when he painted the same subject and location up to fifty times, showing the effects of light at different times of the day.

Try to do a painting in the manner of one specific Impressionist. Van Gogh's swirling lines certainly are different from Cézanne's color "patches," and both differ considerably from Monet's flowing "Water Lily" series. Technically Henri Rousseau and Georges Seurat were Postimpressionist, but both were landscape artists, and offer considerably different techniques.

1. Practice using pastels. Depending on the number of colors you have available, you will probably have to use "unreal" colors. Try placing complementary colors side by side, or cross-hatch with a different color on top of the first one. Consider developing a color scheme by concentrating on certain colors. Use mostly cool or warm colors to achieve entirely different effects.

2. Do thumbnail sketches of different types of landscapes. You may wish to have a specific subject such as a mountain, trees, people on a picnic, or the seashore. It might be helpful to you to look through family photographs for familiar scenes. The Impressionists painted what they were familiar with.

3. *Lightly* sketch your chosen subject onto a piece of drawing paper. To avoid smearing the pastels, you may wish to have a clean sheet of paper to rest your hand on. Oil pastels should be applied intensely to cover the background. Ordinary pastels can be blended, cross hatched, stippled, or scumbled (cross-hatched over a cool or dark color with a warm color).

4. Stand off at a distance and see if you have succeeded in giving your picture a sense of "immediacy." Don't overwork it. As with many painting media, it is possible to go too far. Sometimes you lose the freshness of your work in trying for perfection. There should be differences in value, of course, but see if you have given a feeling of a certain time of day or atmospheric condition.

# PROJECT 9–3: TWO-FIGURE STUDY IN PASTEL

**FOR THE TEACHER**

**Slide # 24: *The Boating Party.*** Mary Cassatt (1845–1926), an American, was trained in Philadelphia. She moved to France, where the quality of her work was so good that she exhibited in the official French Salon. Her work attracted the attention of Edgar Degas, and he became her mentor. In turn, she was influenced by his work, and exhibited with the Impressionists in 1877. She continued to exhibit with them until her death. Although she never married, her best-known work often involves scenes with mothers and children. Because of her connections with many wealthy American collectors, she is credited with promoting Impressionist artwork within the United States. Cassatt worked in both pastel and oils, and was greatly influenced by Japanese Prints.

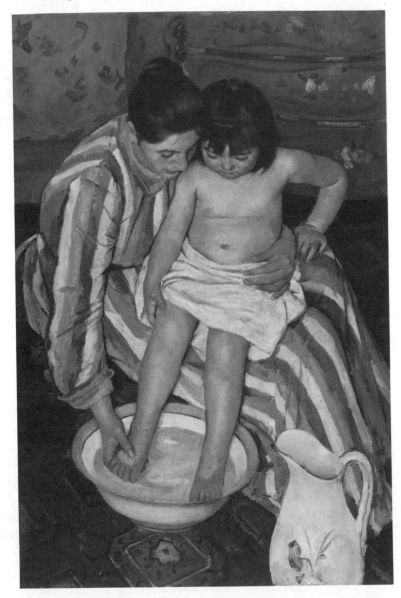

Photo 9-3. *The Bath,* Mary Cassatt, 1891, 39½ × 26 inches, oil on canvas, Robert A. Waller Fund, 1910.2. © 1991 The Art Institute of Chicago. All rights reserved.

## MASTERPIECES OF FIGURE STUDIES

*The Bath,* Mary Cassatt, 1891, The Art Institute of Chicago
*Two Young Ladies in a Loge,* 1882, National Gallery of Art, Washington, D.C.

### PREPARATION

Select two students to model together for the class. One could be seated higher than the other, but they should be next to each other so the artists can solve the problem of how to place them, and how to fill the rest of the picture. If you wish, you could have students do a number of "pair" drawings. If you lack time, it isn't necessary to do the preliminary newsprint drawings.

Point out to students how important pattern is in Cassatt's pictures. Her contrasts of lights and darks, pattern on pattern, near and far, created paintings that fill the eye. Suggest students consider props, diagonal placement of figures, and backgrounds to fill the picture plane.

### FURTHER SUGGESTIONS

- Use black fine-line marker (nonpermanent) to draw the figures. It is not important that the drawings are perfect. Paint over these outlines with watercolor or diluted acrylic paint. The black lines may "bleed," but that is part of the charm of this technique.

- Make the two-figure drawing on pastel colored paper (pink, light blue, light violet, or gray) with Prismacolor® pencils. Use at least three values, and work from dark to light. White pencil can be used to blend or add accents.

- Select an Impressionist masterpiece with more than one figure, and change it slightly by making one of the figures modern (or put yourself in the picture).

Photo 9-4. *Afternoon Tea Party,* Mary Cassatt, 1845–1926, 34.6 × 26.8 cm, drypoint and color aquatint touched with gold paint, The Saint Louis Art Museum. Purchase and funds given by Mr. and Mrs. Warren Mck Shapleigh, Mrs. G. Gordon Hertslet, and Mrs. Richard L. Brumbaugh.

Name: _____   Date: _____

## PROJECT 9–3:  TWO-FIGURE STUDY IN PASTEL

**MATERIALS**

- Pencils
- Drawing paper, 18 × 24 inches
- Pastels

Many of Mary Cassatt's paintings had more than one figure, often mothers and children. Her work was also influenced by Japanese woodcuts, which had an effect of being outlined in dark colors, and filled in with flat (unblended) areas of color. This assignment is to paint two figures within your picture as Cassatt often did.

1. Make light pencil or chalk sketches on drawing paper. *Don't erase.* If you have seen "master drawings," you will notice that many artists keep drawing over until they have it right, not worrying about extra lines, but simply emphasizing the ones that are "correct."

2. Before beginning, consider how you will do the painting. What will the background look like? Will you have pattern on the clothing? Do you want a soft blended effect or a flat unblended color with dark edges? What about a color scheme, perhaps a dominant color? Now, be willing to change your mind.

3. When using pastel, begin with darker colors underneath, placing lighter color on top. You can blend some areas and leave some areas flat (unblended, even color).

4. Pay special attention to having differences in value. Characteristics of many of Mary Cassatt's paintings are light areas next to dark areas, pattern next to pattern, and diagonal lines.

5. To protect the pastel, either spray with hair spray, fixative, or cover with plastic before matting.

    **Caution:** *Be sure to follow all safety precautions when using a spray.*

© 1992 by The Center for Applied Research in Education, Inc.

## PROJECT 9–4: **POINTILLIST POSTCARDS**

**FOR THE TEACHER**

**Slide # 25: *A Sunday Afternoon on the Island of La Grande Jatte.*** Pointillism, Neoimpressionism, or "Divisionism," as Georges Seurat (1859–1891) called it, was seen as a scientific exploration of the theories of color. In place of the colored patches of Cézanne, or brushstrokes of Monet, Seurat worked in small dots of pure colors placed next to each other to create form and shadow, premixing his paint before applying it. He worked masterfully with conté crayon and charcoal, and in fact had been an artist for a number of years before he ever used color. Because he died at age 32 he

Photo 9-5. *Port-en-Bessin: The Outer Harbor, Low Tide,* Georges Seurat, 1888, 21⅛ × 25⅞ cm, oil on canvas, museum purchase, The Saint Louis Art Museum.

created only seven large paintings. On some of the large paintings, he painted borders using the same system of dots. The play, *A Sunday Afternoon in the Park with George*, was written about him and his monumental painting *La Grande Jatte*.

## MASTERPIECES BY SEURAT

*A Sunday Afternoon on the Island of La Grande Jatte*, Georges Seurat, 1884–1886, Chicago Art Institute

*Bathers at Asnieres*, Georges Seurat, 1883–1884, National Gallery, London

*Side Show*, Georges Seurat, 1887–1888, The Metropolitan Museum of Art, New York

## PREPARATION

Pointillism takes infinite patience to do. The postcard size allows students to learn about it without it being a huge project. Many students love doing pointillism, while others will be quite happy with the small postcard size.

Talk with students about the purpose of a postcard. It could be a souvenir of a place one has been, or a scene mailed to show people what you've seen. Suggest they bring in a favorite postcard or a photograph that includes both landscape and people. Show slides of Seurat's work, and discuss how strong variations in value were important in both his early and later work.

## FURTHER SUGGESTIONS

- Have students bring in small gift boxes, and "paint" landscapes on the lids by stamping dots with pencil erasers. (Seurat painted many small paintings on cigar box lids.) Pour tempera paint onto a folded paper towel or dampened sponge to act as a stamp pad. Dip the pencil eraser frequently to stamp a scene to cover the box. (If there is no time to do the entire box, do only the lid.)

- Decorate precut mats for photographs using the pointillist method. (Scrap mats or board are often available for the asking from framing shops.)

## PROJECT 9–4:  POINTILLIST POSTCARDS

**MATERIALS**

- Newsprint
- 5 × 7-inch posterboard
- Tempera paint or Prismacolor® pencils
- Charcoal or pencil
- Brushes, #3 and #7
- Pencils

Imagine yourself on a trip, deciding that you will send a postcard to a friend. Where would you like most to be? If you have a postcard or photograph you would like to reproduce, you could use it, or combine scenes from magazine photos to create an imaginary place. Seurat lived near the sea, and sometimes did sketches of the harbor, or reflections in water.

1. Study a Seurat painting. Make a tree branch or flower of dots of contrasting colors on a 2-inch square, just to get the feel of pointillism.

2. Make a 5 × 7-inch sketch on newsprint to work out in black and white the values of your postcard before you begin to paint it in color. Because you will be creating a little jewel, take the time to work out your colors and values carefully.

3. Plan in advance to make a border (1/4- to 3/8-inch wide) around the edge of the card. This should be the same general color scheme as the postcard, but different enough to look like a border.

4. Think about an overall general color scheme. You might decide to basically use cool colors or warm colors. Experiment placing two opposite colors side by side to create a third color (for example, red and blue together to create violet, or red and yellow together to create orange). Whether you work in pencil or paint, take time to make dots of color. In an area of blue, for example, Seurat might have mixed several shades of blue and placed the individual dots next to each other to show gradations.

5. As you are painting, take time to look at your work from a distance to make sure you are making enough difference in values to create forms such as trees, hills, or clouds.

# PROJECT 9–5: **PORTRAIT IN THE IMPRESSIONIST MANNER**

**FOR THE TEACHER**

**Slide #26: *Portrait of the Artist.*** Although students feel a bit threatened when they are asked to do self-portraits assure them that getting a "likeness" is not terribly important. This project will help them understand how the Impressionists used color to revolutionize the painting world.

A number of the Impressionists painted portraits, and frequently included people in their outdoor paintings. Notable portraitists are listed here. Each of these artists painted a little differently from the others, showing a preference for a specific medium or manner of painting.

Photo 9-6. Student self-portrait in the Impressionist manner.

## MASTERPIECES OF IMPRESSIONIST PORTRAITS

*Lady in Blue,* Henri Matisse, 1937, Collection of Mrs. John Wintersteen, Philadelphia

*Madame Gaudibert,* Claude Monet, 1868, Louvre, Paris

*The Woman with a Coffee Pot,* Paul Cézanne, 1890–1894, Louvre, Paris

*Self-Portrait,* Paul Cézanne, 1877, Bayerische Staatsgemalde Collection, Munich

*The Fifer,* Edouard Manet, 1866, Louvre, Paris

*The Reading,* Edouard Manet, 1868, Louvre, Paris

*Le Moulin de la Galette,* Edouard Manet, 1876, Louvre, Paris

*Singer with Glove,* Edgar Degas, 1878, Fogg Art Museum, Harvard University

*Woman with Parasol,* Georges Seurat, 1884, Emil G. Buehrle Collection, Zurich

*Self-Portrait,* Vincent Van Gogh, 1889, Private Collection, New York

*Girl with Mango,* Paul Gauguin, 1892, Baltimore Museum of Art

## PREPARATION

If possible, have a number of slides, reproductions, and books on Impressionists available for the students to look at. The study sheet on Impressionism would help students see differences in style.

## FURTHER SUGGESTIONS

- Suggest that students do clay sculpture in the Impressionist manner such as that of Auguste Rodin or Edgar Degas. The loose, sketchy application of clay is similar to that of the Impressionists' application of paint.

- Select a picture of a famous person from a magazine cover. Cut it into approximately 1½ × 2-inch pieces, giving each student a portion to enlarge (on proportionally cut paper) in the manner of a different Impressionist. Recombine and tape the pictures together to make one large portrait with each portion representing a different painter.

Name: _____   Date: _____

# PROJECT 9–5:  PORTRAIT IN THE IMPRESSIONIST MANNER

**MATERIALS**

- Tempera
- Brushes
- Pastel
- Acrylic or oil paints
- Paper suitable to the medium

Although most of the Impressionists painted people realistically, this assignment is not to necessarily paint yourself exactly the way they might have, but to use their "technique" in painting. The Impressionists were usually thought of as landscape painters, and several of them specialized in painting outdoors, capturing fleeting effects of the light. They worked generally in small dabs of color, laid side by side, allowing the viewer's eye to mix the colors.

1. Select an artist whose work you like. Some artists specialized in certain media; for example, Degas was a master of pastel. Examine as many photos of work by that artist as you can find. Even if the artist mostly painted landscapes, you will see that he or she applied color in a certain manner.

2. Looking in a mirror, lightly sketch your face with a pencil on white paper. Remember that the head is roughly shaped like an egg (large end up) and that your eyes are halfway between the top and bottom. The mouth is approximately one third of the way between the eyes and the bottom. Don't be too concerned about getting a "likeness." General proportions are shown here.

3. Before painting, examine how your artist applied paint. Some used dots, others used parallel strokes of pastel, and others used small patches of color. Look at the colors they used, and try using some of the colors of their "palette." Very little black was used, and flesh often used tints of greens, pinks, blues, oranges, and yellows.

4. While painting your face, also consider how you will fill in the background. In portraiture, some of the same colors used in the face may also be repeated in the background. Although some portraits were against plain backgrounds, others were quite intricate. These artists were influenced by Japanese woodcuts, and occasionally that influence can be seen in the background, patterns, or composition.

5. To display effectively, make a "museum frame" by shaping a pre-cut mat, which you will color with yellow and gold oil pastels. Look at pictures of frames in books to see how beautifully work was framed at that time.

# PROJECT 9–6: **GAUGUIN LOOK-ALIKES**

## FOR THE TEACHER

**Slide # 27: *Faaturuma (Melancholic).*** Paul Gauguin was a stock broker/Sunday painter who decided at age 35 that he wanted to devote his life to being an artist. He studied with the Impressionist Camille Pissarro, and painted in Paris and Brittany. His early work combined typical scenes of Brittany with themes of religious drama, and showed the influence of Japanese printmakers such as Hokusai, with dark outlines and some flat areas of color. He was a friend and mentor of Van Gogh's, although their quarrels were legendary.

Gauguin moved to Tahiti, where his colors became even richer and further removed from reality. He also made many sculptures and woodcuts in this Tahitian period. His colors were brilliant—many pinks, purples, oranges, combined with darker colors such as dark green or blue—that served to heighten the intensity of color.

## GAUGUIN'S MASTERPIECES

*Vision after the Sermon,* Paul Gauguin, 1888, National Gallery of Scotland, Edinburgh

*La Orana Maria,* Paul Gauguin, 1891, The Metropolitan Museum of Art, New York

*The Day of the God,* Paul Gauguin, 1894, The Art Institute of Chicago

*Fatata te Miti* (By the Sea), Paul Gauguin, 1892, National Gallery of Art, Washington, D.C.

## PREPARATION

Students can do quick sketches of figures (even using magazine photos for inspiration if need be). Use Gauguin's colors and approach to showing nature (mountains, trees, water) combined with figures. Suggest they avoid adding black to a color to make it darker, but instead make it richer by adding the complementary color. (Combine yellow and a small amount of violet to make a grayed violet, or blue and orange to darken orange.)

## FURTHER SUGGESTIONS

- Design Hawaiian shirts with the brilliant colors favored by Gauguin. Cut "shirts" from tagboard, and make a repeat pattern of flowers or trees, painting in the background to complement the flowers.
- Make a "Gauguin lino-cut" featuring waves (based on Japanese woodcuts). For added impact, add boats, trees, or tropical foliage.

# PROJECT 9–6: GAUGUIN LOOK-ALIKES

**MATERIALS**

- Drawing paper
- Pencils
- Tempera paint

Gauguin's paintings are exciting to look at, with their vivid colors and dramatic approach to showing nature. Most of his paintings feature people in a landscape. Because he lived on an island, they often featured water with people near it. Sometimes they were talking, doing chores, or just sitting in the shade.

1. Lightly draw two or more figures on your paper. They might be working or talking together. You could make other figures in the background. Decide what environment they will be in, and draw trees, sea, or mountains (or your local park).

2. Before beginning to paint, select either a warm or cool color scheme, such as blue, green, and violet, or orange, magenta, and pink. The figures can contrast with either background scheme.

3. With dark brown, blue, or black paint, outline everything in the picture. Allow it to dry before painting in the figures and the background.

4. Mix enough tempera to be able to use a similar color in several areas of the painting. It is better to work this way, almost in patches, than to complete one area of a painting before going on to the next. If you use a large area of a bright color (such as red or yellow) in one place, you might want to repeat it elsewhere but in smaller portions.

5. Stand back and look at the painting. Do the figures stand out from the background? Perhaps you have one dominant figure; it might have the brightest clothing, or be the largest one in the group.

# PROJECT 9-7:  VAN GOGH'S BEDROOM

### FOR THE TEACHER

**Slide # 28:** *The Bedroom of the Artist at Arles.* Vincent Van Gogh was one of the group of Postimpressionists whose work was a departure from the colors and method of working of the Impressionists. His vivid colors and swirling brush strokes gave an individual quality to his work that made a strong impact on modern art. He had a short career of only ten years, painting only during the last six. Approximately 900 drawings and 800 paintings have survived, although during his lifetime he sold only one painting.

### POSTIMPRESSIONIST MASTERPIECES

*The Starry Night,* Vincent Van Gogh, 1889, Museum of Modern Art, New York

*The Potato Eaters,* Vincent Van Gogh, 1885, Vincent Van Gogh Foundation, Amsterdam

*Self-Portrait,* Vincent Van Gogh, 1889, collection of Mr. and Mrs. John Hay Whitney, New York

*Vincent's Bedroom at Arles,* Vincent Van Gogh, 1888, Van Gogh Museum, Amsterdam

*The Night Cafe,* Vincent Van Gogh, 1888, Yale University Art Gallery

*Exotic Landscape,* Henri Rousseau, 1910, Norton Simon Foundation, Los Angeles

### PREPARATION

A review of one-point perspective will be of value in helping students see how simple it is to draw things to appear to recede into space. Have them color firmly, with the strokes following the direction of the object being colored (for example, vertical for wood grain). Use a separate class period to quickly apply the tempera paint, so it can be washed off at the end of the period, when it is almost dry. The effect will be a brilliantly colored resist, with tempera clinging to any uncolored areas.

### FURTHER SUGGESTIONS

- Students love trying to imitate Van Gogh's brush strokes. Suggest they use *The Starry Night* as an inspiration for doing a sky painting of a night they remember (such as the Fourth of July), or a very stormy sky.

- Van Gogh's drawings were rich in texture. If you can find examples of his drawings of field or sea, have students try a fine-line marker ink, or pencil drawing with many varieties of texture.

- An exhibition at the Van Gogh Foundation in Arles was entitled "Homage to Van Gogh." Famous artists from all over the world did work in a variety of media, ranging from sculpture and oil paintings to cloth and collage, using Van Gogh's images, colors, and (sometimes) style. His humble chairs, old shoes, self-portraits, all aspects of his art and life were interpreted imaginatively. Challenge students to pay homage to Van Gogh in whatever visual manner they choose.

# PROJECT 9–7:  VAN GOGH'S BEDROOM

## MATERIALS

- Drawing paper
- Crayons or oil crayons
- Tempera paint

The interior of a room has always been a popular subject. Your own bedroom could be drawn from memory, seeing it from a wide angle.

1. Lightly draw details in pencil, trying to depict your room as seen from one corner. One-point perspective will help you draw details.

   a. Draw a horizontal line near the top of your drawing. Place a dot (the vanishing point) somewhere on the line.

   b. With a ruler, draw vertical lines to represent walls, doors, windows and furniture in a room. Vertical and horizontal lines are always parallel to the top, bottom, and sides of the paper.

   c. With a ruler, draw a line from the top of a vertical line and draw to the vanishing point. Do the same with the bottom of the vertical line.

   d. Erase extra lines.

2. Use crayons to apply color (firmly) to various areas in the painting. Choose bright colors that are *not* realistic, such as using a red bedspread, when you really have a blue bedspread, or purple walls instead of green walls. Color in the direction something goes (such as wood grain).

3. Apply tempera paint in realistic colors on top of the colored area. Allow the paint to become almost dry. You will be washing these colors (mostly) off when they are almost dry, but patches of them will cling to the colored background.

4. Hold the almost dry painting under running water. Don't wash it so much that no paint is left, but remove enough of it to allow the undercolors to show through. Pat the picture dry with a paper towel and place on a drying rack.

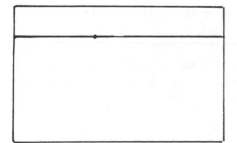
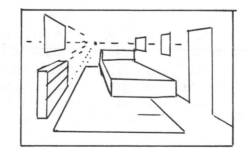

# Unit 3: ART NOUVEAU (1880 TO 1910)

**OVERVIEW OF THE VISUAL ARTS**

The turn of the century spawned innovations in architecture, painting, interior design, commercial art, jewelry, and other applied arts. It was based on natural flower forms, using curved, sinuous, asymmetrical lines. In Germany this period was called "Jugendstil," in France, "Art Nouveau," and in England and America, "Modern." These styles related to the paintings of Henri de Toulouse-Lautrec (1864–1901), Paul Gauguin (1848–1903), Edvard Munch (1863–1944), Vincent van Gogh (1853–1890), Gustav Klimt (1862–1918), and Aubrey Beardsley (1872–1898). Symbolist painters of the time also showed an interest in religious mysticism.

**PAINTING**

Where the Impressionists relied mostly on color to display their departure from established "rules" of painting, the painters of the late nineteenth century relied more on line, perhaps influenced by the Japanese woodcuts that were then popular in Europe. Art Nouveau designs relied heavily on natural forms such as exotic flowers, and particularly used curved lines such as found on stems and buds. In contrast to the stylized work of the Postimpressionists, the work of painters Gustave Klimt, and that of Aubrey Beardsley was truly decorative, employing pattern and design to emphasize figures.

**MASTERPIECES OF ART NOUVEAU PAINTING**

*Orpheus,* Odilon Redon, 1903, The Cleveland Museum of Art

*Profile and Flowers,* Odilon Redon, 1912, McNay Art Institute, San Antonio, Texas

**DECORATIVE ARTS**

An "Arts and Crafts" movement in England was a reaction against what artists saw as industrialization of art. William Morris, an English artist-poet, felt that true art should be both useful and beautiful. He is best known for his designs for wallpaper and furniture. Other decorative arts of the time were graphic design, furniture and textiles, book illustration, glass and ceramic design, and women's fashions.

**MASTERPIECES OF APPLIED DESIGN**

*Entrance to a Metropolitain Station,* Hector Guimard, 1898–1901, Paris

*Detail of "Pimpernel" Wallpaper,* William Morris, 1876, Victoria and Albert Museum, London

*Table Lamp,* Louis Comfort Tiffany, c. 1900, Lillian Nassau Antiques, New York

*Salome with the Head of John the Baptist,* Aubrey Beardsley, 1893, Princeton University Library, Princeton, New Jersey

## ARCHITECTURE

In architecture there was an avoidance of symmetry, straight lines, and flat surfaces. Structural elements became more curvilinear as architects experimented with new materials such as reinforced concrete, metal, and glass. Architects Antoni Gaudi (1852–1926) and Henry Van de Velde (1863–1957) designed buildings that employed the typical curves and lines of Art Nouveau. Louis Sullivan (1885–1910) utilized curving lines from nature and geometric designs as decorations on his revolutionary high rise buildings. Gustave Eiffel's Tower built in 1889 explored the use of iron as a building material.

## MASTERPIECES OF ARCHITECTURE

*Church of the Sagrada Familia,* Antoni Gaudi, 1883–1926, Barcelona

*Case Mila Apartment House,* Antoni Gaudi, 1905–1907, Barcelona

*Eiffel Tower,* Gustave Eiffel, 1889, Paris

*Salon, Van Eetvelde House,* Victor Horta, 1895, Brussels

Photo 9-7. While this cover is attributed to Frank Lloyd Wright, it is not known that Wright actually did the design, which is quite like the geometrical designs of Louis Sullivan. *Air Vent Cover,* c. 1895, American; from the Francis Apartments, Chicago, iron. The Saint Louis Art Museum, Museum Purchase, with funds donated by Mr. and Mrs. Stanley Hanks.

## PROJECT 9–8: **POSTER**

### FOR THE TEACHER

At the time of the French Revolution (1789) and for the next fifty years, political life was changing in much of Europe. "Liberty, Equality, and Fraternity" was the cry for self government. The poster originally served the purpose of informing people, and was later used for propaganda by the leaders. Ultimately it served the same purposes it does today; to advertise products and entertainment, sell an idea, or promote politics.

Toulouse-Lautrec, Alphonse Mucha, Gustav Klimpt, and Aubrey Beardsley were among the fine artists whose posters are sought today by art collectors. Their posters were among the earliest to depict pretty women in order to sell something such as beer, coffee, champagne, or entertainment.

### MASTERPIECES (POSTERS)

*Jane Avril,* Toulouse Lautrec, 1899, Museum of Modern Art, New York

*Salome With the Head of John the Baptist,* Aubrey Beardsley, 1893, Princeton University Library, Princeton, New Jersey

*The Pseudonym and Autonym Libraries,* Aubrey Beardsley, 1895, Museé des Arts Décoratifs, Paris

*Theseus and the Minotaur,* Gustave Klimt, 1898, Hessisches Landesmuseum, Darmstadt

*Vient de Paraitre,* Alphonse Mucha, 1898, Musée des Arts Décoratifs, Paris

### PREPARATION

Ideas for posters are difficult for students. Suggest they think about what they spent their own money for within the last week, or what they *would* have spent it for if they had had enough! Perhaps what they dream about spending on in the future would be something to make a poster about. Thumbnail sketches are very important, and your input while they are doing them will help them clarify ideas in their own minds.

### FURTHER SUGGESTIONS

- Design a book cover in the Art Nouveau manner. Suggest they select lettering, and use a border on the front, spine, and back of the cover. As a challenge, have them think about it as a design for a pocket novel cover that will be eye-catching, yet good design.

- Design a small newspaper advertisement in the Art Nouveau manner for a local business such as a restaurant, beauty salon, or theatre. Because it will be in only black and white, try to make it dramatic, using curved lines in the border that resemble plants.

Photo 9-8. *Sarah Bernhardt as "La Samaritaine,"* Alphonse Mucha, 1897, 67½ × 23½ inches, color lithograph, The Nelson-Atkins Museum of Art, Kansas City, Missouri.

Photo 9-9. *Jane Avril,* Henri de Toulouse-Lautrec, 1893, 128 × 91.4 cm, lithographic poster, The Nelson-Atkins Museum of Art, Kansas City, Missouri.

# PROJECT 9-8:  POSTER

### MATERIALS

- Posterboard
- Long ruler
- Brushes
- Markers
- Fadeless paper
- Rubber cement
- Tempera paint

Many posters that were created around 1900 used a border that became part of the design. These borders usually were at least partially curved, and related closely to the lettering or main motif. Many used black outlines filled in with flat (unshaded) colors. A certain amount of open space draws attention to your message and image.

1. Decide what you will advertise. Some suggestions are an upcoming event, exotic travel, car, video tape, or film.

2. Make several thumbnail sketches (small rectangles). Decide what words you will use. There should be an easily readable main message, and other information in smaller print. Some things to consider:

   a. People should be able to get the message easily: who? what? where? when? why?

   b. Vertical posters have better visual impact.

   c. Think about the poster as a human form: top line, waist line, and a base line.

   d. One important message should be in the largest print.

   e. The lettering should be the same size and color, evenly spaced, not staggered or stacked.

   f. Leave comfortable margins on all sides.

   g. Darker colors show up better from a distance.

   h. Keep the printing simple. Lower case letters are easier to read than upper case (capitals).

   i. The largest letters are often near the bottom of the poster, for visual stability.

   j. Letters could be cut out of construction or fadeless paper, and glued on with rubber cement.

   k. Don't try to crowd too much onto the poster.

3. When you have selected your best thumbnail sketch, draw it onto the posterboard. Take the time to measure so your letters will be exactly the same size and have adequate spacing. Count the number of letters for your main message. Find the middle of the poster, and divide the letters evenly, lightly drawing them in pencil.

4. Add color to the letters and image. This could be done with tempera paint, colored pencil, oil pastels, watercolor, or cut paper.

# PROJECT 9–9:  ART NOUVEAU

**FOR THE TEACHER**

Gustave Klimt was the leader of a group of artists in Vienna, the "Secession," that rejected the preoccupation with light of the Impressionists, and traditional painting. These radical young artists wanted to ally themselves with the international movement of Art Nouveau, which sought to raise the level of arts and crafts.

In addition to his public commissions, which were often controversial, he painted Viennese society women, using themes of motherhood, love, life, and death. He used either very dark or very light backgrounds, tying the subject and background together with rich geometric patterns and gold. His work reflected the European preoccupation with Japanese woodcuts, and quite often he used Japanese motifs to tie the pictures together.

**MASTERPIECES**

*Judith I,* Gustave Klimt, 1901, Osterreichische Galerie, Vienna

*The Kiss,* Gustave Klimt, 1907–1908, Osterreichische Galerie, Vienna

*Baby,* Gustave Klimt, 1917–1918, Private collection, New York

**PREPARATION**

Although most of Klimt's paintings had people in them, they were almost obscured by the masses of surrounding pattern. Have students spend one day making patterns such as swirls, peacock feather concentric circles, squares, triangles, and so on. This is the "reference sheet." Patterned wallpaper samples and tooling foil could also be added to the background.

**FURTHER SUGGESTIONS**

- Make a poster using Klimt's method of design. Although most of his work was not commercial, his divisions of space would make very effective posters.
- Use Klimt's design motifs to design a set of china (plate, cup, and teapot), or to design wallpaper or fabric.

Name: _____     Date: _____

## PROJECT 9–9: **ART NOUVEAU**

**MATERIALS**

- Newsprint
- 12-inch tagboard or posterboard
- Colored pencil or fine-line marker
- Tooling foil, gold or silver color
- Wallpaper samples
- Acrylic paint
- White glue

Gustave Klimt's artworks usually featured people, but they were often a small part of the painting, almost obscured by the richly patterned, often gold-colored backgrounds that were part of Art Nouveau decoration. In collage and design, try to use Klimt's swirling lines and intricate backgrounds to emphasize your people drawings.

1. On a piece of newsprint, make some small sketches of heads and hands, perhaps even using magazine or yearbook photos as your inspiration. On this same sheet of paper, make as many variations of geometric designs as you can think of (triangles, diamonds, circles, half-circles, rectangles, etc.).

2. Cut out the head or figure drawing you like best. Move it around on a sheet of tagboard until you find the best placement for you. Trace it onto the tagboard. Divide the background with curved lines, deciding which ones relate to the figure, and might be robes or clothing, and which ones should be treated as background.

3. If you have wallpaper samples or aluminum tooling foil, pieces can be cut from these and glued onto your background to add richness. Klimt tied the background and foreground together through his use of pattern and color.

4. The robes or clothing surrounding the figure might be slightly different colors, and the designs might become more intricate as they become clothing. Try using concentrations of designs closer to the figure. You must also leave some relatively plain areas to give emphasis to those that have pattern.

# PROJECT 9–10:  FACES AND FLOWERS

## FOR THE TEACHER

Odilon Redon was a Symbolist. He was part of a group that was looking for a new approach to religion or mysticism. His soft, somewhat ethereal paintings were strange, rather surrealistic. He often drew women surrounded in a world of flowers, waves, abstract shapes, and other seemingly unrelated items.

## MASTERPIECES

*The Birth of Venus,* Odilon Redon, 1912, Kimbell Art Foundation, Fort Worth, Texas

*Woman Amidst Flowers,* Odilon Redon, 1909–1910, Jonas collection, New York

*Portrait of Mademoiselle Violette Heymann,* Odilon Redon, 1909, Museum of Art, Cleveland, Ohio

*Orpheus,* Odilon Redon, 1903, The Cleveland Museum of Art

*Roger and Angelica,* Odilon Redon, 1910, The Museum of Modern Art, New York

## PREPARATION

Have each student bring in at least one type of vegetable or fruit (obviously strawberries wouldn't be great for this). This painting could be a team effort, with each member of the team making a "floating face" or human form on a separate piece of paper, each making more than one vegetable stamp and lending each other stamps. The drawing, figure, and background painting should be finished and dried one day, in preparation for the actual stamping to be done on the next. Obviously when you are using vegetables for printing, they are not going to keep very long. Mix tempera paints in advance, and pour them onto "stamp pads" made of folded paper towels, or apply paint to the stamps with brayers.

## FURTHER SUGGESTIONS

- Stamping with vegetables could be done on almost anything. If the surface is washable, such as a tennis shoe or T-shirt, then it is advisable to use acrylic or textile paint. A border for a painting could be stamped, or a precut mat for a picture could be done with vegetables and acrylic paint.

- Use the stamps to entirely create a face (without predrawing). Make it large, with interesting hair or a hat. Students have to work fast.

## PROJECT 9–10: **FACES AND FLOWERS**

**MATERIALS**

- Drawing paper, $18 \times 24$ inches
- Pastels
- Tempera paint (mixed to pastel shades)
- Paper towels
- Vegetables or fruits: green pepper, potatoes, zucchini, carrots, radishes, mushrooms, onions (green and regular), apples, pears, and so on
- X-acto® knives, or nails

It will take some imagination to make abstract "flowers" from cut vegetables such as onions or zucchini.

1. Lightly draw one (or more) faces somewhere on the paper. Size is not important. Fill in the face drawing with pastels.

2. Make an imaginary background for this figure. It could be clouds, the sea, a forest, or a star-filled sky. Leave parts of the background unpainted, because these areas are where you will be stamping "flowers."

3. Cut the vegetables so that after you have a flat edge, there is enough left to grip between your thumb and forefinger (for dipping into the paint). You can shape the printing edge of the vegetable with a knife or nail to resemble a "flower." Different sizes of peppers cut crossways give interesting shapes that could be combined with other vegetables.

4. Saturate a pad made of folded, dampened paper towels with tempera paint. Simply stamp the vegetable onto tempera, then stamp it onto someplace in your painting. If several people in a group make different shapes of flowers, you could probably borrow their "stamps" to use for variety.

5. After the paint has dried, you may wish to go back and fill in with clouds, leaves, or plain or blended areas of pastel.

# PROJECT 9–11: **SULLIVAN'S STENCILS**

## FOR THE TEACHER

Louis Sullivan was an Art Nouveau American architect, best known as a builder of "skyscrapers" (five- or six-story buildings). He was a teacher and mentor of Frank Lloyd Wright.

His work often used decorative elements based on the curves and lines of growing plants. The exterior of buildings such as the department store Carson Pirie Scott in Chicago, or the Wainwright Building in St. Louis, are prime examples of his work. No detail of a building was too small for his attention, and the wrought iron, ceramic, and carved decorative elements of his buildings are avidly catalogued, collected, treasured, and exhibited. At times he designed stencils for the interiors of buildings, and it is these stencils that are the inspiration for this project. The elaborate interlacings are similar to those used in medieval times in illuminated manuscripts such as the *Book of Kells*. Medieval artists were fascinated with the intricate patterns they could make from simple shapes, and carved them on gravestones, placed them on buildings, and painted them on manuscripts.

## MASTERPIECES OF ARCHITECTURE

*Carson Pirie Scott Building,* Louis Sullivan, 1898–1899, Chicago, Ilinois

*Wainwright Building,* Louis Sullivan, 1890–1891, St. Louis, Missouri

## PREPARATION

Before beginning, have students make designs on graph paper so that they have some understanding that these designs are not as complex as they appear to be. They can then make a stencil key to be traced onto the acetate. Other material for stencils could be brown wrapping paper, tagboard (oiled, to make it last longer), frisket paper, and stencil paper.

## FURTHER SUGGESTIONS

- Several students could do "production" stenciling by combining their stencils to make different types of patterns.
- Use acrylic paint to stencil designs onto T-shirts. These designs could be put in bands across the chest, sleeves, or necks.
- Suggest that students find something at home to stencil (getting parents' permission first). It could be the back of a chair, a ceramic mug, a design around a door, a wooden box, etc.

## PROJECT 9–11: **SULLIVAN'S STENCILS**

### MATERIALS

- Graph paper, ½-inch grid
- Acetate: 0.005 gauge, 4 × 6 inches
- Pencils
- Compasses
- Paper punches
- Drawing paper
- Stencil paper

- Masking tape
- Rulers
- Erasers
- X-acto® knives
- Stencil brushes or sponges
- Acrylic paint or watercolor markers

### DIRECTIONS

Interlaced patterns such as those used as decorative building detail by architect Louis Sullivan were also used in the Middle Ages. Sullivan's buildings were rich in such ornament, from doorknobs to elevator grilles, to patterns stenciled on interior walls.

1. Use graph paper to make your design. If you wish it to be larger, make a new one on graph paper, simply using more squares for your design (this will be called a "stencil key").

2. Tape acetate on top of the stencil key. Leave a 1- to 3-inch border around the outside of the design.

3. With an X-acto® knife, cut out your design. Cut the small shapes first, then larger ones. When cutting curves, use your free hand to turn the stencil as you cut. Leave "bridges" to keep the pattern from falling apart. If you happen to tear a stencil, apply tape to both sides, and cut the design through the tape.

   *Safety Note: Always hold your free hand behind the blade.* Hold the knife perpendicular to the stencil paper and always cut toward yourself.

4. To stencil, hold or tape the pattern in place. Dip the stencil brush in paint, and lightly "pounce" it through the stencil. You can "shade" the stencil by making the paint darker at the edges and lighter in the middle. You could also use small sponges for applying paint through the stencil.

**Photo 9-10. Frieze, fragment from the Stock Exchange Building, Chicago, Louis Sullivan, American, 1856–1924. The Saint Louis Art Museum.**

# TRADITIONAL ART OF THE AMERICAS

# THE AMERICAS
## TIME LINE

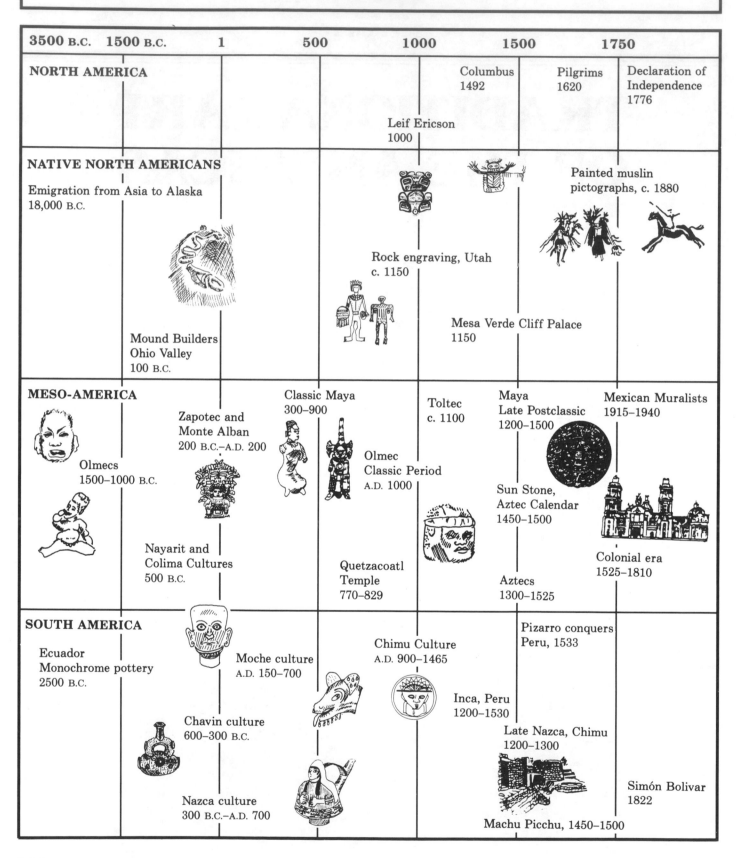

| | 3500 B.C. | 1500 B.C. | 1 | 500 | 1000 | 1500 | 1750 |
|---|---|---|---|---|---|---|---|

**NORTH AMERICA**

Columbus 1492

Pilgrims 1620

Declaration of Independence 1776

Leif Ericson 1000

**NATIVE NORTH AMERICANS**

Emigration from Asia to Alaska 18,000 B.C.

Painted muslin pictographs, c. 1880

Rock engraving, Utah c. 1150

Mesa Verde Cliff Palace 1150

Mound Builders Ohio Valley 100 B.C.

**MESO-AMERICA**

Classic Maya 300–900

Toltec c. 1100

Maya Late Postclassic 1200–1500

Mexican Muralists 1915–1940

Zapotec and Monte Alban 200 B.C.–A.D. 200

Olmecs 1500–1000 B.C.

Olmec Classic Period A.D. 1000

Sun Stone, Aztec Calendar 1450–1500

Nayarit and Colima Cultures 500 B.C.

Quetzacoatl Temple 770–829

Aztecs 1300–1525

Colonial era 1525–1810

**SOUTH AMERICA**

Pizarro conquers Peru, 1533

Chimu Culture A.D. 900–1465

Ecuador Monochrome pottery 2500 B.C.

Moche culture A.D. 150–700

Inca, Peru 1200–1530

Chavin culture 600–300 B.C.

Late Nazca, Chimu 1200–1300

Simón Bolivar 1822

Nazca culture 300 B.C.–A.D. 700

Machu Picchu, 1450–1500

## Unit 1: **MESOAMERICA**

### OVERVIEW OF THE VISUAL ARTS

It is thought that the original inhabitants of the New World emigrated from Asia to Alaska across a land passage (in times of low water) 20,000 years ago. Migrations southward to Mesoamerica continued until the time of the Spanish conquest. Some of the earliest and most advanced civilizations in the western hemisphere began in Mexico where artistic development began in settled agricultural villages approximately 1500 B.C. The inhabitants developed monumental arts such as the pyramids and created intricate stone carvings. Various cultures such as the Olmecs, Mayas, and Aztecs flourished, then disappeared, leaving behind sophisticated architectural complexes and artwork that tell us something of their lives.

It is difficult to generalize about the arts of Mesoamerica because of the long history, the large area covered, and the contributions of various peoples. The highly developed skills and rich heritage of a sophisticated civilization are seen in the carved stone, hand-built pottery, featherwork, painting, textiles, and architecture. The artwork created before the arrival of Columbus (pre-Columbian) was at its finest in Mexico and Peru.

### PAINTING

Richly colored fresco paintings from Mayan times exist in various locations such as those painted at Teotihuacan prior to A.D. 600. Pre-Columbian manuscripts have also been found. These were painted on both sides of gesso-coated deerskin that was accordion-folded and protected by wooden covers. Many Mayan pots were ornamented with a painted stucco that is called "paint cloisonné" because of its resemblance to Chinese cloisonné.

### MASTERPIECES OF PAINTING

*Wall painting of waterside village,* twelfth century, Peabody Museum, Harvard University

*Wall painting,* pre-A.D. 600, Teotihuacan, Mexico

### SCULPTURE

Colossal, helmet-wearing heads are traced to the Olmec culture. Some human forms were represented as werejaguars (like werewolves), recognizable by a cleft in the head. The beautifully carved snake heads at Teotihuacan demonstrate the skill that was achieved with only stone or bone tools. Sculpture was created of many traditional materials such as stone, bone, clay, jade, and gold. A favorite carving material was green jade. The conquistadores found they could trade green glass beads for gold, because the "greenstone" was more valued.

263

## Mexican and South American Archaelogical Sites

## North American Architecture

Log cabin

Adam style—Federal

Revivals: Neoclassicism, Egyptian, Neobaroque
Neogothic, Neoromanesque, Italian Villa,
Neorenaissance, Jacobean, Elizabethan

Colonials: Dutch Colonial, Spanish Colonial,
Georgian Colonial, French Colonial

Styles: Shingle, Pueblo, Mission, Prairie, Ranch

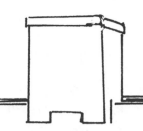

**NORTH AMERICAN**

"Soddy" Sod house

Solomon's Old Log Cabin
1804

Cape Cod style
1686

Farmhouse
c. 1812

Monticello, 1768–1809
Thomas Jefferson

Taos, New Mexico

Frederick C. Robie House
1909, Frank Lloyd Wright

**MESOAMERICAN**

Temple of the Jaguars
Chichén Itzá, Yucatan

Temple of the Warriors
Chichén Itzá, Yucatan

Temple of Kukulkan
Chichén Itzá, Yucatan

Mexico City Cathedral
1563

Pyramid of the Sun
Teotihuacan, Mexico

**SOUTH AMERICAN**

Sacysayhuaman Fortress
Machu Pichu, Peru

Machu Pichu, Peru
Center

Temple of the Sun
Cuzco, Peru

# ARCHITECTURE OF THE AMERICAS

**MASTERPIECES**

*Jaina clay figure,* A.D. 600–950, Museo Nacional, Mexico City

*Limestone plaque,* A.D. 590, Museo Nacional, Mexico City

*Mask of gray-green stone,* Museum für Volkerkunde, Basle, Switzerland

*Chac Mool,* Museo Nacional, Mexico City

*Plate, Cholula Polychrome,* A.D. 1250–1450, Mixtec Culture, St. Louis Art Museum

**ARCHITECTURE**

We are fortunate that we can still see some of the stone architectural complexes erected by the early inhabitants. It helps us to reconstruct their lives and manner of worship. The pyramids at Teotihuacan, Monte Alban, Tula, Chichén Itzá, Yucatan, and Copan, Honduras testify to the building skill, and give some feel for the grandeur that must have existed. The Cholula pyramid near Puebla is larger in volume than Cheop's pyramid in Egypt. The pyramids were part of a large complex that included a ball-playing field, and had a one-story temple on top. It is said that the victors in the ritual ball games were often sacrificed to the gods.

Colonial buildings reflect the heritage of the Spanish and Portugese priests who settled in Mexico and South America. They are often of Baroque design, with brick construction, round arches, tile roofs, and elaborately designed interiors.

**MASTERPIECES**

*Pyramid of the Sun,* c. 100 B.C. to A.D. 600, Teotihuacan, Mexico

*North Pyramid,* c. A.D. 968–1168, Tula, Mexico

*Temple of the Warriors,* Chichén Itzá, Mexico

## PROJECT 10–1: **MAYAN AND AZTEC CIRCLES**

### FOR THE TEACHER

The Mayas kept historical records, beginning about 50 B.C. They accumulated an enormous body of astronomical knowledge and created the most precise calendar known to man. Each day was made into a god. They could predict eclipses of the sun, and had an advanced system of arithmetic. The Aztecs based their calendar on that of the Mayas, and it was virtually identical. The solar year was divided into 18 months of 20 days each.

The circular motif is often seen in paintings and carvings. Their calendar, shields, and sacrificial altars, are arranged geometrically.

### EXAMPLES OF CIRCULAR STONES

*Stone of Tizoc,* c. A.D. 1481–1486, Museo Antropologia, Mexico City

*Chinkultic Disk,* A.D. 590, Museo National de Antropologia, Mexico City

### PREPARATION

If at all possible, have photocopies of some circular designs for students to copy. Modern Mexican design often includes "sun faces," but circular designs are also beautiful with traditional Mayan or Aztec motifs.

### FURTHER SUGGESTION

- Each student could make one of the 20 Aztec day signs in any size. These can be drawn on 5 × 7-inch cards mounted together to make a giant circle. They could also be carved into linoleum for painting, carved on rubber erasers for stamping, or tooled on heavy gold- or silver-colored aluminum foil.

Name: _____   Date: _____

# PROJECT 10–1: **MAYAN AND AZTEC CIRCLES**

## MATERIALS

- Foam picnic plates
- Scissors
- Ink
- Brayers
- Glass for rolling brayers
- Paper
- Compasses

It seems natural when working in a circle to divide it geometrically, as the Aztecs did in their calendar. Traditional designs may help you find a way to decorate a circular motif.

1. Use a compass to make a perfect circle on the bottom of a styrofoam plate. Cut it out with scissors or X-acto® knife. Trace around it on newsprint, and draw a design on the newsprint. Use a compass and ruler if you will be making a geometric design. Cut out the newsprint circle.

   *Safety Note: Always keep your hand behind the blade when you are cutting.*

2. Place the newsprint design on the styrofoam and trace over the design. It will leave a light impression on the styrofoam, which you can go over with a ballpoint pen or pencil to make deeper.

3. Squeeze printing ink from the tube onto a piece of glass. With a brayer, spread the ink around until it is thin enough to spread a thin coat on the styrofoam plate. If the ink is the right consistency, it will not fill in the lines on the plate, but will remain only on the surface.

4. To print, place it ink side down onto the drawing paper. Holding the plate and the paper together, turn it over so the paper is on top. Rub the paper with your hand in order to transfer the picture. Remove the plate and re-ink it.

5. You may choose to not re-ink the plate immediately, but print it again for a "ghost image." If you think of the circle simply as a design, you could get some exciting effects by printing and reprinting the plate, allowing it to overlap. Two or more people could share paper, and print your styrofoam plate on each other's paper.

# PROJECT 10-2: **MURAL (BASED ON MEXICAN MURALISTS)**

## FOR THE TEACHER

**Slide #29:** *Culture of Corn and Preparation of Pancakes.* The Mexican Revolution in 1911 and the overthrow of the dictator Porfirio Diaz inspired a number of artists to paint murals memorializing the Revolution. Foremost among them were painters David Alfaro Siqueiros (1896–1974), José Clemente Orozco (1883–1949), and Diego Rivera (1886–1957). The murals painted by these three artists carried strong messages.

## MASTERPIECES OF MEXICAN MURAL ART

*Zapatistas,* José Orozco, Museum of Modern Art, New York

*The Departure of Quetzalcoatl,* José Orozco, 1932–1934, Dartmouth College, Hanover, New Hampshire

*Liberation of the Peon,* Diego Rivera, 1931, Philadelphia Museum of Art

*Sugar Cane,* Diego Rivera, Ministry of Public Education

*Peasant Mother,* David A. Siqueiros, 1929, National Museum of Fine Arts, Mexico City

*Portrait of the Bourgeoisie,* David A. Siqueiros, 1939, Electrical Workers' Union Building, Mexico City

## PREPARATION

There are several options for this project. You may prefer to simply do small drawings that *could* be applied to a great wall. You could do a mural on roll paper, on posterboard sections hung side by side, on pieces of 4 × 6-foot foamcore, on large white-painted masonite sections, or on a school wall. Teachers are often overjoyed to have a mural painted on a blank classroom wall. The mural needs to relate to its location, not just in size, but also in subject matter. It would be inappropriate, for example, to paint a Mexican mural on a school wall unless you live in Mexico (or teach Spanish). However, the *technique* the Mexican muralists used is very appropriate for a large painting. (The Mexican muralists shared a method of working that was based on the work of Paul Gauguin. There was little detail. The work was outlined in black and had the flat, decorative quality and simplified form of his symbolist work.)

Discuss the purposes of murals. In addition to decorating public places, they sometimes commemorate an event, or are propaganda of one type or another. Ask students to help come up with ideas for a mural that might be suitable for your school. If you do paint a mural in the school, much of the work may end up being done after school. Select one responsible person to be in charge, one who has good judgment and is not afraid to make decisions. I have tried this method three times, and have yet to be disappointed.

## FURTHER SUGGESTIONS

- Another Mexican art form was the mosaic mural such as that seen on the side of a building at the University Library in Mexico City. Have students cut colored construction paper on the paper cutter into "mosaic tiles." Each student could make a small segment of a wall-sized mosaic by gluing small squares onto drawing paper or wide butcher paper. Some of the work could be done in larger geometric shapes such as circles and triangles that could fit together later. (Because this tends to become boring in a very short time, it is suggested that each individual do a piece no larger than $8 \times 10$ inches.)

- Have two students work together to make two easel paintings based on the Mexican Muralists' style. Each one begins a painting, then they trade paintings, allowing the other person to work on theirs. Teamwork of this type can get some very interesting results, and helps teach tolerance for the other person's ideas.

## PROJECT 10-2:  MURAL (BASED ON MEXICAN MURALISTS)

**MATERIALS**

- Newsprint
- Drawing paper
- Colored pencils
- Thin-line black marker
- Overhead transparencies
- Acrylic or latex paint
- Brushes

**Drawing after *The Flower Carrier*, 1935, San Francisco Museum of Art.**

A mural has to be appropriate for its location. The artwork is important, but the mural has to have a theme or idea. If you are doing a mural for your school, it could relate to the history of the region, the people who were there first, or are there now, or the local terrain. If you are doing a mural for a specific classroom, the subject matter might relate to what is taught in that room.

Work with groups of five people. Discuss ideas, then each individual should do a separate *complete* drawing for a mural (in proportion to the available space). Spread out the drawings, and each member of the group should help decide if you should all work on one of the ideas, or if two or more of the drawings could be combined somehow to make a more complex mural.

**Mural Design.** To simply create an idea for a mural design, work in proportion to a wall you might be thinking of using. With colored pencil, completely fill it in, working out a color scheme in advance.

**Posterboard Mural.** To make a mural on posterboard, make a grid by drawing lightly with pencil to enlarge the chosen design in proportion to the posterboard. Several posterboards could be hung side by side, with the mural continuing uninterruptedly. Select a color scheme. This can be painted with acrylic or tempera paint.

**Wall Mural.** After selecting a design, or combining designs, outline the design in black marker and photocopy the design onto an overhead transparency. Place it on an overhead projector and move the projector back and forth until the image is the correct size for the wall. It is possible to photocopy ordinary colored photographs onto transparencies, and these can be placed onto an overhead projector and enlarged. If you choose to use photographs, you must have a unifying idea to pull it together. Acrylic latex paint can be purchased already mixed, or you could buy pure hues, and mix your own paint with white or other hues for different values.

# Unit 2: SOUTH AMERICA

## OVERVIEW OF THE VISUAL ARTS

Civilization existed as early as 2500 B.C. on the coast of Peru, as evidenced by carbon-dating of remnants of textiles that were created at that time. Pottery created as early as 1800 B.C. has been found. Traces are found today of highly civilized cultures that flourished in Peru, Ecuador, Bolivia, and Chile. Pyramids found in Peru were probably influenced by the migrations of people from Mesoamerica.

The Incas were a warlike tribe that conquered the earlier settlers, and by A.D. 1500 ruled a vast empire that included most modern South American countries. They were sun worshippers, and made sacrifices, much as the Mesoamericans made sacrifices to their gods. Because of its rich silver and gold deposits, the empire became attractive to the Spanish conquistadores, and was overtaken by Pizarro in 1533.

## PAINTING

Early adobe pyramids were decorated with wall paintings. Deep shaft graves discovered in Columbia had richly decorated geometric patterns probably derived from weavings. Pottery was frequently painted in colored slip, though not usually in the brilliant colors associated with Mexican pottery.

## MASTERPIECES OF PAINTING

*Shaft grave,* Tierradentro region, Cauca, Columbia

*Rain God with Blue Scrolls,* Tetitla, Teotihuacan, Mexico

*Mixtec Codex Nuttall,* British Museum, c. 1350, London

*Waterside Village,* Temple of the Warriors, twelfth century, Chichén Itzá, Yucatan

## SCULPTURE

Because of their riches of gold, silver, and copper, there was a well developed metal-working technology. Ornaments created from these metals demonstrate their skill. The repoussé technique allowed thin layers of gold to be added to stone or wooden carvings.

Most Peruvian carvings were small, usually in stone or bone. Massive carved stone statues, up to 24 feet in height have been found near Tiahuanaco, Bolivia.

## MASTERPIECES OF SCULPTURE

*Magic Fish,* c. A.D. 800, Museum für Volkerkunde, Berlin

*Moche Sleeping Warrior,* A.D. 300–400, The Metropolitan Museum of Art, New York

*Inca Silver Llama,* A.D. 1440–1532, American Museum of Natural History, New York

*Chibcha Gold Ceremonial Knife,* c. A.D. 1000–1500, University Museum, University of Pennsylvania

*Death Mask in embossed gold plate,* Museum für Volkerkunde, Berlin

## ARCHITECTURE

Ceremonial centers were based on step pyramids. The Incas learned to terrace their hillsides to allow for cultivation, and literally hundreds of miles of terraces still exist. They point to the exceptional skill used by the inhabitants in shaping huge stones to fit together without mortar. It is thought that these were shaped through the use of stone tools. In Cuzco some of the stones were faced with gold plates. Machu Picchu, built around 1450, and one of the most famous Incan remains, perches high on a mountain. One outstanding feature is a semicircular tower of fine masonry. Curious phenomena seen on barren plateaus above the Nasca valley in Peru are vast linear patterns that have been created by removing dark brown pebbles from the yellow, sandy surface. These designs, some resembling animal forms, are similar to those seen painted on Nasca pots. The local people call them "El Calendario" (the calendar), so they may have been used ceremonially.

## MASTERPIECES OF ARCHITECTURE

*Machu Picchu,* c. 1450, Peru

*Sacsahuaman,* c. 1440, Cuzco, Peru

*Tiahuanaco Gateway of the Sun,* A.D. 200–450, Bolivia

*Sun Temple,* Pisac, Peru

## PROJECT 10-3: PERUVIAN PERSONALITY POT

**FOR THE TEACHER**

Vessel forms created in Peru are important to historical knowledge of the Peruvian culture. Making portraits of people on utilitarian vessels goes back hundreds of years. The technique was especially refined in Peru by the Chimu, Mochica, and Nazca peoples. Several forms combining animal or human sculpture with pottery forms were unique. Modeled forms included houses, animals and birds, and humans engaged in every aspect of daily activities. Mochica portrait vases decorated with various colors of clay slip were exceptionally fine.

**PREPARATION**

Most pots made in South America were handbuilt by the coil, modeling, or slab method. The fact that they were vessels appeared to be secondary to the beauty of the objects, and the portrait appeared to be the reason for the pot rather than an added decoration. Suggest that students make a pot that is personal. It could be a favorite animal, or a portrait of a friend or family member.

Photo 10-2. *Male Portrait Jar,* 500–300 B.C., 8 1/8 × 3 15/16 inches, Peru, extreme north coast, gift of Morton D. May, The Saint Louis Art Museum.

Photo 10-3. *Jug—Human Head,* A.D. 600–700, 18.4 cm high, north coast, gift of J. Lionberger Davis, The Saint Louis Art Museum.

## FURTHER SUGGESTIONS

- If it is not possible to do a fired clay project, miniatures could be made the same way with self-hardening clay that can be baked in an oven. Another possibility is to do "ceramics on paper." The drawing for the pot would be the finished product. There are enough possibilities for shapes and designs that a project such as this could give interesting results.

- Repoussé on gold-colored metal would allow students to work with some of the motifs and designs used by the South American metal smiths. Use aqua acrylic paint to make "stones" on the decorative jewelry and pendants made by the Peruvians.

**Photo 10-4. Stirrup-Spout Jar in Shape of the God Ai'apee, A.D. 200–600, 23.4 × 18.9 cm, Mochica culture, Peruvian, North Coast, earthenware, painted. The Saint Louis Art Museum, Gift of J. Lionberger Davis.**

# PROJECT 10–3: PERUVIAN PERSONALITY POT

**MATERIALS**

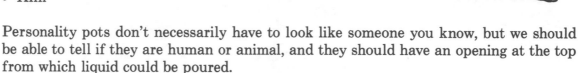

- Red clay, 2 to 3 pounds per person
- White clay to use as slip decoration
- Large pebbles or spoons for polishing clay
- Brushes
- Plastic containers for slip
- Kiln

Personality pots don't necessarily have to look like someone you know, but we should be able to tell if they are human or animal, and they should have an opening at the top from which liquid could be poured.

1. Draw your design before beginning so you will have a plan of action. First draw the "personality" part of the vessel, then decide what type of opening you will have. Several examples are shown on this page of the stirrup pots and other vessels.

2. Wedge the clay thoroughly by kneading, or by slapping the ball of clay between your palms for 10 minutes.

3. Take a piece of clay about the size of a walnut, and lay it on the table. Use the middle part of your fingers next to your palm, and the palm just below fingers to roll the clay to a uniformly sized coil. You can make several coils at a time, but keep them covered with plastic or a damp paper towel so they will not dry out.

4. Start with a spiral coil of clay for the bottom, joining each place where the coils touch by scoring (marking) with a pencil, and adding clay thinned to the consistency of cream (slip) to act as a glue. Continue until the bottom is the size you wish, then start building up the sides. Make your coils go in or out as needed to form the sculpture.

5. Use your forefinger to smooth the coils together on the inside of the pot as you work upward, as you will not be able to do it when the pot gets smaller at the top. The last coils will be quite narrow, as they are the openings of the spout. A "stirrup" spout could be added last.

6. When the clay is "leather hard" (partially dry, and your fingerprints don't show when you touch it), use a stone or the back of a spoon to polish the surface. If you have a second color of clay (such as white, if you are using red clay), make a slip of that color, and paint it on the surface of the pot. Most Peruvian pottery is unglazed, but shiny from such polishing. It generally has a red clay body with white slip decoration.

© 1992 by The Center for Applied Research in Education, Inc.

# Unit 3: NORTHERN NATIVE AMERICANS

## OVERVIEW OF THE VISUAL ARTS

North American cultures have generally been identified as having descended from the Asian migrations across the Bering Strait, although there is another theory that some may have arrived by boat from Oceania. Depending on where they settled, these peoples developed a life style and culture that enabled them to adapt to where they lived. The Northwestern tribes lived near water, and were chiefly hunter-gatherers. Plains cultures followed the buffalo. Other groups practiced agriculture.

As with many other nomadic peoples, the Native North Americans created few monumental works of art other than rock drawings or architectural complexes such as pueblos or mounds. Every object of daily life served a purpose, and there was no separation of art and life. Most of their artwork evolved when utilitarian objects and clothing were carefully created and decorated. The available material determined what artworks were created. Baskets were created by many of the plains Native Americans because of the ready availability of grasses. The Southwestern peoples became expert potters, and Northwestern peoples became master carvers.

In most Native American cultures their rich heritage continues to influence the artwork done today. Pottery and paintings from the Southwestern tribes are valued in museums and collections around the world. Although some of the old ways are lost, a new art is built on heritage of the old.

## PAINTING

Rock paintings and petroglyphs probably served a religious purpose. For painting large rock scenes, mitts were sometimes made of animal skins, with the fur on the outside. In adobe dwellings, murals were often painted on the interior walls. Various surfaces such as buffalo robes, tepees, and traders' muslin were painted by the Plains tribes, not just a way of recording dances, hunts, and war exploits, but also as a recording of group history. As early as the 1770s commercial paints were available. Painting also decorated wooden objects such as drums and plates. In some tribes warriors decorated their bodies with paint so that if they died in battle they were prepared for death.

## PAINTING MASTERPIECES

*Muslin painting,* Kiowa, c. 1875–1885, Nelson-Atkins Gallery of Art, Kansas City, Missouri

*Robe,* Southern Plains, Kansas City Museum of History and Science, Kansas City, Missouri

*Navajo Sand Chant,* The Museum of Navajo Ceremonial Arts, Santa Fe, N.M.

## SCULPTURE

Ready access to wood enabled the Northwestern tribes to develop the carving skills for which they are known today. Their totem poles stood outside their village to symbolize the animals that brought them good luck.

## SCULPTURAL MASTERPIECES

*Carved wood rattle,* Tlingit, c. 1870, Denver Art Museum

*Mask,* Northwest Coast, early nineteenth century, Bella Bella, British Museum

*Shaman's Charm,* Tlingit, Museum of Primitive Art, New York

## ARCHITECTURE

Some of the societal groups of mid-America lived a nomadic life, living in tepees that could be taken along as they moved to follow the buffalo. Other early Native Americans (the mound builders) used upright log structures for their homes and in their burial mounds. In the Southwest, the cultures built masonry and adobe pueblos, sometimes building several stories that must be entered by climbing ladders from the roof of one to another.

## ARCHITECTURAL MASTERPIECES

*Cliff Palace,* c. A.D. 1150, Mesa Verde, Colorado

*Pueblo,* San Ildefonso, New Mexico

## MINOR ARTS

Prestige came from beading, painting, ribbon applique, weaving, and pottery. The materials used were the natural ones available such as pine needles, clay, stone, wood, animal skin, and bone. Many of the artisans had other functions in a tribe, such as a medicine man who might also be a sand painter. Women produced the materials used in everyday life.

**North American Tribal Locations**

## PROJECT 10–4: TLINGIT TOTEMS

**FOR THE TEACHER**

The Native Americans of the Northwest Coast of Canada and the United States developed unique forms of art that are striking in their abstraction and simplicity. The vast majority of these objects are wood carvings that serve a variety of purposes. Many of them were used in religious ceremonies (for example, masks, rattles, or hats) or were used in hunting (clubs and knives). Their homes were built with decorative painted and carved roof supports and entry doors, and their clothing had designs painted or woven into them. One of the outstanding art forms was "kerfed" wood, which was wood steamed and curved to make chests, on which they painted or carved designs.

Religious beliefs were not separated from everyday life, but permeated everything they did. They were dependent on animals and fish for subsistence and consequently painted and carved images of these animals. When they went hunting, they painted

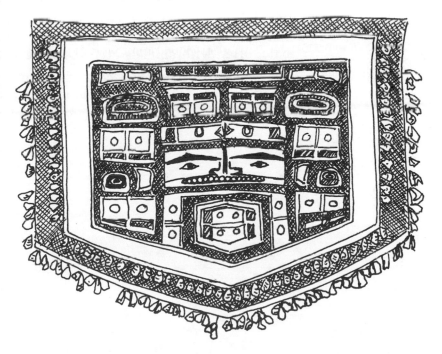

Photo 10-5 (left). *House Post,* mid-nineteenth century, 110 × 37½ × 13 inches (top), 35½ × 36½ × 13 inches (bottom), wood and paint, The Nelson-Atkins Museum of Art, Kansas City, Nelson Fund.

Photo 10-6 (above, right). Rendering of *Blanket,* Chilkat Tribe nineteenth century, 90 cm wide, wool, wood fiber and puffin beaks, gift of Mr. Charles M. Rice, The Saint Louis Art Museum.

their own faces to resemble the animals for which they hunted or fished (such as the wolf, bear, salmon, or whale).

Because of the physical limitations of the land, tribes were small and became identified with specific animals, which they considered their totems (good luck symbols). Totem poles were erected outside their homes, often incorporating more than one animal or carvings of human heads, eyes, or hands.

## PREPARATION

Try to find pictures of items made by the Tlingit and other coastal Native Americans of the Northwest Coast of Canada. Although you could have all the students simply cover boxes, it might be more interesting to have them create a variety of "carved" objects from papier-mâché. They could make "chests," totem poles (from round carpet centers, or round tubes used for mailing posters), masks, hats, rattles, house-posts (large flat boards affixed to upright beams), clubs, or bowls (simply turn a bowl upside down and cover it with papier-mâché strips). The challenge is for them to make a shape that resembles an animal (adding a beak, eyes, hair, feathers), and paint it with the abstract patterns.

## FURTHER SUGGESTIONS

- Have students make Sculpt-tape masks of each other's faces by having one lie down, while the other covers the face and hair (all but the nostrils) with two sheets of plastic wrap long enough to go across the face, reaching the tabletop. Apply several layers of sculpt-tape. When it is dry, paint with tempera paint. These could be made to resemble animals by putting sculpt-tape or papier-mâché features on top.

- The bright colors and simple designs could effectively be made of cut paper and applied to posterboard mask shapes or plain-colored boxes with rubber cement. Rattles could be made of boxes covered in tan paper, with dowel rods coming out of one end.

- Make hats with animal designs by making large circles and cutting out a wedge shape, then decorating before joining the edges to make a conical hat. Their conical hats, often with animals atop them, were carved from a solid block of wood.

- A group totem pole could be made by joining individual sections made on round ice cream cartons. The group would need to decide what animal would be their "totem."

Name: _____     Date: _____

# PROJECT 10–4:  **TLINGIT TOTEMS**

### MATERIALS

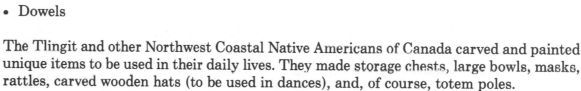

- Boxes of a variety of sizes
- Tagboard
- Newspaper
- Brown kraft paper (or plain grocery sacks)
- Wallpaper paste or Pritt® art paste
- Tempera
- String
- Dowels

The Tlingit and other Northwest Coastal Native Americans of Canada carved and painted unique items to be used in their daily lives. They made storage chests, large bowls, masks, rattles, carved wooden hats (to be used in dances), and, of course, totem poles.

1. If you are working in a group, decide which animal will be your totem. The more common ones used by these people were bears, wolves, mountain sheep, seals, eagles, dogfish, frogs, salmon, beavers and whales. Perhaps each member of the group could make a different item using the same animal interpreted on a different type of object.

2. Make a base to be covered with papier mâché. If you are covering a box, use tagboard to make raised areas, or perhaps have the head of an animal coming from the top of the box. You can make a base shape by wadding paper and taping it with masking tape. Cover the shape with several layers of torn newspaper.

3. To apply paper to the shape, dip the paper in wallpaper paste, and pull it between your first two fingers to remove excess paste. When the shape is finished, apply a final coat or two of smallish (approximately 2 × 2 inches) pieces of torn brown kraft paper, carefully smoothing the edges.

4. Apply finishing details with string or raised areas of cut cardboard. Cover these with kraft paper to make the shape look as if it is carved wood.

5. Allow the shape to dry before applying tempera paint. The colors used are simple: red, black, white, green, and turquoise blue (to resemble the abalone shell that they embedded in their carved pieces). When the paint is dry, apply varnish or polymer medium to give a shiny finish.

# PROJECT 10-5:  TRADERS' MUSLIN PAINTINGS

**FOR THE TEACHER**

Sand painting, which was done for ritualistic purposes may have been the origin of oil painting on surfaces such as buffalo robes and cloth. Oil paints were made by combining pigment with animal fat or oil of piñon seeds. Tempera paints were made by combining pigments with water, yucca syrup, egg (sometimes eagles' eggs), and melon or ground seeds. Pigments were treasured, often stored in special places, and mixed only by certain members of the tribe. Before commercial paints became available (in the 1770s), pigments from clay and minerals and plants were sometimes mixed with ritualistic substances such as eagle feathers, abalone shell, coral, or turquoise.

Some tribes grew cotton and wove cloth from it. Earliest cloth painting was on "mummy" cloth or handwoven cloth. In the Southwest these sometimes were painted as backdrops for an altar. In later times the government issued muslin for sheets to Indians on reservations, and it was also sold by traders. This "traders' muslin" became a natural surface for large paintings. Subjects varied widely, showing riders on horseback, major battles such as the Battle of Little Big Horn, tribal dances, and special festivals. The paintings were recordings of personal and group history. Similar paintings were sometimes done on traders' ledgers, the only available paper.

**Photo 10-7.** *Untitled,* **American Indian, Great Plains (Sioux?), c. 1875–1885, 90 × 200 cm, color and graphite on muslin, The Nelson-Atkins Museum of Art, Kansas City, Missouri. Nelson Fund.**

## PREPARATION

Point out to students that a personal history symbolizes what happened to them, and that the ability to draw is not very important. Most of the paintings on muslin were done by people who had no training in art. There were usually many small figures, in profile, outlined in black, and filled in with color. The background was basically left unpainted. The figures usually were arranged in rows, much as Egyptian tomb paintings.

## FURTHER SUGGESTIONS

- A sand painting can be made by giving each student a sheet of fine (coarse) sandpaper. These can be drawn on with oil pastels.

- Modern Native American painters continued to use pictographic symbols incorporated with modern design. Challenge students to make a composition using at least three pictographs as part of the design. For example, instead of painting standard fluffy clouds, use a cloud symbol to represent clouds, or a tree symbol instead of standard trees. These stylized forms are a good starting point for abstract painting.

- Wet a brown paper bag for 5 minutes. Roll it up, then flatten it to dry. When it is dry, tear it around the sides to resemble an animal skin. Use tempera to outline around the edges in brown, and paint the same subject matter on the "buffalo skin" as could be painted on the muslin.

# PROJECT 10–5: TRADERS' MUSLIN PAINTINGS

**MATERIALS**

- Drawing paper or white muslin
- Black marker
- Watercolor paints
- Crayon or oil crayon

Native Americans of the plains often made autobiographical records of their personal and tribal exploits on muslin, or sometimes on ledger books that they got from traders. They usually had many figures (often on horseback), and the scenes showed battles, dances, tribal encampments, or a personal history. Your personal history could include scenes of your own life, a single incident (such as a swim meet or game), or a "tribal" incident (the family at a reunion or holiday).

1. To do this project on drawing paper, after you decide on your subject, draw it lightly with pencil, then outline it with black marker or black crayon. (If you will be filling in with crayon, outline with black crayon last to avoid smearing.)

2. Fill in with colored crayon, watercolor, or tempera. Leave the background uncolored, except for details such as houses, a mountain range, trees, or water.

3. To paint on muslin, first draw the design on paper with black marker. Lay the muslin on top and tape it to a surface to flatten it. The drawing can be seen through the muslin and traced onto cloth with pencil.

4. Cloth can be colored with crayons, ink, watercolor, acrylic paint, tempera, or colored markers. Many of these paintings were of mixed media such as ink and watercolor, or ink and crayon. Colors generally used by tribal artists were usually "earth" tones, gold, black, brown, white, reddish brown, and occasionally blue or green.

**Drawing after Feather Dance, Big Lefthanded, Navajo, 1905–1912, tempera on cloth. Katherine Harvey collection, Museum of Northern Arizona.**

© 1992 by The Center for Applied Research in Education, Inc.

# Unit 4: PIONEER ART

## OVERVIEW OF THE VISUAL ARTS

The early North American settlers generally had ties to England and Western Europe. They came to this country with little more than the basic necessities, but quickly adapted, learning to make things with the materials on hand to enrich their lives. Many of the pioneer crafts originated in the colonies on the eastern seaboard, but the arts moved westward with the settlers. The necessities of life came first, but humankind seems to need to make even the necessities decorative. Even when working with scraps from clothing, a crazy quilt was often richly embroidered.

## PAINTING

Paintings done early in the history of the United States were traditional landscapes, cityscapes, pictures of individual homes or industry, and portraits. Many so-called early American primitive portraits were done by "limners," itinerant sign painters, who traveled from town to town. Although it has been said that they painted bodies and backgrounds on canvas during the off-season, then simply added heads later, there is no evidence that this was so. "Fireboards" were often painted with scenery such as a view of Mount Vernon. These were kept in front of the fireplace when it was not in use. "Fire fans" were shaped and painted fans to protect the face from the fire in a fireplace.

One interesting type of folk art related to painting was the decorative picture frame. Painting was another of the decorative arts, and students were encouraged to copy engravings and reproductions shown in books as a way of learning. In Victorian times, well bred young ladies learned the "arts," such as painting on satin, velvet, ivory, or paper, and "work in human hair." The "theorem" painting was a form of stencil painting (often on velvet) that used fruit and flower stencils to create perfectly formed objects. Most women could embroider, and many families have heirloom samplers or "mourning" pictures that were embroidered. They sometimes "painted" in embroidery, or applied paint so it looked like embroidery, or (rarely) combined both embroidery and painting in a composition.

## PAINTING EXAMPLES

*Joanna and Elizabeth Perkins* (?), attributed to John Smibert, 1688–1751, The Saint Louis Art Museum

*The Plantation,* artist unknown, c. 1825, The Metropolitan Museum of Art, New York

*The Peaceable Kingdom,* Edward Hicks, c. 1840–1845, Free Library of Philadelphia

*Watching the Cargo,* George Caleb Bingham, 1849, State Historical Society of Missouri, Columbia, Missouri

*After the Hunt,* William Harnett, 1885, California Palace Legion of Honor

## SCULPTURE

Charming folk art sculpture might have been made as toys, or because someone was trying to create a thing of beauty. Some of the better known early American carvings were the wooden weathervanes, ship figureheads, cigar store Indians, and duck decoys.

## EXAMPLES OF SCULPTURE

*Jenny Lind,* Mary E. Humes, 1851, figurehead, Mariners Museum, Newport News, Virginia

*Cigar Store Indian,* Massachusetts, Private Collection

*Cow Weathervane,* nineteenth century, Edison Institute of Technology, Dearborn, Michigan

## ARCHITECTURE

Early homes were based on European designs. Colonial New England homes were two story with a central chimney that also served as a cooking hearth. The "saltbox" house was named for the boxes that salt was kept in. By 1695, fine examples of architecture such as the governor's palace at Williamsburg were being built in centers of population. Thomas Jefferson's Monticello, built in 1796, reflected the neoclassical influence. Pioneers who moved to the west built log cabins if there were trees. Where there were no trees, they dug sod houses into the side of a hill.

## ARCHITECTURAL EXAMPLES

*Ironmaster's House,* c. 1650–1700, Saugus Iron Works National Historical Site, Saugus, Massachusetts

*Farmhouse,* c. 1812, Brookline, Massachusetts

# PROJECT 10–6: THE LOG CABIN PATCHWORK QUILT

### FOR THE TEACHER

Patchwork quilting may have originated in China, Persia, India, or Egypt. The crusaders discovered it and brought it back to Western Europe, where it became popular. The art mostly died out on the continent except for England. When it came to America, it developed into a uniquely American art form, the patchwork quilt. Unlike other art forms, the quilt was something almost anyone could create, and most families own at least one handmade quilt. Making quilts became a social activity that was popular among the pioneers. Museums throughout the country have sponsored shows of old and new quilts, and it is interesting to see how this artform has evolved with modern interpretations. It is still basically a feminine activity, though a number of males have also seen it as a new medium for artwork and are entering the field. I recently saw an exhibition of new African-American quilts, and there is a relationship between the patterns passed down through some African-American families to African kente cloth. Many of the African-American patterns are made in long strips rather than the geometric patches favored by western pioneer families. Applique and embroidery are frequently also seen on quilts.

### QUILT EXAMPLES

*Crazy Quilt,* Celestine Bacheller, c. 1900, Museum of Fine Arts, Boston

*Applique Quilt,* G. Knappenberger, 1876, Museum of American Folk Art, New York City

*Friendship Quilt,* 1848, The Saint Louis Art Museum

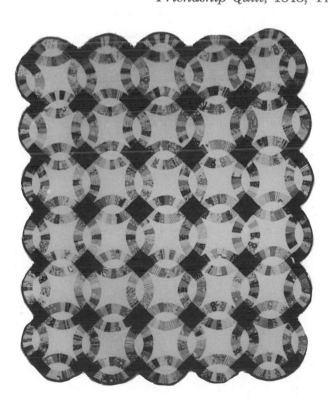 

## PREPARATION

A recent attempt has been made to catalogue quilts within the Pennsylvania area, with people bringing in not only their family quilts to photograph, but also photos of the people who made them, any patterns or information about quilting, and poetry and family stories relating to quilting. This would be a wonderful project for your students. If their own family does not have quilts, suggest they ask among neighbors and friends' families. There are volumes of books about quilts available at the library. Suggest that students check out some of them so you can try to identify the patterns on the quilts they bring in. These could be photographed with an instant camera, and each quilt could have a small history written about it.

To save time you may wish to cut the 4 × 4-inch and 1 × 1-inch paper squares in advance. Allow each student to select one dark and one light color and a different color for the center of each patch. It may help them envision the quilt to work it out on graph paper, but this step is not absolutely necessary.

## FURTHER SUGGESTIONS

- Make one full-sized paper quilt (staple it on a wall) by having each member of the class make at least one 8-inch patch in the log cabin method. This could be done with patterned wallpaper or wrapping paper instead of construction paper.

- Have each student color a different quilt pattern on an 8-inch square of graph paper with colored pencil or crayon.

# PROJECT 10–6: THE LOG CABIN PATCHWORK QUILT

**MATERIALS**

- White drawing paper 18 × 22 inches
- Colored construction paper
- Rulers
- Rubber cement
- Scissors

Your patchwork quilt will be made of paper rather than cloth. Many quilt makers were simply using up scrap cloth, but they became artists at their arrangements of color and pattern. The Log Cabin pattern is one that can be arranged in many different ways. Squares are diagonally divided into half light and half dark patches, with a small square in the center.

1. Select one light and one dark color of construction paper. Cut exact 4 × 4-inch squares. Cut the dark ones diagonally to make triangles. Use rubber cement to glue the dark *triangles* onto the light *squares*. Glue a 1 × 1-inch square of paper of a different color in the center of each patch.

2. Before gluing, try some of the different ways of arranging these squares. The pioneers had many traditional ways of doing it. Some are shown here.

**Straight Furrows**     **Barn Raising**     **Sparkling Diamond**     **Wild Goose Chase**

3. Use a yardstick or ruler to divide the drawing paper into a 1-inch grid to guide you in keeping the patches straight. Arrange and glue the patches onto the drawing paper. To make a border, select one of the colors in your quilt and glue it around the edges.

4. Authentic Log Cabin quilts were made with different sizes and patterns of strips. If you wish to make a patch with strips, cut and assemble the pieces as shown in the diagram below.

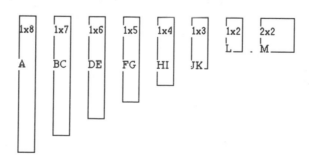

**Photo 10-8.** *White Lily,* **1944–1945, height, 96.0 cm, Alexander Calder, sheet metal, wire, paint, The Saint Louis Art Museum.**

# MODERN ART

# MODERN
## TIME LINE

| | 1880 | 1890 | 1900 | 1910 | 1920 | 1930 | 1940 | 1950 |
|---|---|---|---|---|---|---|---|---|

Art Nouveau
1880–1910

Futurism
1908

Dada 1916–1922
Realism 1920–1940

Surrealism
1922–1940s

Abstract
Expressionism
1945–1960

Miro

Postimpressionism
1886–1920

Fauvism
1905–1907

Armory Show
1913

Henry Moore

Mobile, Calder

Georgia O'Keeffe

De Stijl, 1917

Cubism 1907–1920

German Expressionism
Max Beckmann
1920

Piet Mondrian

The Old Blind
Guitar Player,
1903,
Picasso

The Thinker
Rodin, 1880–1900

First World War
1914–1918

Bauhaus
1925

Maillol

Marino Marini
1949

**Africa**

Aswan Dam
1903

King Tut's Tomb
Discovered 1922

**Americas**

Model T Ford
1908

Wright Brothers
1903

Stock Market
crash 1929

Lindbergh flies
Atlantic 1927

Computer developed
1944

Atom bomb
1945

**Asia**

Ching Dynasty
1644–1911

Russian-Japanese War
1904–1905

Japan invades
Manchuria
1931

People's Republic
of China 1949

**Europe**

Russian Revolution
1917

Georges Rouault
1937

**Near East**

British rule
ends in India
1947

**Other**

# Unit 1: MODERN ART (1900 TO 1950)

## OVERVIEW OF THE VISUAL ARTS

### PAINTING

By the early 1900s, instead of leaving the studio to paint, as the Impressionists did, artists began looking inward, substituting "subconscious" thoughts and dreams for reality. Edvard Munch (1863–1944) was one of the painters who depicted emotionalism in his paintings with such work as *The Scream.*

Each group of artists seemed to inspire the ones to follow them, with the names of specific movements changing frequently. Many of the artists, for example Picasso, Monet, and Matisse, lived and worked during several of these periods, but their work was highly personal, and they were more likely to influence than be influenced by what was happening in the art world.

A brief overview of some of the more notable "isms" of the twentieth century is given here.

**Fauvism (1905–1907).** The Fauves were inspired by the Impressionists and Neo-impressionists. They worked in larger color patches than those of the Impressionists, and in strident colors that often didn't exist in nature. They often dispensed with classical perspective, using color and line to construct their forms.

**Cubism (1908–1914).** Inspired by Cézanne's color patches, the early Cubists broke forms into planes and facets, discarding traditional perspective, modeling, and light effects. Many of the Cubists saw it as a way of simplifying form and strengthening composition.

**Futurism (1909–1918).** This largely Italian art movement, usually sculptural, tried to depict possibilities of the new scientific age, showing the beauty of speed by slowing it down.

**De Stijl (c. 1917).** Primarily Dutch painters, sculptors, architects, designers, and illustrators aimed at evolving a purely abstract art. Examples of the abstraction were the use of primary colors, with strong horizontal and verticals.

**Expressionism (1910–1932).** Emotional expression resulted in the distortion of realism and proportion in the primarily German movement.

**Dada (1916–1922).** Dada is a nonsense word, symbolizing a total breakaway for some artists from making representational work. For some, it was an exploration of the irrational that led to Surrealism.

**Surrealism (1924–1940s).** When André Breton, a poet, founded Surrealism, he envisioned writing poetry based on dreamlike meanderings. This purely literary movement was applied to art, with fantastic subjects sometimes painted in obsessive detail.

## MASTERPIECES OF PAINTING

*Decorative Figure Against an Ornamental Background,* Henri Matisse, 1925, Museé National d'Arte Moderne, Paris

*The Old King,* Georges Rouault, 1937, Museum of Art, Carnegie Institute, Pittsburgh

*Self-Portrait,* Oscar Kokoschka, 1913, Museum of Modern Art, New York

*Nude Descending a Staircase,* Marcel Duchamp, 1912, Philadelphia Museum of Art

*Composition in Line and Color,* Piet Mondrian, 1913, Rijksmuseum, Otterlo, The Netherlands

*Les Demoiselles d'Avignon,* Pablo Picasso, 1907, Museum of Modern Art, New York

*Gypsy Woman with Baby,* Amadeo Modigliani, 1919, National Gallery of Art, Washington, D.C.

*Nighthawks,* Edward Hopper, 1942, The Art Institute of Chicago

*Jukebox,* Jacob Lawrence, 1946, Detroit Institute of Arts

## SCULPTURE

Most of the sculptors of the early period were trained in the tradition of sketching from classical plaster casts, and drawing and sculpting from models. Much of the art done early in the century is forgettable, as monumental art often is. Many of the early sculptors were becoming aware of primitive and prehistoric art with its simplicity and total disregard for reality. They began changing how they sculpted the human form, by exaggerating, making holes in, and eliminating portions altogether.

## MASTERPIECES IN SCULPTURE

*The Kiss,* Constantin Brancusi, 1909, Montparnasse Cemetery, Paris

*Recumbent Figure,* Henry Moore, 1938, The Tate Gallery, London

*Bird in Space,* Constantin Brancusi, 1928, Museum of Modern Art, New York

*Horse,* Raymond Duchamp-Villon, 1914, The Art Institute of Chicago

*Lobster Trap and Fish Tails,* Alexander Calder, 1939, Museum of Modern Art, New York

*The City Rises,* Umberto Boccioni, 1910–1911, Museum of Modern Art, New York

*Head of Fernande Olivier,* Pablo Picasso, 1909, Hirschhorn Museum, Washington D.C.

## ARCHITECTURE

Early twentieth-century buildings, such as the Chrysler and Woolworth Buildings in New York, resemble buildings that are being constructed at the end of the twentieth century. They were functional skyscrapers, but went beyond being vertical boxes. The Art Deco influence is being seen again today. The Bauhaus look (form follows function), the Louis Sullivan and Frank Lloyd Wright influences all transformed what architecture had traditionally been.

## NOTABLE EXAMPLES IN ARCHITECTURE

*Woolworth Building,* Cass Gilbert, 1911–1913, New York

*Chrysler Building,* William Van Alen, 1928–1930, New York

*Schroder House,* Gerrit Rietveld, 1924–1925, Utrecht, Holland

*Notre-Dame-du-Haut,* Le Corbusier, 1950–1954, Ronchamp, France

*Bauhaus,* Walter Gropius, 1925–1926, Dessau, Germany

*Tugendhat House,* Mies van der Rohe, 1930, Brno, Czechoslovakia

*Johnson Wax Building,* Frank Lloyd Wright, 1936–1939, Racine, Wisconsin

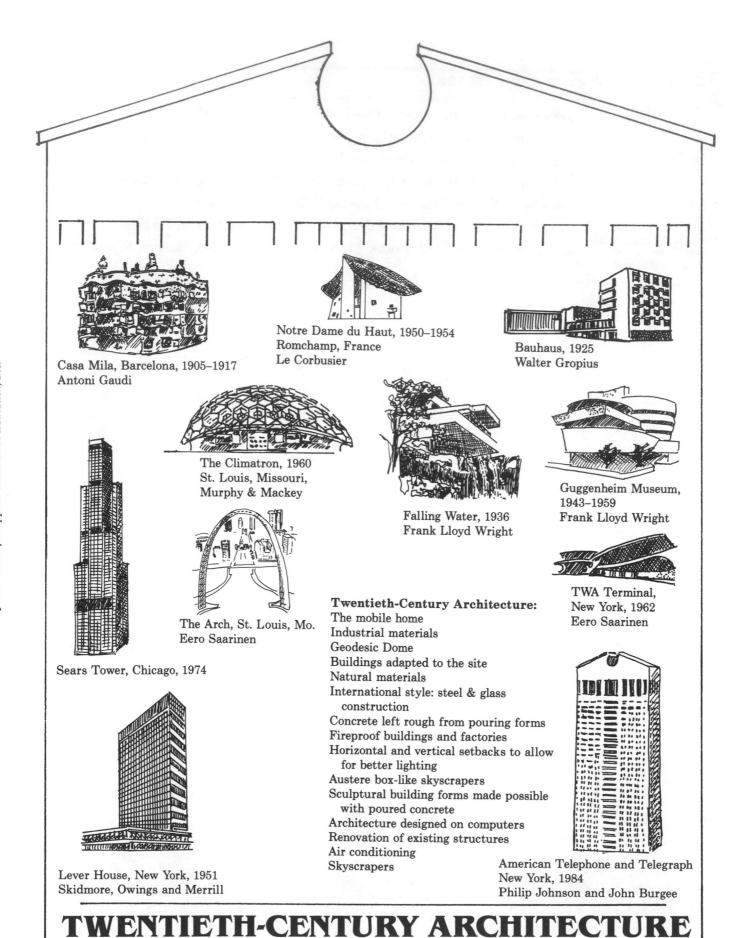

Casa Mila, Barcelona, 1905–1917
Antoni Gaudi

Notre Dame du Haut, 1950–1954
Romchamp, France
Le Corbusier

Bauhaus, 1925
Walter Gropius

The Climatron, 1960
St. Louis, Missouri,
Murphy & Mackey

Falling Water, 1936
Frank Lloyd Wright

Guggenheim Museum,
1943–1959
Frank Lloyd Wright

The Arch, St. Louis, Mo.
Eero Saarinen

TWA Terminal,
New York, 1962
Eero Saarinen

Sears Tower, Chicago, 1974

**Twentieth-Century Architecture:**
The mobile home
Industrial materials
Geodesic Dome
Buildings adapted to the site
Natural materials
International style: steel & glass
   construction
Concrete left rough from pouring forms
Fireproof buildings and factories
Horizontal and vertical setbacks to allow
   for better lighting
Austere box-like skyscrapers
Sculptural building forms made possible
   with poured concrete
Architecture designed on computers
Renovation of existing structures
Air conditioning
Skyscrapers

Lever House, New York, 1951
Skidmore, Owings and Merrill

American Telephone and Telegraph
New York, 1984
Philip Johnson and John Burgee

# TWENTIETH-CENTURY ARCHITECTURE

## PROJECT 11–1: **MATISSE INTERIOR**

### FOR THE TEACHER

Henri Matisse was the acknowledged leader of a movement that was a logical extension of Impressionism and Neoimpressionism. The Fauves (literally translated as "wild beasts" in French) used large vigorous brushstrokes of pure riotous color that reflected their admiration of Vincent Van Gogh, Georges Seurat, Paul Signac, and Paul Gauguin. The Fauve movement, begun in 1905, was supplanted in 1907 by Cubism.

Matisse continued to be a vital force in the art world until his death. He was considered one of the greatest painter-sculptors of the twentieth century.

### FAUVE MASTERPIECES

*The Green Stripe* (Mme Matisse), Henri Matisse, 1905, Royal Museum of Fine Arts, Copenhagen

*Pool of London,* André Derain, 1906, Tate Gallery, London

*Les Bateaux-Lavoirs,* Musée de L'Annonciade, 1906, Saint-Tropez

### PREPARATION

Set up several still-lifes, making a backdrop by putting heavy matboard on an easel for draping fabrics. Ask students to bring in items from home such as green plants, colorful patterned fabric, or kitchen utensils. A discussion of "negative" space prior to beginning will be helpful to students.

### FURTHER SUGGESTIONS

- After completely outlining a still-life pencil drawing in black marker, make several geometric outlines on the paper in pencil, and fill inside or outside the shapes with one or two colors of paint. Erase the pencil-drawn shapes so they do not show. For example, use three to five circles of different sizes, or three identical rectangles, or two triangles and a circle.
- Make a "Matisse-collage" of a room interior, using real fabric or patterned wallpaper and cutouts of construction paper. Include one or more people. This would be a good time to explain how effectively Matisse combined many patterns within one composition.

# PROJECT 11–1:  MATISSE INTERIOR

**MATERIALS**

- 18 × 24-inch newsprint
- 18 × 24-inch drawing paper
- 6 × 8-inch paper
- Oil crayon, colored pencil, or pastels
- Pencils

Henri Matisse often did room interiors, including homey touches such as tables and chairs, depicting many different designs from rugs, wallpaper, and patterned fabric. In some of his detail-filled interiors, Matisse deliberately left unpainted space, and was not concerned with depicting true perspective. A white plant or white easel was often more effective than one that was painted the conventional color.

**Drawing after *Odalisque***

1. Make a viewfinder to aid in selecting a portion of the still life for your drawing (cut a hole 3 × 4 inches in a piece of 6 × 8-inch paper). Hold the viewfinder away from you, close one eye and move it around until you have a pleasing composition (just like looking through a camera viewfinder). Transfer what you see through the viewfinder to the 18 × 24-inch piece of newsprint.

2. Analyze your newsprint drawing. What shapes in the picture could be left uncolored (white), while still resembling the original shape? A teapot? Plant? Chair?

3. Place the front of the drawing on a window (or lightbox), and trace around the drawing on the back with pencil. To transfer it to the drawing paper, tape the newsprint and drawing paper together at the top, and trace around the original drawing on the front of the newsprint.

4. Select a color scheme. Matisse and the other Fauves used brilliant colors, often using complements such as red and green or red and blue. The Fauves did not necessarily paint real colors, but painted real objects in unusual colors.

5. You may wish to select one or more areas to depict pattern. If you are looking at actual fabric while painting it, notice how the pattern changes depending on how it folds and hangs. It is important to paint it the way you see it, not the way you "know" it looks.

# PROJECT 11-2: CUBISM

## FOR THE TEACHER

**Slide # 30: *The Three Musicians.*** Pablo Picasso (1881–1973) was one of the most prolific and creative painter-sculptors of the twentieth century. A fully trained painter by 19, he was already established when he broke new ground with his *Les Demoiselles d'Avignon* (1907). Its planes and deliberate distortions reflect his interest in African sculpture. The large "facets" in this painting were refined in later paintings to smaller divisions of space. He and fellow Cubist George Braque both owed a debt to Cézanne who first reduced shapes to areas of flat color. Both artists created "Collage Cubism," where real objects such as newspaper, wood, imitation caning, or words were glued to backgrounds and combined with painting. Eventually they found they could imitate specific materials by painting patterns to resemble collage. One of Picasso's techniques was to show the front, sides, and occasionally the back appearing simultaneously in an artwork. Although Picasso's paintings were abstract, there is almost always a recognizable subject that he simplified or distorted.

## CUBIST MASTERPIECES

*Les Demoiselles d'Avignon,* Pablo Picasso, 1907, Museum of Modern Art, New York

*Woman's Head,* (sculpture), Pablo Picasso, 1909, Museum of Modern Art, New York

*Man With a Guitar,* Georges Braque, 1911, Solomon Guggenheim Museum, New York

*Three Musicians,* Pablo Picasso, 1921, Philadelphia Museum of Art

*Guernica,* Pablo Picasso, 1937, Prado Museum, Madrid

## PREPARATION

Try to show several aspects of Picasso's Cubism, allowing students to select one aspect for interpretation. They will probably find it much easier to work as "Cubists" by working in a construction paper collage. This allows them to move the paper around to a satisfactory arrangement before gluing. If they have enjoyed making the collage, they might enjoy interpreting it in tempera or acrylic paint.

*Safety Note: Rubber cement fumes can be hazardous. Use in a well ventilated room.*

## FURTHER SUGGESTIONS

- Have one student pose for a figure drawing. Then make it a cubistic drawing by placing straight lines where there are curved ones, and making some boxlike forms. Compare similarities and differences in how each person sees. This could be further developed into a painting.

- This project could be appropriate for a value painting in any color. Simply discuss working from the pure hue from its darkest possible variation to its lightest.

# PROJECT 11–2: CUBISM

## MATERIALS

**Drawing after Picasso's *Man with a Pipe*, 1915.**

- Colored construction paper
- Pencil
- Scissors
- Newsprint
- White drawing paper
- Rubber cement
- Black fine-line marker

Even though you will be making an abstract cubist painting, you need to have a subject to "abstract." Your subject could be your family at dinner, a field trip to a factory, a group of friends watching a film at home, a competition of any kind (professional hockey, for example), or anything you can think of where there is some action.

## CONSTRUCTION PAPER CUBIST COLLAGE

1. Once you have chosen your subject, draw realistic figures or objects at random on a sheet of newsprint. Now simplify and exaggerate the forms with straight or curved lines. Give some thought to where they will be placed on the larger sheet of paper. Cut out the newsprint figures to use as patterns.

**Photo 11-1.** *Guernica,* **Pablo Picasso, 1937, 11 feet 5½ inches × 25 feet 5¾ inches, oil on canvas, Prado Museum, Madrid. Art Resource, NY.**

**300**

## PROJECT 11–2 (Continued)

2. Select a neutral color such as black, brown, or gray as a background. Trace around the newsprint patterns and cut out. In a composition such as this, you must be willing to "fracture" your cut-outs, to substitute other colors of paper for some portions of the figures, to use pattern freely, and to repeat a color in more than one place.

### COLLAGE IN THE MANNER OF *GUERNICA*

Picasso showed the horror of war and saturation bombing in his famous painting of the Spanish Civil War, *Guernica*. Guernica was a small town in Spain that was almost destroyed. You could show action or an event in your life in this project.

1. Select paper in three to four different values of the same general hue; for example, black, white, and gray, or white, light blue, dark blue, and violet.

2. Use one color as your background. Cut several geometric shapes (rectangles, triangles, and irregular shapes) from the lightest and darkest papers.

3. This "action" picture might have real people in motion. How would you show the motion of a track team, or a dance performance, or a concert? Could you "fracture" the forms, or change them from reality in some way in the manner of Picasso?

4. Cut out your forms and move them around on the paper. Try overlapping or adding pattern on top of some areas with related color in marker or crayon. When the composition looks right to you, glue it down.

Photo 11-2. *The Blue Mandolin,* 45⅝ × 34⅝ inches, oil on canvas, 1930, Georges Braque, The Saint Louis Art Museum.

# PROJECT 11–3: **SURREALISTIC PAINTING**

## FOR THE TEACHER

Surrealism did not begin only in the early twentieth century. It existed for many centuries in the work of artists who drew imaginary fantasies. Hieronymus Bosch, the sixteenth-century Dutch painter created a fantasy world in his *Garden of Delights.* Sixteenth-century Italians delighted in the visual pun, such as an island that resembled a man's face, when viewed from a different direction, or Arcimboldo's paintings of faces composed of vegetables or fish. Probably Salvador Dali is the artist most identified with the Surrealist movement, part of which can be attributed to his showmanship, but also to a unique vision. He said, "The difference between a madman and myself is that I am not mad."

Giorgio De Chirico was one of the early twentieth-century artists whose work went beyond reality. Almost everything he painted, including buildings, tiny silhouetted figures, and reclining Greek statues, was realistic. It was the eerie emptiness of city-scapes created through his use of deep shadow and the illusion of perspective that give a "disquieting" feeling to the viewer.

## MASTERPIECES OF SURREALISM

*Nostalgia of the Infinite,* Giorgio de Chirico, 1913, Museum of Modern Art, New York

*The Disquieting Muses,* Giorgio de Chirico, 1916, Gianni Mattioli Foundation, Milan

*Self-Portrait with Seven Fingers,* Marc Chagall, 1912, Stedelijk Museum, Amsterdam

*I and the Village,* Marc Chagall, 1911, Museum of Modern Art, New York

*Large glass,* Marcel DuChamp, 1915, Philadelphia Museum of Art

*Elephant of the Celebes,* Marcel DuChamp, 1921, Museum of Modern Art, New York

*The Persistence of Memory,* Salvador Dali, 1931, Museum of Modern Art, New York

**Photo 11-3.** *The Transformed Dream,* **Georgio de Chirico, oil, The Saint Louis Art Museum.**

## PREPARATION

Show students work by some of the Surrealists. Because the work of these artists was widely divergent and personal, discuss the general appearance of the work of the artists and ask the students to verbally summarize in one sentence what they think the work is about. For example, "Chagall's work shows dreamlike drawings of his life in a small Russian village."

Have students write "stream-of-consciousness" words before painting—it *does* help them come up with ideas. This fantasy "painting" can be done in any dry medium such as pastel, oil pastel, pencil, or cut and pasted paper, or in tempera, watercolor, or oil. The medium is not as important as the idea.

## FURTHER SUGGESTIONS

- Max Ernst explored the method of "Frottage." He made compositions by placing paper on top of textured objects and rubbing with a pencil. Students understand this when you ask them if they ever made a "rubbing" of a penny. Typing paper can be used to make rubbings of various objects in the room with oil pastel or crayon, then these can be emphasized with line to make an abstract, dream-like composition.

- "Decalomania" was a Surrealist technique of placing various colors of paint on a slick paper (such as a magazine page or fingerprint paper), and making a "print" by pressing paper onto the paint while moving it. It is an accidental type of design, but something realistic could be drawn into this background after it has dried.

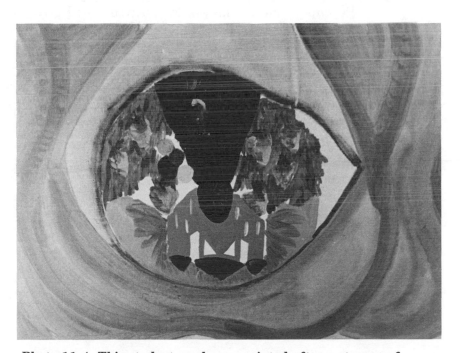

**Photo 11-4. This student work was painted after a stream-of-consciousness writing exercise.**

# PROJECT 11–3: **SURREALISTIC PAINTING**

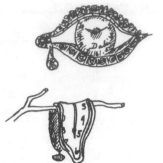

**MATERIALS**

- Newsprint
- Watercolor or drawing paper
- Watercolors, acrylic paint, or tempera
- Pencil

To do a Surrealistic painting, you first have to get your imagination going. There are no limitations. You may think of a place, a person, a priceless object, or ordinary objects arranged in no logical order. Fantasy painters often depicted objects realistically, but in strange juxtapositions.

De Chirico painted realistic city-scapes with eerie shadows and objects. Salvador Dali painted limp watches in normal appearing landscapes with mountains and deserts. Joan Miró took real objects such as screwdrivers, hammers, and pliers, and painted them on canvas as substitutes for people.

1. These two exercises take no more than 10 minutes, to help you develop ideas.

    **a.** For three minutes simply write things as they pop into your mind. This dream-like writing was how the poets came up with a personal vision.

    **b.** Use pencil and paper to "doodle." Simply draw things as they cross your mind. Perhaps some of the words you wrote will give you ideas. You are not at this point trying to make a composition, but just drawing objects as they occur to you. Draw small, quick ideas, without trying to make anything finished.

2. Cut the "doodles" out so you have a number of small drawings. Now move these shapes around on a sheet of newsprint the size of your painting. Group some of them, leave some empty space, and consider balance. You may have to enlarge some of the objects you've drawn, or repeat them someplace else on the drawing. Redraw the shapes or glue them to the drawing.

3. At this point you probably have quite a bit of empty space. Your abstract composition can come alive with a unifying idea. It could be something such as a city-scape (de Chirico), landscape (Dali), or simply lines and circles (Miro).

4. Transfer your drawing to a sheet of watercolor or drawing paper. Whether you use paint or a dry medium such as colored pencil or pastel, you can make this a colorful composition. Try using complementary colors (red/green, violet/yellow), or several values of one hue, and a complementary color.

5. Title your composition. It isn't often that you are asked to name your artwork, but because this is a product of your mind, try saying in a few words what you were trying to show.

© 1992 by The Center for Applied Research in Education, Inc.

## PROJECT 11–4:  BOX ART

**FOR THE TEACHER**

**Slide # 31: *Untitled (Medici Prince).*** Assemblage is a three-dimensional (sculptural) form of collage with related and sometimes unrelated objects put together by an artist. Artist Joseph Cornell, (1903–1972) created assemblages in glass-fronted boxes. His boxes are highly personal, filled with nostalgic and often strange arrangements of objects, maps, and photographs. He had met several of the Surrealists, and his work was often compared to theirs. He began creating assemblage boxes in the 1930s, and continued for another forty years.

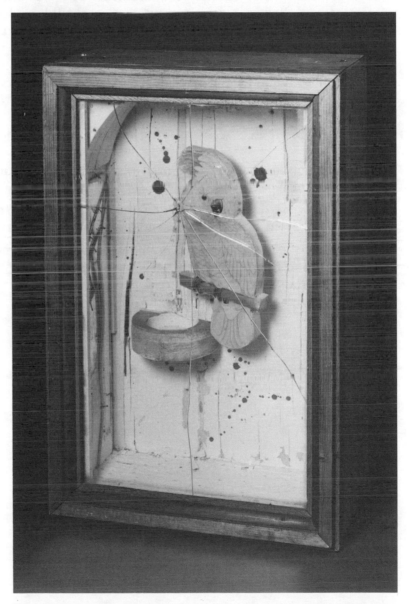

Photo 11-5. *Isabelle* (*Dien Bien Phu* on reverse side), Joseph Cornell, 1954, 18 × 12 × 6 inches, box construction with glass, painted wood, paper collage and mirror, purchase, The Shoenberg Foundation, Inc., The Saint Louis Art Museum.

**MASTERPIECES**

>   *Medici Slot Machine,* Joseph Cornell, 1942, collection of Mr. and Mrs. Bernard J. Reis, New York
>
>   *Soap Bubble Set,* Joseph Cornell, 1950, The Art Institute of Chicago
>
>   *Isabelle (Dien Bien Phu),* Joseph Cornell, 1954, Saint Louis Art Museum
>
>   *Space Object Box,* Joseph Cornell, 1959, Allan Stone Gallery, New York

**PREPARATION**

Show students Surrealist artworks such as Dali's *Persistence of Memory,* so that they will get the idea of unlikely combinations. Suggest that students first locate a box of some type. Size is not important, but it should be sturdy. An old wooden drawer, drinks carton, cigar box, even a plastic box frame would do. If they are in a shop class, they can make a box. Suggest that this is a good time to empty out desk drawers, or ask the family if they would like to get rid of old jewelry or excess materials from a workbench. Bring in art magazines for them to cut up or get ideas from. Before they begin affixing materials to the box, have them discuss their "theme" with you.

**FURTHER SUGGESTIONS**

- Have each student do a colored pencil drawing of his or her own box, or select a portion of it to draw.

- Students can do other forms of assemblage using the same general approach. Marisol did wonderful large-scale assemblages of wooden forms that depicted humans.

- Have all the students bring in any objects they can find. Arbitrarily divide them into groups and have each group create one assemblage using the materials they brought. A certain amount of bartering would be tolerated. It will be a bit chaotic, but it will certainly draw forth creativity.

## PROJECT 11–4:  **BOX ART**

**MATERIALS**

- Box (cigar, wood, plastic)
- Glue (glue gun, white glue)
- Variety of materials (photos, maps, doll parts, toys, etc.)

Assemblage is one of the three types of sculpture. The other two—additive (clay) and subtractive (carving)—are usually created from only one material. In assemblage, you may combine almost any unlikely combination of materials. It is important to first get an idea, then find your materials.

1. Prepare the box. Clean it and figure out how it will be hung or displayed before placing objects in it. If it is a large box, you can drill holes in the back and hang it with rope.

2. Come up with an idea for a theme, perhaps starting with a reproduction of an original work of art, as Cornell did when his theme for a box was based on a reproduction of a portrait of a Medici prince. Once you have your first object, the rest will be easier.

3. Look for materials for the box. It may take some time of looking around for postcards, containers, natural objects, or related objects such as you might find on a workbench or desk. Use humor. Someone will understand visual puns.

4. You could place many small boxes within your large box. Each one could have a related theme. Now that it is easy to have color photocopies made of almost anything, you could have large blowups made of one of your own photos, combining colored images with other materials.

**Drawn after** *Soap Bubble Set,* **1942, Joseph Cornell, Guggenheim Foundation, Venice, Italy.**

**Drawn after Medici,** *Slot Machine,* **1942, Private Collection, N.Y.**

**Drawn from** *Habitat for a Shooting Gallery,* **Joseph Cornell, Des Moines Art Center, Iowa.**

# PROJECT 11-5: **I SAW THE FIGURE FIVE IN GOLD**

**FOR THE TEACHER**

*I Saw the Figure Five in Gold,* a 1928 painting by Charles Demuth (1883–1935), was a forerunner of the use of numbers and letters in artwork. The painting was inspired by a poem written by Demuth's friend, William Carlos Williams, about a fire engine racing through city streets on a wet night. The names "Bill" and "Carlo" refer to the author of the poem, and the "figure five" was on the fire engine. The tilted buildings and rays of color bring to mind how surrealistic such a scene would be at night.

Several artists, including Pop artists Robert Indiana and Jasper Johns, have paid tribute to Demuth through their own work. Indiana's *Demuth 5* is one of a series based on this theme.

**MASTERPIECES**

*Buildings, Lancaster,* Charles Demuth, 1930, Whitney Museum of American Art, New York

*I Saw the Figure Five in Gold,* Charles Demuth, 1928, The Metropolitan Museum of Art, New York

*Report from Rockport,* Stuart Davis, 1940, collection of Mr. & Mrs. Milton Lowenthal, New York

**PREPARATION**

Get wallpaper sample books, portions of wallpaper rolls, or patterned wrapping paper. Discuss how a city can look in the rain, what reflections are like at night. Students might find it easier to do this project if they were given an adjective such as "cloudy" or "sunshiny." Suggest they combine letters or numbers with the collage if they wish.

## PROJECT 11-5: **I SAW THE FIGURE FIVE IN GOLD**

**MATERIALS**

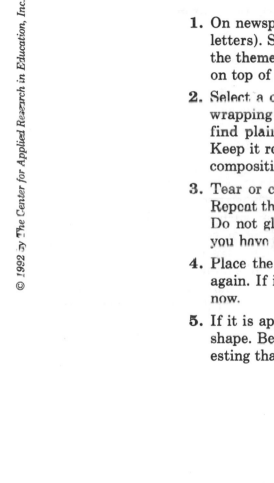

- Wallpaper or wrapping paper
- Plain construction paper
- Glue
- String
- Gilt paint
- Tempera paint

This collage will contain either one or a series of letters or numbers that are significant to you. Select something such as your lucky number, initials, birthday, age, or phone number.

1. On newsprint make a thumbnail sketch. Devise a way of arranging the number (or letters). Select one large shape to be the dominant theme, just as the number 5 was the theme of Demuth's painting. The shape can be the primary subject, or be added on top of a design you have created from pattern and color.

2. Select a color scheme by going through pages of a wallpaper sample book or use wrapping paper to find a printed pattern. When you have selected a pattern, then find plain colors of construction paper that will go with the patterned paper. Keep it relatively simple, but be willing to use one bright color some place in your composition.

3. Tear or cut out pieces of paper, taking care to keep it from being too confusing. Repeat the colors of a pattern, or use string and cut paper to emphasize the pattern. Do not glue anything down until you have moved the pieces around and are sure you have done everything that seems appropriate to it.

4. Place the collage on the floor and walk some distance away from it to look at it again. If it looks good from 10 feet away, then it probably is strong. Glue it down now.

5. If it is appropriate, use gold paint to edge some of the pieces or to paint one large shape. Because gold has always been precious, subtle use of it makes it more interesting than if it is overdone.

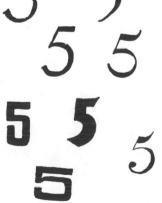

# PROJECT 11–6: **FLOWERS AND BONES**

**FOR THE TEACHER**

**Slide # 32: *Cow's Skull with Calico Roses.*** When Georgia O'Keeffe lived in New York, she painted buildings. When she was in the Southwest, she painted her surroundings. The things she saw and found on her walks through the desert became subjects for her paintings. Many of her works are painted in series, and it is interesting to see how they become progressively simpler as she paints them the third or fourth time.

**O'KEEFFE'S MASTERPIECES**

*Red Hills and Bones*, 1941, Philadelphia Museum of Art

*Cow's Skull-Red, White and Blue*, 1931, The Metropolitan Museum of Art, New York

*Ram's Head with Hollyhock*, 1935, collection of Edith and Milton Lowenthal, New York

*Sky Above Clouds IV*, 1965, Chicago Art Institute

*Two Jimson Weeds*, 1938, collection of Anita O'K. Young

*Black Iris*, 1926, The Metropolitan Museum of Art, New York

**PREPARATION**

Discuss how O'Keeffe demonstrated that the simplest item can be made monumental by how it is shown on a canvas. She sometimes painted vast spaces and large subjects such as mountains, but she also painted small things such as flowers, shells, and rocks that filled the canvas. Most students have also collected such items. Make each student responsible for bringing in a personal item that he or she has collected from nature for the first small study. (You may have to offer extra credit and give them three days' warning, but it can be accomplished.) If at all possible, try to have some real bones available for students to draw. Even fresh bones can have the meat boiled off them if you have the time. Again, ask students to bring some in for your "collection." O'Keeffe said, "My paintings sometimes grow by pieces of what is around."

Name: _____   Date: _____

## PROJECT 11–6: **FLOWERS AND BONES**

### MATERIALS

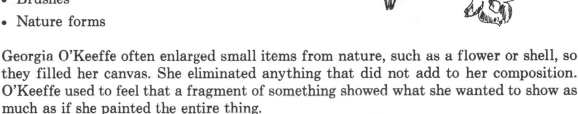

- Drawing paper 6 × 8 inches
- Drawing or watercolor paper 18 × 24 inches
- Newsprint
- Watercolors or pastels
- Brushes
- Nature forms

Georgia O'Keeffe often enlarged small items from nature, such as a flower or shell, so they filled her canvas. She eliminated anything that did not add to her composition. O'Keeffe used to feel that a fragment of something showed what she wanted to show as much as if she painted the entire thing.

1. Select one item from nature such as a piece of driftwood, shell, flower, bone, or rock. Use pencil to draw this one item on the 6 × 8-inch piece of paper, entirely filling the paper. Leave some areas white, make some quite dark, and try to make a range of grays in between. Let this small drawing be a little jewel.

2. Before beginning the large drawing, on newsprint make some thumbnail sketches approximately 3 × 4 inches square. Don't spend much time on these, as they are just a working plan for your large drawing. Consider how you will fill the page. If you intend to combine more than one item, then think about the background. Because of where she lived, O'Keeffe often "floated" items such as cow skulls and flowers in the sky, or above mountains.

3. Lightly draw your design on large paper.

   *Watercolor:*

   Plan ahead which areas will be left light or white. Try colors on newsprint before applying them to the watercolor paper. You can dilute paint that is too dark by adding more water, or blot paint with a paper towel. Work over the entire painting, then go back and build up layers of color before doing details.

   *Pastel:*

   Decide on a general color scheme. Lay in areas of color; the darkest ones first, then the lightest colors last. O'Keeffe would sometimes use only three or four colors, and an accent color (such as red) very sparingly.

# PROJECT 11-7: FRANK LLOYD WRIGHT'S ARCHITECTURE

## FOR THE TEACHER

**Slide # 33: *Kaufmann House, Falling Water.*** Frank Lloyd Wright (1867–1959) was one of the foremost American architects. Many of his low, landscape-hugging suburban homes and innovative skyscrapers are museums today. His "prairie-style" features rooms massed around a central fireplace, and cantilevered roofs shading series of windows. Typical of his construction was that he often eliminated the use of posts and columns. He worked for Louis Sullivan for a time, and in common with Sullivan, designed the interiors so the building would be "all of a piece."

## MASTERPIECES OF ARCHITECTURE

*Frederick C. Robie House,* 1908–1909, Chicago, Illinois

*Ward Willits House,* 1900–1902, Highland Park, Illinois

*Kaufmann House, "Falling Water,"* 1936–1937, Bear Run, Pennsylvania

*Johnson Wax Building,* 1936–1939, Racine, Wisconsin

*Taliesin West,* 1938–1959, Phoenix, Arizona

*Guggenheim Museum,* 1946–1959, New York

## PREPARATION

Students are already used to doing work that ends up being put on the refrigerator door. In this project they will be designing small architectural magnets to hold up other papers. Bring books of architecture into the classroom, or ask students to get them from the library. Ask students to talk about today's buildings. What do they look like? What is the oldest building they've ever seen? Suggest they discuss strip malls, how they would like their own homes to look someday, which buildings in their town should be made into museums to preserve that form of architecture.

## FURTHER SUGGESTIONS

- This project could easily be done in self-hardening clay that can be oven-baked. Paint with acrylic paint and coat with polymer medium to give a shine.
- Architectural pins based on buildings of any styles and age can be miniatures made in either clay or heavy watercolor paper. Glue pins from a hobby shop on back.

## PROJECT 11-7: FRANK LLOYD WRIGHT'S ARCHITECTURE

**MATERIALS**

- Newsprint
- Heavy watercolor paper
- India Ink or black pens
- Circular magnets
- Toothpicks

- Rulers
- Watercolors
- X-acto® knives
- White glue

Modern architecture was influenced by many great designers. Frank Lloyd Wright is one of the best-known American architects. It is said that his work was influenced by the special building blocks he played with as a young child (his mother always knew he would be an architect).

1. On newsprint, draw a 2×3-inch rectangle. Your basic structure should fit within this, or could be smaller. Select a house or skyscraper that appeals to you from a book on architecture. It does not have to be by Frank Lloyd Wright, and could even be a design based on your own house or apartment building. Draw this design carefully, using a ruler, including details such as doors and windows.

2. Tape the newsprint drawing face down on a window or lightbox, and draw along the lines on the back of the drawing.

3. On the piece of watercolor paper, place the newsprint drawing face up. First trace the outline of the house, without any details. Don't draw in pencil on the watercolor paper. In another place, trace portions of the house such as a roof or windows. Try to have three layers of watercolor paper for strength, and because the details are what will make it interesting.

4. Use an X-acto® knife to cut the building and details from the paper (place cardboard on your table to protect it when you cut. Use your finger to spread glue on the backs of details to attach them (to keep the glue from spreading onto the layer underneath). A toothpick or tweezers will help you place the paper. Let it dry.

   *Safety Note: Keep your hand behind the blade when cutting.*

5. With a black pen or India ink, outline and fill in details on the building. If you wish to add color, use watercolor for its soft effect. If the paper building is flimsy, glue it on a piece of posterboard and cut around the outside. Glue a magnet on the back.

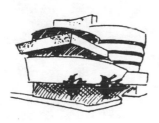

# PROJECT 11–8: ESCHER'S TESSELLATIONS

**FOR THE TEACHER**

Visiting the Alhambra, the Moorish castle in Spain, M. C. Escher (1898–1972) found himself fascinated with the tiled surfaces on the decorated walls and floors. He wanted to use "concrete, recognizable figures of fish, birds, reptiles, or human beings as elements" in the same interlocking manner as the moorish tiles were used. Most of his work was in black and white, largely woodcuts, lithographs, and drawings. His "Relativities" were experiments using perspective and vanishing points to fool the eye. Buildings appeared to go up and down at the same time, showing mirror images. Students are fascinated with his work.

**Photo 11-6. Student work from Judy James' class. Parkway West High School, St. Louis County, Missouri.**

**MASTERPIECES BY ESCHER**

*Day and Night*, 1938, National Gallery of Art, Washington, D.C.
*Metamorphose,* 1939–1940, Vorpal Galleries, San Francisco and Chicago
*Concave and Convex,* 1955, National Gallery of Art, Washington, D.C.
*Drawing Hands,* 1948, Vorpal Galleries, San Francisco and Chicago
*House of Stairs,* 1951, National Gallery of Art, Washington, D.C.

**PREPARATION**

Many of your students may have already done tessellation in their math classes, as working with geometric figures is, after all, a math function. This lesson presents tessellation purely as a visual function. Demonstrate in front of the class using large construction paper and masking tape to demonstrate how to cut from vertex to vertex (a vertex is a corner where two edges come together). Find the midpoint (by folding), and transfer (and tape) the cutout to the opposite side. Make tagboard patterns for the students (approximately 3 inches) of squares, equilateral triangles, rectangles, diamonds, and hexagons.

I am grateful to art teachers Meg Masterman and Mary Anne Haden who demonstrated this technique at a National Art Education Convention, and to Liza Mitchell who shared her expertise with me.

**Photo 11-7.** *Waterfall,* **1961, Maurits Cornelis Escher, 14⅞ × 11¾ inches, lithograph, The Saint Louis Art Museum.**

# PROJECT 11–8: M. C. ESCHER'S TESSELLATIONS

**MATERIALS**

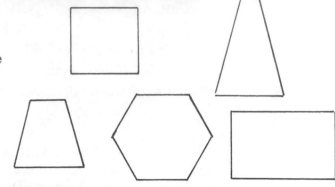

- 3 × 5-inch cards, lined on one side
- 12 × 18-inch construction paper
- 18 × 24-inch construction paper
- Black fine-line marker
- Tagboard geometric patterns
- Scissors

Tessellations are shapes such as squares, triangles, hexagons that fit together into infinity. You see them around you in tile floors, or walls. M. C. Escher was fascinated by tessellation, and created many works of reality and fantasy.

1. Before trying complicated shapes, make a fish the easy way. Use a 3 × 5-inch index card. If you use this as a pattern, and make a second piece identical to the first, you find that when you turn it over, they fit together perfectly.

   **Definition:** A *vertex* is a corner where two edges come together.

   **a.** Cut away one end from corner to corner.
   **b.** Tape the cut-off part on the parallel (opposite) side.
   **c.** Fold the rectangle in half to find the midpoint.
   **d.** Cut a fin from one side to the midpoint.
   **e.** Flip it over and tape it on the parallel side.
   **f.** Decorate with black marker.

**a.**            **b.**            **c.**            **d.**            **e.**            **f.**

2. **Triangle:** Make an equilateral triangle of paper.

   **a.** Find the center point of each side by folding one corner to another.
   **b.** Cut from the centerpoint of an edge to a vertex (corner).
   **c.** Flip the cut-out from the center point and tape it down on the *same* side.
   **d.** Do this on the other two sides.
   **e.** Now examine your shape and see if it looks like anything real.
   **f.** Trace around this paper onto tagboard and carefully cut it out.

**a.**            **b.**            **c.**            **d.**            **e.**            **f.**

3. Select two colors of construction paper. On one color, trace around your tagboard pattern and cut out the shapes. Arrange and carefully glue these shapes onto the other piece of 18 × 24-inch paper. Although you can leave it at that, it is effective to cut the 18 × 24-inch paper around the edges of the shapes. If you wish, draw details with black marker on each piece.

**316**

© 1992 by The Center for Applied Research in Education, Inc.

# PROJECT 11-9: HOMAGE TO HENRY (MOORE)

### FOR THE TEACHER

**Slide # 34: *Three Motives Against Wall, Number 1.*** Henry Moore (1898–1986) was one of the great modern sculptors. While he was a student at the Royal College of Art in London, he developed an interest in pre-Columbian art from examples seen at the British Museum. A reclining figure of Chac Mool, an Aztec god, inspired him in 1929 to do his first reclining figure. During World War II, Moore was employed by the British government to do drawings of people as they rested in subway bomb shelters in London. He was a teacher of drawing for many years after that. Some of his sculpted reclining figures resemble those wartime drawings, showing the softness of draped clothing.

### MASTERPIECES

*Tube Shelter Perspective,* 1941 (drawing), collection of Mrs. Henry Moore, England

*Draped Seated Woman,* 1957–1958, Hebrew University, Jerusalem

*Reclining Figure,* 1929, Leeds City Art Galleries, England

*The King and Queen,* 1952–1953, The Joseph H. Hirschhorn Collection, Washington, D.C.

*Fallen Warrior,* 1956–1957, The Joseph H. Hirschhorn Collection, Washington, D.C.

*Reclining Mother and Child,* 1960–1961, Walker Art Center, Minneapolis

### PREPARATION

Have students bring in cardboard milk cartons—pint, quart, or half-gallon size. These sculptures do not have to be large, so you could mix the plaster for several class members in one batch. The vermiculite (available at garden shops) keeps the plaster light and airy and makes it much easier to carve. Directions for mixing plaster are in Appendix C. Show examples of work by Henry Moore or Barbara Hepworth, so students understand that their carved forms can be quite simple and still look like human figures.

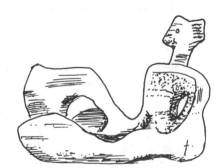

Drawing after *Unesco Reclining Figure,* 1959–1958, Henry Moore, Roman Travertine Marble, 200 inches long.

# PROJECT 11–9: HOMAGE TO HENRY (MOORE)

## MATERIALS

- Cardboard milk cartons
- Vermiculite
- Sandpaper of varying coarseness
- Newspaper
- Bucket or plastic ice cream cartons for mixing the plaster
- Plaster of Paris
- Paring knives
- Brushes
- Polymer medium
- Newsprint

Henry Moore's sculpture is usually based on the human figure, though he might have made holes in the figure (such as the abdomen or breasts). He often used knuckle bones and other bones that he found in his yard as a starting point for his maquettes (small models for his large sculptures). The space that is around the outside of a sculpture (the negative space) is almost as important as the sculpture itself.

*Day 1*

1. Mix plaster by putting warm water in a plastic bucket, and sifting plaster by the handful onto the water's surface. Do not stir the plaster until it has mounded to make a peak showing out of the water (or it may not set up). The proportion is roughly two-thirds water to one-third plaster.

2. Stir it until it begins to turn thick (coating your hand so you cannot see the skin); then add vermiculite (two cups to a quart). *Do not pour excess plaster down the sink, ever!* Pour the plaster-vermiculite mixture into a cardboard container, tap it on the surface to settle it, and allow it to harden overnight.

*Day 2*

3. When it has set up and cooled, tear the cardboard off the outside. Do thumbnail sketches on paper before beginning to carve away plaster. You will find it easier to make if your figure is not too realistic. Almost any carving can take on animal or human characteristics when it is carved with curves and indentations.

4. Begin carving by gently taking away small amounts from the outside. Work over the entire form before trying to do any finishing. Work on a newspaper so that your cleanup will be easy. Make it as smooth as possible with the knife or a plaster rasp.

5. When you have removed as much material as you wish, finish the figure with sandpaper, working from coarse to fine. You can stain or paint the figure, or simply paint several coats of thinned polymer medium on the outside to preserve the finish.

**Drawing after**
***Draped Reclining Woman*, 1957–1958, Neue Staatsgalerie, Munich.**

**Drawing after**
***Reclining Figure*, 1946–1947, collection of Henry R. Hope, Bloomington, Indiana.**

**Drawing after**
***Reclining Figure*, 1963–1965, Lincoln Center.**

# Section 12

# CONTEMPORARY ART

# CONTEMPORARY
## TIME LINE

| | 1950 | 1955 | 1960 | 1965 | 1970 | 1980 | 1990 |
|---|---|---|---|---|---|---|---|

Color Field painting 1950

Pop Art 1950–1960s

Josef Albers Homage to a Square 1963

Conceptual Art, 1970s

Robert Indiana 1966

Smithson Spiral Jetty 1970

Deborah Butterfield 1985

Photorealism 1960–1975

Warhol, 1967

Henri Matisse 1869–1964

Op Art 1960s

Guggenheim Museum 1959

Tourists Duane Hanson 1970

Christo, Surrounded Islands 1983

Helen Frankenthaler Color Field painting, 1961

1967 Louise Nevelson

| | 1950 | 1955 | 1960 | 1965 | 1970 | 1980 | 1990 |
|---|---|---|---|---|---|---|---|
| **Africa** | | | | | Aswan Dam completed 1970 | | |
| **Americas** | Space launch 1957 / School Integration 1954 | J. F. Kennedy died 1963 | | | Man on the moon 1969 / Vietnam War ends, 1974 | Argentina invades Falklands 1982 | |
| **Asia** | Korea, 1950 / People's Republic of China 1949 | | | | China Cultural Revolution 1965–1968 | China, Tianamen Square, 1989 | |
| **Europe** | European Common Market, 1957 | | | | | Berlin Wall comes down, 1990 / Breakup of Soviet Union, 1991 | |
| **Near East** | Israel founded 1948 | | | Israel Seven-Day War 1967 | | Gulf War 1991 | |
| **Other** | | | | | | | |

# Unit 1: CONTEMPORARY ART

## OVERVIEW OF THE VISUAL ARTS

Contemporary twentieth-century art has developed in a logical way. When one looks at movements such as Pop Art, Photorealism, or Appropriationism, it is evident that the use of printed words, and advertising images and symbols began early in the century. The early cubists used "found materials" in their collages. Some of the later work was technically more sophisticated, but not significantly different except for its size. It is interesting that toward the end of the century there is more frequent reference to art of the past, with contemporary artists paying homage to their roots, and a new classicism reappearing.

Artists rely more on computers, copy machines, photography, and sometimes specialized shops to carry out their concepts. The rise of printmaking allows artwork to be widely disseminated, and often is a collaborative effort between the artist and technician. Traditional materials of making art such as oil or pastel on canvas, or bronze casting continue to be used about as often as new materials such as plastics or neon tubing.

## PAINTING

It is often difficult to distinguish whether a painted object that hangs on the wall is a painting or sculpture. Often it is both. Painting once again seems to have developed an "International Style" that was common in the early Renaissance. Easy access to reproductions, travel, and education allow original ways of interpreting art to develop simultaneously in several parts of the world.

Since the early 1950s, no one trend has been in effect for a lengthy period. A brief synopsis of several of the noteworthy developments is given here.

***Pop Art* (1950s and 1960s).** Pop Art is created with a wide range of media, using familiar objects such as soup cans, machinery, or comics combined with words and numbers. These objects are usually magnified, and presented in a variety of media such as photo silkscreen, montage, collage, or combine painting.

***Op Art* (1960s).** Artists used devices such as high contrast, shape, and color to create optical illusions. Moiré patterns or geometric shapes in contrasting colors create the illusion of movement.

***Hard Edge, Shaped, and Color Field* painting (1950s and 1960s).** With the creation of polymer paints, previously difficult-to-create paintings appeared. Masking tape applied to canvas enabled artists to make straight edges. Paintings were not always rectangular, but sometimes shaped to the pattern of the painting. In Color Field painting, large unprimed canvas were stained with acrylic paints without the use of strong tonal contrasts or visible brushstrokes.

***Minimal Art* (1960s to the present).** This mostly three-dimensional work is sometimes shaped by chance (such as a heap of sand), or by an artist (a circle of rocks arranged on a museum floor).

***Photorealism or Hyperrealism* (1967 to 1977).** Artists had as their subject the everyday environment as seen through the eye of a camera. Photorealist artists tended to specialize, with one doing signs, another faces, or another still-lifes.

***Feminist Art* (1970s onward).** A movement of women artists who combined female "subjects" with female objects such as quilts, fibers, and ceramics, to make a statement about feminist art.

***Conceptual Art* (1970s onward).** Conceptual art is often more an idea of art rather than an actual artwork. Sometimes it is written about or drawn (such as Christo's wrapped buildings and bridges), but not always executed.

***Art Povera.*** This largely Italian movement used junk objects in composition, a form of rebellion against materialism.

## SCULPTURE

Sculpture has never had so many materials or forms as it has today. There is no longer one material (stone or bronze) or one subject (the human or animal form) as in the past. It is no longer created for one patron such as the church or government, but for diverse uses, including public and commercial spaces. A wide variety of media fall under the heading of sculpture. Traditional sculptural forms such as bronze castings, and ceramic sculpture are still being done, but many other forms of sculpture exist (such as earthworks, light and space, or neon sculpture).

## MASTERPIECES OF SCULPTURE

*Reclining Figure: Angles,* Henry Moore, 1979, collection of Patsy and Raymond Nasher

*Rush Hour,* George Segal, 1983, Sidney Janis Gallery, New York

*Ohayo,* Judy Pfaff, 1986, Holly Solomon Gallery and Max Protetch Gallery, New York

*Praise for Elohim Adonai,* Mark De Suvero, 1966, The Saint Louis Art Museum

*Untitled,* Donald Judd, 1969, The Saint Louis Art Museum

*Pergusa,* Frank Stella, 1981, collection of Holly Hunt Thackberry, Winnetka, Illinois

*La Riante Contré, Théatres de Mémoirs,* Jean Dubuffet, 1975–1978, collection of Arne and Milly Glimcher, New York

*Head with Blue Shadow,* Roy Lichtenstein, 1965, collection of Patsy and Raymond Nasher

## ARCHITECTURE

After the minimalist art of the skyscraper, with its box form and vast expanses of metal and glass, there seems to be a return to making decorative buildings, with interesting architectural forms. "Disneyesque" architecture is appearing, with bright colors and playful shapes. Strip malls proliferate, many of which appear to go back to the Renaissance shapes of the square, triangle, and rectangle, often as a result of being designed on computers. Many locations continue to cherish their architectural heritage, with even the newest buildings being created to complement their surroundings.

## INNOVATIVE ARCHITECTURE

*Seagram Building,* Mies van der Rohe and Philip Johnson, 1954–1958, New York

*U.S. Pavilion* (Geodesic Dome), R. Buckminster Fuller, 1967, Montreal Expo, Montreal

*Town of Seaside,* Andres Düaney and Elizabeth Plater-Zyberk, 1978–1983, Florida

*AT&T Corporate Headquarters,* Philip Johnson and John Burgee, 1979–1984, New York

*Republic Bank,* Philip Johnson and John Burgee, 1981–1984, Houston, Texas

*Neue Staatsgalerie,* James Stirling and Michael Wilford, 1977–1984, Stuttgart, Germany

*National Gallery of Art,* East Building Addition, I. M. Pei, 1978, Washington, D.C.

*Portland Public Services Building,* Michael Graves, 1980–1982, Portland, Oregon

*Euro Disney Complex* (hotels, yacht club), Robert A. M. Stern, Arata Isozaki, Frank Gehry, Charles Gwathmey & Robert Siegel, and Michael Graves, 1991–1992, Lake Buena Vista, Florida

**Photo 12-1. This sculpture, which makes a sighing noise as it inflates and deflates, is an example of the imaginative sculpture that Claes Oldenburg is noted for. He sometimes changes the scale of an ordinary object to make it monumental.** *Ice Bag,* **Scale B, 1971, diameter 48½ inches, Claes Oldenburg, American, 1929, mechanized sculpture, The Saint Louis Art Museum, gift of Nancy Singer.**

# PROJECT 12–1: **COMBINE PAINTING**

**FOR THE TEACHER**

**Slide # 35:** *Tracer.* Robert Rauschenberg calls his combinations of painting and objects "combine paintings." He freely combines copies of historical artworks with images from newspapers, letters and numbers, and paint. These two-dimensional paintings are often combined with three-dimensional objects such as a stuffed goat with a tire around its middle (as in *Monogram*), or a stuffed rooster. His work has been compared to "Happenings" in the art world.

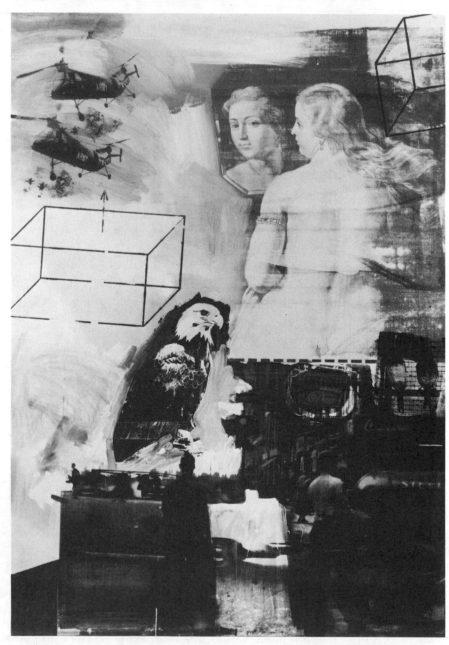

**Photo 12-2.** *Tracer,* **Robert Rauschenberg, 1963, 84 × 60 inches, oil silkscreen on canvas, Nelson Foundation purchase, Nelson-Atkins Museum of Art, Kansas City, Missouri.**

## RAUSCHENBERG'S MASTERPIECES

*Monogram,* 1959, collection of Moderna Museet, Stockholm, Sweden

*Doric Circus,* 1979, National Gallery of Art, Washington, D.C.

*Tracer,* 1964, The Nelson-Atkins Gallery of Art, Kansas City, Missouri

*Odalisk,* 1955–1956, collection of Peter Ludwig, Wallraf-Richartz Museum, Cologne, Germany

*Bed,* 1959, collection of Mr. and Mrs. Leo Castelli, New York

*Trapeze,* 1964, private collection, Turin, Italy

## PREPARATION

Most students have familiarity with collages, from having made them in other classes. Discuss how Rauschenberg worked, visually controlling the spacing of his images with a rough grid, tying elements together with bold splashes of paint. He usually applied the photographic images first with photo silkscreen or lithography, then added numbers, color, or fabric. Because silkscreen is impractical for a large class, your students will transfer images by making rubbings from magazine pictures, as Rauschenberg did in his earliest images.

## FURTHER SUGGESTIONS

- Polymer medium can be painted onto cut-out images from magazines. Allow the polymer to dry, then soak the image in water until you can remove the paper by rubbing with a finger. The ink will stay on the polymer medium. This can be then glued onto paper with polymer medium and used as part of the combine painting.

- Apply magazine pictures by rubbing with silkscreen extender, but use only soft graphite (pencil) to fill in space and tie the images together, experimenting with various densities and strokes.

- Set this up as a three-dimensional problem by stating that after the combine painting is created, a three-dimensional found object(s) must be incorporated into it.

# PROJECT 12–1:  COMBINE PAINTING

**MATERIALS**

- Slick magazines such as *Time*
- Scissors
- Transparent silkscreen extender base
- Spoons (for rubbing paper)
- Drawing paper
- Polymer medium
- Acrylic or tempera paint
- Brushes
- Tissue paper

Robert Rauschenberg was a Pop artist who reveled in combining all kinds of objects (including used tires), with reproductions of artwork, fabric, words and letters, and "the news of the day." His work sometimes made social commentary, as he would show machinery, helicopters, street signs, photos of birds, or nudes.

Remember that when you transfer these items to paper, they will be reversed from the way you see them. Depending on the size of your paper, you will not want to overdo the number of printed images that you are transferring, to leave room to do other types of collage and painting.

1. Go through magazines (such as *Art News* and *Time*), and select the major images that you will use to transfer. Find other images that might work for you. Use printed words (which will be seen backwards, don't forget), or visual puns.

2. Think of the page of drawing paper as divided into a large grid. It isn't necessary to place things squarely, or divide the page evenly, but this will help you organize the items as you place them.

3. Use your finger to apply a thin layer of silkscreen extender on the front of the picture. Place it on the paper where you want it to be. You might mask the drawing paper around it to protect it from getting dirty. Apply a small amount of silkscreen extender on the back of the magazine cut-out to allow the spoon to move easily and avoid tearing the paper. Rub the back of the picture with the spoon until the ink has transferred onto the drawing paper (you can peek from time to time, it could take up to 15 minutes).

4. Continue placing images on the paper in this manner until you are satisfied that you have enough. You could now use cloth or tissue paper (applied with polymer medium), or opaque paint such as tempera or acrylic to use color that relates in some way to the pictures. Emphasize some images with colored pencil.

© 1992 by The Center for Applied Research in Education, Inc.

# PROJECT 12-2: ANDY WARHOL AND THE COPY MACHINE

## FOR THE TEACHER

**Slide # 36: 20 Marilyns.** Andy Warhol was certainly one of the best known Pop artists. He began his career as a shoe illustrator, eventually experimenting with film making and photo silkscreening. He is best known for his photo silkscreens of famous people or objects (such as his series of electric chairs, Campbell soup cans, and Brillo box sculptures). In his series pictures he experimented with grouping identical or similar photos which had each been inked differently. The smears and printing errors were allowed to show, giving variations in each picture. The repetition in these Pop Art experiments has been likened to the repetition of commercials and sitcoms on television.

## WARHOL'S MASTERPIECES

*Marilyn Monroe,* 1962, collection of Jasper Johns, New York

*Green Coca-Cola Bottles,* 1962, private collection, New York

*Dollar Bills,* 1962, collection of Mr. and Mrs. Robert C. Scull, New York

*Campbell's Soup Can,* 1964, collection of Alberto Ulrich, Milan, Italy

## PREPARATION

Discuss the Pop Art trend, and ask students their opinions about prints of subject matter such as soup cans, stacks of Brillo boxes, or pictures of celebrities. Students can use their own photos (even colored school photos work), and do a series of their own pictures in any size, though the 5 × 7-inch size is best. Groups enjoy individually transforming identical pictures, then mounting them together on one board.

Allow time for photocopying. When copying, it seems to work best to use the lightest possible copying exposure on the copy machine. I have found that if I work with a black and white photo it should be developed a little lighter than normal. Even if the photo seems a little dark, it is effective to color even on top of the darkest areas. It would be best to have eight photocopies of each student's photo for a group project. Encourage the use of pattern and imagination; there really is no right or wrong in a project such as this.

## FURTHER SUGGESTIONS

- Find and discuss potential items from today's culture that might have been used by Andy Warhol as subject matter. What or who might be parodied in art?
- A sheet of small school photos can be photocopied before it is cut up, and each student can do variations on only his or her own face.

# PROJECT 12-2: ANDY WARHOL AND THE COPY MACHINE

**MATERIALS**

- Student photos (black and white or color)
- Waxy colored pencils such as Prismacolor®
- Posterboard for mounting
- Rubber cement

Andy Warhol did his multiple prints of people such as Marilyn Monroe, Elizabeth Taylor, and Mao Tse-Tung in photo silkscreen. He was also well-known for making series photos of Campbell soup cans and even an electric chair!

1. Obtain photocopies of your own photo. Trim them so they are all the same size (approximately 5 × 7 inches). It is also possible to work with much smaller photos. Sheets of school photos can be copied before cutting them apart.

2. For best results use three to five colors. Some suggestions for hand-coloring are:
   a. Make all lines go the same slanting direction.
   b. Make patterned backgrounds.
   c. Use patterned dots of different colors and sizes in clothing.
   d. Leave the black and white of the photocopy showing some places.
   e. Color on top of black in some places; it still shows.
   f. Use overlapping geometric shapes to partially cover the face and background.
   g. Avoid coloring too lightly or fast. Careful work shows!
   h. Don't attempt to cover the entire thing.
   i. Try cross-hatching.
   j. Try not to make a cartoon of it by coloring teeth or crossing eyes.

3. When the pictures are colored, arrange them on the mount board. Move them around until you like the looks of the arrangement. You may find one or more of the pictures doesn't "go." Don't hesitate to throw it out and do another one that complements the others.

4. Attach them to the background with rubber cement. For a permanent bond, coat the back of the mount board and the photocopy, allowing them both to dry before placing them together.

# PROJECT 12-3: **THE INCREDIBLE INEDIBLE**

## FOR THE TEACHER

Claes Oldenburg (born in 1929) is a Pop Art sculptor whose artwork recreates familiar items in unlikely materials. He literally opened a "store" in New York that was filled with models of clothing, fragments of signs, and food items executed in plaster, painted in garish colors. For a later show he created gigantic food items (huge hamburgers) in "soft" sculpture (vinyl stuffed with kapok). He continued to translate ordinary objects such as a pay telephone, toilet, and drum set into soft, sagging sculpture. A fertile imagination is shown by his large mechanically powered ice bag that inflates and collapses, and a gigantic lipstick tube mounted on a tank and painted bright pink.

## OLDENBURG'S MASTERPIECES

*Lipstick Ascending on Caterpillar Tracks,* 1969, Yale University Art Gallery

*Soft Giant Drum Set,* 1967, collection of Kimiko and John G. Powers, New York

*Soft Toilet,* 1966, collection of Mr. and Mrs. Victor W. Ganz, New York

*Soft Pay Telephone,* 1963, collection of William Zierler, New York

*The Stove,* 1962, private collection

*Giant Ice Bag,* 1969-1970, Thomas Segal Gallery, Boston

## PREPARATION

Have students talk about transforming ordinary objects into public sculpture. Does sheer scale make it an outstanding piece of sculpture? If your class wishes to make huge objects, divide them into groups to work together. If you wish to make plaster objects as Oldenburg did, use plaster-impregnated gauze over a papier-mâché base. While the project is titled for a food item, it could easily be almost any ordinary object that would look unusual because of sheer size.

## FURTHER SUGGESTIONS

- Students can sew vinyl to make small soft sculptures in the manner of Oldenburg. If canvas is available, make the forms of canvas, stuffing them tightly, coating the outside with gesso, and painting in fluorescent colors mixed with polymer medium.

- Passable large stuffed sculpture can be made with colored 36-inch-wide roll paper. The paper can be wrapped around cardboard or tagboard cut-outs and glued over the edges. A hamburger made in layers in this method is impressive. Imagine the puffy bun, hamburger, lettuce, tomato, and cheese.

- Two sheets of colored roll paper can be cut out together and stapled almost all the way around the edges. Decorate before lightly stuffing newspapers inside, and staple the form shut. Trim the edges and suspend from the ceiling.

- Students can make human forms such as those by George Segal by encasing different body parts in sculpture tape, and joining them together. I never cease to be amazed at the clever sculptures students make when they do this; they go far beyond simple representation.

## PROJECT 12–3: THE INCREDIBLE INEDIBLE

**MATERIALS**

- Newspaper
- Wallpaper or Pritt® paste
- Tempera
- Polymer medium
- Masking tape

Claes Oldenburg has made a career of taking ordinary objects and combining them to make gigantic sculptures. He began by making small plaster food, then went on to make gigantic food such as hamburgers or bacon-lettuce-tomato sandwiches.

1. Depending on the size of the sculpture, one of these methods of forming the underlying structure for papiér-mâché should be followed.

    a. For a relatively small shape, make the base by lightly wadding newspaper, using string or masking tape to form a basic shape.

    b. Form tagboard into the basic shape and tape it well.

    c. Styrofoam or cardboard boxes and cartons can be part or all of the base.

    d. For a large sculpture, use chicken wire (available at a hardware store) to define the shape.

    e. If you are making a huge sculpture, make a rough armature of $1 \times 2$-inch wood, then cover it with chicken wire, stapling or nailing the wire onto the wood. Make sure it is sturdy and well balanced.

2. Mix the wallpaper or Pritt® paste in a bucket of water, stirring until it is creamy, but not too thick. It keeps for several days. Tear the newspaper vertically (with the grain) into strips approximately $1\frac{1}{2} \times 12$ inches. Tear enough to work in one class period.

3. Dip a strip of paper in the paste. Holding it over the bucket, pull it between your fingers to eliminate excess paste before applying it to the armature. If you have indentations where you don't want them, you can lightly wad a piece of newspaper and hold it in place with strips of newspaper. It will take at least three layers of newspaper all over to give the strength that is needed.

4. For a final coat, *tear* grocery bags or kraft paper into roughly 3-inch shapes, and apply all over, smoothing and overlapping as you go. These feathered edges will give a strong, smooth finish to the outside. Allow it to dry several days.

5. Use house paint, tempera, or acrylic to paint the outside. If you use tempera, you might wish to paint a coat of polymer medium on the outside, or take it outside and use spray varnish to make it shiny.

# PROJECT 12-4: BLACK, WHITE, OR GOLD

## FOR THE TEACHER

Louise Nevelson (1900–1988) was born in Russia, coming to the United States in 1905. As a young sculptor, she started out with rather traditional cubistic forms, but became well-known in the 1950s for her painted wood assemblages. Like Joseph Cornell, she gave structure to her work by containing many disparate scraps of wood inside boxes (old milk crates) which then were grouped together. She did have some pieces that were free-standing, but the straight edges of boards visually gave structure to the bits and pieces that she used. Her assemblages are painted entirely in one of three colors— black (the earliest color), white, or gold. She was said to have actually had a different studio for each of these three colors, as she found it too difficult to think in more than one color at a time. The interplay of light and shadow was always a factor in her work. In later years she used materials such as Lucite®, aluminum, Formica®, Cor-ten steel, or epoxy in boxlike assemblages that resembled her wooden constructions.

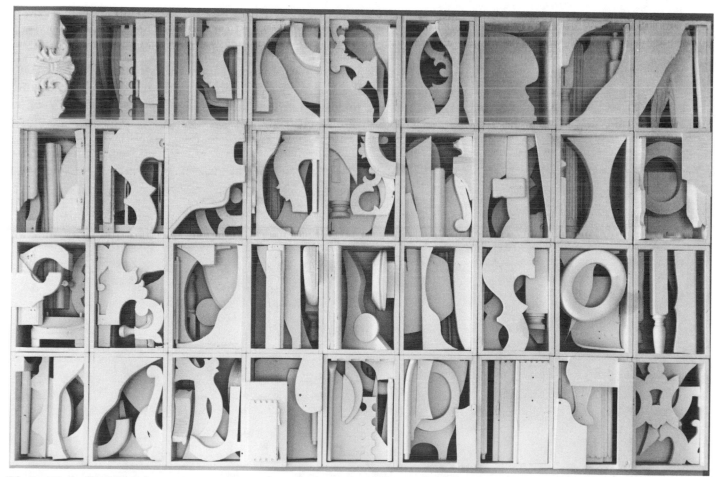

Photo 12-3. *New Continent,* Louise Nevelson, 1962, 77¾ × 121¾ × 10⅛ inches, wood painted white, The Saint Louis Art Museum. Purchase and funds given by Miss Martha I. Love, Mr. and Mrs. George S. Rosborough, Jr., The Weil Charitable Foundation, Mr. and Mrs. Warren Shapleigh, Mr. Henry B. Pflager, the Lea-Thi-Ta Study.

## NEVELSON'S MASTERPIECES

*An American Tribute to the British People,* 1960–1965, Tate Gallery, London

*Sun Garden, No. 1,* 1964, collection of Mr. and Mrs. Charles M. Diker

*Black Chord,* 1964, collection of Joel Ehrenkranz

*New Continent,* 1962, The Saint Louis Art Museum

*Transparent sculpture VI,* 1967–1968, Whitney Museum of American Art, New York

## PREPARATION

Discuss with students what it will take to make a one-color material used in sculpture interesting (for example, deep shadows, textural variety, repetition and space). Students may or may not choose to work within a box form, but announce in advance that all the work will hang together on a wall. It will take approximately two days. Allow time when they are all done to look at and talk about them. Which ones are effective because they were restrained? Which ones were "busy"? How do they go together as a group? If you use tagboard, you may wish to spray paint all the sculptures one color.

## FURTHER SUGGESTIONS

- With the trend toward Disneyesque architecture, and the variety of new materials available, sculptors are now using color more freely. Challenge students to try this sculpture project using colored posterboard and pattern effectively.
- Nevelson made wonderful junk jewelry with bits and pieces of wood, and metal that she wore with her elegant black evening gowns (along with her cowboy hat and boots). Suggest that students make either an "assemblage" piece of jewelry or a "miniature masterpiece" from found materials.

## PROJECT 12–4:  **BLACK, WHITE, OR GOLD**

**MATERIALS**

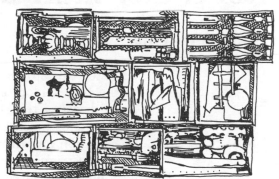

- Black or white posterboard
- White glue
- Cigar or shoe boxes
- Straight pins
- Spray paint: matte black, white, or gold

Although it is not absolutely necessary to work within a box form, it is nevertheless a good organizational tool. If the cardboard pieces you make overflow the box, you might add more boxes to the sculpture to complete it. You can use an existing box such as a cigar or shoe box, make your own, or use heavier cardboard pieces as a base.

1. Here are several suggestions for ways to transform cardboard:
    a. Curl it. Take one end of a piece of posterboard in each hand, and firmly pull it up and down over the edge of a table. As you do this, it will start to curl inward.
    b. Score it. With a straightedge ruler or yardstick, use the tip of a pair of scissors to make a straight line. This will enable you to fold it inward. You can score to make columns or edges.
    c. Cut and fold back. Make shapes such as small triangles. Cut them on two sides, and either fold them back or curl them by pushing them up and over a pencil. This will create shadows inside.
    d. Make similar forms such as pyramids or tiny boxes and assemble them all together.
    e. Take apart paper tubes from towels or toilet paper, cut holes in them, or somehow alter them, reassembling them to make monumental appearing structures.

2. Move the pieces around for some time before assembling. In place of advance planning, this is more a trial and error type of project. You may have to add more forms or take some away. When you are certain it couldn't possibly look better, then glue it with white glue. You may have to hold pieces in place with straight pins until the glue dries.

3. At this point make a decision about whether you want to spray paint it or not. Several of you in a class could spray yours all the same color, and display them together, making a gigantic assemblage like Louise Nevelson's wall sculptures.

# PROJECT 12–5: WRAP A BUILDING

## FOR THE TEACHER

Christo (Christo Javacheff, born in 1935) has made his place in art history with art-works that seldom endured more than two weeks. His works are not quite "happen-ings," because they have a longer-lasting visible effect, and in fact a few of his more famous ones (such as the *Wrapped Bundestag*) never actually took place except in his imagination and drawings. His earth works are well-known, with a *Running Fence*, or *Canyon Curtain*, putting pink ballet skirts around several islands in the Caribbean, wrapping sidewalks in Loose Park in Kansas City, Missouri, in yellow plastic, and wrapping the Pont Neuf bridge in Paris. He began by wrapping things on a small scale (such as humans), then worked up to the imaginary! The works are not salable, obvi-ously, but they are sometimes privately funded, and often what is sold are his mock-up drawings beforehand and photographs afterwards.

## CHRISTO'S MASTERWORKS

*Surrounded Islands, Biscayne Bay* 1983 (drawing), Miami, private collection, New York

*Strip-tease* ("empaquetage"), 1963, private collection

*Package on Wheelbarrow*, 1963, The Museum of Modern Art, New York

## FURTHER SUGGESTIONS

- So that students can appreciate the time period when many artists wrapped things in plastic and twine, assign each student to bring in a wrapped object from home. (Everyone has plastic cleaner bags or paper bags and string.) Put them all in one place and discuss them. Are some better "works of art" than others? Are they art at all? The whole idea of earning money for doing something that doesn't last and isn't particularly beautiful boggles the minds of secondary students.

- Have them do pencil drawings of their wrapped packages.

Name: _____     Date: _____

# PROJECT 12–5:   **WRAP A BUILDING**

**MATERIALS**

- Plastic
- String
- Drawing paper
- Conté crayon (or pencil)
- Glue
- Tagboard

This is your preliminary mock-up for a proposed wrapped place.

1. Select a real structure somewhere in the world. It could be a church, pyramid, bridge, skyscraper, the White House, your school—someplace that actually exists. Draw the outline of this structure on tagboard (much smaller than the drawing paper) and cut it out.

2. Decide what color the plastic will be that you use for wrapping. There are many types of plastic available, and you might wish to hunt around for an unusual color. The same is true for string. While you may just want clear plastic and white string, there might be more mystery if all that could be seen was the outline. Wrap your building, keeping the package as flat as possible.

3. Glue your architectural "package" to the paper. Place it carefully so that you can draw some other buildings or background around it. You want to have your drawing resemble the real location.

4. You would probably not draw on the plastic, but draw on the paper. Think carefully before beginning to draw. Sometimes it is what you leave out that makes a composition more exciting than what you put in. You might choose to do one or two buildings in great detail, and others only very sketchily.

5. When you are finished, put them on a wall and decide which one would be most likely to get public funding, or which ones might remain conceptual only.

# PROJECT 12–6: FINGERPRINT REALISM

**FOR THE TEACHER**

Chuck Close (born in 1940) was an abstract painter when he chose to eliminate working with color or brushes, and paint only faces of close friends. He is a Photorealist, but he is more interested in "making marks" with various tools and media than in exploring various subjects. Rather than directly projecting a slide onto canvas, he superimposes a grid over the surface of the photograph, and enlarges the photo by making a matching grid on a larger surface.

Before doing his large acrylic paintings (averaging 9 × 7 feet, often in color now), he frequently enlarges to smaller grids in various media, such as pastel on watercolor paper, pastels on paper that was first watercolored, colored pencil on paper, or ink and graphite on paper. He also sometimes uses fingerprints to apply paint (as in his painting, *Fanny*).

Photo 12-4. *Fanny/Finger-painting,* Chuck Close, 1985, 102 × 84 × 2½ inches, gift of Lila Acheson Wallace, National Gallery of Art, Washington, D.C.

## MASTERPIECES BY CHUCK CLOSE

*Self-Portrait,* 1968, Walker Art Center, Minnesota

*Leslie,* 1973, collection of Edmund P. Pillsbury, Connecticut

*Susan,* 1971, collection of Mr. and Mrs. Morton G. Neumann, Illinois

*Keith,* 1970, St. Louis Art Museum

### PREPARATION

Have students bring in the largest picture of themselves or a family member that they have available. This will be translated into a "painting" using only black ink, applied in different values by using fingertips as the painting tool. If only color photos are available, students may find it easier to transfer values to black and white by making a photocopy of their portrait (it could even be enlarged if it is too small). They could then make the grid directly on the photocopy rather than drawing the face on tracing paper.

Purchase (through a school store) or borrow enough stamp pads for two students to share. Also buy refill ink, as it will be used up. If this is not possible, make "pads" of felt or folded paper towels.

### FURTHER SUGGESTIONS

- Make one giant face by projecting an overhead transparency of a face (of the principal?) on the wall and outlining in pencil. Alternatives are to project it onto canvas, or onto 18 × 24-inch sheets of taped-together drawing paper, which are then taken apart for working. Have fifteen different students work on it at a time by applying fingerprints.

- Any subject such as a landscape or still-life is appropriate for stamping with fingerprints (or a pencil eraser).

Photo 12-5. *Keith,* 1970. Chuck Close, 275.0 × 212.5 cm, acrylic on gessoed canvas. The Saint Louis Art Museum, funds given by the Schoenberg Foundation, Inc.

# PROJECT 12–6: FINGERPRINT REALISM

**MATERIALS**

- Ink stamp pad
- Alcohol (for cleaning fingers)
- Drawing paper 18 × 24 inches
- Rulers
- Pencils

To make an enlargement of a face, you may rely on a photograph of yourself or a friend, as Chuck Close did. If you look at your face in a mirror, you will notice that some areas are lighter than others, such as the forehead, cheeks, chin, and nose. If you look at a photograph, you will observe this also. In painting with fingerprints rather than a brush, you will simply use less ink on your fingers to do these lighter areas.

1. Place tracing paper over your photo. Draw as carefully as possible, trying to make details realistic. When you have finished, compare your drawing and the photo, and make the drawing as detailed as you can.

2. To make a grid, use a ruler to make lines on the tracing paper around the outside of the drawing. If this is a small photo, you will probably divide the drawing into ¼-inch squares by making lines vertically and horizontally, ¼ inch apart.

3. On the larger drawing paper, enlarge the grid in proportion. For example, ¼ inch on the small drawing could be equal to 1 inch or 2 inches on the large paper. Depending on the shape of your photo, you may have to trim your paper when you are finished.

4. Each time you touch your finger on the ink stamp pad, it will then print darkly. Begin fingerprinting in the darkest areas, then as the ink wears off, apply it to the lighter areas. If you are not certain how much ink will be applied, test it on a piece of paper.

5. From time to time, walk away from your photo and look at it from a distance. You will not be able to see the fingerprints, but you will know whether the values are "working" or not, or whether you need to make the dark areas darker yet.

© 1992 by The Center for Applied Research in Education, Inc.

## PROJECT 12–7: **PHOTOREALISM**

**FOR THE TEACHER**

**Slide # 37: *Buddha.*** Except for their large size, Photorealist paintings look like photographs, complete with the flatness and the varying focal quality of a photograph. Most photo realists take photographs of their subjects and project the photo onto canvas. Each of the original Photorealists (those who painted from 1977 to 1987) tended to select a certain type of subject to be explored, such as Richard Estes' city-scapes, Charles Bell's children's toys, Don Eddy's cars and silver displays, or Richard McLean's horses.

Audrey Flack is one of the leading Photorealists. Her work shows her fascination with the opulence of the Baroque still life, the detail-filled "Vanitas" paintings. At times she appropriates photographs from news sources, as in her well-known work *Kennedy Motorcade,* 1964. Most of the large still-lifes (sometimes as large as 8 feet square) are compositions she sets up and photographs as transparencies that are projected onto the canvas. Flack paints with an airbrush to get the brilliant coloring and varied textural effects for which her work is known.

**PHOTO-REALIST MASTERPIECES**

*Jolie Madame,* Audrey Flack, 1972, Australian National Gallery, Canberra, Australia

*Leonardo's Lady,* 1975, Audrey Flack, The Museum of Modern Art, New York

*Marilyn* (Monroe), (Vanitas), Audrey Flack, 1977, University of Arizona Museum of Art, Tucson

Photo 12-6. *Buddha,* Audrey Flack, 1975, 70 × 96 inches, airbrushed acrylic over polymer emulsion on canvas, purchase and funds given by the Contemporary Art Society, The Saint Louis Art Museum.

*Buddha,* Audrey Flack, 1975, St. Louis Museum of Art

*New Shoes for H,* Don Eddy, 1973, Cleveland Museum of Art, Ohio

*Keith,* Chuck Close, 1970, The St. Louis Art Museum, St. Louis

*Drugs,* Richard Estes, c. 1970, Art Institute of Chicago

## PREPARATION

Discuss the work of Photorealists. A relatively recent trend in art is that of appropriating images from outside sources. You might get a lively discussion started if you discuss the difference between appropriating and plagiarizing.

## FURTHER SUGGESTIONS

- Janet Fish is a painter who selects "tabletop" arrangements as her subject matter. She paints glass objects, food, (sometimes still in its cellophane wrapping) and flowers, showing her fascination with reflections and the play of light. The interrelationships of these objects to each other is of primary importance to her. Simply set up a still-life that contains almost nothing but reflective items such as mirrors, glass bottles and other containers. Painting glass or other reflective materials is a matter of putting on canvas *exactly* what is seen. Almost any medium is suitable for this assignment, though Janet Fish often works in oil or watercolor.

- Ask students to bring in their own favorite snapshot and enlarge it as precisely as possible by using a grid system.

**Photo 12-7.** *Private Parking X,* **Don Eddy, 1971, 167 × 238.8 cm, acrylic on canvas, gift of Leila and Monroe R. Meyerson, The Saint Louis Art Museum.**

Name: _____    Date: _____

## PROJECT 12–7: **PHOTOREALISM**

**MATERIALS**

- Still life materials or magazine cut-outs
- Tracing paper
- 9 × 12 inch drawing paper
- Polaroid or other camera
- Photoflood lights or lamps
- Colored pencils

The Photorealists usually project their photographs onto the canvas to help them to be totally accurate. Although most of the Photorealists use acrylic paint, you could use colored pencil, watercolor, pencil, or any combinations of these materials to make your enlargement.

Several alternatives for interpreting a Photorealist composition are given here.

1. *Colored pencil:* To make brilliantly colored accurate interpretations, the firm application of colored pencil will probably give the best results. By working relatively small, you will be able to give the energy that is needed to work in this manner.

   a. Make a collage still life of colored magazine photos. Try to have a theme of some sort in mind such as cars, animals, city, or something else that is of interest to you.

   b. Either trace direct onto drawing paper, or (if you can't see through it) photocopy the collage and trace around the photocopy. It is also possible to color directly on a photocopy with pencil, but the results will be entirely different than if you work on good drawing paper.

2. *Original photograph or slide of a still-life:* Set up a still-life and photograph it. Your photo can be enlarged on a copy machine, and you can trace your copy, while using your original photo for color matching. If you take slides, they can be projected.

3. *Collage from appropriated items:* In this project you may or may not choose to make a drawing or painting from the collage you have made. Perhaps you can learn the problems facing a Photorealist if your collage is the finished product. Audrey Flack sometimes uses a photograph of a real person, such as Marilyn Monroe, or a portrait by Leonardo da Vinci as the theme of a collage. When you have selected a theme, find other pictures that relate, sometimes strangely, but sometimes just to repeat a shape of something else you have put in the picture.

# PROJECT 12-8: FEMININE OR MASCULINE ART?

**FOR THE TEACHER**

**Slide # 38: *Conservatory.*** While much of the art created through the years by women or men is unidentifiable by gender, artists do try to create what is meaningful to them. Many women artists have been surrounded by things of the home such as children and family, and consequently have often been inspired by these as subjects. Successful female artists are often not as well known as men for a variety of reasons, but research is finding they have existed throughout the history of art.

Miriam Shapiro is a "feminist" artist. She says, "All of my work is responsive to my being female in a patriarchal society." She taught a course at the California Institute of Arts for women only, and "wanted to be known as a woman artist." Her very large paintings/collages, which she calls "femmages" (because of the consciously feminine materials used in them) incorporate such feminine images as hearts, costumes, fans, flowers, patchwork motifs, or crocheted fabrics.

**WELL KNOWN WORKS BY MIRIAM SHAPIRO**

*Murmur of the Heart,* 1980, collection of the artist

*The Azerbajani Fan,* 1980, collection of the artist

*Conservatory,* 1988, collection of the artist

*I'm Dancin' as Fast as I Can,* 1980s, collection of the artist

Photo 12-8. *Pas de Deux,* Miriam Shapiro.

**PREPARATION**

What are little girls made of? What are little boys made of? What is "feminine" furniture or a "masculine" room? Most of us have a combination of feminine and masculine preferences. One of my university teachers brought up that he had seen separate entrance doors for men and women into a meeting house in a Shaker community. Our assignment (in a sculpture class) was to make a feminine or masculine door (many of the women made "male" doors, and vice-versa). Have students bring in materials from home, and in one location gather the "feminine" objects, and in another place the "masculine."

In this assignment students may make feminine or masculine collages, or a combination of each, but these should be conscious decisions rather than just putting anything they feel like on the collage. Suggest that they can be "appropriationists" (as many artists have been over the centuries, using something done by an artist whom they admire) as an inspiration for their theme.

You will have missed a great opportunity if you do not evaluate this work as a class when it is done. This is an issue that will raise their consciousness of contemporary art and why and how artists sometimes select their themes.

# PROJECT 12–8:  FEMININE OR MASCULINE?

## MATERIALS

- Feminine or masculine collage materials
- Canvas board or 14-ply matboard
- Scissors
- Polymer medium
- Acrylic paints
- Brushes

Before making a collage, get the materials together. What is interesting today is that many of these materials are seen on the clothing of both men and women, and there is often little difference between the types of clothing they wear (androgynous). These lists contain a few suggestions for "gender" materials:

Feminine collage materials—glitter, fabric, lace, ruffles, jewels

Masculine collage materials—nails, leather, denim, wood

1. Without a theme, your collage will look like everyone else's. You need to "reach within yourself" to find something that is special about you. Think about someone you admire . . . something you aspire to someday . . . a dream that you often have . . . an incident in your past—something that is unique to *you.*

2. When you have settled on an idea, look at the collage materials (masculine, feminine, or both) to find materials that might fit into your collage. This will be most effective if it has some elements of realism combined with collage materials. Magazine pictures (or painted copies of them) could be part of your collage. Use these sparingly.

3. Move materials around on the board's surface. Either walk off, or place the collage on the floor to see it from a distance.

   a. Check it from several angles to see if it is visually effective.

   b. Does it have a center of interest—the brightest, lightest, immediately seen area?

   c. Do the other materials add to or detract from the center of interest?

   d. Can you add anything or take anything away that would make it better?

4. With a brush, apply polymer medium (or thinned white glue) to affix items to the board. You may also brush the polymer on top of the collage material to give a sheen, and to act as a varnish.

5. If you then find that you wish to paint on top of these materials with acrylic paint, the polymer medium keeps the materials from absorbing the paint. Acrylic paint and polymer work well together, and you can continue to build up your surface with either paint or more collage materials.

## PROJECT 12-9:  LIME GREEN CATS

**FOR THE TEACHER**

**Slide # 39: *Radioactive Cats*.** Many contemporary artists work simultaneously in various media. A prime example of this work is that of Sandy Skoglund, a west coast artist. Skoglund specializes in creating environments, or installations, using multiple sculptured images which she then photographs. Her sculptural, painterly photographic work is startling and unforgettable. She uses a monochromatic background filled with brightly colored objects such as those in *Radioactive Cats*. This installation features a brownish room, with an old couple whose skin is almost salmon in color. Throughout the room are lime green cats.

A similar installation is titled *Revenge of the Goldfish*. It features a blue bedroom with brightly painted orange fish hanging on the walls and from the ceiling. She makes models of such things as cats, fish, baby dolls (as in her environment *Maybe Babies*, or the electric blue leaves of the installation *A Breeze at Work*). Skoglund also creates monochromatic Photorealistic paintings from photomontages.

**Photo 12-9. *Revenge of the Goldfish*, Sandy Skoglund, The Saint Louis Art Museum.**

**PREPARATION**

This transformation of the environment could be an all-class project. It could be done on a small scale by creating an environment in a large carton such as a refrigerator box or a corner of the room. Show the slide of Skoglund's work, and "brainstorm" about living creatures or objects that could be made in multiples. Talk about what could be part of this environment besides the brightly colored forms? Should there be people in it? How should they be dressed, and what should they be doing?

If at all possible, when you are done, have someone take a roll of color prints so that each student would have an original photograph of the installation.

**FURTHER SUGGESTIONS**

- Make individual two-dimensional "environments" by having students repeatedly trace the same object, color them brightly with one color, then cut them out and paste them onto a background made of a black-and-white magazine picture.

- Have students make individual miniature environments in a box that is open in the front and on the top. Think of it as a gallery installation, considering the size of the "room" and the effect it would have on the public that would come to see it. In a photograph of the miniature environment, scale could have been life-size.

**Photo 12-10.** *Radioactive Cats,* 1980, Sandy Skoglund, 76.2 × 94.6 cm, Cibachrome print, The Saint Louis Art Museum.

# PROJECT 12–9:  **LIME GREEN CATS**

## MATERIALS

*Stuffed Paper Form*

- Fadeless paper in bright colors
- Newspaper
- Staplers
- Staples
- Scissors
- String
- Newsprint or tagboard pattern

*Papier-Mâché*

- Clay
- Kraft paper or paper bags
- Wallpaper paste
- Tempera paint
- Petroleum Jelly or vegetable shortening
- X-acto® knife

Color and repetition are going to be an important part of your environmental installation. You will be making many similar images, and while they can vary somewhat in shape, they should all be the same bright color. Sandy Skoglund's installations use color combinations that usually are of complementary colors, such as orange and blue, lime green and salmon, yellow and violet. Directions will be given for two different types of materials:

*Stuffed Paper Forms*

1. Make a pattern of newsprint or tagboard (fish, for example). The size will vary depending on whether you are transforming an entire room or only a small version of one. These will be effective if hung from a ceiling or stapled on the walls. They would not be self-supporting.

2. Cut two identical pieces of fadeless or roll paper for each form. Use staples closely together around the edges, sealing all but an opening 4 to 5 inches. Tear newspaper into smallish pieces, crumple, and stuff into the opening. Use staples to close it entirely. If necessary, trim the edges. Staple string onto the form to hang it from a ceiling or wall.

*Papier-Mâché Forms*

1. To make similar "castings," make the original forms of clay. Oil or grease the clay so it will release the papier-mâché forms.

2. Tear kraft paper (or grocery bags) into pieces approximately 2 × 2 inches. Dip a piece in wallpaper paste, and pull it between the first two fingers of your hand to remove excess paste. Totally cover the original clay form, using at least three thicknesses of paper. When it is dry, use an X-acto® knife to cut it apart to remove from the clay form. Place the parts together, and use more pieces of kraft paper to hold the seams together. To make identical forms, keep the clay form covered in plastic for reuse.

   ***Safety Note:*** *Use extreme care when cutting.*

3. When it is dry, paint with tempera or spray paint and arrange a suitable environment. You may wish to have people in the environment also. Make photographs to record your installation.

**347**

# PROJECT 12–10: COCKFIGHT

**FOR THE TEACHER**

**Slide # 40: _Zaga._** Nancy Graves (born in 1940) began her career as a sculptor, using soft materials to make models of life-sized camels! After studying in Italy, she learned the technique of lost wax casting. Her sculptures are composed of natural and found objects that have been coated with investment compound (somewhat like plaster of Paris), and the coated form is then placed in a "burn-out furnace" where intense heat incinerates the material inside, leaving a hollow shell. Molten bronze is poured into the shell, and when it cools, the investment is removed, and the bronze sprues (vents) are filed off. When Nancy Graves creates her assemblages, she chooses from literally hundreds of bronze objects, welding them together to create the light, airy, apparently weightless forms. By applying ground glass onto the surface and heating it, so that it becomes part of the surface or painting, the sculptures have color that is part of the finish. Her work is known for its imagination and humor.

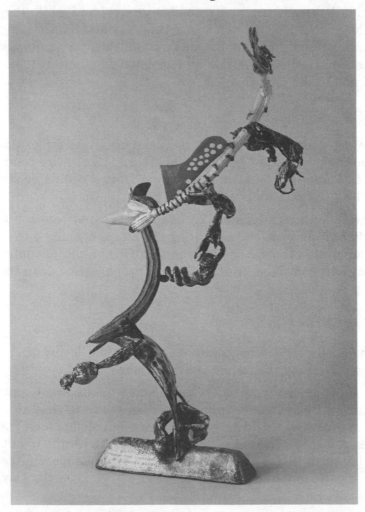

**Photo 12-11.** _Fought Cight Cockfight,_ **Nancy Graves, 1984, 33½ × 16½ × 13½ inches, bronze with polychrome patina, enamel and acrylic lacquer, The Saint Louis Art Museum, Schoenberg Foundation, Inc.**

## GRAVES' MASTERWORKS

*Zaga,* 1983, Nelson-Atkins Art Museum, Kansas City, Missouri

*Fought Cight Cockfight,* 1984, St. Louis Art Museum

### PREPARATION

Talk about the *possible* with the students. You will not have the benefit of being able to weld objects together, so you will have to weld with glue, stick things into styrofoam, or whatever works! Have the students gather objects from home and nature, bringing in as many objects as they can find. What may be abundant in one location (such as pinecones), someone else might not have access to. The one criteria is that the objects should be firm enough to handle so they don't disintegrate when they are glued on.

### ANOTHER SUGGESTION

- Suggest that each student bring in *one* type of material from which to create an individual assemblage of units. This could be cotton swabs, toothpicks, cotton balls, styrofoam cups, pinecones, marbles, tiny styrofoam balls, jewelry boxes, shells—whatever is available. For almost every material made, there is a glue that will hold it together.

**Photo 12-12.** *Cockfight,* **David Smith, 1945,**
**45$^{1}/_{16}$ × 21$^{1}/_{2}$ × 10$^{1}/_{2}$ inches, steel, The Saint Louis**
**Art Museum.**

Name: _____ Date: _____

# PROJECT 12–10: **COCKFIGHT**

**MATERIALS**

- Wood bases (a 2 × 4-inch board cut into 4-inch squares)
- Nails (for attaching wire to the base)
- Wire
- Gesso
- Acrylic paint
- Glue: glue gun, epoxy, white glue
- Spray paint
- Found objects such as tagboard, pretzels, styrofoam cups, baskets, dowels, plastic flowers or leaves, sticks, branches, pinecones, shells, miscellaneous sturdy dried flowers such as lotus pods

**Drawing after *Fought Cight Cockfight*, 1984, Nancy Graves.**

**Drawing after *Cockfight*, 1945, David Smith.**

Nancy Graves' assemblages may *look* like twigs, leaves, and pretzels, but they are natural objects that have been cast in bronze, welded together, and painted. You will have to settle for *real* pretzels, twigs, dried cones, and so on that you will assemble and spray paint to preserve.

It may help you when you assemble all these elements to have something real (such as a person or animal) in your mind as a subject for an abstract sculpture.

1. Nail wire to a board. You can attach some of the items by wrapping them with wire and attaching them, or can attach them with a glue gun or white glue.

2. Because not all real tropical leaves and plant life are strong enough to support themselves, you may prefer to attach plastic reproductions or cut leaves from tag board. Yours will not have the strength that bronze ones would, which is the reason for a wire or tagboard armature (structure).

3. As you are assembling the materials, take the time to step back and look at the work to see if it yet resembles anything in particular. It isn't a necessity for it to be something like a human or animal, but it may look that way in spite of what you are doing (or because of it).

4. When you are satisfied that you cannot add more without destroying the charm and humor of your sculpture, you might wish to spray paint it or paint it with tempera. Fluorescent or regular tempera can be added to polymer medium to give a paint that has a built-in varnish.

# PROJECT 12–11: THE T-SHIRT GENERATION

### FOR THE TEACHER

Wearable art is seen at art openings, museum shops and exhibits, special art festivals, and galleries that feature "art to wear." Almost any art exhibit at a museum has T-shirts for sale based on the featured artists' work. Students especially enjoy designing their own artwork. They see "designer" T-shirts, and might as well be their own designers.

### PREPARATION

Display art reproductions around the room. If this is the culminating project to a unit, these posters will help students see unifying characteristics. Because students will probably be buying their own T-shirts, they may prefer to select their own time period or artist, but they may appreciate the limitation of reproducing a work of art.

You could inspire them by suggesting that a major museum has "commissioned" them to design the shirt to sell at the opening of an exhibit of (for example) Impressionism or Monet. Remind them that this shirt might be purchased and worn by both males and females. After making the first shirt, allow them to create their own designs.

Photo 12-13. *Student artwork.* Grant Kniffen's students from Parkway North High School, St. Louis County, Missouri created masterpieces on T-shirts using acrylic paint.

**FURTHER SUGGESTIONS**

- Students could make a cloth wallhanging using only hand-painted reproductions of artwork, "signed" by the featured artist. Each student could do a separate one, or these could be joined together to make a monumental work of art for the school. This should be lined and given a border for a finished look.

- Hand painting could be done on shoes, jeans, or sweatshirts.

- This project has the potential to be a major fundraiser for departmental needs through sales of T-shirts to other students.

**Photo 12-14. This T-shirt is also by Grant Kniffen's student.**

Name: _____ Date: _____

## PROJECT 12–11: THE T-SHIRT GENERATION

### MATERIALS

- T-shirts
- Brushes (large, fine, stencil, brights)
- Styrofoam egg cartons or small painting cups
- 18 × 24-inch newsprint
- Cleaners' bags
- Acrylic or textile paints

- Hangers
- Water
- Tagboard
- X-acto® knife
- Stencil brush

Select an artist or time period whose work you would like to reproduce. It is not necessary to reproduce an entire work of art, but only a portion of it. Prepare a shirt for painting by washing it in hot water to remove sizing.

1. Put at least three layers of newsprint inside the shirt to prevent paint from going through to the back. Loosely stuff the sleeves by making a roll of paper inside them.

2. Plan a design on newsprint. To base the design on the work of one particular artist, find one whose work you like. Use only a portion of the design. You could even "sign" the painting with a signature like that of the artist.

3. Paint can be applied in a number of ways. The thinner the paint, the softer and more comfortable the shirt will be. Small areas can be painted with intense color, but the shirt will be stiff if too much pigment is applied.

   a. Dilute the paint with water and almost "stain" the cloth with light color. You can go back and make it darker if you wish, or paint more intense color back into the stained areas.

   b. Make a stencil by cutting a design into tagboard with an X-acto® knife. Use a stiff brush to dab the paint onto the shirt through the openings made. The stencil pattern may be repeated all over the T-shirt, or just on the front.

   *Safety Note: Be careful when using the knife.*

   c. Cut a design on an art gum eraser and apply paint, and repeatedly stamp the same design to make a "picture." Letters of the alphabet are very effective. The stamp needn't have fresh paint applied each time, because the differences in value are interesting.

   d. Dilute the paint and pour the "colored water" onto the shirt. It can be painted back into with thin lines if you wish.

   e. Spatter paint by dipping the brush in very thin paint and splashing it around.

4. Hang the shirt to dry with paper or plastic cleaner bag inside to prevent paint from going through to the other side. If you wish to add further decoration, you can paint sparkles or add "jewels" to accent certain parts of the design when it is dry. (Both these items can be purchased at hobby shops.)

# APPENDICES

A: How to Create Slides from Books or Magazines
B: Ceramics Basics
C: How to Mix Plaster
D: Artists' Birthdays
E: How to Plan a Party
F: Famous Artists
G: Famous Buildings and Their Architects

# A:  HOW TO CREATE SLIDES FROM BOOKS OR MAGAZINES

This is the least expensive way to build your slide collection. My students have put together "slide shows" using this method, and the slide library is improving considerably as a result.

**MATERIALS**

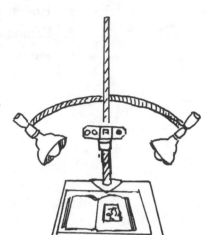

- 35-mm camera (for up to 14 inches)
- Macro lens or close-up rings
- Color slide film for *tungsten lighting* or a blue filter that converts film for tungsten lighting
- Two photo flood lamps, 3200 K
- 18% gray card (photo shop)
- Sheet of glass (to hold book flat at times)
- Copy stand (a tripod could substitute)
- Two L-shaped 3-inch wide pieces of black matboard or construction paper

1. Place book or magazine on a flat surface. If it won't lie flat because of the spine of the book, place a clean piece of sheet glass on it to hold it flat. If you do not have a copy stand, the camera can be put on a tripod or may be hand-held provided you don't shoot below 30 ($1/30$th of a second).

2. Place the flood lamps above and to the sides of the artwork at a 45° angle. If these are carefully directed, you can avoid glare.

3. Raise or lower the camera to eliminate white edges as much as possible. If these still show, use the L-shaped pieces of cardboard to surround the painting to avoid uneven borders.

4. Look through your lens to see if there is glare on the picture. Move the lamps slightly if there is. It will show as a lighter area unless you eliminate the glare.

5. Place the gray card on top of the picture and take a "reading" on it. When you remove the gray card, the camera's meter may show that the picture is overexposed or underexposed. Trust the gray card. It will give you very true colors. If the first roll is over or underexposed, then next time compensate accordingly for your camera. You could also "bracket" each picture by taking one photo at exactly the gray card reading, then take one overexposed, and one underexposed, but this method uses considerably more film.

# B: CERAMICS BASICS

Wedging is done to remove air bubbles from clay. Large amounts of clay can be kneaded like dough, or slammed on a table. One of my colleagues prefers to have students make a ball and slap it between their hands to hold down on noise. Use a wire to cut wedged clay apart to see if there are bubbles. If they are there, continue wedging. Ten minutes is average. Keep clay moist while working by placing damp paper towels around it and covering it with plastic when not being worked on.

If clay dries out too much, it can be recycled by putting it in a barrel with water, then after a couple of days, taking it out to drain excess water.

## COIL BUILDING

Wedge the clay. Roll out even coils from 1/4- to 1-inch thick. The bottom of a pot can be a coil or slab. Make several uniform coils. Join coils together by cutting a slanted end one way on one coil, and the opposite way on the other before joining. Each time two coils are joined, the two surfaces should be scored and slip-coated. Add three coils at a time, then smooth them inside and outside. Use a flat wooden stick to paddle them smooth on the outside. When the pot is leather-hard (firm to the touch), you could polish it on the outside with the back of a spoon or a stone.

## SLAB BUILDING

### MATERIALS

- Rolling pin or 1 × 12-inch dowels
- 1/4 × 12-inch wood lathing strips
- Knife
- Slip (mix clay and water to thickness of white glue)
- Needle tool
- Canvas or newsprint
- Metal scraper

Make thumbnail sketches, then a tagboard pattern of your idea. For uniform slabs, place a ball between two parallel wooden strips, and roll it out. If there are visible bubbles, they can be pricked with a needle tool. Cut vertically around the pattern with a knife. Join slabs together by scoring (making marks) on the two edges, and applying slip to the joints. Smooth the edges by hand or with a metal scraper. For extra strength, a thin coil of clay can be placed inside right angle slabs.

### FINISHING

Allow the clay to dry totally before firing. Underglazes can be painted on while greenware (unfired clay) is drying. After a bisque (first) firing, underglazes or regular glazes can be applied. Bisqueware pieces could be painted with acrylic paints, spray painted, or stained with shoe polish.

# C: HOW TO MIX PLASTER

## MATERIALS

- Plaster of paris
- Plastic bucket (or small plastic container)
- Milk cartons, pie tins

This is a chemical reaction, and proper mixing will get the best results. Once you have begun mixing, do not add more plaster. It may seem too thin, but it will set up eventually. If you wish to have it thick enough to control during a one-hour period, it will take approximately 15 minutes. Exact measurements are not possible because much depends on the weather, the heat of the water, the type of plaster, and so on. Plaster can be mixed by the bucketful or the small buttertubful. A rough proportion is 1/3 water to 2/3 plaster.

*Note: Do not stir until you have all the plaster in the water.*

1. Depending on the amount you need, put *warm* water in the bottom of a bucket or other container. Cold water may be used, but it takes longer to set up. Use a scoop (a small plastic margarine container will do) to sift plaster onto the surface of the water. It will settle to the bottom as you do this. Continue to add plaster until it forms a mound that sticks above the surface of the water.

2. Mix the plaster by placing your hand on the bottom of the container and gently mixing it between your fingers. The idea is to avoid creating bubbles. If you intend to carve it, it can be poured into containers while it is still quite liquid. (It is easier to carve if vermiculite—available in garden supply stores—is added when it is thicker.)

3. You will know it is within minutes of setting up when it coats your hand so the skin doesn't show and begins to be the thickness of whipping cream. When it leaves a path where you move your hand, then you have approximately two minutes to work before it sets up. Always have containers (such as aluminum pie pans to make plaster bats) to put excess plaster into.

4. Always get as much of it out of the bucket with your hand as you can. Allow the residue to dry in the bucket; you can give it a thump later, and it will flake into the wastebasket. You will need to wash your hands, of course, but allow water to keep running in the sink so it does not clog the drain.

*Note: Never pour excess plaster down a sink!*

# D: ARTISTS' BIRTHDAYS

## JANUARY
10. Barbara Hepworth, 1903
11. Alexander Calder, 1870
12. John Sargent, 1856
14. Berthe Morisot, 1841
19. Paul Cezanne, 1839
23. Edouard Manet, 1832
28. Jackson Pollock, 1912
28. Claes Oldenburg, 1929

## FEBRUARY
3. Norman Rockwell, 1894
4. Fernand Leger, 1881
8. Franz Marc, 1880
12. Max Beckmann, 1884
13. Grant Wood, 1892
21. Constantin Brancusi, 1876
24. Winslow Homer, 1836
25. Pierre A. Renoir, 1841

## MARCH
1. Oscar Kokoschka, 1886
6. Michelangelo, 1475
7. Piet Mondrian, 1872
9. David Smith 1906
19. Josef Albers, 1888
20. George C. Bingham, 1811
21. Hans Hofmann, 1880
22. Anthony van Dyck, 1599
23 Juan Gris, 1887
30 Francisco de Goya
30 Vincent van Gogh, 1853

## APRIL
2. Max Ernst, 1891
4. Edward Hicks, 1780
6. Raphael, 1483
12. Robert Delaunay, 1885
15. Leonardo da Vinci, 1452
15. Theodore Rousseau, 1812
20. Joan Miro', 1893
22. Odilon Redon, 1840
23. J.M.W. Turner, 1775
26. Eugene Delacroix, 1798

## MAY
6. Ernst Kirchner, 1880
13. Joseph Stella, 1877
13. Georges Braque, 1882
15. Jasper Johns, 1930
21. Albrecht Durer, 1471
21. Henri Rousseau, 1844
22. Mary Cassatt, 1844
22. Marisol, 1930
23. Franz Kline, 1910
27. Georges Rouault, 1871

## JUNE
1. Red Grooms, 1937
3. Raoul Dufy, 1877
6. Velasquez, 1599
7. Paul Gauguin, 1848
13. Christo, 1935
16. Jim Dine, 1935
25. Sam Francis, 1923
28. Peter Paul Rubens, 1577

## JULY
7. Marc Chagall, 1887
8. Kathe Kollwitz, 1867
9. David Hockney, 1937
10. Camille Pissarro, 1830
10. J. M. Whistler, 1834
10. Georgio de Chirico, 1888
12. Amedeo Modigliani, 1884
12. Andrew Wyeth, 1917
14. Gustav Klimt, 1862
15. Rembrandt, 1606
19. Edgar Degas, 1834
22. Edward Hopper, 1882
22. Alexander Calder, 1898
28. Marcel Duchamp, 1887
30. Henry Moore, 1898

## AUGUST
5. George Tooker, 1920
7. Emile Nolde, 1867
8. Andy Warhol, 1931
21. Aubrey Beardsley
24. Alphonse Mucha, 1860
27. Man Ray, 1890

## SEPTEMBER
2. Romare Bearden, 1914
3. Louis Sullivan, 1856
7. Grandma Moses, 1860
7. Jacob Lawrence, 1917
12. Ben Shahn, 1898
13. Robert Indiana
23. Paul Delvaux, 1897
25. Mark Rothko, 1903

## OCTOBER
4. Frederick Remington, 1861
10. Antoine Watteau, 1684
19. Umberto Boccioni
21. Katsushika Hokusai, 1760
22. Robert Rauschenberg, 1925
25. Pablo Picasso, 1881
27. Roy Lichtenstein, 1923
28. Francis Bacon, 1909
31. Joannes Vermeer, 1632

## NOVEMBER
2. Jean Baptiste Chardin, 1699
7. Francisco de Zurbaran, 1598
8. Charles Demuth, 1883
11. Paul Signac, 1863
11. Edouard Vuillard, 1868
12. Auguste Rodin, 1840
14. Claude Monet, 1840
15. Georgia O'Keeffe, 1887
21. Rene' Magritto, 1890
24. H. Toulouse-Lautrec, 1864
26. George Segal, 1924
28. Morris Louis, 1912

## DECEMBER
1. Georges Seurat, 1859
3. Gilbert Stuart, 1755
4. Wassily Kandinsky, 1866
5. Walt Disney, 1901
7. Stuart Davis, 1894
8. Aristide Maillol, 1861
8. Diego Rivera, 1886
12. Edvard Munch, 1863
12. Helen Frankenthaler, 1928
18. Paul Klee, 1879
20. Pieter de Hooch, 1629
24. Joseph Cornell, 1903
31. Henri Matisse, 1869

# E: HOW TO PLAN A PARTY

**FOR THE TEACHER**

Students are always looking for a reason to have a party, and what better reason than to celebrate the birthday of an artist. This could be a celebration of Youth Art Month, a theme for an art club reception, or a classroom end-of-unit or end-of-year project, and could become an annual tradition at your school.

This project was created by Pamela Hellwege of the Saint Louis Art Museum Education Department for a teacher workshop, and is used with her permission and the permission of the Museum. Pam photocopied a life-size picture of Picasso's face, and each person was given a copy. These were mounted on tagboard and suitable Picasso-esque headdresses were made.

**MATERIALS**

- Tagboard
- Scissors
- Markers
- Glue
- Colored fadeless paper

Once you have decided on a specific artist, show slides of his or her work. Talking about the images and setting up committees is fun because imagination can run wild, and there are no limitations. Get students to volunteer to be on a committee such as:

1. Refreshments: Based on nationality, colors, or shapes used in artwork, what colors should they be? What is appropriate food?

2. Table decoration

3. Room decorations: Draw a life-sized outline of a human figure that resembles the person. A group can take charge of "dressing" it appropriately.

4. Entertainment: A tableau based on artwork? Skits? Music? Games?

5. Invitations: Invite parents, faculty, administration, or just yourselves to your celebration.

6. Personal adornment: hats, costumes, or masks.

7. Party favors: souvenirs of the party for everyone to take home.

Have someone in charge of photographs so you will have a record of the event for the following year.

# F:   FAMOUS ARTISTS

**Pre-Renaissance (c.1250 to 1470)**
ITALY
   Giotto, c. 1267–1337
   Cimabue, 1251–1302
   Simone Martini, 1315–1344
   Paolo Uccello, 1397-1475
   Fra Angelico, c. 1400–1455
   Masaccio, c. 1401–1469
   Fra Filippo Lippi, c. 1406–1469
   Castagno, c. 1410–1457
   A. del Pollaiuolo, c. 1431–1498
NETHERLANDS
   Jan van Eyck, c. 1390–1441
   Robert Campin, 1375–1444
   Limbourg brothers, fl. 1400–1430
   R. van der Weyden, c. 1399–1464
   Hieronymus Bosch, c. 1450–1516
   Hans Memling, c. 1430-1494
   Hugo van der Goes, c. 1440–1482
   Pieter Brueghel, c. 1525–1569

**Renaissance (1450 to 1520)**
ITALY
   Sandro Botticelli, 1444–1510
   Leonardo da Vinci, 1452–1519
   Piero di Cosimo, 1462–1521
   Verrocchio, 1435–1488
   Donato Bramante, 1444–1514
   Michelangelo, 1475–1564
   Raphael, 1483–1520
   Piero Della Francesca 1416–1492
   Mantegna, 1431–1506
   Correggio, 1494–1534
GERMANY
   Matthias Grünewald, c. 1455–1528
   Albrecht Dürer, 1471–1528
   Lucas Cranach, 1472–1553
   Albrecht Altdorfer, c. 1480–1538
   Adam Elsheimer, 1578–1610
   Hans Holbein, Younger, 1497–1543

**Mannerism (1525 to 1600)**
ITALY
   Titian, 1488/90–1576
   Andrea Palladio, 1508–1580
   Jacopo Tintoretto, 1518–1594
   Paolo Veronese, 1528–1588
   Vasari, 1511–1574
FRANCE
   Jean Clouet, c. 1486–1541

**Baroque, (1590 to 1750)**
ITALY
   M. da Caravaggio, 1573–1610
   Gianlorenzo Bernini, 1598–1680
   Annibale Carracci, 1560–1609
HOLLAND
   Gerrit von Honthorst, 1590–1656
   Rembrandt van Rijn, 1606–1669
   Jacob van Ruisdael, 1628–1682
   Mcindert Hobbema, 1638–1709
   Frans Hals, 1580–1666
   Willem Claez Heda, 1594–1680/2
   Pieter Saenredam, 1597–1662
   Pieter de Hooch, 1629–1684
   Jan Vermeer, 1632–1675
   Jan Steen, 1626–1679
SPAIN
   El Greco, (born Greek) 1541–1614
   Jusepe Ribera, 1588–1652
   Francisco de Zurburan, 1598 1661
   Diego Velásquez, 1599–1660
   Bartolomé Murillo, 1617–1690
FLANDERS
   Jan Brueghel, 1568–1625
   Peter Paul Rubens, 1577–1640
   Anthony van Dyck, 1599 1641
FRANCE
   Louis Le Nain, 1593–1648
   Georges de la Tour, 1593–1652
   Nicolas Poussin, 1594–1665
   Claude Lorrain, 1600–1682

**Neoclassicism (1770 to 1820)**
AMERICA
   Thomas Jefferson, 1743–1826
FRANCE
   Jacques Louis David, 1748–1825
   Jean Ingres, 1780–1867
SPAIN
   Francisco Goya, 1746–1828

**Romanticism (c. 1800 to 1850)**
FRANCE
   Eugene Delacroix, 1798–1863
   Theodore Gericault, 1791–1834
   Gustave Moreau, 1826–1898
BRITAIN
   J.M.W. Turner, 1775–1851

**Romanticism (c. 1800 to 1850)** (continued)

BRITAIN (continued)
John Constable, 1776–1837
Thomas Gainsborough, 1727–1788

AMERICA
Benjamin West, 1738–1820
John S. Copley, 1738–1815
G. C. Bingham, 1811–1879

**Realism (c. 1850 to 1880)**

FRANCE
Jean Francois Millet, 1814–1875
Jean Baptiste Corot, 1796–1875
Honoré Daumier, 1808–1879
Gustave Courbet, 1819–1877
Eugene Boudin, 1824–1898
Jean Antoine Houdon, 1741–1828

AMERICA
Winslow Homer, 1836–1910
Thomas Eakins, 1844–1916

**Impressionism (c. 1870 to 1905)**

FRANCE
Edouard Manet, 1832–1883
Claude Monet, 1840–1926
Camille Pissarro, 1830–1903
Edgar Degas, 1834–1917
Berthé Morisot, 1841–1895
Pierre-Auguste Renoir, 1841–1919
Paul Cézanne, 1839–1906
Alfred Sisley, 1839–1899
Auguste Rodin, 1840–1917

AMERICA
Mary Cassatt, 1845–1926

**Postimpressionism (c. 1886 to 1920)**

FRANCE
H. Toulouse-Lautrec, 1864–1901
Paul Gauguin, 1848–1903
Georges Seurat, 1855–1891
Henri Rousseau, 1844–1910
Henri Matisse, 1869–1954
Paul Cézanne, 1839–1906
Odilon Redon, 1840–1916
Edward Vuillard, 1868–1940
Bonnard, 1867–1947

HOLLAND
Vincent van Gogh, 1863–1890

NORWAY
Edvard Munch, 1863–1944

**Art Nouveau (c. 1880 to 1910)**

AUSTRIA
Gustave Klimt, 1862–1918
Alphonse Mucha, 1860–1939

BRITAIN
Aubrey Beardsley, 1872–1898

**Fauvism (1905 to 1907)**

FRANCE
Henri Matisse, 1869–1954
André Derain 1880–1954
Raoul Dufy, 1877–1953
Georges Braque, 1882–1963

BELGIUM
Maurice Vlaminck, 1876–1958

**Expressionism (1890–1940s)**

NORWAY
Edvard Munch, 1863–1944

GERMANY
Ernst Ludwig Kirchner, 1880–1938
Emil Nolde, 1867–1956
Max Beckmann, 1844–1950
Franz Marc, 1880–1916
Lyonel Feininger, 1871–1956

AUSTRIA
Oscar Kokoschka, 1886–1980

BELGIUM
James Ensor 1860–1949
Constant Permeke, 1886–1952

RUSSIA
Wassily Kandinsky, 1866–1944
Alexei von Jawlensky, 1864–1941
Chaim Soutine, 1894–1943
Kasimir Malevich, 1878–1935

SWITZERLAND
Paul Klee, 1879–1940

FRANCE
Georges Rouault, 1871–1958

ITALY
Amadeo Modigliani 1884–1920

**Cubism (1907 to 1920s)**

SPAIN
Pablo Picasso, 1881–1973
Juan Gris, 1887–1927

FRANCE
Georges Braque, 1882–1963
Robert Delaunay, 1885–1941
Jacques Villon, 1875–1963
Marcel Duchamp, 1887–1968
Fernand Leger, 1881–1955

**Futurism (c. 1908)**

ITALY
  Umberto Boccioni, 1882–1916
  Gino Severini, 1883–1966

**Abstraction (c. 1930s to 1960s)**

HOLLAND
  Piet Mondrian, 1872–1944

RUSSIA
  Kasimir Malevich, 1878–1935
  Wassily Kandinsky, 1866–1944
  El Lissitsky, 1890–1941

FRANCE
  Robert Delaunay, 1885–1941

BRITAIN
  Barbara Hepworth, 1903–1975
  Henry Moore, 1898–1986

ITALY
  Alberto Giacometti, 1901–1966

AMERICA
  Claes Oldenburg, 1929

**De Stijl (c. 1917–   )**

HOLLAND
  Theo van Doesburg, 1883–1931
  Piet Mondrian, 1872–1944
  Gerit Rietveld, 1888–1964

ROMANIA
  Constantin Brancusi, 1876–1957

**Dada (1916 to 1922)**

FRANCE
  Marcel Duchamp, 1887–1968
  Francis Picabia, 1879–1953
  Hans Arp, 1887–1966

GERMANY
  George Grosz, 1893–1959
  Kurt Schwitters, 1887–1948

**Surrealism (1922 to 1940)**

GERMANY
  Max Ernst, 1891–1975

SPAIN
  Salvador Dali, 1904–1988
  Joan Miró, 1893–1983

ITALY
  Giorgio di Chirico, 1888–1978

BELGIUM
  Yves Tanguy, 1900–1955
  René Magritte, 1898–1967
  Paul Delvaux, b. 1897

**Surrealism (1922 to 1940)** (continued)

GERMANY
  Jean Arp, 1887–1966
  Kurt Schwitters, 1887–1948

SWITZERLAND
  Paul Klee, 1879–1940

RUSSIA
  Marc Chagall, 1887

FRANCE
  Marcel Duchamp, 1887–1968

AMERICA
  Man Ray, 1890–1976
  Joseph Cornell, 1903–1972

**Realism (1920 to 1940)**

AMERICA
  Georgia O'Keeffe, 1887–1986
  George Bellows, 1882–1925
  Stuart Davis, 1894 1964
  Ben Shahn, 1898–1969
  Edward Hopper, 1882–1967
  Thomas Hart Benton, 1889–1975
  Grant Wood, 1892–1942
  Anna Mary Moses, 1860 1961
  Charles Demuth, 1883–1935
  Charles Sheeler, 1883–1965
  John Marin, 1870–1953

MEXICO
  Orozco, 1883–1949
  Rivera 1886–1957
  David A. Siqueiros, 1896–1974
  Rufino Tamayo, 1899–

FRANCE
  Maurice Utrillo, 1883–1955

**Abstract Expressionism (1945 to 1960)**

AMERICA
  Hans Hofmann, 1880–1966
  Arshile Gorky, 1904–1948
  Alexander Calder, 1898–1976
  Willem de Kooning, 1904–1988
  Franz Kline, 1910–1962
  Clyfford Still, 1904–1980
  Robert Motherwell, 1915
  Joseph Cornell, 1903–1972
  Louise Nevelson, 1900–1988
  Mark Rothko, 1903–1970
  Jackson Pollok, 1912–1956
  Bernard Dubuffet, 1901–1985
  Sam Francis, 1923
  Frank Stella, 1936
  David Smith, 1906–1965
  Dan Flavin, 1923

**Abstract Expressionism (1945 to 1960)** (continued)

BRITAIN
Francis Bacon, 1910

HOLLAND
Karel Appel, 1921

ITALY
Alberto Giacometti, 1901–1966
Amadeo Modigliani, 1884–1920

SWITZERLAND
Alberto Burri, 1915

**Constructivism (c. 1917–1930s)**

RUSSIA
Naum Gabo, 1890–1977
Alexander Rodchenko, 1891–1956
Anton Pevsner, 1886–1962
Kasimir Malevich, 1878–1935

**Color Field Painting (1950–present)**

AMERICA
Morris Louis, 1912–1962
Kenneth Noland, 1924
Ellsworth Kelly, 1923
Helen Frankenthaler, 1928
Sam Francis, 1923

**New Realism, Pop Art (1950s–late 60's)**

AMERICA
Robert Rauschenberg, 1925
Jasper Johns, 1930
Jim Dine, 1935
Marisol Escobar, 1930
Alice Neel, 1900–1984
Andrew Wyeth, 1917
Janet Fish, 1938
Andy Warhol, 1930–1988
Roy Lichtenstein, 1923
Tom Wesselman, 1931
James Rosenquist, 1933
Ernest Trova, 1927
Claes Oldenburg, 1929
George Segal, 1924
Robert Indiana, 1928

BRITAIN
David Hockney, 1937
Richard Chamberlain

ITALY
Piero Mazoni, 1913
Lucio Fontana, 1899–1968

MEXICO
Frieda Kahlo, 1910

**Op Art (1960's)**

AMERICA
Richard Anuszkiewicz, 1930

BRITAIN
Bridget Riley, 1931

FRANCE
Victor Vasarely, 1908

**Hyperrealism**

AMERICA
Duane Hanson, 1925
Chuck Close, 1940

**Conceptual Art (c. 1970–present)**

AMERICA
Joseph Beuys, 1921
Christo (Javacheff), 1935
Robert Smithson, 1928–1973
Richard Serra, 1939

**Photorealism (c. 1967 to 1977)**

AMERICA
Audrey Flack, 1931
Don Eddy, 1944
Richard Estes, 1932
Robert Bechtle, 1932

**Post Modern**

AMERICA
Julian Schnabel, 1957
Judy Pfaff, 1946
Edward Keinholz, 1927
Miriam Shapiro, 1923

GERMANY
Anselm Kiefer, 1945

**Modern Sculptors**

AMERICA
Carl Andre, 1935
Alexander Archipenko, 1887–1964
Alexander Calder 1898–1976
Naum Gabo, 1890–1977
Donald Judd, 1928–
Roy Lichtenstein, 1923
Jacques Lipchitz, 1891–1973
Isamu Noguchi, 1904
Claes Oldenburg, 1929
George Segal, 1924
Richard Serra, 1939
David Smith, 1906–1965
Tony Smith, 1912–1980
Frank Stella, 1936
Mark Di Suvero, 1933

**Modern Sculptors** (continued)

SWITZERLAND
Jean Arp, 1887–1966
Alberto Giacometti, 1901–1966

GERMANY
Joseph Beuys, 1921–1986

FRANCE
Constantin Brancusi, 1876–1957
Jean Dubuffet, 1901–1985
R. Duchamp-Villon, 1876–1918
Max Ernst, 1891–1976
Henri Laurens, 1885–1954
Aristide Maillol, 1861–1944

FRANCE (continued)
Henri Matisse 1869–1954
Antoine Pevsner, 1884–1962
Auguste Rodin, 1840–1917

BRITAIN
Barbara Hepworth, 1903–1975
Richard Long, 1945
Henry Moore, 1898–1986
Jacob Epstein, 1880–1959

SPAIN
Joan Miró, 1893–1983
Pablo Picasso, 1881–1973

# G: FAMOUS BUILDINGS AND THEIR ARCHITECTS

## Ancient Architecture

Parthenon, 448–432 B.C., Ictinus and Callicrates
Colosseum, A.D. 72–80
Pyramids, 2470–2530 B.C.
Stonehenge, c. 2000 B.C.

## Gothic

Abby Church of St. Denis, master builder of St. Denis. 1122, Abbot Suger

## Renaissance

### ITALY

Dome for the Florence Cathedral, 1420–1436, Filippo Brunelleschi
Tempietto, 1500–1502, Donato Bramante
Dome of St. Peter's, Rome, 1506–1546, Michelangelo Buonarroti
Villa Rotonda, 1550, Andrea Palladio, Vicenza

### ENGLISH

Whitehall Banqueting Hall, 1619–1622, Inigo Jones, London

## Baroque

### ITALY

Capitoline Hill, 1538–1561, Michelangelo Buonarroti
New St. Peter's facade, 1607–1615, Carlo Maderno, Rome
St. Peter's Colonnade, 1656–1663, Gian Lorenzo Bernini
Sant' Agnese, Piazza Navone, 1653–1663, Francesco Borromini, Rome

### AUSTRIA

Karlskirche, 1715, Johann B.F. von Erlach, Vienna

### FRANCE

City plan of Washington, D.C., 1791, Pierre Charles L'Enfant
Versailles, 1669–1685, Louis LeVau, Jules Hardouin Mansart
Louvre, 1667–1670, Louis LeVau, Charles Le Brun, and Claude Perrault
Church of Les Invalides, 1706, Jules Hardouin Mansart

### BRITISH

New St. Paul's, 1675, Christopher Wren, London

## Modern Architecture

### BELGIUM

House, #4 Avenue Palmerson, 1894, Victor Horta, Brussels

### SPAIN

Casa Mila, 1905–1910, Antonio Gaudí, Barcelona, Spain

## Modern Architecture (continued)

### AUSTRIA

Steiner House, 1910, Adolf Loos, Vienna

### GERMANY

A.E.G. Turbine factory, 1909, Peter Behrens, Berlin
Fagus Factory, 1910–1914, Walter Gropius and Hannes Meyer, Alfeld-an-der-Leine
Bauhaus, 1925–26, Walter Gropius, Dessau
German Pavilion, International Exposition, 1929, Mies van der Rohe, Barcelona
Seagram Building, 1958, Mies van der Rohe and Philip Johnson, New York

### HOLLAND

Café de Unie, 1925, J.J.P.Oud, Rotterdam
Schroder House, 1924–1925, Gerrit Rietveld, Utrecht

### BRITAIN

Crystal Palace, 1851, John Paxton, London

### FRANCE

Ozenfant House, 1922, Le Corbusier, Paris
Notre Dame de Haute, Le Corbusier, Ronchamp, France
Capitol Buildings, 1951–1957, Le Corbusier, Chandigarh, India
Galerie des Machines, International exposition, 1889, Ferdinand Dutert, Paris
L'Opera, 1861–1874, Charles Garnier, Paris
Eiffel Tower, 1889, Gustave Eiffel, Paris

### FINLAND

Civic Center, 1950–1951, Alvar Aalto, Saynatsalo, Finland

## American Architecture

University of Virginia, c. 1817, Thomas Jefferson, Charlottesville, Virginia
Monticello, 1770–1782, Thomas Jefferson, near Charlottesville, Virginia
Quincy Market, 1825–1826, Alexander Parris, Boston, Massachusetts
Fanueuil Hall, 1740–1742, John Smibert, Boston, Massachusetts
United States Capitol, 1855–1864, Thomas Ustick Walter, Washington, D.C.
New York University, 1832–1837, Alexander Jackson Davis
The Smithsonian Institute, 1846–1855, James Renwick, Washington, D.C.
Bank of Pennsylvania, 1798–1800, Benjamin Henry Latrobe, Philadelphia, Pennsylvania
Baltimore Cathedral, 1804–1821, Benjamin Henry Latrobe, Baltimore, Maryland

## American Architecture (continued)

Pennsylvania Academy of Fine Arts, 1871–1876, Frank Furness, Philadelphia, Pennsylvania

Woolworth Building, 1911–1913, Cass Gilbert, New York, New York

Biltmore, 1888–1895, Richard Morris Hunt, Asheville, North Carolina

Pennsylvania Station, 1902–1910, McKim, Mead and White, New York, New York

National Gallery Addition, 1968–1978, I.M. Pei & Partners, Washington, D.C.

Yale Center for British Art, 1969–1972, Louis I. Kahn, New Haven, Connecticut

Marshall Field Warehouse, 1885–1957, Henry Hobson Richardson, Chicago, Illinois

Wainwright Building, 1890–1891, Adler and Sullivan, St. Louis, Missouri

Carson, Pirie and Scott Department store, 1899–1904, Louis Sullivan, Chicago, Illinois

Ward Willitts House, 1900–1902, Frank Lloyd Wright, Highland Park, Illinois

Robie House, 1908–1909, Frank Lloyd Wright, Chicago, Illinois

Dr. Edith Farnsworth House, 1945–1951, Ludwig Mies van der Rohe (he emigrated to America), Plano, Illinois

Kaufmann House, "Falling Water," 1936–37, Frank Lloyd Wright, Bear Run, Pennsylvania

Philip Johnson House, 1949, Philip Johnson, New Caanan, Connecticut

United States Embassy, 1957–1959, Edward Stone, New Delhi, India

Kresge Auditorium, 1955, Eero Saarinen, M.I.T., Cambridge, Massachusetts

Lever House, 1952, Skidmore, Owings & Merrill

United States Air Force Academy, 1955–1958, Skidmore, Owings, and Merrill

Richards Medical Research Building and Laboratories, 1957–1960, Louis I. Kahn, U. Of Penn., Philadelphia

Seagram Building, 1954–1958, Mies van der Rohe and Philip Johnson, New York

AT & T Headquarters, 1979–1984, Philip Johnson and John Burgee, New York

National Gallery of Art, East Building, 1978, I.M. Pei, Washington, D.C.

Portland Public Services Building, Michael Graves, Portland, Oregon

Swan and Dolphin Hotels, 1991, Michael Graves, Lake Buena Vista, Florida

Euro Disney Complex, 1991–1992, Robert A.M. Stern, Arata Isozaki, Frank Gehry, Charles Gwathmey, Robert Siegel, and Michael Graves

## Canada

Habitat, 1967, Moshe Safdie (b. Israel), Montreal, Canada

U.S. Pavilion, 1967, R. Buckminster Fuller, Montreal, Canada

# SLIDE CREDITS

1. *Horses, Bull and Stags*, c. 14,000-13,500 B.C. Lascaux Cave Paintings. Dordogne, France. Art Resource, NY.
2. *The Goddess Hathor Places the Magic Collar on Sethi I*, New Kingdom, 19th dyn. From Thebes. 226m high. Louvre, Paris. Giraudon/Art Resource, NY.
3. *Mummy Cartonnage of Amen-Nestawy-Nahkt, Priest of Amun*, c. 1000 B.C., Thebes. 71″ × 19″. St. Louis Art Museum Gift of Mr. & Mrs. Barney A. Ebsworth for the children of St. Louis.
4. *Saying Farewell at Hsün-yang* (detail). Ch'iu Ying. Ming Dynasty. Handscroll. 157¼″ × 13½″. Nelson-Atkins Museum of Art, Kansas City, MO (Nelson Fund) 46-50.
5. *Dipylon Vase*, c. 700 B.C. Krater, 42½″ b. The Metropolitan Museum of Art, NY. Art Resource, NY.
6. *Parthenon* (Acropolis, Parthenon and Erechtheum). 448-432 B.C. Athens. Vanni/Art Resource, NY.
7. *Winged Victory of Samothrace*, c. 200 B.C. Marble, 108⅓″ b. Louvre, Paris. Art Resource, NY.
8. *Colosseum*, 80 A.D. Rome. Vanni/Art Resource, NY.
9. *African Mask*, Nigeria, Ibo Tribe. Wood with multicolored patina, 26¼″ h., 8″ w. The Saint Louis Art Museum. Gift of Dr. Donald Suggs.
10. *Les Très Riches Heures de Duc de Berry. May*, Pol de Limbourg, 1413-16. Illuminated manuscript. Museé de Condé, Chantilly, France. Giraudon/Art Resource, NY.
11. *The Fleet Crosses the Channel, Sept. 27, 1066*, c. 1080, Bayeaux, France. Bayeaux tapestry, 230′ long × 20′ high. Scala/Art Resource, NY.
12. *Chartres Cathedral*, Facciata, 1215-20. Chartres, France. Scala/Art Resource, NY.
13. *The Blue Cloak (Netherlandish Proverbs)*, Pieter Brueghel, 1599. State Museum, Berlin. Scala/Art Resource, NY.
14. *The Last Supper (Ultima Cena)*, Leonardo da Vinci, c. 1495-98. S. Maria delle Grazie, Milan. Scala/Art Resource, NY K40168.
15. *David*, Michelangelo, 1501-04. 14′ high. Academia, Florence. Scala/Art Resource, NY.
16. *The Sistine Chapel, detail (Creation of Man)*, Michelangelo, 1508-12. Fresco. The Vatican, Rome. Scala/Art Resource, NY.
17. *The School of Athens*, Raphael, 1510-11. Fresco. Stanza della Segnatura. Vatican Museum, Rome. Art Resource, NY.
18. *Still Life*, Pieter Claesz, 1643. Oil on wood panel, 24½″ × 19″. The Saint Louis Art Museum. Museum purchase.
19. *The Night Watch (The Company of Captain Frans Banning Cocq)*, Rembrandt van Rijn, 1642. Oil on canvas, 359 × 438cm. The Rijksmuseum, Amsterdam. Scala/Art Resource, NY.
20. *Viaduct of the Ducal Palace of Venice*, Antonio Canaletto. Uffizzi Palace, Florence. Scala/Art Resource, NY.
21. *Yacht Approaching the Coast*, J.M.W. Turner, c. 1935-40. Oil on canvas, 40½″ × 56″. Tate Gallery, London. Art Resource, NY.
22. *Mont St. Victoire*, Paul Cézanne, 1885-87. Stedelijk Museum, Amsterdam. Art Resource, NY.
23. *Charing Cross Bridge*, Claude Monet, 1903. St. Louis Art Museum.
24. *The Boating Party*, Mary Cassatt, 1893-94. Canvas, 35½″ × 46⅛″. National Gallery of Art, Washington, D.C. Chester Dale Collection.
25. *A Sunday Afternoon on the Island of La Grande Jatte*, Georges Seurat, 1884-86. Photograph © 1991, The Art Institute of Chicago. All Rights Reserved. Helen Birch Bartlett Memorial Collection.
26. *Self-Portrait*, Vincent van Gogh, 1889-90. Oil on canvas, 650 × 545 cm. Musee d'Orsay, Paris. Scala/Art Resource, NY.
27. *Faaturuma (Melancholic)*, Paul Gauguin, 1891. Oil on canvas, 37″ × 26⅞″. Nelson-Atkins Museum of Art, Kansas City, MO (Nelson Fund) 38-5.
28. *Vincent's Bedroom in Arles*, Vincent van Gogh, 1888. Oil on canvas, 575 × 740cm. van Gogh Museum, Amsterdam. Art Resource, NY.
29. *Culture of Corn and Preparation of Pancakes*, Diego Rivera, 1950. Fresco. National Palace, Mexico City. Giraudon/Art Resource, NY.
30. *The Three Musicians*, Pablo Picasso, 1921. Museum of Modern Art, NY. Copyright 1992 ARS, NY/SPADEM.
31. *Untitled (Medici Prince)*, Joseph Cornell, c. 1953. Mixed media, 17″ × 10⅝″ × 4⅜″. National Gallery of Art, Washington, D.C. Gift of Collectors Committee.
32. *Cow's Skull with Calico Roses*, Georgia O'Keeffe, 1931. Oil on canvas, 91.2 × 61cm. Photograph © 1991, The Art Institute of Chicago. All Rights Reserved. Gift of Georgia O'Keeffe, 1947.712.
33. *Kaufmann House, Falling Water*, Frank Lloyd Wright, 1936. Bear Run, PA. Art Resource, NY.
34. *Three Motives Against Wall, Number 1*, Henry Moore, 1958-59. Bronze, 19⅞″ × 42¼″ × 17¼″. National Gallery of Art, Washington, D.C. Gift of Enid A. Haupt.
35. *Tracer*, Robert Rauschenberg, 1963. Oil/silkscreen on canvas, 84″ × 60″. Nelson-Atkins Museum of Art, Kansas City, MO (Nelson Gallery Foundation Purchase) F84-70.
36. *Twenty Marilyns*, Andy Warhol, 1962. Private Collection, Paris. Copyright 1991 Estate and Foundation of Andy Warhol/ARS, NY.
37. *Buddha*, Audrey Flack, 1975. Air brushed acrylic over polymer emulsion on canvas, 70″ × 96″. The Saint Louis Art Museum. Purchase and funds given by the Contemporary Art Society.
38. *Conservatory*, Miriam Schapiro, 1988. Acrylic/fabric on canvas, 72″ × 152″. Collection: Miami University Art Museum, Oxford, OH. Courtesy of Bernice Steinbaum Gallery, NY.
39. *Radioactive Cats*, Sandy Skoglund, 1980. Cibachrome print, 30″ × 37¼″. The Saint Louis Art Museum. Purchase.
40. *Zaga*, Nancy Stevenson Graves, 1983. Cast bronze with polychrome chemical patination, 72″ × 49″ × 32″. The Nelson-Atkins Museum of Art, Kansas City, MO (Gift of the Friends of Art) F84-27.